D0753370

NOAH'S ARK

NOAH'S ARK

words from the Book of Genesis

illustrated by JANE RAY

DUTTON CHILDREN'S BOOKS NEW YORK

For Clara

The words from the Book of Genesis have been taken from the Authorized King James Version of the Bible.

CIP data is available.

First published in the United States 1990 by
Dutton Children's Books,
a division of Penguin Books USA Inc.

Originally published 1990 in Great Britain by
Orchard Books, The Watts Group,
96 Leonard Street, London EC2A 4RH

First American Edition   Printed in Belgium
10 9 8 7 6 5 4 3 2 1
ISBN 0-525-44653-2

God saw that the wickedness of man was great
in the earth, and it grieved him at his heart.

And the Lord said, I will destroy man, and beast,
and the creeping thing, and the fowls of the air;
for it repenteth me that I have made them.

But Noah found grace in the eyes of the Lord. Noah was a just man, and walked with God. And Noah begat three sons, Shem, Ham, and Japheth.

And God said unto Noah, I will cause it to rain upon the earth forty days and forty nights; and every thing that is in the earth shall die. But with thee will I establish my covenant.

Make thee an ark of gopher wood. Rooms shalt thou make in the ark, and shalt pitch it within and without with pitch. The length of the ark shall be three hundred cubits, the breadth of it fifty cubits, and the height of it thirty cubits.

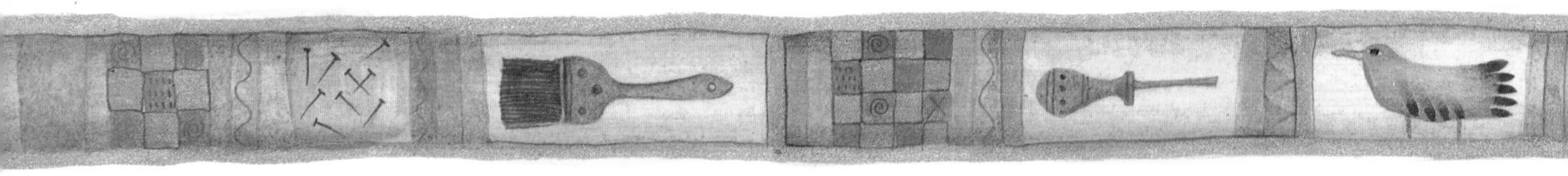

A window shalt thou make to the ark; and the
door of the ark shalt thou set in the side thereof;
with lower, second, and third stories shalt thou
make it.

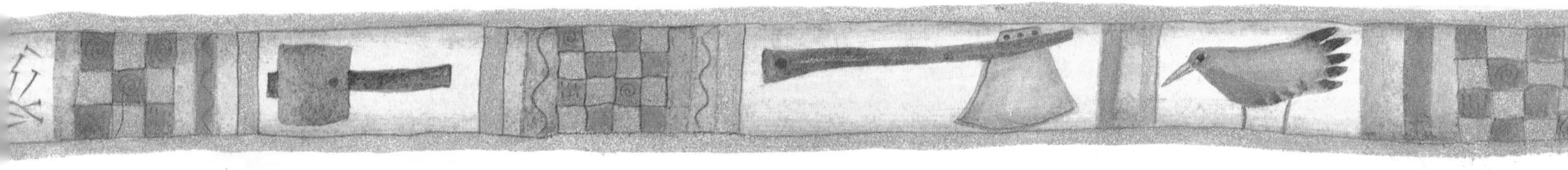

And thou shalt come into the ark, thou, and thy sons,

and thy wife, and thy sons' wives with thee.

And of every living thing of all flesh, two
of every sort shalt thou bring into the ark,

to keep them alive with thee; they shall be male and female.

Of fowls of the air

and of beasts, and of every thing

that creepeth upon the earth.

And take thou unto thee of all food that is eaten; and it shall be for food for thee, and for them. Thus did Noah, according to all that God commanded him.

And it came to pass after seven days, that the waters of the flood were upon the earth. The windows of heaven were opened; and the ark went upon the face of the waters.

And all the high hills, that were
under the whole heaven, were covered.

And the mountains were covered.

Every living substance was destroyed which was upon the ground, both man, and cattle, and the creeping things, and the fowl of the heaven; and

Noah only remained alive, and they that were with him in the ark.

And God remembered Noah, and made a wind to pass over the earth. The rain from heaven was restrained, and the ark rested upon the mountains of Ararat. And the waters decreased continually until the tops of the mountains were seen.

And at the end of forty days Noah opened the window of the ark and sent forth a dove,

to see if the waters were abated from off the ground. But she found no rest for the sole of her foot and returned into the ark.

And again Noah sent forth the dove; and the dove came in to him in the evening; and in her mouth was an olive leaf: so Noah knew that the waters were abated from off the earth. And at the end of seven days Noah again sent forth the dove, which returned not unto him any more.

And Noah removed the covering of the ark, and looked, and, behold, the face of the ground was dry. And God spake unto Noah, saying, I will set my bow in the cloud, and it shall be a token of a covenant between me and you and every living creature.

Go forth of the ark, thou, and thy wife, and thy sons, and thy sons' wives with thee. Bring forth with thee every living thing that is with thee, both of fowl, and of cattle, and of every creeping thing

that creepeth upon the earth. Be fruitful, and multiply, and replenish the earth, for I will not curse the ground any more.

And while the earth remaineth, seedtime and
harvest, and cold and heat, and summer and
winter, and day and night shall not cease.

OCA/OCP:
Oracle9i™ DBA Fundamentals I
Study Guide

Biju Thomas
Bob Bryla

San Francisco • London

Associate Publisher: Neil Edde
Acquisitions and Developmental Editor: Jeff Kellum
Editor: Pat Coleman
Production Editor: Elizabeth Campbell
Technical Editor: Ashok Hanumath, Betty MacEwan
Graphic Illustrator: Tony Jonick
Electronic Publishing Specialist: Interactive Composition Corporation
Proofreaders: Dave Nash, Laurie O'Connell, Yariv Rabinovitch
Indexer: Jerilyn Sprotson
CD Coordinator: Erica Yee
CD Technician: Kevin Ly
Book Designer: Bill Gibson
Cover Designer: Archer Design
Cover Photographer: Photo Researchers

Library of Congress Card Number: 2001099340

ISBN: 0-7821-4063-7

Manufactured in the United States of America

10 9 8

To Our Valued Readers:

In a CertCities.com article dated December 15, 2001, Oracle certification was ranked #2 in a list of the "10 Hottest Certifications for 2002." This shouldn't come as a surprise, especially when you consider the fact that the OCP program nearly tripled in size (from 30,000 to 80,000) in the last year. Oracle continues to expand its dominance in the database market, and as companies begin integrating Oracle9i systems into their IT infrastructure, you can be assured of high demand for professionals with the Oracle Certified Associate and Oracle Certified Professional certifications.

Sybex is proud to have helped thousands of Oracle certification candidates prepare for the exams over the years, and we are excited about the opportunity to continue to provide professionals like you with the skills needed to succeed in the highly competitive IT industry.

Our authors and editors have worked hard to ensure that the Oracle9i Study Guide you hold in your hands is comprehensive, in-depth, and pedagogically sound. We're confident that this book will meet and exceed the demanding standards of the certification marketplace and help you, the Oracle9i certification candidate, succeed in your endeavors.

Good luck in pursuit of your Oracle9i certification!

Neil Edde
Associate Publisher—Certification
Sybex, Inc.

Software License Agreement: Terms and Conditions

The media and/or any online materials accompanying this book that are available now or in the future contain programs and/or text files (the "Software") to be used in connection with the book. SYBEX hereby grants to you a license to use the Software, subject to the terms that follow. Your purchase, acceptance, or use of the Software will constitute your acceptance of such terms.

The Software compilation is the property of SYBEX unless otherwise indicated and is protected by copyright to SYBEX or other copyright owner(s) as indicated in the media files (the "Owner(s)"). You are hereby granted a single-user license to use the Software for your personal, noncommercial use only. You may not reproduce, sell, distribute, publish, circulate, or commercially exploit the Software, or any portion thereof, without the written consent of SYBEX and the specific copyright owner(s) of any component software included on this media.

In the event that the Software or components include specific license requirements or end-user agreements, statements of condition, disclaimers, limitations or warranties ("End-User License"), those End-User Licenses supersede the terms and conditions herein as to that particular Software component. Your purchase, acceptance, or use of the Software will constitute your acceptance of such End-User Licenses.

By purchase, use or acceptance of the Software you further agree to comply with all export laws and regulations of the United States as such laws and regulations may exist from time to time.

Software Support

Components of the supplemental Software and any offers associated with them may be supported by the specific Owner(s) of that material, but they are not supported by SYBEX. Information regarding any available support may be obtained from the Owner(s) using the information provided in the appropriate read.me files or listed elsewhere on the media.

Should the manufacturer(s) or other Owner(s) cease to offer support or decline to honor any offer, SYBEX bears no responsibility. This notice concerning support for the Software is provided for your information only. SYBEX is not the agent or principal of the Owner(s), and SYBEX is in no way responsible for providing any support for the Software, nor is it liable or responsible for any support provided, or not provided, by the Owner(s).

Warranty

SYBEX warrants the enclosed media to be free of physical defects for a period of ninety (90) days after purchase. The Software is not available from SYBEX in any other form or media than that enclosed herein or posted to www.sybex.com. If you discover a defect in the media during this warranty period, you may obtain a replacement of identical format at no charge by sending the defective media, postage prepaid, with proof of purchase to:

SYBEX Inc.
Product Support Department
1151 Marina Village Parkway
Alameda, CA 94501
Web: http://www.sybex.com

After the 90-day period, you can obtain replacement media of identical format by sending us the defective disk, proof of purchase, and a check or money order for $10, payable to SYBEX.

Disclaimer

SYBEX makes no warranty or representation, either expressed or implied, with respect to the Software or its contents, quality, performance, merchantability, or fitness for a particular purpose. In no event will SYBEX, its distributors, or dealers be liable to you or any other party for direct, indirect, special, incidental, consequential, or other damages arising out of the use of or inability to use the Software or its contents even if advised of the possibility of such damage. In the event that the Software includes an online update feature, SYBEX further disclaims any obligation to provide this feature for any specific duration other than the initial posting.

The exclusion of implied warranties is not permitted by some states. Therefore, the above exclusion may not apply to you. This warranty provides you with specific legal rights; there may be other rights that you may have that vary from state to state. The pricing of the book with the Software by SYBEX reflects the allocation of risk and limitations on liability contained in this agreement of Terms and Conditions.

Shareware Distribution

This Software may contain various programs that are distributed as shareware. Copyright laws apply to both shareware and ordinary commercial software, and the copyright Owner(s) retains all rights. If you try a shareware program and continue using it, you are expected to register it. Individual programs differ on details of trial periods, registration, and payment. Please observe the requirements stated in appropriate files.

Copy Protection

The Software in whole or in part may or may not be copy-protected or encrypted. However, in all cases, reselling or redistributing these files without authorization is expressly forbidden except as specifically provided for by the Owner(s) therein.

To my family

—Biju Thomas

To Mary Christine

—Bob Bryla

Acknowledgments

Thank you Sybex for trusting me to work on two books at the same time. I would like to thank the following wonderful people at Sybex for their support, patience, and hard work: Jeff Kellum (Development Editor) for his support, valuable comments, and getting us going; Elizabeth Campbell (Production Editor) for her patience and understanding and for making sure every piece of the book ties together and is on schedule. I know many more people from Sybex contributed to this book; I thank each one of them for their hard work and the high quality of work.

I thank Pat Coleman (Editor) for her hard work. Pat, your edits made a difference in the chapters. I thank Ashok Hanumanth and Betty MacEwan for their technical review and comments. Bob, thank you for completing the chapters well ahead of schedule.

It would not have been possible for me to participate in this project if my parents had not come over to the United States from India to take care of our son Joshua. I thank my parents for taking care of the baby and house for the past five months. Thank you, Shiji, for your endless support and love.

Last, but not least, I thank my colleagues for their support and friendship. Thank you, Wendy, for understanding me so well and all the help you provided. Thank you all—you are the best to work with.

—Biju Thomas

I would like to thank all the folks at Sybex that made this a most enjoyable and rewarding experience, including Elizabeth Campbell and Jeff Kellum, who reinforced my attention to detail. Thanks go to Biju for not letting me write too many of these chapters myself. Thanks also to Pat Coleman, who filled in the gaps from my college writing courses, and to Ashok and Betty for their insightful comments and suggestions.

This book wouldn't be possible without the love and support from my family throughout the long nights and weekends when I still managed to find time to give the kids a bath and read books before bedtime. I loved every minute of it.

Thanks also to my professional colleagues, both past and present, who provided me with inspiration, support, and guidance and pushed me a little further to take a risk now and then: Joe Johnson, Julie Krause, Karen Kressin, Chuck Dunbar, and that math teacher in high school, whose name eludes me at the moment, who introduced me to computers on a DEC PDP-8 with a teletype and a paper tape reader.

—Bob Bryla

Contents at a Glance

Contents

Introduction

There is high demand for professionals in the information technology (IT) industry, and Oracle certifications are the hottest credential in the database world. You have made the right decision to pursue certification, because being Oracle certified will give you a distinct advantage in this highly competitive market.

Many readers may already be familiar with Oracle and do not need an introduction to the Oracle database world. For those who aren't familiar with the company, Oracle, founded in 1977, sold the first commercial relational database and is now the world's leading database company and second-largest independent software company, with revenues of more than $10 billion, serving more than 145 countries.

Oracle databases are the de facto standard for large Internet sites, and Oracle advertisers are boastful but honest when they proclaim, "The Internet Runs on Oracle." Almost all big Internet sites run Oracle databases. Oracle's penetration of the database market runs deep and is not limited to dot-com implementations. Enterprise resource planning (ERP) application suites, data warehouses, and custom applications at many companies rely on Oracle. The demand for DBA resources remains higher than others during weak economic times.

This book is intended to help you on your exciting path toward becoming an Oracle9i Oracle Certified Associate (OCA), which is the first step on the path toward Oracle Certified Professional (OCP) and Oracle Certified Master (OCM) certification. Basic knowledge of Oracle SQL is an advantage when reading this book but is not mandatory. Using this book and a practice database, you can start learning Oracle and pass the IZ0-031 test: Oracle9i Database: Fundamentals I.

Why Become an Oracle Certified Professional?

The number one reason to become an OCP is to gain more visibility and greater access to the industry's most challenging opportunities. Oracle certification is the best way to demonstrate your knowledge and skills in Oracle database systems. The certification tests are scenario-based, which is the most effective way to assess your hands-on expertise and critical problem-solving skills.

Certification is proof of your knowledge and shows that you have the skills required to support Oracle core products. The Oracle certification program can help a company to identify proven performers who have demonstrated their skills and who can support the company's investment in Oracle technology. It demonstrates that you have a solid understanding of your job role and the Oracle products used in that role.

OCPs are among the best paid in the IT industry. Salary surveys consistently show the OCP certification to yield higher salaries than other certifications, including Microsoft, Novell, and Cisco.

So, whether you are beginning a career, changing careers, securing your present position, or seeking to refine and promote your position, this book is for you!

Oracle Certifications

Oracle certifications follow a track that is oriented toward a job role. There are database administration, database operator, and developer tracks. Within each track, Oracle has a three-tiered certification program:

- The first tier is the Oracle Certified Associate (OCA). OCA certification typically requires you to complete two exams, the first via the Internet and the second in a proctored environment.
- The next tier is the Oracle Certified Professional (OCP), which builds upon and requires an OCA certification. The additional requirements for OCP certification are additional proctored exams.
- The third and highest tier is the Oracle Certified Master (OCM). OCM certification builds upon and requires OCP certification. To achieve OCM certification, you must attend two advanced Oracle Education, classroom courses (from a specific list of qualifying courses) and complete a practicum exam.

The following material will address only the database administration track, because at the time of this writing, it was the only 9i track offered by Oracle. The other tracks have 8 and 8i certifications and will undoubtedly have 9i certifications. See the Oracle website at `http://www.oracle.com/education/certification` for the latest information.

Oracle9i Certified Database Associate

The role of the database administrator (DBA) has become a key to success in today's highly complex database systems. The best DBAs work behind the scenes, but are in the spotlight when critical issues arise. They plan, create, maintain, and ensure that the database is available for the business. They are always watching the databaseµ for performance issues and to prevent unscheduled downtime. The DBA's job requires broad understanding of the architecture of Oracle database and expertise in solving problems.

The Oracle9i Certified Database Associate is the entry-level certification for the database administration track and is required to advance toward the more senior certification tiers. This certification requires you to pass two exams that demonstrate your knowledge of Oracle basics:

- 1Z0-007: Introduction to Oracle9i: SQL
- 1Z0-031: Oracle9i Database: Fundamentals I

The 1Z0-007 exam, Introduction to Oracle9i: SQL, is offered on the Internet. The 1Z0-031 exam, Oracle9i Database: Fundamentals I, is offered at a Sylvan Prometric facility.

Oracle9i Certified Database Administrator (DBA)

The OCP tier of the database administration track challenges you to demonstrate your continuing experience and knowledge of Oracle technologies. The Oracle9i Certified Database Administrator certification requires achievement of the Certified Database Associate tier, as well as passing the following two exams at a Sylvan Prometric facility:

- 1Z0-032: Oracle9i Database: Fundamentals II
- 1Z0-033: Oracle9i Database: Performance Tuning

Oracle9i Certified Master

The Oracle9i Certified Master is the highest level of certification that Oracle offers. To become a certified master, you must first achieve Certified Database Administrator status, then complete two advanced instructor-led classes at an Oracle education facility, and finally pass a hands-on exam at Oracle Education. The classes and practicum exam are offered only at an Oracle education facility and may require travel. The advanced classes that will count toward your OCM requirement include the following:

- Oracle9i: Program with PL/SQL
- Oracle9i: Advanced PL/SQL
- Oracle9i: SQL Tuning Workshop
- Oracle9i: High Availability in an Internet Environment
- Oracle9i: Database: Implement Partitioning
- Oracle9i: Real Application Clusters Implementation
- Oracle9i: Data Warehouse Administration
- Oracle9i: Advanced Replication
- Oracle9i: Enterprise Manager

Passing Scores

The 1Z0-031: Oracle9i Database: Fundamentals I exam consists of two sections—basic and mastery. The passing score for basic section is 71 percent and for mastery section is 56 percent at the time of writing this book. Please download and read the Oracle9i Certification candidate guide before taking the exam. The basic section covers the fundamental concepts, and the mastery section covers more difficult questions, mostly based on practice and experience. You must pass both sections to pass the exam. The objectives, test scoring, number of questions, and so on are listed at `http://www.oracle.com/education/certification`.

More Information

You can find the most current information about Oracle certification at `http://www.oracle.com/education/certification`. Follow the Certification link and choose the track that interests you. Read the Candidate Guide for the test objectives and test contents, and keep in mind that they can change at any time without notice.

OCA/OCP Study Guides

The Oracle9i database administration track certification consists of four tests: two for OCA level and two more for OCP level. Sybex offers several study guides to help you achieve this certification:

- *OCA/OCP: Introduction to Oracle9i™ SQL Study Guide* (exam 1Z0-007: Introduction to Oracle9i: SQL)
- *OCA/OCP: Oracle9i™ DBA Database Fundamentals I Study Guide* (exam 1Z0-031: Oracle9i Database: Fundamentals I)

- *OCP: Oracle9i™ DBA Database Fundamentals II Study Guide* (exam 1Z0-032: Oracle9i Database: Fundamentals II)
- *OCP: Oracle9i™ DBA Performance Tuning* (exam 1Z0-033: Oracle9i Database: Performance Tuning)

Additionally, these four books are offered in a boxed set: *OCP: Oracle9i™ DBA Certification Kit.*

Skills Required for DBA Certification

To pass the certification exams, you need to master the following skills:

- Write SQL SELECT statements that display data from either single or multiple tables.
- Restrict, sort, aggregate, and manipulate data using both single and group functions.
- Create and manage tables, views, constraints, synonyms, sequences, and indexes.
- Create users and roles to control user access and maintain security.
- Understand Oracle Server architecture (database and instance).
- Understand the physical and logical storage of the database, and be able to manage space allocation and growth.
- Manage data, including its storage, loading, and reorganization.
- Manage redo logs, automatic undo, and rollback segments.
- Use globalization features to choose a database character set and National Language Support (NLS) parameters.
- Configure Net8 on the server side and the client side.
- Use backup and recovery options.
- Archive redo log files and hot backups.
- Perform backup and recovery operations using Recovery Manager (RMAN).
- Use data dictionary views and set database parameters.
- Configure and use multithreaded server (MTS) and Connection Manager.
- Identify and tune database and SQL performance.

- Use the tuning/diagnostics tools STATSPACK, TKPROF, and EXPLAIN PLAN.
- Tune the size of data blocks, the shared pool, the buffer caches, and rollback segments.
- Diagnose contention for latches, locks, and rollback segments.

Tips for Taking the OCP Exam

Use the following tips to help you prepare for and pass each exam.

- Each OCP test contains about 55–80 questions to be completed in 90 minutes. Answer the questions you know first so that you do not run out of time.
- The answer choices for many questions on the exam look identical at first. Read the questions carefully. Do not just jump to conclusions. Be sure that you clearly understand exactly what each question asks.
- Most of the test questions are scenario-based. Some scenarios contain nonessential information and exhibits. You need to be able to identify what's important and what's not important.
- Do not leave any questions unanswered. There is no negative scoring. After selecting an answer, you can mark a difficult question or one that you're unsure of and come back to it later.
- When answering questions that you are not sure about, use a process of elimination to get rid of the obviously incorrect answers first. Doing this greatly improves your odds if you need to make an educated guess.
- If you're not sure of your answer, mark it for review and then look for other questions that might help you eliminate any incorrect answers. At the end of the test, you can go back and review the questions that you marked for review.

Where Do You Take the Exam?

You take the Introduction to Oracle9i: SQL exam (1Z0-007) via the Internet. To register for an online Oracle certification exam, you will need an Internet connection of at least 33Kbps, but a 56Kbps, LAN, or broadband connection is recommended. You will also need either Internet Explorer 5 (or later) or Netscape 4.*x* (Oracle does not recommend Netscape 5.*x* or 6.*x*). At the time of this writing, the online 1Z0-007 exam is $90. If you do not have a credit card to use for payment, you will need to contact Oracle to purchase a voucher. You can pay with a certification voucher, promo codes, or credit card.

You can take the other exams at any of the more than 800 Sylvan Prometric Authorized Testing Centers around the world. For the location of a testing center near you, call 1-800-891-3926. Outside the United States and Canada, contact your local Sylvan Prometric Registration Center. Usually, you can take the tests in any order.

To register for a proctored Oracle Certified Professional exam at a Sylvan Prometric test center, do the following:

- Determine the number of the exam you want to take.
- Register with Sylvan Prometric online at `http://www.2test.com` or, in North America, by calling 1-800-891-EXAM (800-891-3926). At this point, you will be asked to pay in advance for the exam. At the time of this writing, the exams are $125 each and must be taken within one year of payment.

When you schedule the exam, you'll get instructions regarding all appointment and cancellation procedures, the ID requirements, and information about the testing-center location. You can schedule an exam as much as six weeks in advance or as soon as one working day before the day you want to take it. If something comes up and you need to cancel or reschedule your exam appointment, contact Sylvan Prometric at least 24 hours in advance.

What Does This Book Cover?

This book covers everything you need to pass the Oracle9i Database: Fundamentals I exam. This exam is part of the Oracle9i Certified Database Associate certification tier in the database administration track. It teaches you the basics of Oracle Architecture and Administration. Each chapter begins with a list of exam objectives.

Chapter 1 Discusses the new features of Oracle9i database compared with the previous versions.

Chapter 2 Explains the Oracle9i architecture and its main components.

Chapter 3 Discusses the various tools available to DBAs, connecting to the Oracle database, and startup/shutdown of the database.

Chapter 4 Discusses how to create a database manually as well as how to use the Database Configuration Assistant. It also discusses the Oracle data dictionary.

Chapter 5 Explains the uses and contents of the control files and redo log files.

Chapter 6 Discusses tablespaces and data files. The logical structure of the tablespace within he database and Oracle Managed Files are discussed.

Chapter 7 Explains logical storage structures such as blocks, extents, and segments and managing undo data.

Chapter 8 Discusses creating tables with the various datatypes and options available to store data. Creating and managing indexes and constraints are discussed.

Chapter 9 Introduces database and data security. Setting up profiles, users, privileges, and roles are discussed. It also discusses the Globalization Support.

Each chapter ends with Review Questions that are specifically designed to help you retain the knowledge presented. To really nail down your skills, read and answer each question carefully.

How to Use This Book

This book can provide a solid foundation for the serious effort of preparing for the OCA database administration exam track. To best benefit from this book, use the following study method:

1. Take the Assessment Test immediately following this introduction. (The answers are at the end of the test.) Carefully read over the explanations for any questions you get wrong, and note which chapters the material comes from. This information should help you plan your study strategy.
2. Study each chapter carefully, making sure that you fully understand the information and the test objectives listed at the beginning of each chapter. Pay extra close attention to any chapter related to questions you missed in the Assessment Test.
3. Complete all hands-on exercises in the chapter, referring to the chapter so that you understand the reason for each step you take. If you do

not have an Oracle database available, be sure to study the examples carefully. Answer the Review Questions related to that chapter. (The answers appear at the end of each chapter, after the "Review Questions" section.)

4. Note the questions that confuse or trick you, and study those sections of the book again.

5. Before taking the exam, try your hand at the Bonus Exams included on the CD that comes with this book. The questions on these exams appear only on the CD. This will give you a complete overview of what you can expect to see on the real test.

6. Remember to use the products on the CD included with this book. The electronic flashcards and the Edge Test exam preparation software have been specifically designed to help you study for and pass your exam. You can use the electronic flashcards n your Windows computer or on your Palm device.

To learn all the material covered in this book, you'll need to apply yourself regularly and with discipline. Try to set aside the same time period every day to study, and select a comfortable and quiet place to do so. If you work hard, you will be surprised at how quickly you learn this material. All the best!

What's on the CD?

We have worked hard to provide some really great tools to help you with your certification process. All the following tools should be loaded on your workstation when you're studying for the test.

The EdgeTest for Oracle Certified DBA Preparation Software

Provided by EdgeTek Learning Systems, this test-preparation software prepares you to pass the Oracle9i Database: Fundamentals I exam. In this test, you will find all the questions from the book, plus two Bonus Exams that appear exclusively on the CD. You can take the Assessment Test, test yourself by chapter, take either of the Bonus Exams, or take an exam randomly generated from all the questions.

Electronic Flashcards for PC and Palm Devices

After you read the *OCA/OCP: Oracle9i Database: Fundamentals I Study Guide*, read the Review Questions at the end of each chapter, and take the Bonus Exams which appear only on the CD. But wait, there's more! Test yourself with the flashcards included on the CD. If you can get through these difficult questions and understand the answers, you'll know that you're ready for the exam.

The flashcards include 150 questions specifically written to hit you hard and make sure you are ready for the exam. With the Review Questions, Bonus Exams, and flashcards, you should be more than prepared for the exam.

OCA/OCP: Oracle9i Database: Fundamentals I Study Guide in PDF

Sybex is now offering the Oracle certification books on CD so you can read the book on your PC or laptop. It is in Adobe Acrobat format. Acrobat Reader 5 is also included on the CD. This will be extremely helpful to readers who fly or commute on a bus or train and don't want to carry a book, as well as to readers who find it more comfortable reading from their computer.

How to Contact the Authors

To contact Biju Thomas, you can e-mail him at `biju@bijoos.com` or visit his website for DBAs at http://`www.bijoos.com/oracle`.

To contact Bob Bryla, you can e-mail him at `rjbryla@mhtc.net`.

About the authors

Biju Thomas is an Oracle9i certified professional with eight years of Oracle database management and application development experience. He has written articles for *Oracle Magazine*, *Oracle Internals*, and *Select Magazine*. He maintains a website for DBAs at `http://www.bijoos.com/oracle`.

Bob Bryla is an Oracle9i certified professional with more than ten years of database design, database application development, and database administration experience in a variety of fields. He is currently an Internet Database Analyst and DBA at Lands' End, Inc. in Dodgeville, Wisconsin.

Assessment Test

1. Multiple ___________ can share an SGA.

   A. PMON processes

   B. Server processes

   C. Instances

   D. Databases

   E. Tablespaces

2. Which component in the following list is not part of the SGA?

   A. Database buffer cache

   B. Library cache

   C. Sort area

   D. Shared pool

   E. Java pool

3. Which background process updates the online redo log files with the redo log buffer entries when a `COMMIT` occurs in the database?

   A. DBW*n*

   B. LGWR

   C. CKPT

   D. CMMT

4. How do you change the status of a database to restricted availability, if the database is already up and running? (Choose the best answer.)

   A. Shut down the database and start the database using `STARTUP RESTRICT`.

   B. Use the `ALTER DATABASE RESTRICT SESSIONS` command.

   C. Use the `ALTER SYSTEM ENABLE RESTRICTED SESSION` command.

   D. Use the `ALTER SESSION ENABLE RESTRICTED USERS` command.

5. When you connect to a database by using `CONNECT SCOTT/TIGER AS SYSDBA`, which schema are you connected to in the database?

   A. `SYSTEM`

   B. `PUBLIC`

   C. `SYSDBA`

   D. `SYS`

   E. `SCOTT`

6. Suppose the database is in the `MOUNT` state; select two statements from the options below that are correct.

   A. The control file is open; the database files and redo log files are closed.

   B. You can query the SGA by using dynamic views.

   C. The control file, data files, and redo log files are open.

   D. The control file, data files, and redo log files are all closed.

7. Which of the following clauses will affect the size of the control file when creating a database? (Choose two.)

   A. `MAXLOGFILES`

   B. `LOGFILE`

   C. `ARCHIVELOG`

   D. `MAXDATAFILES`

8. Which script creates the data dictionary tables?

   A. `catalog.sql`

   B. `catproc.sql`

   C. `sql.bsq`

   D. `dictionary.sql`

9. Which files can be multiplexed?

   A. Data files

   B. Parameter files

   C. Redo log files

   D. Alert log files

10. What happens when one of the redo members of the next group is unavailable when LGWR has finished writing the current log file?

    A. Database operation will continue uninterrupted.

    B. The database will hang; do an `ALTER DATABASE SWITCH LOGFILE` to skip the unavailable redo log.

    C. The instance will be shut down.

    D. LGWR will create a new redo log member, and the database will continue to be in operation.

11. When you multiplex the control file, how many control files can you have for one database?

    A. Four

    B. Eight

    C. Twelve

    D. Unlimited

12. Which initialization parameter specifies that no more than the specified number of seconds will elapse during an instance recovery? (Choose the best answer.)

    A. `FAST_START_IO_TARGET`

    B. `FAST_START_MTTR_TARGET`

    C. `LOG_CHECKPOINTS_TO_ALERT`

    D. `CHECKPOINT_RECOVERY_TIME`

    E. `LOG_CHECKPOINT_TIMEOUT`

13. Which SQL*Plus command can you use to see whether the database is in `ARCHIVELOG` mode?

    A. `SHOW DB MODE`

    B. `ARCHIVELOG LIST`

    C. `ARCHIVE LOG LIST`

    D. `LIST ARCHIVELOG`

14. Which initialization parameter must be set to create a control file using OMF?

    A. `DB_CREATE_SPFILE`

    B. `DB_CREATE_FILE_DEST`

    C. `DB_CREATE_ONLINE_LOG_DEST_`*n*

    D. `CONTROL_FILES`

15. The following are the steps required for relocating a data file belonging to the `USERS` tablespace. Choose the correct order in which the steps are to be performed.

    1. Copy the file `/disk1/users01.dbf` to `/disk2/users01.dbf` using an operating system command.

    2. `ALTER DATABASE RENAME FILE '/disk1/users01.dbf' TO` '/disk2/users01.dbf'

    3. `ALTER TABLESPACE USERS OFFLINE`

    4. `ALTER TABLESPACE USERS ONLINE`

    A. 1, 2, 3, 4

    B. 3, 1, 2, 4

    C. 3, 2, 1, 4

    D. 4, 2, 1, 3

16. Which storage parameter is used to make sure that each extent is a multiple of the value specified?

A. MINEXTENTS

B. INITIAL

C. MINIMUM EXTENT

D. MAXEXTENTS

17. Choose two extent management options available for tablespaces.

A. Dictionary-managed

B. Data file-managed

C. Locally managed

D. Remote managed

E. System-managed

18. Which dictionary views would give you information about the total size of a tablespace? (Choose two.)

A. DBA_TABLESPACES

B. DBA_TEMP_FILES

C. DBA_DATA_FILES

D. DBA_FREE_SPACE

19. Which parameter is used to set up the directory for Oracle to create data files, if you do not specify a file name in the DATAFILE clause when creating or altering tablespaces?

A. DB_FILE_CREATE_DEST

B. DB_CREATE_FILE_DEST

C. DB_8K_CACHE_SIZE

D. USER_DUMP_DEST

E. DB_CREATE_ONLINE_LOG_DEST_1

20. Select the invalid statements from the list below regarding undo segment management. (Choose all that apply.)

    A. ALTER SYSTEM SET UNDO_TABLESPACE = ROLLBACK;

    B. ALTER DATABASE SET UNDO_TABLESPACE = UNDOTBS;

    C. ALTER SYSTEM SET UNDO_MANAGEMENT = AUTO;

    D. ALTER SYSTEM SET UNDO_MANAGEMENT = MANUAL;

21. Which statement allows specifying the parameters PCTFREE and PCTUSED?

    A. CREATE TABLE

    B. ALTER INDEX

    C. ALTER TABLESPACE

    D. All the above

22. Choose two space management parameters used to control the free space usage in a data block.

    A. PCTINCREASE

    B. PCTFREE

    C. PCTALLOCATED

    D. PCTUSED

23. Which data dictionary view would you query to see the temporary segments in a database?

    A. DBA_SEGMENTS

    B. V$SORT_SEGMENT

    C. DBA_TEMP_SEGMENTS

    D. DBA_TABLESPACES

24. The ALTER INDEX   REBUILD command cannot ___________.

    A. Move index to a new tablespace

    B. Change the INITIAL extent size of the index

    C. Collect statistics on the index

    D. Specify a new name for the index

25. Which command do you use to collect statistics for a table?

    A. ALTER TABLE *<TABLE_NAME> COMPUTE STATISTICS*

    B. ANALYZE TABLE *<TABLE_NAME> COMPUTE STATISTICS*

    C. ALTER TABLE *<TABLE_NAME> COLLECT STATISTICS*

    D. ANALYZE TABLE *<TABLE_NAME> COLLECT STATISTICS*

26. How do you prevent row migration?

    A. Specify larger PCTFREE

    B. Specify larger PCTUSED

    C. Specify large INITIAL and NEXT sizes

    D. Specify small INITRANS

27. Which data dictionary view can you query to find the primary key columns of a table?

    A. DBA_TABLES

    B. DBA_TAB_COLUMNS

    C. DBA_IND_COLUMNS

    D. DBA_CONS_COLUMNS

    E. DBA_CONSTRAINTS

28. Choose three valid partitioning methods available in Oracle9i.

    A. RANGE

    B. BINARY

    C. LIST

    D. COMPOUND

    E. HASH

29. If you run the ALTER SESSION SET NLS_DATE_FORMAT = 'DDMMYY' statement, which dictionary view would you query to see the value of the parameter?

    A. V$SESSION_PARAMETERS

    B. NLS_SESSION_PARAMETERS

C. NLS_DATABASE_PARAMETERS

D. V$SESSION

30. Which NLS parameter can be specified only as an environment variable?

A. NLS_LANGUAGE

B. NLS_LANG

C. NLS_TERRITORY

D. NLS_SORT

31. Look at the result of the following query and choose the best answer.

```
SELECT PROPERTY_VALUE FROM database_properties
WHERE  property_name = 'DEFAULT_TEMP_TABLESPACE';

PROPERTY_VALUE
--------------------------
APP_TEMP_TS
```

A. Newly created users in the database will be assigned APP_TEMP_TS as their temporary tablespace.

B. Newly created users in the database will be assigned APP_TEMP_TS as their temporary tablespace if the TEMPORARY TABLESPACE clause is omitted in the CREATE USER statement.

C. Newly created users in the database will be assigned APP_TEMP_TS as their temporary tablespace even if the TEMPORARY TABLESPACE clause is specified in the CREATE USER statement.

D. Newly created users in the database will be assigned APP_TEMP_TS as their default as well as temporary tablespace, if the DEFAULT TABLESPACE and TEMPORARY TABLESPACE clauses are omitted in the CREATE USER statement.

Answers to Assessment Test

1. B. The background processes and the SGA constitute an instance. An instance can have only one PMON process, but can have many server processes. An instance can only be associated with one database. See Chapter 2 for more information.

2. C. The sort area is not part of the SGA; it is part of the PGA. The sort area is allocated to the server process when required. See Chapter 2 for more information on the components of the SGA and an overview of the Oracle database architecture.

3. B. The LGWR process is responsible for writing the redo log buffer entries to the online redo log files. The LGWR process writes to the redo log files when a `COMMIT` occurs, when a checkpoint occurs, when the DBW*n* writes dirty buffers to disk, or every three seconds. To learn more about the background processes and database configuration, refer to Chapter 2.

4. C. Though answer A is correct, the more appropriate answer is C. You can use the `ALTER SYSTEM` command to enable or disable restricted access to the database. To learn about sessions and database startup/shutdown options, turn to Chapter 3.

5. D. When you connect to the database by using the `SYSDBA` privilege, you are really connecting to the SYS schema. If you use `SYSOPER`, you will be connected as `PUBLIC`. To learn more about administrator authentication methods, refer to Chapter 3.

6. A and B. When the database is in the `MOUNT` state, the control file is opened to get information about the data files and redo log files. You can query the SGA information by using the `V$` views as soon as the instance is started, that is, in the `NOMOUNT` state. More information about database start-up steps is in Chapter 3.

7. A and D. The clauses `MAXDATAFILES`, `MAXLOGFILES`, `MAXLOGMEMBERS`, `MAXINSTANCES`, and `MAXHISTORY` affect the size of the control file. Oracle pre-allocates space in the control file for the maximums you specify. To learn more about database creation, refer to Chapter 4.

8. C. The script `sql.bsq` is executed automatically by the `CREATE DATABASE` command, and it creates the data dictionary base tables. The `catalog.sql` script creates the data dictionary views. To learn more about the other scripts and data dictionary, refer to Chapter 4.

9. C. Redo log files and control files can be multiplexed. There should be a minimum of two control files and two redo log members on different disks. See Chapter 4 for more information about multiplexing database files.

10. A. When one of the redo log members becomes unavailable, Oracle writes an error message in the alert log file and the database operation continues uninterrupted. When all the redo log members of a group are unavailable, the instance shuts down. For more information, see Chapter 5.

11. B. You can have a maximum of eight control files per database. It is recommended that you keep the control files on different disks. For more information, see Chapter 5.

12. B. `FAST_START_MTTR_TARGET` ensures that no more than the specified number of seconds will elapse until the instance recovery is complete. `FAST_START_IO_TARGET and LOG_CHECKPOINT_TIMEOUT` are deprecated in Oracle 9i. `LOG_CHECKPOINTS_TO_ALERT` is `TRUE` if database checkpoints are logged in the alert log file. See Chapter 5.

13. C. The `ARCHIVE LOG LIST` command shows whether the database is in `ARCHIVELOG` mode, whether automatic archiving is enabled, the archival destination, and the oldest, next, and current log sequence numbers. Refer to Chapter 5.

14. C. The parameter `DB_CREATE_ONLINE_LOG_DEST_`*n* gives the directory location for the control file and redo log files. Oracle automatically generates the control filename itself.

    The parameter `DB_CREATE_SPFILE` is a nonexistent parameter. OMF uses `DB_CREATE_FILE_DEST` to specify the location of datafiles. The `CONTROL_FILES` parameter must NOT be present for OMF to automatically create the control file. See Chapter 5 for more information about maintaining the control file.

15. B. To rename a data file, you need to make the tablespace offline, so that Oracle does not try to update the data file, while you are renaming. Using OS commands copy the data file to the new location and using the ALTER DATABASE RENAME FILE command or the ALTER TABLESPACE RENAME FILE command, rename the file in the database's control file. To rename the file in the database, the new file should exist. Bring the tablespace online for normal database operation. For more information, refer to Chapter 6.

16. C. Use the `MINIMUM EXTENT` parameter to ensure that each extent is a multiple of the value specified. This parameter is useful for reducing fragmentation in the tablespace. For more information, refer to Chapter 6.

17. A, C. When the extent management options are handled through the dictionary, the tablespace is known as dictionary managed. When the extent management is done using bitmaps in the data files belonging to the tablespace, it is known as locally managed. The default is locally managed. For more information, see Chapter 6.

18. B, C. The `DBA_DATA_FILES` view has the size of each data file assigned to the tablespace; the total size of all the files is the size of the tablespace. Similarly, if the tablespace is locally managed and temporary, you need to query the `DBA_TEMP_FILES` view. For more information, refer to Chapter 6.

19. B. `DB_CREATE_FILE_DEST` specifies the directory to create data files and temp files. This directory is also used for control files and redo log files if the `DB_CREATE_ONLINE_LOG_DEST_1` parameter is not set. For more information, refer to Chapter 6.

20. B, C, D. Choice A is the only valid statement, because the undo tablespace can have any name that follows Oracle object-naming conventions. Choice B is incorrect because undo segments are not managed with `ALTER DATABASE`. Choices C and D are incorrect because the `UNDO_MANAGEMENT` parameter cannot be changed dynamically. Undo tablespace creation and management is discussed in Chapter 7.

21. A. You can specify PCTFREE and PCTUSED for creating or altering tables or clusters. You can specify PCTFREE for indexes. Creating or altering tablespaces does not allow the specification of free space management parameters. See Chapter 7 for more information on data block space management.

22. B and D. PCTFREE and PCTUSED are the space management parameters that control space in a block. PCTFREE specifies the percentage of space that should be reserved for future updates (which can increase the length of the row), and PCTUSED specifies when Oracle can start reinserting rows to the block once PCTFREE is reached. PCTFREE and PCTUSED together cannot exceed 100. To learn about space management parameters, refer to Chapter 7.

23. A. To see all the temporary segments in the database, use the DBA_SEGMENTS view and restrict the query using SEGMENT_TYPE = 'TEMPORARY'. The V$SORT_SEGMENT view shows only the temporary segments created in TEMPORARY tablespaces. To learn about the types of segments, see Chapter 7.

24. D. To rename an index, you use the ALTER INDEX *<old_name> RENAME TO <new_name>* command, but you cannot combine a rename with any other index operation. When rebuilding an index, you can specify a new tablespace and new storage parameters. The index can be rebuilt in parallel, and you can specify COMPUTE STATISTICS to collect statistics. For information about indexes, refer to Chapter 8.

25. B. You use the ANALYZE command to collect statistics on a table. COMPUTE STATISTICS reads all the blocks of the table and collects the statistics. ESTIMATE STATISTICS takes a few rows as a sample and collects statistics. For information about collecting statistics and validating structure by using the ANALYZE command, refer to Chapter 8.

26. A. PCTFREE specifies the free space reserved for future updates to rows. By specifying a larger value for PCTFREE, more free space is available in each block for updates. Row migration occurs when a row is updated and there is not enough space to hold the row; Oracle then moves the entire row to a new block, leaving a pointer in the old block. For information about data block free space management, refer to Chapter 8.

27. D. The DBA_CONS_COLUMNS view has the column name and position that belongs to the constraint. To find the primary key constraint name, query the DBA_CONSTRAINTS view with CONSTRAINT_TYPE and TABLE_NAME in the WHERE clause. To learn about constraints, refer to Chapter 8.

28. A, C, E. Oracle9i has four partitioning methods available: RANGE, HASH, COMPOSITE, and LIST. In range partitioning, rows with a range of values are mapped to a partition. In hash partitioning, rows are mapped to a partition using a derived hash value. In composite partitioning, range is used for partitions, and hash is used for sub-partitions. In list partitioning, rows are mapped to partitions based on discrete column values. For information about partition, refer to Chapter 8.

29. B. The NLS_SESSION_PARAMETERS view shows information about the NLS parameter values that are in effect in the session. For more information, see Chapter 9.

30. B. NLS_LANG is specified as an environment variable. The parameter specifies a language, a territory, and a character set. For more information, see Chapter 9.

31. B. The query shows the tablespace name specified for the DEFAULT TEMPORARY TABLESPACE clause of the CREATE DATABASE or ALTER DATABASE statement. Prior to Oracle9i, if you omit the TEMPORARY TABLESPACE clause in the CREATE USER statement, SYSTEM tablespace was the default. In Oracle9i, you can define a default temporary tablespace for the database. For more information, see Chapter 9.

Oracle9i New Features for Administrators

The Oracle9i platform picks up where Oracle8i left off. The Oracle9i database was enhanced across all major functional areas: server availability, scalability, performance, security, and manageability.

Of course, as an Oracle Certified DBA candidate, you need to know about all aspects of the Oracle database, not just the new features; however, if you have a good background in previous Oracle versions, you can certainly benefit from an Oracle9i new-features overview.

Although the Oracle9i platform is also enhanced in the application server and development tools areas, this chapter focuses on the new features of Oracle9i that are database-related.

As with any new release of the Oracle Server, a lot of the new features replace or make obsolete features that exist in previous versions of the Oracle Server. The last section of this chapter discusses the deprecated and unsupported features in Oracle9i.

High Availability

The Oracle9i database was enhanced in a number of areas to make sure that the database is available during maintenance operations, even if those maintenance operations are occurring on the user objects currently in use.

The Oracle DBA has more control over the recovery of the database in the case of instance failure, and the user has more options to re-create data even after changes or deletions have been committed.

More flexibility has been added to the import/export process, and LogMiner has been expanded to include DDL (Data Definition Language) statement support. RMAN (Recovery Manager) is more automated and more efficient; it is also easier to use with the new OEM (Oracle Enterprise Manager) interface.

You can perform additional operations on Index Organized Tables (IOTs), as well as redefinition operations on regular tables without any downtime for the users of those tables. The flexibility of the SPFILE initialization file option frees the DBA from having to edit a text-based initialization file and having to wait for a shutdown and restart for the new parameter values to take effect.

Disaster Recovery

In previous versions of Oracle, the DBA had to contend with a number of different parameters to strike a balance between high performance, availability, and minimal recovery time. Oracle9i introduces the new parameter `FAST_START_MTTR_TARGET` to allow the DBA to specify the maximum number of seconds that a crash recovery should take.

Database users can implement their own style of disaster recovery by using *Oracle Flashback Query*. A user can essentially move back to a particular point of time in the past and view the contents of a table or tables. Using this feature, users can "undo" changes made in the past by seeing which operations led to the change and then manually re-inserting or repairing the changes to the database. This feature can also be used as a historical query tool, for example, to give a bank customer an account balance as of a particular time in the past. This flashback capability is supported by the new system package `DBMS_FLASHBACK`.

Oracle Data Guard makes standby databases easier to use, with more robust failover features and an easy to use GUI interface. It essentially combines the primary and standby databases into a single "high availability" resource. Oracle's native standby database functionality (which can be managed under the Data Guard umbrella) has been enhanced to allow the primary database to be used as the new standby, instead of being discarded as in previous versions of Oracle.

Import/Export

Oracle9i contains a number of enhancements to make the Import and Export utilities more precise and efficient. Instead of having to manually recalculate table statistics after an import, the DBA can use statistics that were saved with the table during the export with the *STATISTICS* import parameter. This feature goes well beyond a simple "yes" or "no": the DBA can trust the Import engine to reject the saved statistics if they are questionable and to recalculate appropriately.

Another "fine-grained" enhancement to the Export utility is the ability to specify the tables to be exported by specifying the tablespace(s) that contain the tables to export. In addition to exporting all tables within a given tablespace, all indexes are exported with their corresponding tables regardless of where the index itself is stored.

The new Export and Import utilities support components of the Oracle Flashback Query feature, in which parts of an export can be extracted using new flashback parameters.

LogMiner

LogMiner, already a robust tool in previous versions of Oracle, has been significantly enhanced in Oracle9i. Unlike previous versions, the new version can support DDL statements, chained or migrated rows, and direct path inserts. Additionally, you can extract the database's data dictionary to the redo logs and analyze the logs with LogMiner.

In previous versions of LogMiner, all DDL statements were indirectly represented in the log files as several transactions against the data dictionary, making it difficult for the DBA to determine what the actual DDL statement was. Now, LogMiner will log both the DDL statement that the DBA or user typed, plus the multiple DML (Data Manipulation Language) statements run against the data dictionary.

Being able to extract the dictionary to a flat file or redo logs has several advantages:

- There is no performance hit against the live data dictionary, reducing dictionary contention with other transactional users of the database.
- Because all the information needed is in the redo logs, the database need not be open to use LogMiner.
- In a quickly changing data dictionary, the table metadata in the redo logs may not match what is currently in the live data dictionary.

A couple of other features are worthy of mention. In previous versions of LogMiner, the analysis stopped when a corrupted redo log file was encountered. In the new version of LogMiner, the SKIP_CORRUPTION option in the DBMS_LOGMNR.START_LOGMNR procedure notes and ignores the bad block(s). The other new option in this procedure is COMMITTED_DATA_ONLY. With this option enabled, any LogMiner operation will return results only from committed transactions.

Backup and Recovery

The enhancements to Recovery Manager (RMAN) are numerous. They fall into three basic categories:

- Persistent configuration parameters
- General enhancements to backup and restore
- A redesigned, easier-to-use graphical interface

RMAN now supports the *CONFIGURE* command, which allows the DBA to set the backup parameters persistently across backup sessions. Once all the appropriate parameters are set correctly, the DBA can do a full backup with one command, BACKUP DATABASE. The CONFIGURE command applies to many RMAN operations: backup retention policies, channel allocations, device type specifications, backup copies, and control file backups.

General enhancements to RMAN include *long-term backups*, *mirrored backups*, *restartable backups*, and *archive log backups*. Long-term backups are backups that you can explicitly archive for longer than the default retention policy. Mirrored backups are an enhanced version of the duplexing option originally released in Oracle8i, with the added capability to specify different formats (destinations) for backup copies. Time savings can be realized with the new restartable backup feature of RMAN. When you restart a backup with the NOT BACKED UP option, only missing or incomplete files are backed up, based on backup time. And finally, you can now include archive logs that have not been backed up in a datafile backup, instead of or in addition to using a BACKUP ARCHIVELOG command.

A significantly enhanced user interface to RMAN makes the DBA's job even easier. All the new options available in the command line interface are also available in the GUI version of the tool.

Online Operations

Many of the new features in Oracle9i allow online operations to proceed without interruption; in other words, access to tables and other database objects is continuously available to users even though redefinition and reorganization operations may be going on in the background. Of particular note are high availability enhancements related to *Index-Organized Tables* (IOTs), online reorganization of tables, and server-side parameter files (SPFILEs).

In previous versions of the Oracle database, an IOT was unavailable for most reorganization and index operations. In Oracle9i, a number of operations on IOTs are allowed while the table is in use. For example, you can create and rebuild IOT secondary indexes; you can update stale logical ROWIDs; you can rebuild IOTs by using the `ALTER TABLE ... MOVE` option, which can not only rebuild the primary key index but also rebuild the overflow data segment.

Problematic for an enterprise DBA are large tables that are heavily used around the clock and occasionally need some kind of modification or reorganization. In Oracle9i, many of the common operations that would previously have made the table unavailable can now be done "on the fly" with minimal impact to the table's users. For example, you can convert non-partitioned tables to partitioned tables, and vice versa. You can convert IOTs to heap-based tables. You can drop non-primary key columns, add new columns, and rename columns. In addition, you can modify storage parameters for a table. Tables without a primary key or tables with user-defined data types cannot be altered in this way, however.

SPFILEs enhance the online availability of databases by no longer requiring manual parameter file edits that may necessitate a restart of the database. An SPFILE is binary, not directly editable, and resides on the server. When you change SPFILE parameters with an `ALTER SYSTEM` command, they can be changed for the current instance only, the next restart of the instance (in other words, in the SPFILE), or both.

Scalability

The scalability of the Oracle9i Server is improved in three areas:

- Changes to the internal database structures to keep downtime to a minimum

- Expansion of the Oracle clustering technology (Real Application Clusters) to add additional resources without changes to application programs
- More flexibility in user session management to use session memory resources more efficiently

Architecture

Numerous changes to the Oracle9i architecture make the Oracle database even more scalable as the enterprise grows, with little or no changes to applications or procedures. In many cases, these new features smooth the operation and maintenance of the database for the DBA. These features include global index architecture changes, metadata extraction capabilities, and tablespace block management changes along with various memory management enhancements.

Global index improvements allow users and DBAs to execute DDL commands without invalidating the entire global index. This keeps the availability of the index as high as possible while at the same time making the DBA's life easier by reducing the number of steps and commands required to keep the indexes valid.

Extracting the *metadata* from a database was a complicated task in previous versions of Oracle, involving multiple queries or doing special export/import operations. Oracle9i adds a new package called `DBMS_METADATA` to either browse all metadata or to extract metadata for specific database objects. The output can be in either SQL or XML format.

The use of *external tables* in Oracle9i extends the reach of SQL select statements to external files. Although there are a number of restrictions on how external tables can be accessed, external tables provide a useful way to stage intermediate tables for data warehouse ETL (extract, transform, load) operations without loading the intermediate data into the database itself.

Automatic segment space management within a tablespace makes the DBA's life easier by essentially eliminating a lot of the guesswork when attempting to specify the default segment parameters in the tablespace. The free and used space is managed with bitmaps instead of free lists; tablespaces whose segment space is automatically managed must also be locally managed (that is, not managed in the data dictionary).

In the area of memory management, major changes were made in Oracle9i to ease the maintenance and improve the utilization of memory in the SGA (System Global Area). In essence, SGA memory and its sub-components can grow or shrink in response to changes in load or types of database operations being performed at the time. Memory in the SGA is now allocated in units called *granules*, whose size depends on the total estimated size of the SGA itself. In response to changing conditions, the DBA can dynamically change memory in each of the sub-components, such as the shared pool and buffer cache. To help the DBA in specifying an optimal buffer cache size, statistics collection can be enabled using the buffer cache advisory feature.

Real Application Clusters

In a nutshell, *Real Application Clusters* (RACs) allows multiple instances to run against the same database. Special hardware is required to allow a group of shared disks to be accessed at a very high throughput rate by each node in the cluster. Each node in the cluster can have more than one CPU.

There are a couple of benefits to using RACs. It's easy to add an additional node when the workload increases, without having to change any application code or operational procedures. Additionally, as each node is added to the cluster, the total availability of the database increases, as an instance failure on any particular node automatically initiates transparent application failover on one of the other nodes.

Cache Fusion, one of the new features included with RACs, allows data blocks to be shared between instances without the use of the shared disk resources. Retrieving a block from another instance's cache is significantly faster than retrieving that same block from a disk subsystem.

Session Management

Oracle Shared Server, formerly known as multithreaded server (MTS), contains many enhancements to further increase the performance and reduce the overhead of shared server connections. Changes to the connection establishment process reduce the total number of messages required to establish the connection between the client and the dispatcher. The new Common Event Model in the dispatcher handles both network and database events similarly, reducing overhead and the amount of polling required to capture the event notifications.

OCI (Oracle Call Interface) connection pooling allows middle-tier products to more efficiently manage a pool of connections for an application, rather than having the middleware explicitly manage the connections to the database.

Performance

Performance gains in the Oracle9i Server are realized with new features that are highly visible to the user or application developer. Conformance to the latest SQL standards makes coding more efficient for the developer and makes the execution of this code potentially more efficient on the server side. The DBA has a new feature set to help monitor index usage, allowing the DBA to drop indexes that are used infrequently or not at all.

SQL and PL/SQL Optimization

Oracle9i complies much closer with the SQL:1999 standards and syntax. Some of the standards now reflected in the Oracle SQL processor include enhancements to join operations, case statements, FK (foreign key) and PK (primary key) caching operations, and multi-table inserts. Significant enhancements to the PL/SQL processor allow for dramatic decreases in execution time for PL/SQL procedures, especially those that do not have SQL references.

You can now explicitly specify query join types in `FROM` clauses, rather than in the `WHERE` clause. The join types supported include *cross joins* (Cartesian products), *natural joins* (equijoins), and full, left, and right *outer joins*.

Oracle9i expands on the `CASE` expression that has been available since Oracle8i. A new type of `CASE` expression, a *searched `CASE`* expression, operates much like an `IF...THEN...ELSE` construct and allows for multiple predicates within the `WHEN` clauses. The *`NULLIF`* and *`COALESCE`* functions operate much like "abbreviated" `CASE` statements for returning and evaluating null values.

Unindexed foreign keys still require table-level share locks when an update or delete on the primary key takes place; however, the overhead is reduced and availability increased because the lock is immediately released after it is obtained. Foreign key creation is faster because Oracle9i caches the first 256 primary key values for DML statements that process at least two rows.

The new *multi-table insert* feature allows for easier coding and less SQL processing overhead, because all source and destination tables are specified in the same `INSERT` statement. You can also use this feature to easily refresh materialized views in a data warehouse environment.

PL/SQL execution is significantly more efficient in Oracle9i because the byte code generated in previous Oracle versions has been replaced by native C code. Additional performance gains are a result of the compiled code residing in the PGA (Program Global Area) rather than in the SGA, reducing contention in the SGA.

I/O Performance

The presence of too many indexes can negatively impact performance when you are inserting or updating rows, especially in an OLTP (Online Transaction Processing) environment. In addition, significant amount of disk space may be wasted if these indexes are not needed. You can gather new statistics at query parse time to help identify which indexes are used during a particular query. You can alter indexes directly with the `ALTER INDEX ... MONITORING USAGE` clause; new data dictionary views such as `V$OBJECT_USAGE` indicate whether a particular index has been used in the specified time frame.

Cursor sharing, a feature introduced in Oracle8i, has been enhanced in Oracle9i. In Oracle8i, you could reuse SQL statements in the shared pool if only the literal values in the SQL statement were different. In many cases, this reuse improved memory utilization in the shared pool, but risked some performance degradation when the values in the keyed column were skewed in terms of the histogram statistics. As a result, using only one execution plan for these queries was a potentially inefficient operation. In Oracle9i, the execution plans are reused only if the optimizer has determined that the execution plan is independent of the literal value(s) used in the query. The parameter `CURSOR_SHARING` can now have the value `SIMILAR` in addition to the already available `FORCE` and `EXACT` values.

To make Oracle's Cost Based Optimizer (CBO) more accurate, three new columns have been added to the `PLAN_TABLE`: `CPU_COST`, `IO_COST`, and `TEMP_SPACE`. In other words, the new Oracle9i cost model now takes into account the estimated CPU cost of the operation, the effect of caching, and the effect of using temporary segments for pre-fetching index blocks.

Java Enhancements

The internal Java engine has better garbage collection and native compilation. The performance has been enhanced by the use of object sharing and session pinning. Middle-tier operations have also been enhanced by internal improvements to JDBC (Java Database Connectivity) and SQLJ (SQL embedded in Java applications).

Security

Oracle9i adds a number of security related features to make random numbers more random, make rows of a table accessible only to those who need access, and allow the DBA to more easily audit table access based on an expanded set of conditions.

Data Encryption

Oracle9i introduces a new function, `GETKEY`, in the package `DBMS_OBFUSCATION_TOOLKIT`. Provided that the encryption keys themselves are stored securely, `GETKEY` will generate a random number that is significantly more secure than a number generated from `DBMS_RANDOM`.

Label Security

Oracle9i provides *Label Security*, a more secure and "fine-grained" approach to controlling access to rows in a database by the use of a special label in each row of the database. This new access control method is based on Oracle's Virtual Private Database (VPD) features and is facilitated by the use of a new set of PL/SQL packages.

Fine-Grained Auditing

Automatic auditing of the database has been enhanced in Oracle9i. In Oracle8i, auditing could be triggered only at a very high level: access of privileges or objects. In addition, the data returned in the audit table only contained a limited set of facts such as the username, date and time, and the object or privilege accessed. Using *Fine-Grained Auditing* (FGA), you can specify conditions on a given row of a table and record them in the audit table when those conditions are satisfied. In addition, user-defined procedures can be triggered when an audit condition is satisfied to perform additional processing, for example, to page the DBA when a particular row or set of rows is accessed in a table.

Manageability

The new manageability features of Oracle9i simplify the life of the DBA by centralizing the locations where various database-related files are stored. The enhanced *undo tablespace* (rollback) features eliminate much of the guesswork when setting up the proper undo structures for various database scenarios. DBAs also have more control over how resources are used within a resource consumer group. All these enhancements are fully supported through a simplified and streamlined Oracle Enterprise Manager (OEM).

Oracle Managed Files (OMF)

Oracle Managed Files (OMF) provides an easy way for the DBA to manage the locations of many types of database files by using two new initialization parameters. The DBA specifies only operating system locations for certain types of files, and the Oracle Server handles the unique naming of the operating system files themselves.

The two new parameters are `DB_CREATE_FILE_DEST` and `DB_CREATE_ONLINE_LOG_DEST_n`. The parameter `DB_CREATE_FILE_DEST` defines the default location for storing new datafiles associated with a given tablespace as well as for temporary files. The second parameter, `DB_CREATE_ONLINE_LOG_DEST_n`, provides similar functionality except that this location is specified for new control files and online redo log files. You manage archived redo log files as you did in previous Oracle versions.

Using OMF for one group of files does not prevent the DBA from continuing to use the older methods for naming files in the database; both methods can coexist nicely, and you can convert to a completely OMF-based database in stages.

Undo Tablespace Management

Automatic Undo Management provides yet another way to ease the administrative burden for the DBA. In previous Oracle versions, managing space for undo (rollback) segments was complex and error prone. In Oracle9i, managing space is almost as simple as creating an undo tablespace big enough to handle the maximum number of undo entries at the busiest time of the day and letting the Oracle database handle the rest. Another "fine-grained" enhancement to undo management is the ability for the DBA to specify how long to keep undo data before it is overwritten, potentially avoiding the classic, yet dreaded, "Snapshot too old" error.

You can create the undo tablespace when you create the database or later if migration from manual undo (rollback) management cannot be implemented immediately. Multiple undo tablespaces can exist in the database, although only one can be active at any given time.

Fine-Grained User Policy Management

User security has been strengthened with more restrictive, and therefore more secure, default values. Most of the accounts created by the Database Configuration Assistant (DBCA) are initially locked with expired passwords. The initialization parameter `O7_DICTIONARY_ACCESSIBILITY` now defaults to `FALSE`, unlike previous versions of Oracle. As a result, only users with the SYSDBA privilege can see the contents of the data dictionary.

The *Secure Application Role* feature of Oracle9i extends the functionality of Application Context first introduced in Oracle8i. To enable an application role in Oracle8i required using a password as authentication for a role; this practice can be a big security problem if the password itself is breached, therefore allowing any application to access the restricted data via the role. Instead, in Oracle9i, the role is enabled by calling a stored procedure, which can validate the user based on a number of criteria, such as the IP address of the user or the time of day.

The Oracle *Enterprise Login Assistant* (ELA) improves enterprise user security and ease of use by allowing users to have only one username and password (stored in the Oracle Internet Directory). In addition, because SSL (Secure Sockets Layer) and wallets on the client side are not required, user administration is further simplified for the DBA. Even previous versions of the Oracle client can use ELA to utilize single sign-on functionality.

Fine-Grained Resource Management

In Oracle9i, DBAs can further restrict or fine-tune resource usage by resource consumer group. The new *Active Session Pool* feature of the Database Resource Manager can now restrict how many active sessions can exist from users within a particular resource consumer group. If this limit is reached, the new user must wait until another user's session has completed. The data dictionary views `V$SESSION` and `V$RSRC_CONSUMER_GROUP` have new columns that show how many consumer group sessions are waiting for resources and how long they have been waiting.

You can use the new Oracle9i feature *Automatic Consumer Group Switching* to switch a particular session's consumer group on the fly. You can temporarily switch long-running daytime queries to a resource group that is normally used for nightly batch jobs if the session is active for more than a particular length of time. As a result, the session will not be terminated, but switched to another consumer group that will have less impact on OLTP transactions during the day.

On a similar note, you can also restrict the amount of undo space used by a session for a given consumer group by using the new plan directive `UNDO_POOL`. When this limit is exceeded, no further statements (other than `SELECT`) will be allowed for the session until other sessions within the same group release some undo segments or until the DBA manually increases the amount of undo quota allowed for the consumer group.

Enterprise Manager

Oracle Enterprise Manager (OEM) has had a major facelift in terms of look and feel. Instead of the four-pane format of previous versions of OEM, the new Oracle9i OEM has a simpler, two-pane master/detail layout. Many of the functions that were available by launching a separate executable in previous versions are now tightly integrated into a single OEM console. For example, the database administration functions previously available in DBA Studio are now a component of OEM.

As with previous versions of OEM, you can launch the console in standalone or via an Oracle Management Server (OMS). Connecting standalone does not require the middle-tier services nor do the target databases need the Intelligent Agent installed; however, the DBA cannot use many of the advanced features of OEM. These features include functionality such as Web-enabled applications, paging, backup tools, and access to events, jobs, and groups, to name a few.

Globalization Support

Previously known as National Language Support (NLS), *Globalization Support* is now the term that describes the features of Oracle9i that facilitate the use of the Oracle database with applications across all languages, continents, and time zones without having to customize the application for each locale in which the application is used.

New timestamp data types, such as TIMESTAMP and INTERVAL, are both more precise than the DATE data type in previous Oracle versions, but also allow the option to store a timestamp value as non-globalized, absolute within a specified time zone, or relative to the time zone of the user retrieving the data.

Along with the new TIMESTAMP and INTERVAL data types in Oracle9i are the operations and functions that support these types. "Common sense" operations between TIMESTAMP and INTERVAL are allowed, such as calculating an INTERVAL from two TIMESTAMP variables or adding an INTERVAL to a TIMESTAMP. A full complement of predefined functions are included to process these types, such as DBTIMEZONE to retrieve the value of the database time zone or TO_TIMESTAMP to convert a string representation of a timestamp to the internal representation.

Oracle9i supports Unicode version 3. New functions such as COMPOSE and DECOMPOSE handle characters with diacritical marks, and other new functions such as UNISTR convert a string to a Unicode string. And finally, expanded sorting options provide new sorts as well as a fourth level of sorting that can be user-defined using Oracle's Locale Builder.

Unsupported and Deprecated Features

Many of the changes to the Oracle9i Server that enhance the performance or increase the ease of use for both administrators and users can unfortunately require changes to features or changes in how a task is accomplished in Oracle9i. *Unsupported* features are not available at all; *deprecated* features are still available for sites that need to spread out the conversion over a period of time and more than one release of the Oracle Server.

Some of the key changes in Oracle9i are in the areas of backup and recovery, security, initialization parameter changes, network enhancements, and Unicode datatype handling.

Backup and Recovery

The Export/Import utilities still support the `INCREMENTAL` option, but this option may be removed in a future release. The `INCREMENTAL` option backed up an entire table even if only one row in the table was changed. You can still specify individual tables in an export operation, but administrators are encouraged to use RMAN (Recovery Manager) instead to back up and recover database tables and entire databases.

Using a clone database for tablespace point-in-time recovery (TSPITR) is deprecated in Oracle9i. Using the transportable tablespace (TTS) feature is recommended instead. For the same reason, the `FOR RECOVER` clause of `ALTER TABLESPACE ... OFFLINE` is supported only for backward compatibility.

Security

The `CONNECT INTERNAL` and `CONNECT INTERNAL/PASSWORD` commands are not supported in Oracle9i. Instead, you use the syntax `CONNECT / AS SYSDBA` or `CONNECT username/password AS SYSDBA`.

Server Manager is no longer supported. Use SQL*Plus for all DBA maintenance operations. Any automated scripts that were written for use with Server Manager should run in SQL*Plus with only minor modifications.

Network

The following services previously supported under Oracle Net8 (now known as Oracle Net Services) are no longer supported in Oracle9i: NDS External Naming and Authentication, the SPX protocol, Net8 `OPEN`, the authentication methods Identix and SecurID, and the use of a `protocol.ora` file.

In addition, no new features have been added to Oracle Names, and in the future, Oracle Names will no longer be used as a centralized naming method for name resolution. Instead, administrators should use Oracle Internet Directory (OID) for name resolution. Oracle Internet Directory uses LDAP (Lightweight Directory Access Protocol) version 3 and provides a high level of scalability, security, and availability that Oracle Names cannot provide.

Initialization Parameters

The initialization parameters in the following lists have been either deprecated or are not supported in Oracle9i. The replacements for these parameters are discussed in more detail in the other chapters of this book and the other books in the OCA/OCP series.

Deprecated Initialization Parameters

ROLLBACK_SEGMENTS

FAST_START_IO_TARGET

TRANSACTIONS_PER_ROLLBACK_SEGMENT

LOG_CHECKPOINT_INTERVAL

DB_BLOCK_BUFFERS

BUFFER_POOL_KEEP

BUFFER_POOL_RECYCLE

Unsupported Initialization Parameters

ALWAYS_ANTI_JOIN

ALWAYS_SEMI_JOIN

JOB_QUEUE_INTERVAL

OPTIMIZER_PERCENT_PARALLEL

HASH_MULTIBLOCK_IO_COUNT

DB_BLOCK_LRU_LATCHES

DB_BLOCK_MAX_DIRTY_TARGET

SORT_MULTIBLOCK_READ_COUNT

DB_FILE_DIRECT_IO_COUNT

GC_DEFER_TIME

GC_RELEASABLE_LOCKS

GC_ROLLBACK_LOCKS

LM_LOCKS

LM_RESS

USE_INDIRECT_DATA_BUFFERS

National Character Set

Various changes have been made to simplify and unify the use of Unicode characters in an Oracle database. The Unicode datatypes NCHAR, NVARCHAR2, and NCLOB can only be used as Unicode types in Oracle9i. The national character sets for these types can only be AL16UTF16 or UTF8; the AL24UTFFSS character set has been replaced by UTF8.

Summary

The new features in Oracle9i focus on two high levels: improvements to the "user experience" and improvements to make the life of a DBA less stressful. From the user's point of view, the Oracle Server is available when the user needs it, and the performance improvements keep up with their query processing needs, both from an OLTP and a data warehousing point of view. From the DBA's point of view, the database is more secure, easier to manage, and easier to upgrade without noticeable changes to applications or operations.

The Oracle9i server is more available than ever. Failover support is more robust and automatic, and the DBA's job is more streamlined by enhancements to the GUI for these new availability features. Database users are able to be more self-sufficient with the new features of LogMiner and Oracle Flashback Query feature, maximizing database availability while reducing the dependency on the DBA for routine historical data requests. In addition, many of the operations that required the database to be shut down can now be done online with minimal impact to ongoing user activity.

Many of the changes to the Oracle9i architecture facilitate both the performance and scalability of the Oracle server. Memory management is more flexible, allowing many of the SGA memory structures to grow and shrink as the demand on the system changes during the day. Access to external data is improved by treating some external data tables as if they were native Oracle tables.

The coding of SQL and PL/SQL statements is more streamlined for the application developer by higher conformance to the SQL:1999 standards. Additions to the supported join types, along with a more versatile CASE statement, and multi-table insert makes both the application developer and the Oracle server more efficient.

In terms of overall security, the Oracle9i Server provides more "fine-grained" enhancements: a better random number generator, the ability to more tightly control access to rows in a table, and a more useful and flexible means of auditing access to the database.

The Oracle9i Server is much easier to manage from a DBA perspective with the new Oracle Managed Files (OMF) and the automated undo features. Security is further enhanced by the Secure Application Role feature, which replaces a relatively weak password authentication method with a more robust and secure stored procedure methodology for enabling roles. DBAs can also control resource usage more easily by using the Active Session Pool feature to limit resource consumption by consumer group.

Globalization Support (formerly known as National Language Support) has been expanded well beyond the role of supporting different character sets. It now includes additional data types and predefined functions to support applications that will be run simultaneously in different languages and different time zones, with no changes to the application programs.

Many of the new features in Oracle9i either replace or make obsolete features in previous Oracle releases.

Key Terms

Before you take the exam, be certain you are familiar with the following terms:

Active Session Pool

archive log backups

Automatic Consumer Group Switching

Cache Fusion

`COALESCE`

`CONFIGURE`

cross joins

cursor sharing

Enterprise Login Assistant

external tables

Fine-Grained Auditing

global index

Globalization Support

granules

Index-Organized Table

Label Security

LogMiner

long-term backups

metadata

mirrored backups

multi-table insert

natural joins

`NULLIF`

Oracle Data Guard

Oracle Flashback

Oracle Managed Files

Oracle Shared Server

outer joins

Real Application Clusters

restartable backups

searched `CASE`

Secure Application Role

`STATISTICS`

undo tablespace

Review Questions

1. Which new feature of Oracle9i allows users to view the contents of a table at some point in the past?

   A. LogMiner

   B. Import

   C. Metadata Viewer

   D. Oracle Flashback

2. Choose the statement below that is true regarding enhancements to shared SQL statements in the shared pool.

   A. The cursor sharing feature can re-use a SQL statement even if the columns in the statement are in a different order or the `GROUP BY` clause is different.

   B. The new columns `CPU_COST`, `IO_COST`, and `TEMP_SPACE` in `PLAN_TABLE` help the rule-based optimizer (RBO) to be more accurate.

   C. Even if the only difference in SQL statements is in the literal values, the SQL statement may not be re-used if the histogram statistics are skewed for a column in the `WHERE` clause.

   D. The `CURSOR_SHARING` parameter now supports the `SIMILAR` and `DERIVED` values.

3. Given the table declaration below, identify invalid use of timestamp datatypes in an expression or function. (Choose two.)

```
CREATE TABLE TRANSACTIONS
(TRANS_ID          NUMBER,
AMOUNT             NUMBER(10,2),
TRANS_START TIMESTAMP,
TRANS_END          TIMESTAMP,
SHIP_DATE          DATE,
EXPIRE_DATE INTERVAL DAY(0) TO SECOND(0));
```

A. `TRANS_START - TRANS_END`

B. `TO_TIMESTAMP(AMOUNT, 'YY-MM-DD HH:MI:SS')`

C. `TRANS_START + INTERVAL '4' DAY`

D. `TRANS_START + SHIP_DATE`

4. Which of the following operations cannot be performed online without any disruption to ongoing online transactions?

A. Dropping a user-defined column

B. Rebuilding secondary IOT indexes

C. Adding new columns to a heap-based table

D. Rebuilding a primary IOT index

5. Which of the following types of joins are now allowed in the `FROM` clause of a SQL statement? (Choose all that apply.)

A. cross joins

B. inner joins

C. full outer joins

D. left outer joins

6. How many panes exist in the new version of Oracle Enterprise Manager (OEM)?

A. One, with pop-up windows

B. Four, as in previous versions

C. Two, in a master/detail format

D. Two, with DBA tools in the right-hand pane

7. The DBA is importing a table and an index from a dump file that was exported from another Oracle9i database. Which options does the DBA have when using the statistics from this dump file? (Choose all that apply.)

A. Explicitly accept all statistics

B. Explicitly reject all statistics

C. Let `IMPORT` decide if the statistics are safe; otherwise recalculate

D. Accept statistics only for non-partitioned tables

E. Explicitly re-calculate statistics, regardless of whether the original statistics are good or bad

8. The Secure Application Role feature in Oracle9i allows a user to authenticate role privileges by doing which of the following?

   A. Calling a stored procedure

   B. Using OS authentication

   C. Using PWFILE authentication

   D. Using an encrypted role password

9. Chad normally runs queries against very small tables, but has informed the DBA that he will soon be running some queries against the data warehouse tables for the operations manager. What can the DBA do to make sure that these new queries won't slow down OLTP operations? (Choose the best answer.)

   A. The DBA can use the Active Session Pool feature to put Chad's session on hold until another user in the same consumer group finishes their session.

   B. The DBA can use the Automatic Consumer Group Switching feature to switch Chad's consumer group to the same group as the OLTP users.

   C. The DBA can use the Active Session Pool feature to suspend the session if there are too many active OLTP sessions.

   D. The DBA can use the Automatic Consumer Group Switching feature to switch Chad's consumer group to a secondary group that has a lower priority.

10. Which of the following is not an advantage of having the data dictionary in the redo logs when using LogMiner for DML and DDL activity?

A. The LogMiner activity will not impact other users' activity against the data dictionary.

B. The LogMiner reports will be more accurate against a snapshot of the data dictionary rather than a constantly changing live data dictionary.

C. Bad blocks in one of the redo logs will not stop the LogMiner analysis with a static data dictionary.

D. The database does not need to be open to use LogMiner, since all needed information is in the redo logs.

11. Which of the new RMAN options can the DBA use to save time when a backup does not complete successfully?

A. Restart the backup with the `NOT BACKED UP` option.

B. Use mirrored backups to send the backup to two different device types.

C. Include the archive logs in the backup.

D. There is no alternative to a failed backup other than to restart the backup.

12. Identify the true statement regarding binary SPFILEs.

A. All changes to an SPFILE are implemented only after the instance is restarted.

B. Changes made to an SPFILE with the `ALTER SYSTEM` command can be made simultaneously with the change to the memory copy of the parameter.

C. An SPFILE can exist on the client side.

D. SPFILEs can be used in conjunction with a text-format PFILE.

13. Place the following block read options in order of access time, shortest to longest.

A. Block is read from remote cache without Cache Fusion

B. Block is read from a local cache

C. Block is read from a remote cache with Cache Fusion

D. Block is read from a shared disk

14. PL/SQL execution is significantly more efficient at runtime for which of the following reasons? (Choose two.)

A. Native C code is generated for PL/SQL procedures.

B. The compiled code resides in the SGA.

C. Byte code is generated by the compiler and therefore can easily be re-used by different transactions.

D. The compiled code resides in the PGA.

Answers to Review Questions

1. D. The package DBMS_FLASHBACK allows the user to view the contents of a table or tables at a specified time in the past.

2. C. If the execution plan is independent of the literal values used in the query, it is likely that the query can be re-used.

   The new columns in the PLAN_TABLE assist the cost-based optimizer, not the rule-based optimizer, and the CURSOR_SHARING parameter does not have DERIVED as a possible value.

3. B, D. Any reasonable combination of date and time data types is allowed. However, date fields cannot be added together, and dollar amounts are not valid arguments to date conversion functions.

4. A. Primary keys cannot be dropped nor can columns with user-defined data types be dropped without making a table unavailable.

5. A, B, C, D. All the above joins are now specified in the WHERE clause. Previous versions of Oracle supported all these join types other than the full outer join in the WHERE clause.

6. C. The new OEM not only uses a cleaner, easier-to-use two-pane layout, it integrates all the tools previously available through DBA Studio.

7. A, B, C, E. IMPORT cannot reject statistics based on whether the table is partitioned.

8. A. The stored procedure can restrict access to the role in a number of ways, such as by date and time or by the IP address of the user requesting access to the role.

9. D. Switching to another consumer group with a lower priority will allow the query to finish while minimizing the impact on the ongoing OLTP transactions.

   The Active Session Pool feature controls resource usage within the same consumer group and will not necessarily reduce the contention with OLTP transactions.

10. C. Bad blocks can be ignored in LogMiner; however this feature is independent of where LogMiner retrieves the data dictionary information.

11. A. Running RMAN with the `NOT BACKED UP` option backs up only the missing or incomplete files.

12. B. The changes to an SPFILE may be made at the same time the change is made to the memory copy of the parameter. SPFILEs only exist on the server side and are created using a PFILE. Once the SPFILE is activated, the PFILE is no longer needed.

13. B, C, D, A. Blocks read from a remote cache without Cache Fusion must be written to the shared disk by the remote instance before the blocks can be retrieved by the local instance.

14. A, D. The compiled code is moved to the PGA to reduce contention on the SGA; interpreted byte code is inherently less efficient to execute than native compiled C code.

Oracle Overview and Architecture

ORACLE9i FUNDAMENTALS I EXAM OBJECTIVES COVERED IN THIS CHAPTER:

- ✓ **Describe the Oracle architecture and its main components**
- ✓ **Describe the structures involved in connecting a user to an Oracle instance**

Exam objectives are subject to change at any time without prior notice and at Oracle's sole discretion. Please visit Oracle's Training and Certification website (`http://www.oracle.com/education/certification/`) for the most current exam objectives listing.

The Oracle9i database is filled with many features that enhance the functionality and improve the performance of the database. It is feature-rich with objects, Java, and many Internet programming techniques. The DBA Fundamentals I exam of the OCP (Oracle Certified Professional) certification tests your knowledge of the Oracle Server architecture and the most common administration tasks. This chapter begins by discussing the components that constitute the Oracle database and the way the database functions. Administering an Oracle database requires that you know how these components interact and how to customize them to best suit your requirements.

Oracle9i Server: An Overview

The Oracle Server consists of two major components—the database and the instance. *Database* is a confusing term that is often used to represent different things on different platforms; the only commonality is that it is something to do with data. In Oracle, the term *database* represents the physical files that store data. An *instance* comprises the memory structures and background processes used to access data (from the physical database files). Each database should have at least one instance associated with it. It is possible for multiple instances to access a single database; this is known as the Real Application Cluster configuration.

Oracle Objective **Describe the Oracle server architecture and its main components**

You use the Oracle database, which is a collection of data, to store and retrieve information. The database consists of logical structures and physical structures. *Logical structures* represent the components that you can see in the Oracle database (such as tables, indexes, and so on), and *physical structures* represent the method of storage that Oracle uses internally (the physical files). Oracle maintains the logical structure and physical structure separately, so that the logical structures can be defined identically across different hardware and operating system platforms.

Logical Storage Structures

Oracle logically divides the database into smaller units to manage, store, and retrieve data efficiently. The following paragraphs give you an overview of the logical structures; they are discussed in detail in the coming chapters.

Tablespaces The database is logically divided into smaller units at the highest level called tablespaces. A *tablespace* commonly groups related logical structures together. For example, you might group data specific to an application or a function together in one or more tablespaces. This logical division helps to administer a portion of the database without affecting the rest of it. Each database should have one or more tablespaces. When you create a database, Oracle creates the SYSTEM tablespace as a minimum requirement.

Blocks A *block* is the smallest unit of storage in Oracle. A block is usually a multiple of the operating system block size. A data block corresponds to a specific number of bytes of storage space. The block size is based on the parameter DB_BLOCK_SIZE and is determined when the database is created.

Extents An *extent* is the next level of logical grouping. It is a grouping of contiguous blocks, allocated in one chunk.

Segments A *segment* is a set of extents allocated for logical structures such as tables, indexes, clusters, and so on. Whenever you create a logical structure, Oracle allocates a segment, which contains at least one extent, which in turn has at least one block. A segment can be associated to only one tablespace. Figure 2.1 shows the relationship between tablespaces, segments, extents, and blocks.

FIGURE 2.1 Logical structure

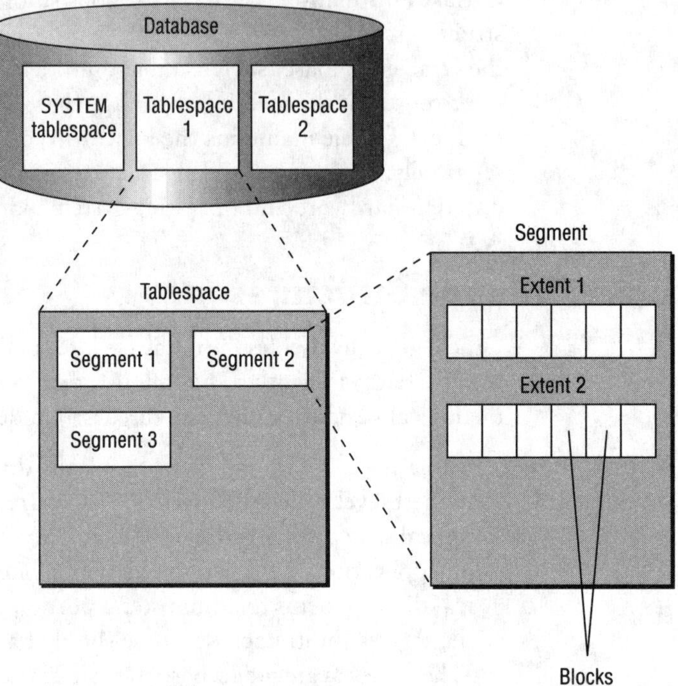

There are four types of segments:

Data segments Store the table (or cluster) data. Every table created will have a segment allocated.

Index segments Store the index data. Every index created will have an index segment allocated.

Temporary segments Are created when Oracle needs a temporary work area, such as for sorting, during a query, and to complete execution of a SQL statement. These segments are freed when the execution completes.

Undo segments Store undo information. When you roll back the changes made to the database, undo records in the undo tablespace are used to undo the changes.

Segments and other logical structures are discussed in detail in Chapter 6, "Logical and Physical Database Structures."

A *schema* is a logical structure that groups the database objects. A schema is not directly related to a tablespace or to any other logical storage structure. The objects that belong to a schema can reside in different tablespaces, and a tablespace can have objects that belong to multiple schemas. Schema objects include structures such as tables, indexes, synonyms, procedures, triggers, database links, and so on.

Physical Storage Structures

The physical database structure consists of three types of physical files:

- Data files
- Redo log files
- Control files

The purpose and contents of each type of file are explained in the following paragraphs. Figure 2.2 shows the physical structures and how the database is related to the memory structures and background processes. This figure also shows the relationship between tablespaces and data files.

Data files contain all the database data. Every Oracle database should have one or more data files. Each data file is associated with one and only one tablespace. A tablespace can consist of more than one data file.

Redo log files *Redo log files* record all changes made to data. Every Oracle database should have two or more redo log files, because Oracle writes to the redo log files in a circular fashion. If a failure prevents a database change from being written to a data file, you can obtain the changes from the redo log files; therefore changes are never lost. Redo logs are critical for database operation and recovery from a failure. Oracle allows you to have multiple copies of the redo log files (preferably on different disks). This feature is known as *multiplexing* of redo logs, a process in which Oracle treats the redo log and its copies as a group identified with an integer, known as a redo log group. Redo log files are discussed in detail in Chapter 5, "Control Files and Redo Log Files."

FIGURE 2.2 Oracle Server physical structures

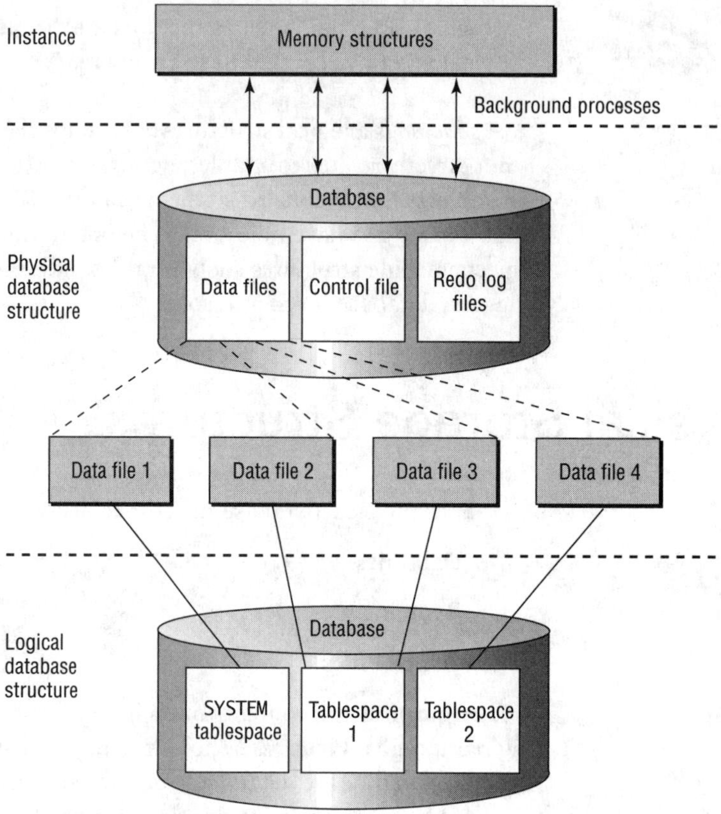

Instance
Memory structures
Background processes
Database
Physical database structure
Data files
Control file
Redo log files
Data file 1
Data file 2
Data file 3
Data file 4
Database
Logical database structure
SYSTEM tablespace
Tablespace 1
Tablespace 2

Control files Every Oracle database has at least one *control file*. It maintains information about the physical structure of the database. The control file can be multiplexed, so that Oracle maintains multiple copies. It is critical to the database. The control file contains the database name and timestamp of database creation as well as the name and location of every data file and redo log file. Control files are discussed in detail in Chapter 5, "Control Files and Redo Log Files."

The size of a tablespace is determined by the total size of all the data files associated with the tablespace. The size of the database is the total size of all its tablespaces.

Oracle Memory Structures

The memory structures are used to cache application data, data dictionary information (metadata—information about the objects, logical structures, schemas, privileges, and so on—discussed in Chapter 3, "Creating a Database and Data Dictionary"), Structured Query Language (SQL) commands, PL/SQL and Java program units, transaction information, data required for execution of individual database requests, and other control information. Memory structures are allocated to the Oracle instance when the instance is started. The two major memory structures are known as the *System Global Area* (also called the *Shared Global Area*) and the *Program Global Area* (also called the *Private Global Area* or the *Process Global Area*). Figure 2.3 illustrates the various memory structures in Oracle.

FIGURE 2.3 Oracle memory structures

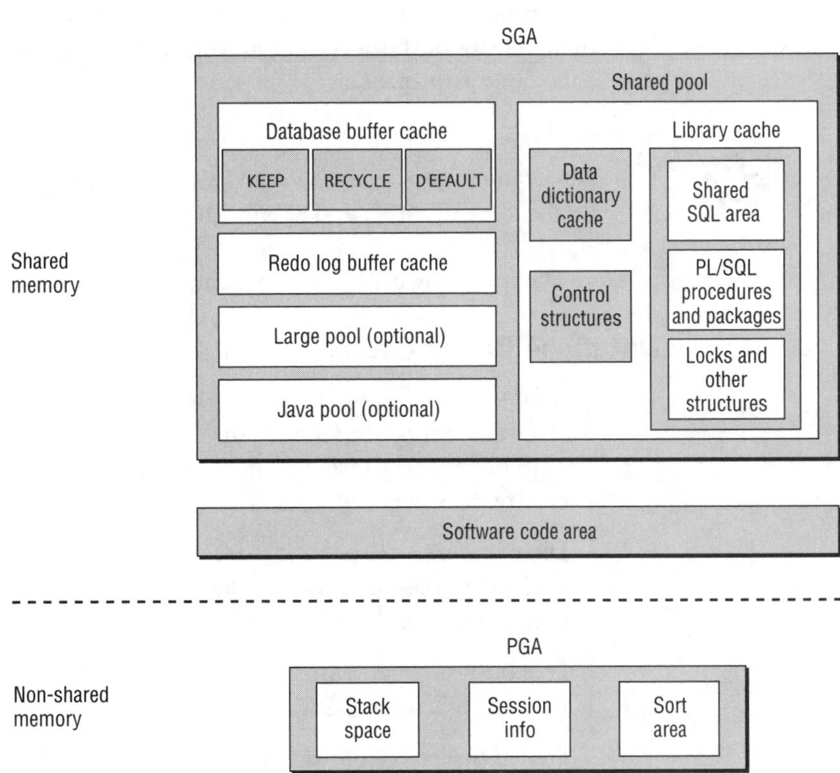

System Global Area

The *System Global Area (SGA)* is a shared memory area. All users of the database share the information maintained in this area. The SGA and the background processes constitute an Oracle instance. Oracle allocates memory for the SGA when an Oracle instance is started and de-allocates it when the instance is shut down. The information stored in the SGA is divided into multiple memory structures that are allocated space when the instance is started. These memory structures are dynamic in Oracle9i, in which the total size cannot exceed the value specified in the initialization parameter SGA_MAX_SIZE.

Memory in the SGA is allocated in units of contiguous memory called *granules*. The size of a granule depends on the parameter SGA_MAX_SIZE; if the SGA size is less than 128MB, each granule is 4MB; otherwise, each granule is 16MB.

A minimum of three granules are allocated for the SGA: one for the fixed part of the SGA (redo buffers, locking information, database state information), one for the buffer cache, and one for the shared pool (library cache and data dictionary cache).

The dynamic performance view V$BUFFER_POOL tracks the granules allocated for the DEFAULT, KEEP, and RECYCLE buffer pools.

The following are the components of the SGA.

Database Buffer Cache

The *database (DB) buffer cache* is the area of memory that caches the database data, holding blocks from the data files that have been read recently. The DB buffer cache is shared among all the users connected to the database. There are three types of buffers:

Dirty buffers *Dirty buffers* are the buffer blocks that need to be written to the data files. The data in these buffers has changed and has not yet been written to the disk.

Free buffers *Free buffers* do not contain any data or are free to be overwritten. When Oracle reads data from disk, free buffers hold this data.

Pinned buffers *Pinned buffers* are the buffers that are currently being accessed or explicitly retained for future use (for example, the KEEP buffer pool).

Oracle maintains two lists to manage the buffer cache. The *write list* (dirty buffer list) contains the buffers that are modified and need to be written to the disk (the dirty buffers). The *least recently used (LRU)* list contains free buffers, pinned buffers, and the dirty buffers that have not yet been moved to the write list. Consider the LRU list as a queue of blocks, in which the most recently accessed blocks are always in the front (known as the most recently used, or MRU, end of the list; the other end, where the least recently accessed blocks are, is the LRU end). The least-used blocks are thrown out of the list when new blocks are accessed and added to the list.

When an Oracle process accesses a buffer, it moves the buffer to the MRU end of the list so that the most frequently accessed data is available in the buffers. When new data buffers are moved to the LRU list, they are copied to the MRU end of the list, pushing out the buffers from the LRU end. An exception to this procedure occurs when a full table is scanned; in this case, the blocks are written to the LRU end of the list. When an Oracle process requests data, it searches the data in the buffer cache, and if it finds data, the result is a cache hit. If it cannot find the data, the result is a cache miss, and data then needs to be copied from disk to the buffer.

Before reading a data block into the cache, the process must first find a free buffer. The server process on behalf of the user process searches either until it finds a free buffer or until it has searched the threshold limit of buffers. If the server process finds a dirty buffer as it searches the LRU list, it moves that buffer to the write list and continues to search. When the process finds a free buffer, it reads the data block from the disk into the buffer and moves the buffer to the MRU end of the LRU list. If an Oracle server process searches the threshold limit of buffers without finding a free buffer, the process stops searching and signals the DBW*n* background process to write some of the dirty buffers to disk. The DBW*n* process and other background processes are discussed in the next section.

Oracle9i allows for three independent sub-caches within the database buffer cache: The KEEP buffer pool retains the data blocks in memory; they are not aged out. The RECYCLE buffer pool removes the buffers from memory as soon as they are not needed. The DEFAULT buffer pool contains the blocks that are not assigned to the other pools. The parameters DB_CACHE_SIZE, DB_KEEP_CACHE_SIZE, and DB_RECYCLE_CACHE_SIZE determine the size of the buffer cache. DB_RECYCLE_CACHE_SIZE determines the size to be allocated to the RECYCLE pool, and DB_KEEP_CACHE_SIZE determines the size to be allocated to the KEEP pool, in the buffer cache. The DB_BLOCK_SIZE parameter defines the size of an Oracle block in the buffer cache. When creating or altering tables and indexes, you can specify the BUFFER_POOL in the STORAGE clause.

To allow the DBA (database administrator) to size the components of the buffer cache efficiently, Oracle9i provides the "buffer cache advisory feature" to maintain the statistics associated with different cache sizes. This feature does incur a small performance hit on both memory and CPU, however.

You use the parameter DB_CACHE_ADVICE to enable or disable statistics collection; its values can be ON, OFF, or READY. The view V$DB_CACHE_ADVICE is available for displaying the cache statistics.

Redo Log Buffer

The *redo log buffer* is a circular buffer in the SGA that holds information about the changes made to the database data. The changes are known as redo entries or change vectors and are used to redo the changes in case of a failure. Changes are made to the database through INSERT, UPDATE, DELETE, CREATE, ALTER, or DROP commands.

The parameter LOG_BUFFER determines the size of the redo log buffer cache.

Shared Pool

The *shared pool* portion of the SGA holds information such as SQL, PL/SQL procedures and packages, the data dictionary, locks, character set information, security attributes, and so on. The shared pool consists of the library cache and the data dictionary cache.

Library Cache

The *library cache* contains the shared SQL areas, private SQL areas, PL/SQL procedures and packages, and control structures such as locks and library cache handles.

The shared SQL area is used for maintaining recently executed SQL commands and their execution plans. Oracle divides each SQL statement that it executes into a shared SQL area and a private SQL area. When two users are executing the same SQL, the information in the shared SQL area is used for both. The shared SQL area contains the parse tree and execution plan, whereas the private SQL area contains values for the bind variables (persistent area) and runtime buffers (runtime area). Oracle creates the runtime area as the first step of an execute request. For INSERT, UPDATE, and DELETE statements, Oracle frees the runtime area after the statement has been executed. For queries, Oracle frees the runtime area only after all rows have been fetched or the query has been canceled.

Oracle processes PL/SQL program units the same way it processes SQL statements. When a PL/SQL program unit is executed, the code is moved to the shared PL/SQL area, and the individual SQL commands within the program unit are moved to the shared SQL area. Again, the shared program units are maintained in memory with an LRU algorithm. If another process requires the same program unit, Oracle can omit disk I/O and compilation, and the code that resides in memory will be executed.

The instance maintains the third area of the library cache for internal use. Various locks, latches, and other control structures reside here, and any server processes that require this information can freely access it.

Data Dictionary Cache

The *data dictionary* is a collection of database tables and views containing metadata about the database, its structures, its privileges, and its users. Oracle accesses the data dictionary frequently during the parsing of SQL statements. The *data dictionary cache* holds the most recently used database dictionary information. The data dictionary cache is also known as the *row cache* because it holds data as rows instead of buffers (which hold entire blocks of data).

The parameter SHARED_POOL_SIZE determines the size of the shared pool and can be dynamically altered.

Large Pool

The *large pool* is an optional area in the SGA that the DBA can configure to provide large memory allocations for specific database operations such as an Oracle backup or restore. The large pool allows Oracle to request large memory allocations from a separate pool to prevent contention from other applications for the same memory. The large pool does not have an LRU list.

The parameter LARGE_POOL_SIZE specifies the size of the large pool and can be dynamically altered.

Java Pool

The *Java pool* is another optional area in the SGA that the DBA can configure to provide memory for Java operations, just as the shared pool is provided for processing SQL and PL/SQL commands.

The parameter JAVA_POOL_SIZE determines the size of the Java pool, but can not be dynamically altered.

Program Global Area

The *Program Global Area (PGA)* is the area in the memory that contains the data and process information for one process, and this area is non-shared memory. The contents of the PGA depend on the server configuration. For a dedicated server configuration (one dedicated server process for each connection to the database—dedicated server and shared server configurations are discussed later in this chapter), the PGA holds stack space and session information. For shared server configurations, in which user connections are pooled through a dispatcher, the PGA contains the stack space information, and the session information is in the SGA. *Stack space* is the memory allocated to hold variables, arrays, and other information that belongs to the session. A PGA is allocated for each server process and de-allocated when the process is completed. Unlike the SGA that is shared by several processes, the PGA provides sort space, session information, stack space, and cursor information for a single server process.

Sort Area

The memory area that Oracle uses to sort data is known as the *sort area*, and it uses memory from the PGA for a dedicated server connection. For shared server configurations, the sort area is allocated from the SGA. Shared and dedicated server configurations are discussed later in this chapter. Sort area size can grow depending on the need; you use the SORT_AREA_SIZE parameter to set the maximum size. The parameter SORT_AREA_RETAINED_SIZE determines the size to which the sort area is reduced after the sort operation. The memory released from the sort area is kept with the server process; it is not released to the operating system.

If the data to be sorted does not fit into the memory area defined by SORT_AREA_SIZE, Oracle divides the data into smaller pieces that do fit and sorts these individually. These individual sorts are called *runs*, and the sorted data is held in the user's temporary tablespace using temporary segments. When all the individual sorts are complete, Oracle merges these runs to produce the final result. Oracle sorts the result set if the query contains a DISTINCT, ORDER BY, or GROUP BY operator or any set operators (UNION, INTERSECT, MINUS).

Managing SORT_AREA_SIZE in a large enterprise environment may be challenging. The trick is trying to maximize performance without using up too many system resources. Oracle9i provides an automatic method for managing PGA memory. The two key initialization parameters used to automate PGA memory management are PGA_AGGREGATE_TARGET and WORKAREA_SIZE_POLICY. The value for PGA_AGGREGATE_TARGET specifies the *total* amount of memory that can be used by all server processes, and the value for WORKAREA_SIZE_POLICY is either MANUAL or AUTO.

Software Code Area

Software code areas are the portions of memory that store the code that is being executed. Software code areas are mostly static in size and depend on the operating system. These areas are read-only and can be shared (if the operating system allows), so multiple copies of the same code are not kept in memory. Some Oracle tools and utilities (such as SQL*Forms and SQL*Plus) can be installed as shared, but some cannot. Multiple instances of Oracle can use the same Oracle code area with different databases if they are running on the same computer.

Oracle Background Processes

A *process* is a mechanism used in the operating system to execute a series of tasks. Oracle starts multiple processes in the background when the instance is started. Each background process is responsible for specific tasks. The following sections describe each process and its purpose. All the background processes need not be present in every instance. Figure 2.4 shows the Oracle background processes.

FIGURE 2.4 The Oracle background processes

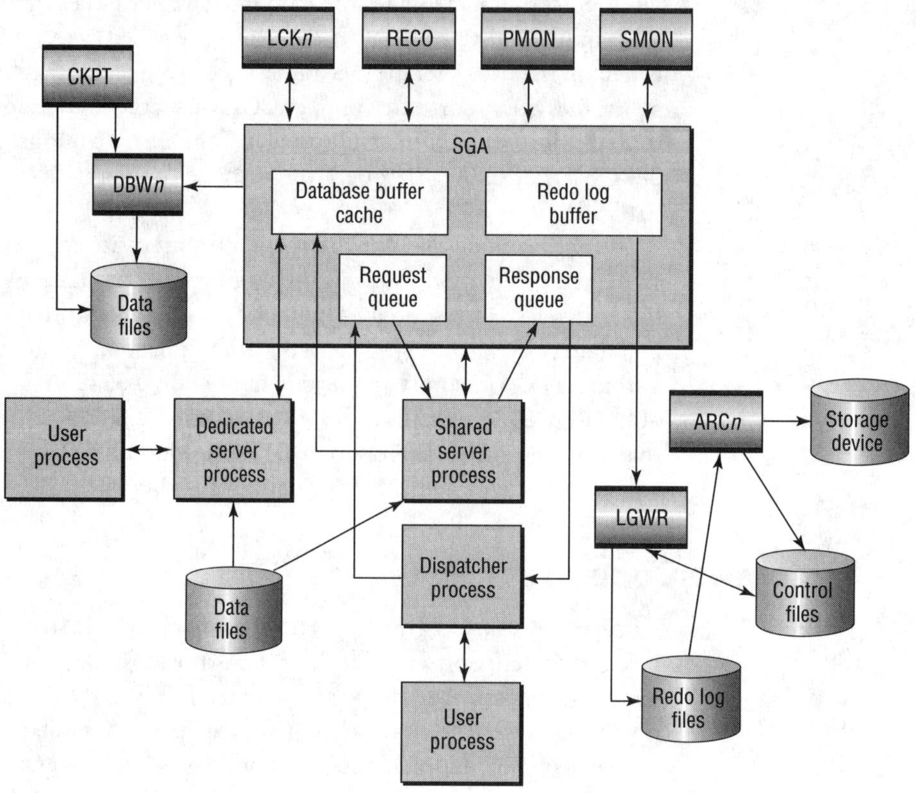

A user (client) process is initiated from the tool that is trying to use the Oracle database. A *server process* accepts a request from the *user process* and interacts with the Oracle database. On dedicated server systems, there will be one server process for each client connection to the database.

Database Writer (DBW*n*)

The purpose of the *database writer process (DBWn)* is to write the contents of the dirty buffers to the data file. By default, Oracle starts one database writer process (DBW0) when the instance starts; for multi-user and busy systems, you can have nine more database writer processes (DBW1 through

DBW9) to improve performance. The parameter DB_WRITER_PROCESSES determines the additional number of database writer processes to be started.

The DBW*n* process writes the modified buffer blocks to disk, so more free buffers are available in the buffer cache. Writes are always performed in bulk to reduce disk contention; the number of blocks written in each I/O is operating system dependent. The DBW*n* process initiates writing to data files under these circumstances:

- When the server process cannot find a clean buffer after searching the set threshold of buffers, it initiates the DBW*n* process to write dirty buffers to the disk, so that some buffers are freed.
- When a checkpoint occurs, DBW*n* periodically writes buffers to disk.
- When a timeout occurs.
- When you change a tablespace to read-only.
- When you place a tablespace offline.
- When you drop or truncate a table.
- When you place a tablespace in BACKUP mode.

Writes to the data file(s) are independent of the corresponding COMMIT performed in the SQL code.

Log Writer (LGWR)

The *log writer process (LGWR)* writes the blocks in the redo log buffer in the SGA to the online redo log files. The redo log buffer is circular. When the LGWR writes log buffers to the disk, Oracle server processes can write new entries in the redo log buffer. LGWR writes the entries to the disk fast enough to ensure that room is available for the server process to write log information. The log writer process writes the buffers to the disk under the following circumstances:

- When a user transaction issues a COMMIT
- When the redo log buffer is one-third full
- When the DBW*n* process writes dirty buffers to disk

- Every three seconds
- When there is one megabyte of redo records

LGWR writes simultaneously to the multiplexed online redo log files. Even if one of the log files in the group is damaged, LGWR continues writing to the available file. LGWR writes to the redo logs sequentially so that transactions can be applied in order in the event of a failure.

By writing the committed transaction to the redo log files, the change to the database is never lost (that is, it can be recovered if a failure occurs).

Checkpoint (CKPT)

Checkpoints help to reduce the time required for instance recovery. A *checkpoint* is an event that flushes the modified data from the buffer cache to the disk and updates the control file and data files. The *checkpoint process (CKPT)* updates the headers of data files and control files; the DBW*n* process writes the actual blocks to the file.

If checkpoints occur too frequently, disk contention becomes a problem with the data file updates. If checkpoints occur too infrequently, the time required to recover a failed database can be significantly longer. Checkpoints occur automatically when an online redo log file fills (log switch). A log switch occurs when Oracle finishes writing one file and starts the next file.

System Monitor (SMON)

The *system monitor process (SMON)* performs instance or crash recovery at database start-up by using the online redo log files. SMON is also responsible for cleaning up temporary segments in the tablespaces that are no longer used and for coalescing the contiguous free space in the tablespaces. If any dead transactions were skipped during crash and instance recovery because of file-read or offline errors, SMON recovers them when the tablespace or file is brought back online. SMON wakes up regularly to check whether it is needed. Other processes can call SMON if they detect a need for SMON to wake up.

SMON coalesces the contiguous free space in a tablespace only if its default PCTINCREASE value is set to a nonzero value.

Process Monitor (PMON)

The *process monitor process (PMON)* cleans up failed user processes and frees up all the resources used by the failed process. It resets the status of the active transaction table and removes the process ID from the list of active processes. It reclaims all resources held by the user and releases all locks on tables and rows held by the user. PMON wakes up periodically to check whether it is needed.

DBW*n*, LGWR, CKPT, SMON, and PMON processes are the default processes associated with all instances.

Archiver (ARC*n*)

When the Oracle database is running in *ARCHIVELOG* mode, the online redo log files are copied to another location before they are overwritten. You can use these archived log files to recover the database. When the database is in ARCHIVELOG mode, you can recover the database up to the point of failure. The *archiver process (ARCn)* performs the archiving function. Oracle9i can have as many as 10 ARC*n* processes (ARC0 through ARC9). The LGWR process starts new ARC*n* processes whenever the current number of ARC*n* processes is insufficient to handle the workload. The ARC*n* process is enabled only if the database is in ARCHIVELOG mode and automatic archiving is enabled (parameter LOG_ARCHIVE_START = TRUE).

Recoverer (RECO)

The *recoverer process (RECO)* is used with distributed transactions to resolve failures. The RECO process is present only if the instance permits distributed transactions and if the DISTRIBUTED_TRANSACTIONS parameter is set to a nonzero value. If this initialization parameter is zero, RECO is not created during instance start-up. This process attempts to access databases involved in in-doubt transactions and resolves the transactions. A transaction is in doubt when you change data in multiple databases and a failure occurs before you save the changes. The failure can be the result of a server crash or a network problem.

Lock (LCK*n*)

LCKn processes (LCK0 through LCK9) are used in the Real Application Cluster environment, for inter-instance locking. The Real Application Cluster option lets you mount the same database for multiple instances.

Queue Monitor (QMN*n*)

The *queue monitor process* is used for Oracle Advanced Queuing, which monitors the message queues. You can configure as many as 10 queue monitor processes (QMN0 through QMN9). Oracle Advanced Queuing provides an infrastructure for distributed applications to communicate asynchronously using messages. Oracle Advanced Queuing stores messages in queues for deferred retrieval and processing by the Oracle Server. The parameter `AQ_TM_PROCESSES` specifies the number of queue monitor processes.

Failure of an SNP process or a QMN process does not cause the instance to crash; Oracle restarts the failed process. If any other background process fails, the Oracle instance fails.

Dispatcher (D*nnn*)

Dispatcher processes are part of the shared server architecture. They minimize the resource needs by handling multiple connections to the database using a limited number of server processes. You can create multiple dispatcher processes for a single database instance; you must create at least one dispatcher for each network protocol used with Oracle.

Shared Server (S*nnn*)

Shared server processes provide the same functionality as the dedicated server processes, except that shared server processes are not associated with a specific user process. You create shared server processes to manage connections to the database in a shared server configuration. The number of shared server processes that you can create ranges between the values of the parameters SHARED_SERVERS and MAX_SHARED_SERVERS.

Real World Scenario

Managing and Monitoring Background Processes

Over the last couple of weeks, the users have reported that the system is slowing down. Your system hardware manager had just added a second CPU and some additional disk drives to handle the space needed by some new applications that use your database. The users always seem to get their reports, and their sessions never terminate abnormally. You suspect that one of the background processes may be at fault.

As an experienced DBA, you know that the first place you should look is the alert log. There might be a trace file in the user dump area, but the users are not reporting anything abnormal other than the increase in response time. The alert log indicates that your log switches are occurring every couple of minutes, and you're occasionally getting "Checkpoint not complete" messages. Because of the increase in the number of users, the online log files (discussed in later chapters) are filling up too fast and causing unnecessary delays for the users. You decide to automate the review of these logs in the future so you can catch these problems before the users notice a problem.

Keeping the background processes straight can be a challenge. Some of them exist as single background processes (for example, LGWR), while other background processes may have multiple copies for a given instance (for example, DBWn). The alert log, the process-specific logs, and the user logs are the key to detecting and preventing performance problems.

Daily "cron" jobs or some of the newer features of Oracle Enterprise Manager (OEM) can easily automate the review of the logs and e-mail the results to the DBA or operations group. In addition, these jobs can clean up, truncate, or archive the logs if the size of the log file becomes unmanageable.

Many third-party tools can also help manage these tasks, but knowing what's going on "under the hood" is required to use these tools effectively.

Connecting to an Oracle Instance

Before discussing the actual mechanism for connecting to an Oracle database, let us review the terms *user process* and *server process*.

An application program (such as Pro*C) or an Oracle tool (such as SQL*Plus) starts the user process when you run the application tool. The user process may be on the same machine where the instance/database resides, or it may be initiated from a client machine in a client/server architecture.

Oracle Objective — **Describe the structures involved in connecting a user to an Oracle instance**

A server process gets requests from the user process and interacts with the Oracle instance to carry out the requests. On some platforms, it is possible to combine the user process and the server process (single task) to reduce system overhead if the user process and the server process are on the same machine. The server process is responsible for the following:

- Parsing and executing SQL statements issued via the application or tool
- Reading the data files and bringing the necessary data blocks into the shared buffer cache if the data blocks requested are not already in the SGA
- Returning the results to the user process in such a way that it can understand the data

In client/server architecture, OracleNet is commonly used to communicate between the client and the server. The client process (user process) attempts to establish a connection to the database using the appropriate OracleNet driver, and then OracleNet communicates with the server and assigns a server process to fulfill the request on behalf of the user process. OracleNet has a listener on the server that constantly waits for connection requests from client machines (client and server can be on the same machine).

Depending on the architecture of the network, the distribution of the employees, the response time requirements, and the security requirements, different users may connect to the database using different methods. The next two sections describe the ways in which an Oracle user can connect to the database using either a dedicated server connection or a multithreaded (shared server) connection. For certain DBA operations, dedicated server connections are required.

Dedicated Server Configuration

In a dedicated server configuration, one server process is created for each connection request. Oracle assigns a dedicated server process to take care of the requests from the user process. The server process is terminated when the user process disconnects from the database. Even if the user process is not making any requests, the server process will be idling and waiting for a request. Refer to Figure 2.4 for a diagram of how a user process interacts with Oracle by using a dedicated server process.

The following steps detail how a dedicated server process takes the request from a user process and delivers the results (the background processes are not discussed in these steps):

1. The client application or tool initiates the user process to connect to the instance.
2. The client machine communicates the request to the server machine by using OracleNet drivers. The OracleNet listener on the server detects the request and starts a dedicated server process on behalf of the user process after verifying the username and password.
3. The user issues a SQL command.
4. The dedicated server process determines whether a similar SQL is in the shared SQL area. If not, it allocates a new shared SQL area for the command and stores the parse tree and execution plan. During parsing, the server process checks for syntactic correctness of the statement, checks whether the object names are valid, and checks privileges. The required information is obtained from the data dictionary cache. A PGA is created to store the private information of the process.

5. The server process looks for data blocks that need to be changed or accessed in the buffer cache. If they are not there, it reads the data files and brings the necessary blocks to the SGA.
6. The server process executes the SQL statement. If data blocks need to be changed, they are changed in the buffer cache (the DBW*n* process updates the data file). The change is logged in the redo log buffer.
7. The status of the request or the result is returned to the user process.

The Shared Server (Multithreaded) Configuration

If many users are connecting to the dedicated server database, there will be many server processes. Most of the time, these server processes will be idle for Online Transaction Processing (OLTP) applications. You can configure Oracle to have one server process manage multiple user processes. This configuration is known as the *shared server* or *multithreaded configuration*.

In a shared server configuration, Oracle starts a fixed number of server processes when the instance starts. These processes work in a round-robin fashion to serve requests from the user processes. The user processes connect to a dispatcher background process, which routes client requests to the next available shared server process. One dispatcher process can handle only one communication protocol; hence, there should be at least one dispatcher process for every protocol used.

The shared server configuration requires all connections to use OracleNet. So, for establishing a connection to the instance using a shared server configuration, three processes are involved: an OracleNet listener process, a dispatcher process, and a shared server process.

When a user makes a request, the dispatcher places the request on the request queue; an available shared server process picks up the request from this queue. When the shared server process completes the request, it places the response on the calling dispatcher's response queue. Each dispatcher has its own response queue in the SGA. The dispatcher then returns the completed request to the appropriate user process. Figure 2.4 shows the connection using a shared server configuration and the associated processes.

The following steps detail how a shared server process takes the request from a user process and delivers the results:

1. When the instance is started, one or more shared server processes and dispatcher processes are started. The OracleNet listener is running on the server. The request and response queues are created in the SGA.
2. The client application or tool initiates the user process to connect to the instance.
3. The client machine communicates the request to the server machine by using OracleNet drivers. The OracleNet listener on the server detects the request and identifies the protocol that the user process is using. It connects the user process to one of the dispatchers for this protocol (if no dispatcher is available for the requested protocol, a dedicated server process is started by the listener).
4. The user issues a SQL command.
5. The dispatcher decodes the request and puts it into the request queue (at the tail) along with the dispatcher ID.
6. The request moves up the queue as the server processes serve the previous requests. The next available shared server process picks up the request.
7. The shared server process determines whether a similar SQL statement is there in the shared SQL area. If not, it allocates a new shared SQL area for the command and stores the parse tree and execution plan. During parsing, the server process checks for syntactic correctness of the statement, validity of the object names, and privileges. The required information is obtained from the data dictionary cache. A PGA is created to store the private information of the process.
8. The server process looks for data blocks that need to be changed or accessed in the buffer cache. If they are not there, it reads the data files and brings the necessary blocks into the SGA.

9. The server process executes the SQL statement. If data blocks need to be changed, they are changed in the buffer cache (the DBW*n* process updates the data file). The change is logged in the redo log buffer.

10. The status of the request or the result is returned to the response queue for the dispatcher.

11. The dispatcher periodically checks the response queue. When it finds a response, it sends it to the requested user process.

Processing SQL Statements

You use Structured Query Language (SQL) to manipulate and retrieve data in an Oracle database. Data Manipulation Language (DML) statements query or manipulate data in existing database objects. `SELECT`, `INSERT`, `UPDATE`, `DELETE`, `EXPLAIN PLAN`, and `LOCK TABLE` are DML statements. These are the most commonly used statements in the database. In this section, we'll explain how Oracle processes the queries and other DML statements. We'll also discuss what happens when a user makes the changes they made to the database permanent (issues a `COMMIT`), or decides to undo the changes (issues a `ROLLBACK`).

This section on processing SQL statements is primarily for background information. More than likely you will not come across a question on processing SQL statements in the Oracle9i Fundamentals I exam.

SQL Parse, Execute, and Fetch Stages

SQL statements are processed in either two or three steps, or stages. Each SQL statement passed to the server process from the user process goes through parse and execute phases. In the case of queries (`SELECT` statements), an additional phase of fetch is done to retrieve the rows. We will look at each of these in the following sections.

Parse *Parsing* is one of the first stages in processing any SQL statement. When an application or tool issues a SQL statement, it makes a parse call to Oracle, which does the following:

- Checks the statement for syntax correctness and validates the table names and column names against the dictionary
- Determines whether the user has privileges to execute the statement
- Determines the optimal execution plan for the statement
- Finds a shared SQL area for the statement

If there is an existing SQL area with the parsed representation of the statement in the library cache, Oracle uses this parsed representation and executes the statement immediately. If not, Oracle generates the parsed representation of the statement, allocates a shared SQL area for the statement in the library cache, and stores its parsed representation there. Oracle's parse operation allocates a shared SQL area for the statement, which allows the statement to be executed any number of times without parsing repeatedly.

Execute Oracle executes the parsed statement in the *execute* stage. For `UPDATE` and `DELETE` statements, Oracle locks the rows that are affected, so that no other process is making changes to the rows until the transaction is completed. Oracle also looks for data blocks in the data buffer cache. If it finds them, the execution will be faster; if not, Oracle has to read the data blocks from the physical data file to the buffer cache. If the statement is a `SELECT` or an `INSERT`, no rows need to be locked because no data is being changed.

Fetch The *fetch* operation follows the execution of a SQL `SELECT` command. After the execution completes, the rows identified during the execution stage are returned to the user process. The rows are ordered (sorted) if requested by the query. The results are always in a tabular format; rows may be fetched (retrieved) one row at a time or in groups (array processing).

Figure 2.5 shows the steps required in processing a `SELECT` query.

FIGURE 2.5 Query processing stages

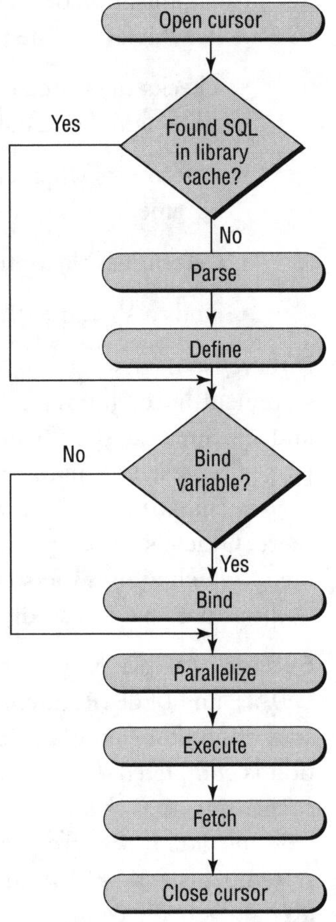

1. Create a cursor. The cursor may be explicit or implicit.
2. Parse the statement.
3. Define output: specify location, type, and data type of the result set, and convert the data type if necessary. This step is required only when the results are fetched to variables.
4. Bind variables; if the query is using any variables, Oracle should know the value for the variables.

5. See whether the query can be run in parallel, that is, whether multiple server processes can be working to complete the query.
6. Execute the query.
7. Fetch the rows.
8. Close the cursor.

Figure 2.6 shows the steps required to process one of the DML statements `INSERT`, `UPDATE`, or `DELETE`.

FIGURE 2.6 DML processing stages

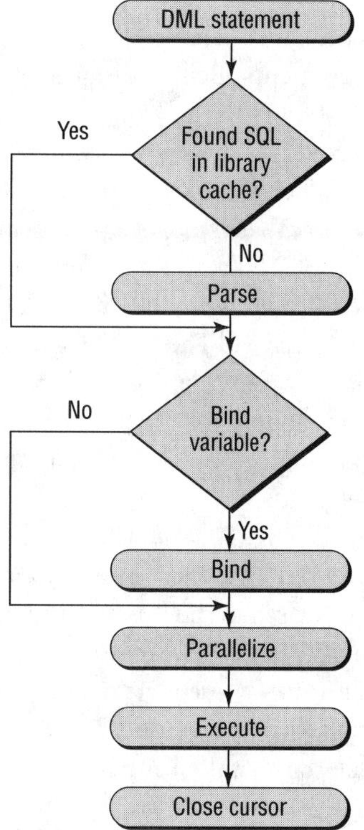

1. Create a cursor; Oracle creates an implicit cursor.
2. Parse the statement.

3. Bind variables; if the statement is using any variables, Oracle should know the value for the variables.
4. See whether the statement can be run in parallel (multiple server processes working to complete the work).
5. Execute the statement.
6. Inform the user that the statement execution is complete.
7. Close the cursor.

Processing a *COMMIT or ROLLBACK*

You have seen how the server process processes a query and other DML statements. Before discussing the steps in processing a `COMMIT` or a `ROLLBACK`, let's look at an important mechanism that Oracle uses for recovery—the *system change number (SCN)*.

When a transaction commits, Oracle assigns a unique number that defines the database state at a precise moment in time, acting as an internal timestamp. The SCN is a serial number, unique and always increasing. SCNs provide a read-consistent view of the database. The database is always recovered based on the SCN. The SCN is also used to provide a read-consistent view of the data. When a query reaches the execution stage, the current SCN is determined; only the blocks with an SCN less than or equal to this SCN are read—for changed blocks (with a higher SCN), data is read from the rollback segments.

The SCN is recorded in the control file, data file headers, block headers, and redo log files. The redo log file has a low SCN (the lowest change number stored in the log file) and high SCN (the highest change number in the log file—assigned when the file is closed, before opening the next redo log file). The SCN value is stored in every data file header, which is updated whenever a checkpoint is done. The control file records the SCN number for each data file that is taken offline.

Steps in Processing a *COMMIT*

Oracle commits a transaction when you do the following:

- Issue a `COMMIT` command
- Execute a DDL statement
- Disconnect from Oracle

The following are the steps for processing a COMMIT, that is, making the changes to the database permanent:

1. The server process generates an SCN number and is assigned to the rollback segment; then it marks in the rollback segment that the transaction is committed.
2. The LGWR process writes the redo log buffers to the online redo log files along with the SCN number.
3. The user is notified that the COMMIT is complete.
4. The server process releases locks held on rows and tables.
5. The server process marks the transaction as complete.

Oracle defers writes to the data file to reduce disk I/O. The DBW*n* process writes the changed blocks to the data file independent of any COMMIT. By writing the change vectors and the SCN number to the redo log files, Oracle ensures that the committed changes are never lost. This process is known as the *fast commit*—writes to redo log files are faster than writing the blocks to data files.

Steps in Processing a *ROLLBACK*

If the transaction has not been committed, it can be rolled back; that is, the state of the database tables for the session are restored to their original values. Oracle rolls back a transaction when:

- You issue a ROLLBACK command.
- The server process terminates abnormally.
- The DBA kills the session.

The following steps are used in processing a ROLLBACK, that is, in undoing the changes to the database:

1. The server process undoes all changes made in the transaction by using the undo segment entries.
2. The server process releases all locks held on tables and rows.
3. The server process marks the transaction as complete.

Summary

This chapter introduced you to the Oracle architecture and configuration. The Oracle Server consists of a database and an instance. The database consists of the structures that store the actual data. The instance consists of the memory structures and background processes. The database has logical structures and physical structures. Oracle maintains the logical structures and physical structures separately, so they can be managed independently of each other.

The database is divided logically into multiple tablespaces. Each tablespace can have multiple segments. Each database table or index is allocated a segment. The segment consists of one or many extents. The extent is a contiguous allocation of blocks. A block is the smallest unit of storage in Oracle.

The physical database structures include data files, control files, and redo log files. The data files contain all the database data. The control file keeps information about the data files and redo log files in the database, as well as the database name, creation timestamp, and so on. The redo log files keep track of the database changes. You can use the redo log files to recover the database in case of instance or media failure.

The memory structures of an Oracle instance include the System Global Area (SGA) and Program Global Area (PGA). The SGA is shared among all the database users; the PGA is not. The SGA consists of the database buffer cache, shared pool, and redo log buffers.

The database buffers cache the recently used database blocks in memory. The dirty buffers are the blocks that are changed and need to be written to the disk. The DBW*n* process writes these blocks to the data files. The redo log buffers keep all changes to the database; these buffers are written to the redo log files by the LGWR process. The shared pool consists of the library cache, dictionary cache, and other control structures. The library cache contains parsed SQL and PL/SQL codes. The dictionary cache holds the most recently used dictionary information.

The application tool (such as SQL*Plus or Pro*C) communicates with the database by using a server process on the server side. Oracle can have dedicated server processes, whereby one server process takes requests from one user process. In a multithreaded configuration, the server processes are shared.

Parse, execute, and fetch are the major steps used in processing queries. For other DML statements (other than SELECT), the stages are parse and execute. The parse step compiles the statement in the shared pool, checks the user's privileges, and arrives at an execution plan. In the execute step, the parsed statement is executed. During the fetch step, data is returned to the user.

Exam Essentials

Identify the three types of database files that constitute the database. Briefly describe the purpose and key differences between control files, data files, and redo log files. Describe other essential files that are needed to start up the database but are not considered a part of the database.

Explain and categorize the SGA memory structures. Identify the SGA areas along with the sub-components contained within each of these areas. Be able to place a database-related object (for example, a SQL statement or a data file block) into its appropriate SGA area.

Understand the steps involved in processing a SQL statement. Understand which server components do and do not participate in processing SQL, and understand the steps required when a DML statement is executed.

Enumerate and explain the primary (required) background processes. Identify each process with its primary purpose, its interaction with other background processes, and when the background process is active.

Understand the purpose of the PGA. List the components of the PGA, as well as understand the conditions under which PGA components are stored in the SGA.

Identify the initialization parameters related to the SGA and buffer pool sizing. Understand which parameters can be dynamically altered and which parameters are optional.

Key Terms

Before you take the exam, make sure you're familiar with the following terms:

- ARCHIVELOG
- archiver process (ARCn)
- block
- checkpoint process (CKPT)
- control file
- data dictionary
- data dictionary cache
- data file
- database
- database buffer cache
- database writer process (DBWn)
- dirty buffer
- execute
- extent
- fetch
- free buffer
- granules
- instance
- Java pool
- large pool
- library cache
- log writer process (LGWR)
- logical structures
- multithreaded configuration
- parsing
- physical structures
- pinned buffer
- Private Global Area
- Process Global Area
- process monitor process (PMON)
- Program Global Area
- recoverer process (RECO)
- redo log buffer
- redo log file
- runs
- schema
- segment
- server process
- Shared Global Area
- shared pool
- shared server configuration
- software code areas
- sort area
- system change number (SCN)
- System Global Area (SGA)
- system monitor process (SMON)
- tablespace
- user process

Review Questions

1. Which component is not part of the Oracle instance?

   A. System Global Area

   B. Process monitor

   C. Control file

   D. Shared pool

2. Which background process and associated database component guarantee that committed data is saved even when the changes have not been recorded in the data files?

   A. DBW*n* and database buffer cache

   B. LGWR and online redo log file

   C. CKPT and control file

   D. DBW*n* and archived redo log file

3. What is the maximum number of database writer processes allowed in an Oracle instance?

   A. 1

   B. 10

   C. 256

   D. Limit specified by an operating system parameter

4. Which background process is not started by default when you start up the Oracle instance?

   A. DBW*n*

   B. LGWR

   C. CKPT

   D. ARC*n*

5. Which of the following best describes a Real Application Cluster configuration?

   A. One database, multiple instances

   B. One instance, multiple databases

   C. Multiple databases on multiple servers

   D. Shared server process takes care of multiple user processes

6. Choose the correct hierarchy, from largest to smallest, from this list of logical database structures.

   A. Database, tablespace, extent, segment, block

   B. Database, tablespace, segment, extent, block

   C. Database, segment, tablespace, extent, block

   D. Database, extent, tablespace, segment, block

7. Which component of the SGA contains the parsed SQL code?

   A. Buffer cache

   B. Dictionary cache

   C. Library cache

   D. Parse cache

8. Julie, one of the database analysts, is complaining that her queries are taking longer and longer to complete, although they seem to produce the correct results. The DBA suspects that the buffer cache is not sized correctly and is causing delays due to data blocks not being available in memory. Which initialization parameter should the DBA use to monitor the usage of the buffer cache?

   A. `BUFFER_POOL_ADVICE`

   B. `DB_CACHE_ADVICE`

   C. `DB_CACHE_SIZE`

   D. `SHARED_POOL_SIZE`

9. Which background process is responsible for writing the dirty buffers to the database files?

   A. DBW*n*

   B. SMON

   C. LGWR

   D. CKPT

   E. PMON

10. Which component in the SGA has the dictionary cache?

    A. Buffer cache

    B. Library cache

    C. Shared pool

    D. Program Global Area

    E. Large pool

11. When a server process is terminated abnormally, which background process is responsible for releasing the locks held by the user?

    A. DBW*n*

    B. LGWR

    C. SMON

    D. PMON

12. What is a dirty buffer?

    A. Data buffer that is being accessed

    B. Data buffer that is changed but is not written to the disk

    C. Data buffer that is free

    D. Data buffer that is changed and written to the disk

13. If you are updating one row in a table using the `ROWID` in the `WHERE` clause (assume that the row is not already in the buffer cache), what will be the minimum amount of information read to the database buffer cache?

    A. The entire table is copied to the database buffer cache.

    B. The extent is copied to the database buffer cache.

    C. The block is copied to the database buffer cache.

    D. The row is copied to the database buffer cache.

14. What happens next when a server process is not able to find enough free buffers to copy the blocks from disk?

    A. Signals the CKPT process to clean up the dirty buffers

    B. Signals the SMON process to clean up the dirty buffers

    C. Signals the CKPT process to initiate a checkpoint

    D. Signals the DBW*n* process to write the dirty buffers to disk

15. Which memory structures are shared? Choose two.

    A. Sort area

    B. Program Global Area

    C. Library cache

    D. Large pool

16. Which of the following initialization parameters does NOT determine the size of the buffer cache?

    A. `DB_KEEP_CACHE_SIZE`

    B. `DB_CACHE_SIZE`

    C. `DB_BLOCK_SIZE`

    D. `DB_RECYCLE_CACHE_SIZE`

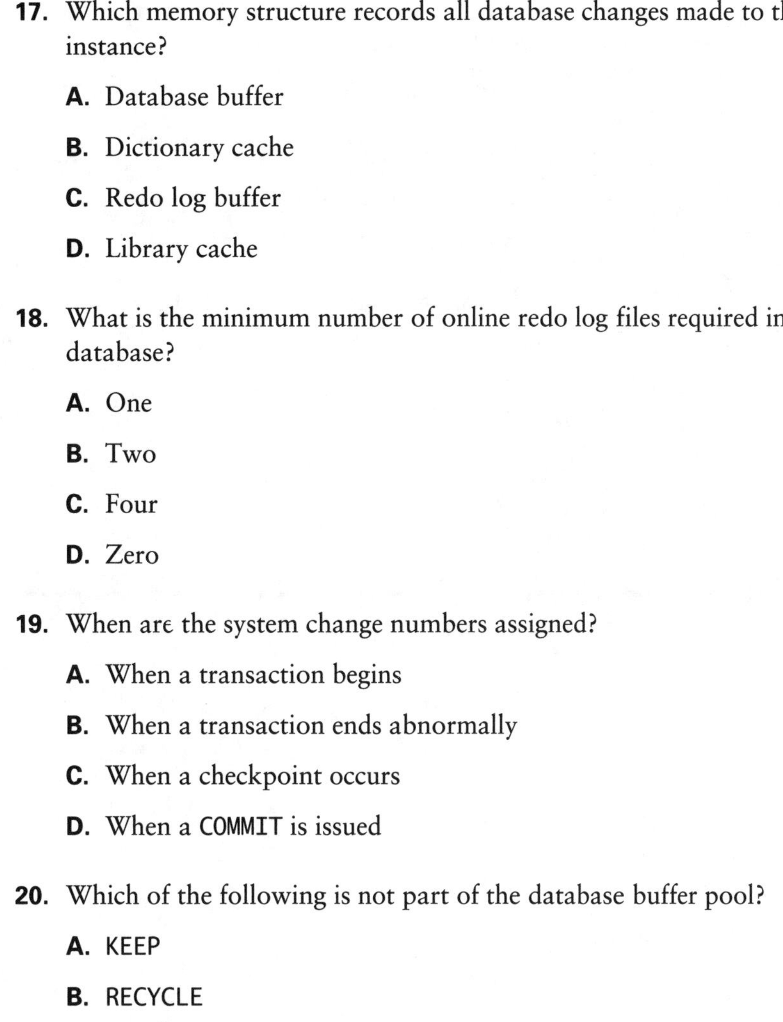

17. Which memory structure records all database changes made to the instance?

A. Database buffer

B. Dictionary cache

C. Redo log buffer

D. Library cache

18. What is the minimum number of online redo log files required in a database?

A. One

B. Two

C. Four

D. Zero

19. When are the system change numbers assigned?

A. When a transaction begins

B. When a transaction ends abnormally

C. When a checkpoint occurs

D. When a `COMMIT` is issued

20. Which of the following is not part of the database buffer pool?

A. `KEEP`

B. `RECYCLE`

C. `LIBRARY`

D. `DEFAULT`

21. Memory granules are not allocated at instance startup for which of the following SGA components?

    A. Database buffer cache

    B. Shared pool

    C. Redo log buffers

    D. Large pool

    E. None of the above

Answers to Review Questions

1. C. The Oracle instance consists of memory structures and background processes. The Oracle database consists of the physical components such as data files, redo log files, and the control file. The System Global Area and shared pool are memory structures. The process monitor is a background process.

2. B. The LGWR process writes the redo log buffer entries when a `COMMIT` occurs. The redo log buffer holds information on the changes made to the database. The DBW*n* process writes dirty buffers to the data file, but it is independent of the `COMMIT`. The dirty buffers can be written to the disk before or after a `COMMIT`. Writing the committed changes to the online redo log file ensures that the changes are never lost in case of a failure.

3. B. By default, every Oracle instance has one database writer process—DBW0. Additional processes can be started by setting the initialization parameter `DB_WRITER_PROCESSES`(DBW1 through DBW9).

4. D. ARC*n* is the archiver process, which is started only when the `LOG_ARCHIVE_START` initialization parameter is set to `TRUE`. DBW*n*, LGWR, CKPT, SMON, and PMON are the default processes associated with all instances.

5. A. In a Real Application Cluster configuration, multiple instances (known as nodes) can mount one database. One instance can be associated with only one database. In a multithreaded configuration, one shared server process takes requests from multiple user processes.

6. B. The first level of logical database structure is the tablespace. A tablespace may have segments, segments have one or more extents, and extents have one or more contiguous blocks.

7. C. The library cache contains the parsed SQL code. If a query is executed again before it is aged out of the library cache, Oracle will use the parsed code and execution plan from the library cache. The buffer cache has data blocks that are cached. The dictionary cache caches data dictionary information. There is no SGA component named parse cache.

8. B. The parameter `DB_CACHE_ADVICE` can be set to `YES` to enable cache usage monitoring. `DB_CACHE_SIZE` and `SHARED_POOL_SIZE` are sizing parameters for SGA structures; the parameter `BUFFER_POOL_ADVICE` does not exist.

9. A. The DBW*n* process writes the dirty buffers to the data files under two circumstances—when a checkpoint occurs or when the server process searches the buffer cache for a set threshold.

10. C. The shared pool has three components: the library cache, the dictionary cache, and the control structures.

11. D. PMON, or the process monitor, is responsible for cleaning up failed user processes. It reclaims all resources held by the user and releases all locks on tables and rows held by the user.

12. B. Dirty buffers are the buffer blocks that need to be written to the data files. The data in these buffers has changed and is not yet written to the disk. A block waiting to be written to disk is on the dirty list and cannot be overwritten.

13. C. The block is the smallest unit that can be copied to the buffer cache.

14. D. To reduce disk I/O contention, the DBW*n* process does not write the changed buffers immediately to the disk. They are written only when the dirty buffers reach a threshold, when there are not enough free buffers available, or when the checkpoint occurs.

15. C and D. The sort area is allocated to the server process as part of the PGA. The PGA is allocated when the server process starts and is de-allocated when the server process completes. The library cache and the large pool are part of the SGA and are shared. The SGA is created when the instance starts.

16. C. The parameter `DB_BLOCK_SIZE` does not change the size of the buffer cache. It changes only the size of each Oracle block written to and read from disk.

17. C. The redo log buffer keeps track of all changes made to the database before writing them to the redo log files. The database buffer contains the data blocks that are read from the data files, and are most recently used. The dictionary cache holds the most recently used data dictionary information. The library cache holds the parsed SQL statements and PL/SQL code.

18. B. There should be at least two redo log files in a database. The LGWR process writes to the redo log files in a circular manner, so there should be at least two files.

19. D. A system change number (SCN) is assigned when the transaction is committed. The SCN is a unique number acting as an internal timestamp, used for recovery and read-consistent queries.

20. C. There is no database buffer cache named `LIBRARY`. The DBA can configure multiple buffer pools by using the appropriate initialization parameters for performance improvements. The `KEEP` buffer pool retains the data blocks in memory; they are not aged out. The `RECYCLE` buffer pool removes the buffers from memory as soon as they are not needed. The `DEFAULT` buffer pool contains the blocks that are not assigned to the other pools.

21. E. All of these SGA components are allocated in granule units. A minimum of three granules are allocated for the SGA at instance startup: one for the fixed portion of the SGA, one for the database buffer cache, and one for the shared pool.

Installing and Managing Oracle

ORACLE9i DBA FUNDAMENTALS I EXAM OBJECTIVES OFFERED IN THIS CHAPTER:

- ✓ Identify common database administrative tools available to a DBA
- ✓ Identify the features of the Oracle Universal Installer
- ✓ Explain the benefits of Optimal Flexible Architecture (OFA)
- ✓ Set up password file authentication
- ✓ List the main components of the Oracle Enterprise Manager and their uses
- ✓ Create and manage initialization parameter files
- ✓ Configure Oracle Managed Files (OMF)
- ✓ Start up and shut down an instance
- ✓ Monitor the use of diagnostic files

Exam objectives are subject to change at any time without prior notice and at Oracle's sole discretion. Please visit Oracle's Training and Certification website (`http://www.oracle.com/education/certification/`) for the most current exam objectives listing.

Oracle9i uses Java-based tools to install Oracle software and create databases. Java gives the same look and feel for the installer across all platforms. The Oracle Enterprise Manager utility comes with many user-friendly database administration tools. In this chapter, you will be introduced to the features of the Oracle Universal Installer and Enterprise Manager utilities. You will also learn to use parameters and to start up and shut down an Oracle instance.

The Oracle Universal Installer

To install Oracle9i, you use the *Oracle Universal Installer (OUI)*, a GUI-based Java tool that has the same look and functionality across all platforms. On Windows platforms, you invoke the installer by running the executable `setup.exe`. On Unix platforms, you invoke the installer by running the script `runInstaller`. Figure 3.1 shows the installation location screen when you invoke the OUI. You can install new Oracle9i products or remove installed Oracle9i products by using the OUI.

Oracle Objective — **Identify the features of the Oracle Universal Installer**

FIGURE 3.1 The Oracle Universal Installer

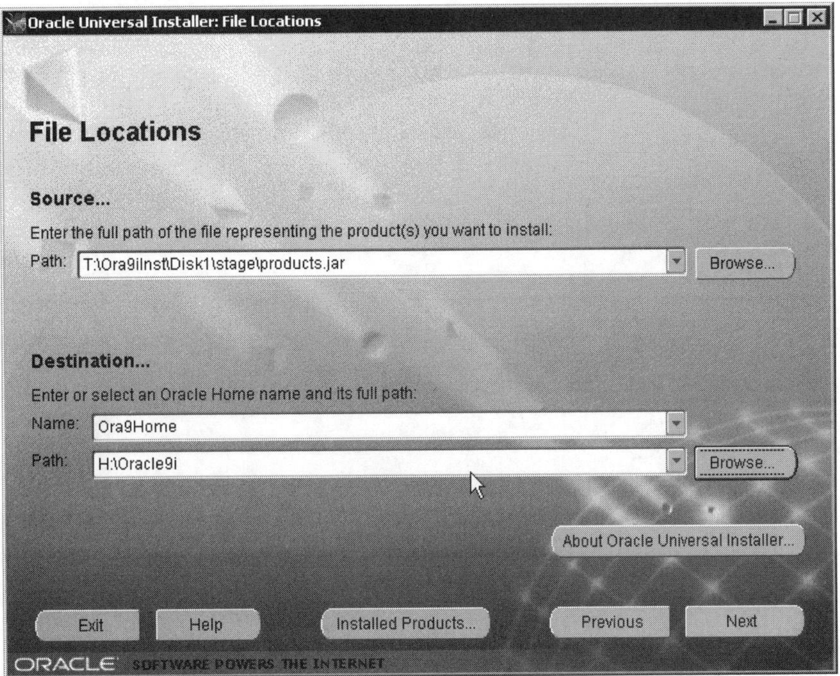

The OUI accepts minimal user inputs for a typical installation, and you can choose the desired products by using the custom installation. OUI supports multiple Oracle homes in case you need to install different versions of Oracle under different Oracle homes. OUI resolves the dependencies among various Oracle products automatically.

OUI allows silent installation, which is especially useful for workstations that do not support a graphical interface. You can capture the response to each installer question in a response file and use the file for future installations. Installer activities and result statuses are logged into files that you can review after installation.

The installer can start other Oracle tools such as the Database Configuration Assistant to create a new database or the Oracle Net Configuration Assistant to configure the listener for the database.

Oracle Enterprise Manager

Oracle Enterprise Manager (OEM) is a graphical system management tool used to manage components of Oracle and to administer the databases from one session. OEM comprises a console and management utilities, a repository in which to save all the metadata information, and the actual nodes (databases and other components) that need to be managed. Figure 3.2 shows the three-tier architecture of OEM.

Oracle Objective — **List the main components of the Oracle Enterprise Manager and their uses**

FIGURE 3.2 The OEM three-tier architecture

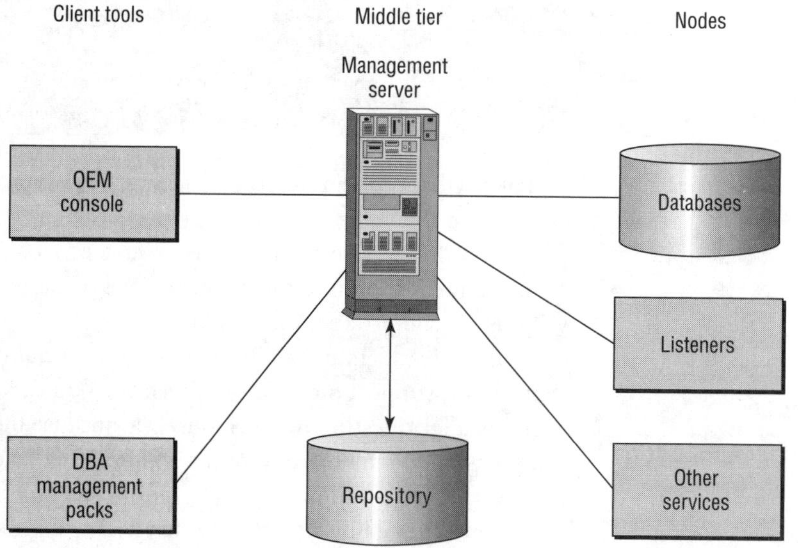

The basic components of the OEM are:

- Console
- Management Server
- Common services
- DBA Tools

The Console

The console is a client GUI tool that provides a single point of access to all the databases, network, and management tools. The console consists of two panes, which can be seen in Figure 3.3.

FIGURE 3.3 The OEM console

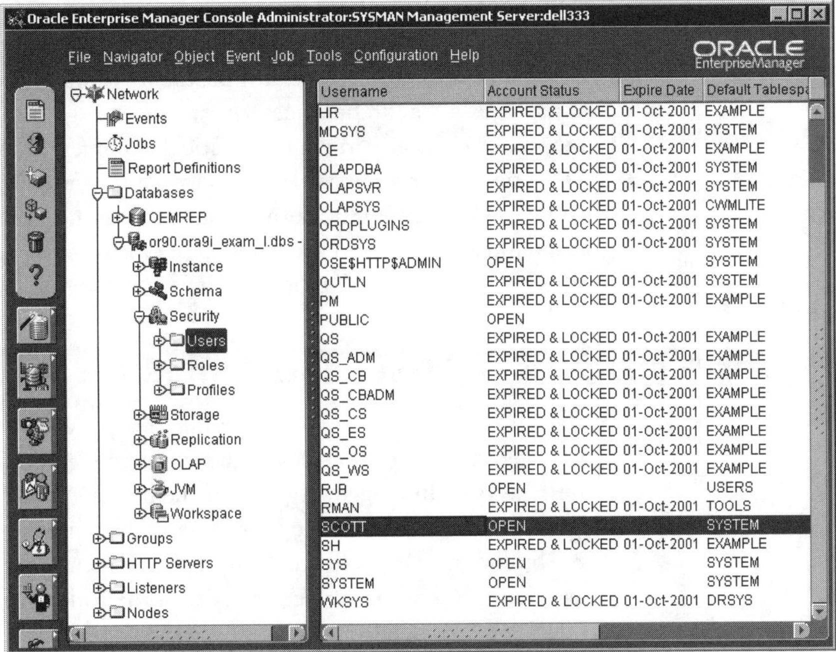

The Navigator pane displays a hierarchical view of all the databases, listeners, nodes, and other services in the network and their relationships. You can drill down the branches and see the database users, roles, groups, events, and so on.

The Group branch enables you to graphically view and construct logical administrative groups of objects for more efficient management and administration. You can group objects together based on any criteria, such as department, geographical location, or function. The Group branch is especially useful for managing environments that include large numbers of databases and other services or for seeing the relative location of managed services. To create a group, you first name and register a group in the Group branch, and then you drag objects that you want to manage as a unit from the Navigator branch and drop them into the Group branch. Groups can consist of similar or dissimilar targets; for example, a group might have two database servers, a management server, and an application server. You can display these groups on top of a graphical image of your choice, such as a geographical map, a building blueprint, or an organization chart.

The Jobs branch is the user interface to the Job Scheduling System, which you can use to automate repetitive tasks at specified times on one or multiple databases. A job consists of one or more tasks. You can build dependencies within the tasks, and you can specify that certain tasks execute as a result of the outcome of another task.

The Events branch is the user interface to the Event Management System, which monitors the network for problem events. An event is made up of one or more tests that an Intelligent Agent checks against one or more of its managed services in monitoring for critical occurrences. When the Intelligent Agent detects a problem on the services, it notifies the console and the appropriate DBA based on the permissions set up. The Intelligent Agents are local to a database node and are responsible for monitoring the databases and other services on the database node.

The Management Server and Common Services

The Management Server is the middle tier between the console GUI and managed nodes. It processes all system management tasks and distributes these tasks to Intelligent Agents on the nodes. You can use multiple Management Servers to balance workload and to improve performance.

The common services are the tools and systems that help the Management Server. The common services consist of the following:

Repository The repository is a set of tables that store the information about the managed nodes and the Oracle management tools. You can create this data store in any Oracle database, but preferably on a node that does not contain a critical Oracle instance to be monitored.

Service discovery OEM discovers all databases and listeners on a node, once the node is identified. The Intelligent Agent finds the services and reports them back to the Oracle Management Server. These discovered services are displayed in the Navigation pane of the console.

Job Scheduling System Using the Job Scheduling System, you can schedule and execute routine or repetitive administrative tasks. You can set up the system to notify you upon completion, failure, or success of a job through e-mail or a pager.

Event Management System The Event Management System in the OEM monitors the resource problems, loss of service, shortage of disk space, or any other problem detected on the node. You can set these occurrences up as events, and the Intelligent Agent tests periodically to monitor them.

Notification system You can specify that the notification about the status of jobs or events can be sent to the console, via e-mail, or to a pager. You can select the notification procedures when you set up the job or event.

Paging/e-mail blackout This feature prevents the administrator from receiving multiple e-mails or pages when a service is brought down for maintenance or for a scheduled period of downtime.

Security Security parameters in OEM are defined for services, objects, and administrators. A *super administrator* is someone who creates and defines the permissions of all the repository's administrators. The super administrator can access any object and control its security parameters, including objects owned by other administrators.

DBA Tools

The *DBA Tools* are integrated with the OEM, which helps the administrators with their daily routine tasks. These tools provide complete database administration using GUI tools rather than using SQL*Plus. You access the tools in the left pane of the OEM console under each database instance.

Oracle Objective

Identify common database administrative tools available to a DBA

Using the DBA Tools, you can administer the following:

Instance You can start up and shut down an instance; modify parameters; view and change memory allocations, redo logs, and archival status; view user sessions and their SQL; see the execution plan of SQL; and manage resource allocations and long-running sessions.

Schema You can create, alter, or drop any schema object, including advanced queues and Java-stored procedures. You can clone any object.

Security You can change the security privileges for users and roles, and you can create and alter users, roles, and profiles.

Storage You can manage tablespaces, data files, undo segments, redo log groups, and archive logs.

SQL*Plus Worksheet You can issue SQL statements against any database, in a graphical environment that is much easier to use than the command line version of SQL*Plus.

Optimal Flexible Architecture (OFA)

The *Optimal Flexible Architecture (OFA)* is a set of guidelines specified by Oracle to better manage the Oracle software and the database. OFA enforces the following:

- A consistent naming convention
- Separating Oracle software from the database
- Separating the Oracle software versions
- Separating the data files belonging to different databases
- Separating parameter files and database creation scripts from the database files and software
- Separating trace files, log files, and dump files from the database and software

Oracle Objective **Explain the benefits of Optimal Flexible Architecture (OFA)**

Figure 3.4 shows the software installation and database files on a Windows 2000 platform conforming to the OFA. Here the `ORACLE_BASE` directory is `G:\oracle`, which has four branches—`admin`, `ora90`, `ora91`, and `oradata`. The `ora90` and `ora91` folders are software installations. If you separate the versions, upgrading the database is easy. The `admin` and `oradata` folders have subfolders for each database on the server. In Figure 3.4, `oradb01` and `oradb02` are two databases. Under the `admin` branch, for each database, are subfolders for administrative scripts (`adhoc`), background dump files and the alert log file (`bdump`), core dump files (`cdump`), database creation scripts (`create`), export files (`exp`), parameter files (`pfile`), and a user dump folder (`udump`). The `oradata` folder has the data files, redo log files, and control files belonging to the database, separated at the database level by using subfolders.

FIGURE 3.4 OFA directory structures

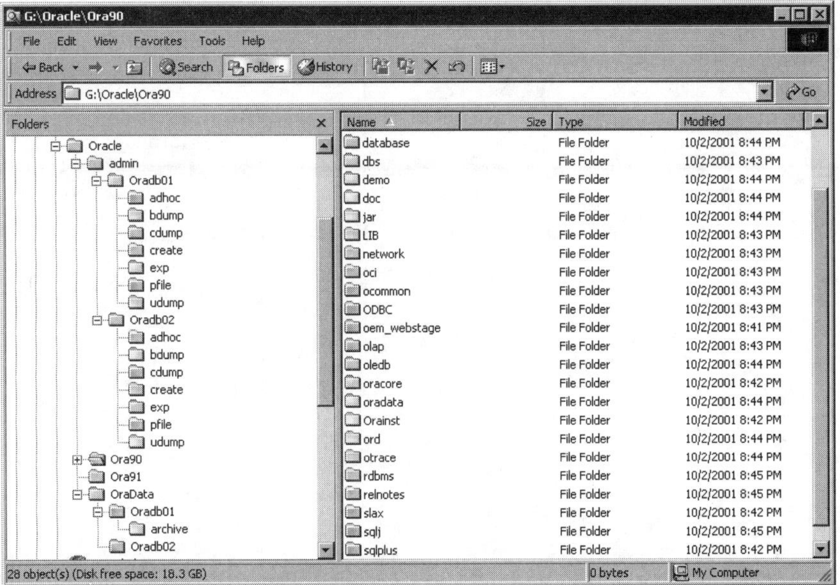

For performance reasons, the OFA architecture can be slightly extended to include multiple disks and to spread out the data files. Figure 3.5 shows such a layout, in which `oradata01`, `oradata02`, `oradata03`, `oradata04`, and so on can be on separate disks and can hold separate types of files (data files separate from redo log files) or different tablespaces (data tablespace separate from the index tablespace, and separate from the system tablespace).

FIGURE 3.5 OFA using multiple disks

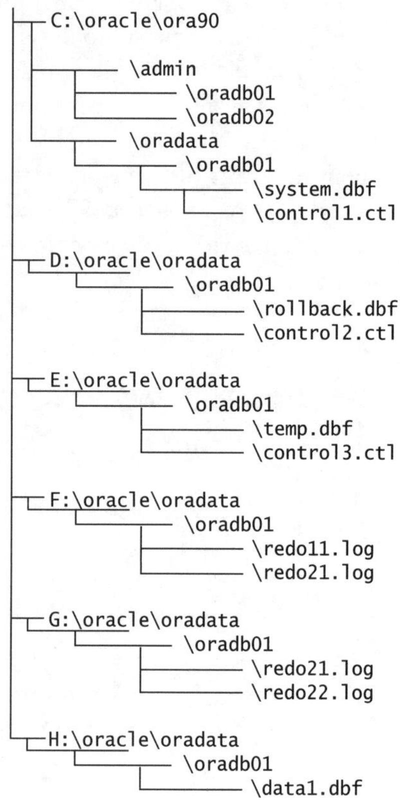

Administrator Authentication Methods

In this section, we will discuss the privileges and authentication methods available when using the administration tools described in the previous section. You can allow administrators to connect to the database by using operating system authentication or password file authentication. For remote or local database administration, you can use either method, but you can use the operating system authentication method with remote administration only if you have a secured network connection. To use remote authentication of users through Remote Dial-In User Service (RADIUS—a standard lightweight protocol used for user authentication and authorization) with Oracle, you need Oracle9i Enterprise Edition with the Advanced Security option.

When you create a database, Oracle automatically creates two administrator login IDs—SYS and SYSTEM. The initial password for SYS is CHANGE_ON_INSTALL, and the initial password for SYSTEM is MANAGER. For security reasons, change these passwords as soon as you finish creating the database. Oracle recommends that you create at least one additional user to do the DBA tasks, rather than using the SYS or SYSTEM account. A predefined role, DBA, is created with all databases and has all database administrative privileges.

Operating System Authentication

Oracle can verify your operating system privileges and connect you to the database to perform database operations. To connect to the database by using *operating system authentication*, you must be a member of the OSDBA or OSOPER operating system group. On most Unix systems, this is the *dba* group. You can specify the name of the OSDBA and OSOPER groups when you install Oracle by using the OUI.

OSDBA and OSOPER are not Oracle privileges or roles that you grant through the Oracle database. The operating system manages them. When you connect to the database by using the OSOPER privilege (or SYSOPER privilege), you can perform STARTUP, SHUTDOWN, ALTER DATABASE [OPEN/MOUNT], ALTER DATABASE BACKUP, ARCHIVE LOG, and RECOVER, and SYSOPER includes the RESTRICTED SESSION privilege. When you connect to the database by using the OSDBA privilege (or SYSDBA privilege), you have all system privileges with ADMIN OPTION, the OSOPER role, CREATE DATABASE, and time-based recovery.

To use operating system authentication, set the REMOTE_LOGIN_PASSWORDFILE parameter to NONE, which is the default.

Operating system authenticated users can connect to the database by using CONNECT / AS SYSDBA or CONNECT / AS SYSOPER. You do not need a user created in the Oracle database to use operating system authentication. Here is an example from a Windows platform, making a local operating system authentication connection to the database to perform administration operations:

```
Microsoft(R) Windows DOS
(C)Copyright Microsoft Corp 1990-1999.

E:\>sqlplus /nolog
```

```
SQL*Plus: Release 9.0.1.0.1 - Production on Tue Oct 2
20:53:08 2001

(c) Copyright 2001 Oracle Corporation.  All rights
reserved.

SQL> connect / as sysdba
Connected.
SQL> archive log list
Database log mode              No Archive Mode
Automatic archival             Disabled
Archive destination            H:\Oracle9i\RDBMS
Oldest online log sequence     0
Current log sequence           1
SQL>
```

Password File Authentication

When using *password file authentication*, the user connects to the database by specifying a username and a password. The user needs to have been granted the appropriate privileges in the database.

Oracle Objective

Set up password file authentication

To use password file authentication, follow these steps:

1. Using the ORAPWD utility, create a password file with the SYS password. When you change the password in the database, the password in this file is automatically updated.
2. Set the `REMOTE_LOGIN_PASSWORDFILE` parameter.
3. Grant the appropriate users `SYSDBA` or `SYSOPER` privilege. When you grant this privilege, these users are added to the password file.

When you invoke the ORAPWD utility without any parameters, the syntax for creating the password file is displayed.

```
$ orapwd
Usage: orapwd file=<fname> password=<password>
  entries=<users>
  where
    file - name of password file (mand),
    password - password for SYS and INTERNAL (mand),
    entries - maximum number of distinct DBAs and
  OPERs (opt),
  There are no spaces around the equal-to (=) character.
```

The FILE parameter specifies the name of the parameter file. Normally the file is created in the dbs directory under ORACLE_HOME (the directory where Oracle software is installed). The PASSWORD parameter specifies the SYS password, and ENTRIES specifies the maximum number of users you will be assigning the SYSOPER or SYSDBA privileges. If you exceed this limit, you will need to re-create the password file. ENTRIES is an optional parameter.

You can set the parameter REMOTE_LOGIN_PASSWORDFILE to either EXCLUSIVE or SHARED. If you set the parameter to EXCLUSIVE, the password file can be used for only one database; you can add users other than SYS and INTERNAL to the password file. If you set the parameter to SHARED, the password file is shared among multiple databases, but you cannot add any user other than SYS or INTERNAL to the password file.

When you connect to the database by using the SYSDBA privilege, you are connected to the SYS schema, and when you connect by using the SYSOPER privilege, you are connected to the PUBLIC schema.

The view V$PWFILE_USERS has the information on all users granted either SYSDBA or SYSOPER privileges. The view has the username and a value of TRUE in column SYSDBA if the SYSDBA privilege is granted, or it has a value of TRUE in column SYSOPER if the SYSOPER privilege is granted.

Starting Up the Oracle Instance

To start or stop an Oracle instance, you must have the SYSDBA or SYSOPER privilege. To start up a database, you can use either the Instance branch of OEM or SQL*Plus to connect with a user account that has SYSDBA or SYSOPER privileges. The database start-up is done in three stages. First, you start an instance associated with the database, then the instance mounts the database, and finally you open the database for normal use. The examples discussed in this section use SQL*Plus to start up the database.

Oracle Objective — **Start up and shut down an instance**

The instance can start, but not mount, the database by using the STARTUP NOMOUNT command. Normally you use this database state for creating a new database or for creating new control files. When you start the instance, Oracle allocates the SGA and starts the background processes.

The instance can start and *mount* the database without opening it by using the STARTUP MOUNT command. This state of the database is used mainly for performing specific maintenance operations such as renaming data files, enabling or disabling archive logging, renaming, adding, or dropping redo log files, or for recovering a full database. When you mount the database, Oracle opens the control files associated with the database. Each control file contains the names and locations of database files and online redo log files.

You use STARTUP OPEN or STARTUP to start the instance, mount a database, and open the database for normal operations. When you open the database, Oracle opens the online data files and online redo log files. If any of the files are not available or are not in synch with the control file, Oracle returns an error. You may have to recover one of the files before you can open the database.

Issuing the ALTER DATABASE MOUNT command when the database is not mounted will mount the database in a previously started instance. ALTER DATABASE OPEN will open a closed database. You can open a database in read-only mode by using the ALTER DATABASE OPEN READ ONLY command. When you start the database in read-only mode, no redo information is generated because you cannot modify any data. The following example shows how to start a database by using the SQL*Plus utility.

```
E:\>sqlplus /nolog

SQL*Plus: Release 9.0.1.0.1 - Production on Tue Oct 2
21:05:53 2001

(c) Copyright 2001 Oracle Corporation.  All rights
reserved.

SQL> connect / as sysdba
Connected to an idle instance.
SQL> startup
ORACLE instance started.

Total System Global Area  118255568 bytes
Fixed Size                   282576 bytes
Variable Size              83886080 bytes
Database Buffers           33554432 bytes
Redo Buffers                 532480 bytes
Database mounted.
Database opened.
SQL> exit
Disconnected from Oracle9i Enterprise Edition Release
9.0.1.1.1 - Production
With the Partitioning option
JServer Release 9.0.1.1.1 - Production

E:\>
```

Sometimes you may have problems starting up an instance. In those cases, you can use `STARTUP FORCE` to start a database that will not shut down or start up gracefully. Use this option only if you could not shut down the database properly; `STARTUP FORCE` shuts down the instance if it is already running and then restarts it.

You can restrict access to the database by using the command `STARTUP RESTRICT` to start the database in restricted mode. Only users with the `RESTRICTED SESSION` system privilege can connect to the database. You can also use `ALTER SYSTEM [ENABLE/DISABLE] RESTRICTED SESSION` to enable or disable restricted access after opening the database. Put the database in restricted mode if you want to make any major structure modifications or to get a consistent export.

You need to have the ALTER SYSTEM privilege to change the database availability by using the ALTER SYSTEM [ENABLE/DISABLE] RESTRICTED SESSION command.

You can start an Oracle instance with one of two types of parameter files: a text-based PFILE or a binary SPFILE. The SPFILE parameter file is new in Oracle9i, which not only eases the administration of parameter files, but also gives the DBA more flexibility when specifying the persistence of parameter values.

When an instance is started in the NOMOUNT state, you can access only the views that read data from the SGA. V$PARAMETER, V$SGA, V$OPTION, V$PROCESS, V$SESSION, V$VERSION, V$INSTANCE, and so on are dictionary views that read from the SGA. When the database is mounted, information can be read from the control file. V$THREAD, V$CONTROLFILE, V$DATABASE, V$DATAFILE, V$DATAFILE_HEADER, V$LOGFILE, and so on all read data from the control file.

The Parameter File: PFILE

Oracle uses a *parameter file* when starting up the database, either a text-based PFILE or a binary SPFILE (discussed in the next section). The *PFILE* is a text file containing the parameters and their values for configuring the database and instance. The default location and name of the file depend on the operating system; on Unix platforms, by default Oracle looks for the parameter file by the name init<*SID*>*.ora* (*SID* is the name of the instance) under the $ORACLE_HOME/dbs directory. You can specify the parameter file location and name when starting up the database by using the PFILE option of the STARTUP command. The following command starts up the database in restricted mode by using the parameter file initORADB01.ora under the /oracle/admin/ORADB01/pfile directory.

```
STARTUP PFILE=/oracle/admin/ORADB01/pfile/initORADB01.ora
  RESTRICT
```

Oracle Objective | **Create and manage initialization parameter files**

The parameter files tell Oracle the following when starting up an instance:

- The name of the database and the location of the control files
- The location of the archived log files and whether to start the archival process
- The size of the SGA
- The location of the dump and trace files
- The parameters to set limits and that affect capacity

If you do not specify a parameter in the parameter file, Oracle assumes a default value for the parameter. You can structure a custom parameter file liberally, but certain syntax rules are enforced for the files. The syntax rules are:

- Precede comment lines with a pound sign (#).
- All parameters are optional. When parameters are omitted, defaults will be applied.
- Parameters and their values are generally not case sensitive. Parameter values that name files can be case sensitive if the host operating system's filenames are case sensitive.
- You can list parameters in any order.
- Parameters that accept multiple values, such as the `CONTROL_FILES` parameter, can list the values in parentheses delimited by commas or with no parentheses delimited by spaces.
- The continuation character is the backslash character (\). Use the backslash when a parameter's list of values must be continued on a separate line.
- Enclose parameter values that contain spaces in double quotes.
- Use the equal sign (=) to delimit the parameter name and its associated value.

The Parameter File: SPFILE

The other type of parameter file that Oracle9i supports is a *persistent* parameter file, otherwise known as an *SPFILE*. This file is located in the same directory as a PFILE, in the `$ORACLE_HOME/dbs` directory.

The SPFILE is a binary file and is not meant to be edited by a standard text editor; it is created from a standard PFILE and then modified by the ALTER SYSTEM command thereafter. In the case of an SPFILE, the ALTER SYSTEM command can change the value of an initialization parameter either for the life of the instance, or across a shutdown and restart, or both.

To initially create an SPFILE, a PFILE must exist first; the following example creates an SPFILE in the default location from an initSID.ora PFILE that resides in the same default location:

```
SQL> CREATE SPFILE FROM PFILE;
```

The next time the instance is restarted, only the SPFILE will be used to initialize the database.

Get Parameter Values

You can get the value of a parameter by using the SHOW PARAMETERS command. When this command is used without any arguments, Oracle displays all the parameters in alphabetic order and their values. To get the value for a specific parameter, use the SHOW PARAMETERS command with the parameter name as the argument. For example, to view the value of the DB_BLOCK_SIZE parameter, use the following:

```
SQL> show parameters db_block_size
NAME                         TYPE      VALUE
---------------------------- --------- ---------------------
db_block_size                integer   8192
SQL>
```

The argument in the SHOW PARAMETERS command is a filter; you can specify any string, and Oracle displays the parameters that match the argument string anywhere in the parameter name. The argument is not case sensitive. In the following example, all parameters with OS embedded somewhere in the name are shown.

```
SQL> show parameters OS
NAME                         TYPE      VALUE
---------------------------- --------- ---------------------
optimizer_index_cost_adj     integer   100
os_authent_prefix            string
os_roles                     boolean   FALSE
```

```
remote_os_authent            boolean   FALSE
remote_os_roles              boolean   FALSE
timed_os_statistics          integer   0
SQL>
```

You can also get the parameter values by querying the V$PARAMETER view. V$PARAMETER shows the parameter values for the current session. V$SYSTEM_PARAMETER has the same structure as the V$PARAMETER view, except that it shows the system parameters. The columns in the V$PARAMETER view are shown in Table 3.1.

TABLE 3.1 *V$PARAMETER* View

Column Name	Data Type	Purpose
NUM	NUMBER	Parameter number.
NAME	VARCHAR2 (64)	Parameter name.
TYPE	NUMBER	Type of parameter: 1—Boolean, 2—string, 3—integer, 4—file.
VALUE	VARCHAR2 (512)	Value of the parameter.
ISDEFAULT	VARCHAR2 (9)	Whether the parameter value is the Oracle default. FALSE indicates that the parameter was changed during start-up.
ISSES_ MODIFIABLE	VARCHAR2 (5)	TRUE indicates that the parameter can be changed by using an ALTER SESSION command.
ISSYS_ MODIFIABLE	VARCHAR2 (9)	FALSE indicates that the parameter cannot be changed by using the ALTER SYSTEM command. IMMEDIATE indicates that the parameter can be changed, and DEFERRED indicates that the parameter change takes effect only in the next session.

TABLE 3.1 *V$PARAMETER* View *(continued)*

Column Name	Data Type	Purpose
ISMODIFIED	VARCHAR2 (16)	MODIFIED indicates that the parameter was changed by using ALTER SESSION. SYSTEM_MOD indicates that the parameter was changed by using ALTER SYSTEM.
ISADJUSTED	VARCHAR2 (5)	TRUE indicates that Oracle adjusted the value of the parameter to be a more suitable value.
DESCRIPTION	VARCHAR2 (64)	A brief description of the purpose of the parameter.
UPDATE_COMMENT	VARCHAR2 (255)	Set if a comment has been supplied by the DBA for this parameter.

To get the parameter names and their values for the parameter names that *start* with OS, perform this query:

```
SQL> col name format a30
SQL> col value format a25
SQL> SELECT name, value
  2  FROM   v$parameter
  3  WHERE  name like 'os%';

NAME                           VALUE
------------------------------ -------------------------
os_roles                       FALSE
os_authent_prefix

SQL>
```

You can also use the GUI tool in OEM to see the values of parameters. The description shown in this tool is more elaborate than the description you would see in the V$PARAMETER view.

Set Parameter Values

When you start up the instance, Oracle reads the parameter file and sets the value for the parameter. For the parameters that are not specified in the parameter file, Oracle assigns a default value. The parameters that are modified at instance start-up can be displayed by querying the V$PARAMETER view for a FALSE value in the ISDEFAULT column.

```
SQL> SELECT name, value
  2  FROM   v$parameter
WHERE  isdefault = 'FALSE';
```

Certain parameters can be changed dynamically by using the ALTER SESSION or ALTER SYSTEM command. To identify such parameters, query the view V$PARAMETER.

You can change the value of a parameter system-wide by using the ALTER SYSTEM command. A value of DEFERRED or IMMEDIATE in the ISSYS_MODIFIABLE column shows that the parameter can be dynamically changed by using the command ALTER SYSTEM. DEFERRED indicates that the change you make does not take effect until a new session is started. The existing sessions will use the current value. IMMEDIATE indicates that as soon as you change the value of the parameter, it is available to all sessions in the instance. A *session* can be a job or a task that Oracle manages. When you log in to the database by using SQL*Plus or any client tool, you start a session. Sessions are discussed in the next section. Here is an example of modifying a parameter by using ALTER SYSTEM.

```
SQL> ALTER SYSTEM SET log_archive_dest =
  '/oracle/archive/DB01';
```

The following example will set the TIMED_STATISTICS parameter to TRUE for all future sessions.

```
SQL> ALTER SYSTEM SET timed_statistics =
  TRUE DEFERRED;
```

A value of TRUE in the ISSES_MODIFIABLE column indicates that the parameter can be changed by using ALTER SESSION. When you change a parameter by using ALTER SESSION, the value of the parameter is changed only for that session. When you start the next session, the parameter will have the original value (the Oracle default, the value set in the parameter file, or the value set by ALTER SYSTEM). Here is an example of modifying a parameter by using ALTER SESSION:

```
SQL> ALTER SESSION SET nls_date_format =
  'MM-DD-YYYY';
```

Using an SPFILE, the DBA has more flexibility as to when the parameter takes effect in the instance: in effect for the current instance only, in effect only after the instance is restarted, or is both in effect immediately and after the instance is restarted.

The following example changes the value of MAX_DUMP_FILE_SIZE; this new value will take effect only after the instance is shut down and restarted:

```
SQL> ALTER SYSTEM SET MAX_DUMP_FILE_SIZE=20000
SCOPE=SPFILE;
```

The other two options for the SCOPE clause are MEMORY (for the life of the current instance only) and BOTH (for the current instance and across shutdown and restart). The default is BOTH.

Managing Sessions

Oracle starts a session when a database connection is made. The session is available as long as the user is connected to the database. When a session is started, Oracle allocates a session ID to that session. To display the user sessions connected to a database, query the view V$SESSION. In V$SESSION, the session identifier (SID) and the serial number (SERIAL#) uniquely identify each session. The serial number guarantees that session-level commands are applied to the correct session objects if the session ends and another session begins with the same session ID.

The V$SESSION view contains a lot of information about a session. The username, machine name, program name, status, and login time are a few of the useful pieces of information in this view. For example, if you need to know which users are connected to the database and the program they are running, execute the following query.

```
SQL> SELECT username, program
  2  FROM   v$session;
```

Sometimes it may be necessary to terminate certain user sessions. You can terminate a user session by using the ALTER SYTEM command. The SID and SERIAL# from the V$SESSION view are required to kill the session. For example, to kill a session created by user JOHN, you do the following.

```
SQL> SELECT username, sid, serial#, status
  2  FROM   v$session
  3  WHERE  username = 'JOHN';
```

```
USERNAME                         SID    SERIAL# STATUS
------------------- ---------- --------- --------
JOHN                               9          3 INACTIVE

SQL> ALTER SYSTEM KILL SESSION '9, 3';

System altered.

SQL> SELECT username, sid, serial#, status
  2  FROM   v$session
  3  WHERE  username = 'JOHN';

USERNAME                         SID    SERIAL# STATUS
------------------- ---------- --------- -------
JOHN                               9          3 KILLED

SQL>
```

When you kill a session, first Oracle terminates the session to prevent the session from executing any more SQL statements. If any SQL statement is in progress when the session is terminated, the statement is terminated, and all changes are rolled back. The locks and other resources used by the session are also released.

If you kill an INACTIVE session, Oracle terminates the session and marks the status in the V$SESSION view as KILLED. When the user subsequently tries to use the session, an error is returned to the user, and the session information is removed from V$SESSION.

If you kill an ACTIVE session, Oracle terminates the session and issues an error message immediately to the user that the session is killed. If Oracle cannot release the resources held by the session in 60 seconds, Oracle returns a message to the user that the session has been marked for kill. The status in the V$SESSION view will again show as KILLED.

If you want the user to complete the current transaction and then terminate their session, you can use the DISCONNECT SESSION option of the ALTER SYSTEM command. If the session has no pending or active transactions, this command has the same effect as KILL SESSION. Here is an example:

```
ALTER SYSTEM DISCONNECT SESSION '9,3' POST_TRANSACTION;
```

You can also use the IMMEDIATE clause with the KILL SESSION or DISCONNECT SESSION to roll back ongoing transactions, release all session locks, recover the entire session state, and return control to you immediately. Here are some examples:

```
ALTER SYSTEM DISCONNECT SESSION '9,3' IMMEDIATE;
ALTER SYSTEM KILL SESSION '9,3' IMMEDIATE;
```

Shutting Down the Oracle Instance

Similar to the stages in starting up a database, there are three stages to shutting down a database. First, you close the database, then the instance dismounts the database, and finally you shut down the instance.

Oracle Objective — **Start up and shut down an instance**

When closing the database, Oracle writes the redo buffer to the redo log files and the changed data in the database buffer cache to the data files, and closes the data files and redo log files. The control file remains open, but the database is not available for normal operations. After closing the database, the instance dismounts the database. The control file is closed at this time. The memory allocated and the background processes still remain. The final stage is the instance shutdown. The SGA is removed from memory and the background processes are terminated when the instance is shut down.

To initiate a database shutdown, you can use the SHUTDOWN command in SQL*Plus or use the Instance branch of the OEM GUI tool. You need to connect to the database by using a dedicated server process with an account that has SYSDBA privileges to shut down the database. Once the shutdown process is initiated, no new user sessions are allowed to connect to the database.

You can shut down the database by using the SHUTDOWN command with any of four options. These options and the steps that Oracle takes are as follows.

SHUTDOWN NORMAL

When you use the SHUTDOWN command without any options, the default option is NORMAL. When you issue SHUTDOWN NORMAL, Oracle does the following:

- Does not allow any new user connections.
- Waits for all users to disconnect from the database. All connected users can continue working.
- Closes the database, dismounts the instance, and shuts down the instance once all users are disconnected from the database.

SHUTDOWN IMMEDIATE

You use SHUTDOWN IMMEDIATE to bring down the database as quickly as possible. When you issue SHUTDOWN IMMEDIATE, Oracle does the following:

- Does not allow any new user connections
- Terminates all user connections to the database
- Rolls back uncommitted transactions
- Closes the database, dismounts the instance, and shuts down the instance

SHUTDOWN TRANSACTIONAL

You use SHUTDOWN TRANSACTIONAL to bring down the database as soon as the users complete their current transaction. This is a mode that fits between IMMEDIATE and NORMAL. When you issue SHUTDOWN TRANSACTIONAL, Oracle does the following:

- Does not allow any new user connections.
- Does not allow any new transactions in the database. When a user tries to start a new transaction, the session is disconnected.
- Waits for the user to either roll back or commit any uncommitted transactions.
- Closes the database, dismounts the instance, and shuts down the instance once all transactions are complete.

The following example shows a SHUTDOWN TRANSACTIONAL command using SQL*Plus.

```
E:\>sqlplus /nolog

SQL*Plus: Release 9.0.1.0.1 - Production on Tue Oct 2
21:30:55 2001

(c) Copyright 2001 Oracle Corporation.  All rights
reserved.

SQL> connect / as sysdba
Connected.
SQL> shutdown transactional
Database closed.
Database dismounted.
ORACLE instance shut down.
SQL> exit
Disconnected from Oracle9i Enterprise Edition Release
9.0.1.1.1 - Production
With the Partitioning option
JServer Release 9.0.1.1.1 - Production

E:\>
```

SHUTDOWN ABORT

When any of the other three shutdown options does not work, you can bring down the database abruptly by using the SHUTDOWN ABORT command. An instance recovery is needed when you start up the database next time. When you issue SHUTDOWN ABORT, Oracle does the following:

- Terminates all current SQL statements that are being processed
- Disconnects all connected users
- Terminates the instance immediately
- Will not roll back uncommitted transactions

When the database is started up after a SHUTDOWN ABORT, Oracle has to roll back the uncommitted transactions by using the online redo log files.

Instance Messages and Instance Alerts

Oracle writes informational messages and alerts to different files depending on the type of message. These messages are useful when you're troubleshooting a problem. Oracle writes to these files in locations that are specific to the operating system; you can specify the locations in the initialization parameters. You alter these parameters by using the ALTER SYSTEM command.

Oracle Objective

Monitor the use of diagnostic files

The three variables used to specify the locations are as follows:

BACKGROUND_DUMP_DEST Location to write the debugging trace files generated by the background processes and the alert log file.

USER_DUMP_DEST Location to write the trace files generated by user sessions. The server process, on behalf of the user sessions, writes trace files if the session encounters a deadlock or encounters any internal errors. The user sessions can be traced. The trace files thus generated are also written to this location.

CORE_DUMP_DEST Location to write core dump files, primarily used on Unix platforms. Core dumps are normally produced when the session or the instance terminates abnormally with errors. This parameter is not available on Windows platforms.

All databases have an *alert log file*. An alert log file in the directory specified by BACKGROUND_DUMP_DEST logs significant database events and messages. The alert log stores information about block corruption errors, internal errors, and the non-default initialization parameters used at instance start-up. The alert log also records information about database start-up, shutdown, archiving, recovery, tablespace modifications, rollback segment modifications, and data file modifications.

The alert log is a normal text file. Its filename depends on the operating system. For Unix platforms, it takes the format alert_*<SID>.log* (*SID* is the instance name). During the start-up of the database, if the alert log file is not available, Oracle creates one. This file grows slowly, but without limit, so you might want to delete or archive it periodically. You can delete the file even when the database is running.

Oracle Managed Files (OMF)

In previous versions of the Oracle Server, maintaining the physical operating system files associated with logical database objects was problematic. Dropping a logical database object (such as a tablespace) did not delete the associated operating system file, and therefore an extra step was performed to manually delete the files formerly associated with database objects.

Oracle Objective

Configure Oracle Managed Files (OMF)

The *Oracle Managed Files (OMF)* feature of Oracle9i addresses this issue. You can use two new initialization parameters to define the location of files in the operating system: `DB_CREATE_FILE_DEST` and `DB_CREATE_ONLINE_LOG_DEST_`*n*.

The parameter `DB_CREATE_FILE_DEST` specifies the default location for new datafiles. The actual operating system file is created with the prefix `ora_` and a suffix of `.dbf`. If the `CREATE DATABASE` command (or any other commands that use the OMF initialization parameters) fails, the associated data files are removed from the server file system.

The parameter `DB_CREATE_ONLINE_LOG_DEST_`*n* specifies as many as five locations for online redo log files and control files. The online redo log files have a suffix of `.log`, and the control files have a suffix of `.ctl`.

You don't have to use both parameters, and you can dynamically change the values of these parameters with the `ALTER SYSTEM` command.

Real World Scenario

OMF Time-Saving Benefits

Consider how much OMF helps the busy DBA. Quite often, I forget to delete the datafile(s) associated with a dropped tablespace, causing problems with operating system backups and using disk space that could otherwise be used for other database objects.

> Before OMF, I would occasionally perform a manual audit, comparing file listings at the operating system level with the results from querying the views V$DATAFILE, V$CONTROLFILE, and V$LOGFILE.
>
> Yet another immediate benefit of using OMF is to store a "base" directory pathname in a single initialization parameter. This makes database creation scripts easier to maintain, allowing for easy re-use in different environments by merely changing one or two initialization parameters.

Summary

This chapter briefly discussed the Universal Installer and Enterprise Manager, two of Oracle's Java-based GUI tools. The OUI has the same interface across all platforms and is used to install multiple products. Oracle Enterprise Manager is a system management tool used to manage components of Oracle and to administer many local and remote databases at one location. OEM comprises a console and management utilities, a repository to save all the metadata information, and the actual nodes (databases and other components) that need to be managed.

For connecting to the database as administrator, Oracle has two authentication methods. Operating system authentication is allowed if you are local to the computer where the database is situated or if you have a secure network connection. Password file authentication creates a password file at the server with the SYS password. Users can be granted SYSDBA or SYSOPER privilege, and they can connect to the database with appropriate privileges. You need either of these privileges to shut down or start up the database.

Starting up Oracle involves three stages. First, you start the instance, then the instance mounts the database, and finally you open the database. You can start up the database in any of these stages by using the start-up options. The database availability can also be controlled by enabling restricted access.

Shutting down the database also involves three stages, but in reverse order. You can shut down the database in four ways. SHUTDOWN NORMAL, the default, waits for all users to log out before shutdown. SHUTDOWN IMMEDIATE disconnects all user sessions and shuts down the database. SHUTDOWN TRANSACTIONAL waits for the users to complete their current transaction and then shuts down the database. SHUTDOWN ABORT simply terminates the instance immediately.

When you start up the database, Oracle uses different parameters to configure memory, to configure the database, and to set limits. These parameters are saved in a file called the parameter file (PFILE), which is read by Oracle during instance start-up. Many of these parameters can be changed dynamically for the session by using the `ALTER SESSION` command or for the database by using the `ALTER SYSTEM` command. The alternative parameter file, SPFILE, is a binary file that can be modified on the fly and whose parameters can take effect either for the life of the instance only, after the next restart only, or both.

The Optimal Flexible Architecture (OFA) is a set of guidelines specified by Oracle to better manage the Oracle software and the database. OFA enforces a consistent naming convention as well as separate locations for Oracle software, database, and administration files.

The database constantly writes information about major database events in a log file called the alert log file. Oracle also writes trace and dump information for debugging session problems.

Exam Essentials

Understand the purpose and benefits of OFA. Be able to describe how different types of database and database-related files are stored in different locations.

Identify the default database administrator users. Enumerate the two primary default users and the slightly different roles these users play in the database. Identify the role that is granted to other users to allow similar functionality.

Be able to create a password file. Know how to specify the location of the password file, the method for adding users to the password file, and the initialization parameter that needs to be modified to allow SYSDBA access to non-default users.

Understand the three-tier OEM architecture. Identify the three levels of the hierarchy and their roles. Identify special components that need to be created in each tier to facilitate ease of use for DBAs.

Describe the differences and similarities between the two types of initialization files. Be able to list the key parameters found in both files and the way in which these files are maintained.

Understand how OMF simplifies operating system file administration. Be able to identify the two new initialization parameters associated with OMF. Know how the filenames are constructed at the operating system level.

Enumerate the steps involved in startup and shutdown of the database. Describe each step by what resources are available at that step. Understand the circumstances under which a DBA would use a particular STARTUP option. Understand the consequences of placing the database in read-only mode.

Identify the three categories of diagnostic files. Understand how the locations of these files are specified, in addition to how these files are created and what is stored in each of these files.

Key Terms

Before you take the exam, make sure you're familiar with the following terms:

alert log file	Oracle Universal Installer (OUI)
DBA Tools	operating system authentication
Management Server	parameter file
mount	password file authentication
Optimal Flexible Architecture (OFA)	PFILE
Oracle Enterprise Manager (OEM)	session
Oracle Managed Files (OMF)	SPFILE

Review Questions

1. Which of the following is an invalid database start-up option?

   A. STARTUP NORMAL

   B. STARTUP MOUNT

   C. STARTUP NOMOUNT

   D. STARTUP FORCE

2. Which two values from the V$SESSION view are used to terminate a user session?

   A. SID

   B. USERID

   C. SERIAL#

   D. SEQUENCE#

3. To use operating system authentication to connect to the database as an administrator, what should the value of the parameter REMOTE_LOGIN_PASSWORDFILE be set to?

   A. SHARED

   B. EXCLUSIVE

   C. NONE

   D. OS

4. What information is available in the alert log files?

   A. Block corruption errors

   B. Users connecting and disconnecting from the database

   C. All user errors

   D. The default values of the parameters used to start up the database

5. Which parameter value is used to set the directory path where the alert log file is written?

   A. ALERT_DUMP_DEST

   B. USER_DUMP_DEST

   C. BACKGROUND_DUMP_DEST

   D. CORE_DUMP_DEST

6. Which SHUTDOWN option requires instance recovery when the database is started the next time?

   A. SHUTDOWN IMMEDIATE

   B. SHUTDOWN TRANSACTIONAL

   C. SHUTDOWN NORMAL

   D. None of the above

7. Which SHUTDOWN option will wait for the users to complete their uncommitted transactions?

   A. SHUTDOWN IMMEDIATE

   B. SHUTDOWN TRANSACTIONAL

   C. SHUTDOWN NORMAL

   D. SHUTDOWN ABORT

8. How do you make a database read-only? (Choose the best answer.)

   A. STARTUP READ ONLY

   B. STARTUP MOUNT; ALTER DATABASE OPEN READ ONLY

   C. STARTUP NOMOUNT; ALTER DATABASE READ ONLY

   D. STARTUP; ALTER SYSTEM ENABLE READ ONLY

9. Which role is created by default to administer databases?

   A. DATABASE_ADMINISTRATOR

   B. SUPER_USER

   C. DBA

   D. No such role is created by default; you need to create administrator roles after logging in as SYS.

10. Which parameter in the ORAPWD utility is optional?

A. `FILE`

B. `PASSWORD`

C. `ENTRIES`

D. All the parameters are optional; if you omit a parameter, Oracle substitutes the default.

11. Which privilege do you need to connect to the database, if the database is started up by using `STARTUP RESTRICT`?

A. `ALTER SYSTEM`

B. `RESTRICTED SESSION`

C. `CONNECT`

D. `RESTRICTED SYSTEM`

12. At which stage of the database start-up is the control file opened?

A. Before the instance start-up

B. Instance started

C. Database mounted

D. Database opened

13. User `SCOTT` has opened a SQL*Plus session and left for lunch. When you queried the `V$SESSION` view, the `STATUS` was `INACTIVE`. You terminated `SCOTT`'s session. What will be the status of `SCOTT`'s session in `V$SESSION`?

A. `INACTIVE`

B. There will be no session information in `V$SESSION` view

C. `TERMINATED`

D. `KILLED`

14. Which command will "bounce" the database—that is, shut down the database and start up the database in a single command?

    A. `STARTUP FORCE`

    B. `SHUTDOWN FORCE`

    C. `SHUTDOWN START`

    D. There is no single command to "bounce" the database; you need to shut down the database and then restart it

15. When performing the command `SHUTDOWN TRANSACTIONAL`, Oracle performs the following tasks in what order?

    A. Terminates the instance

    B. Performs a checkpoint

    C. Closes the data files and redo log files

    D. Waits for all user transactions to complete

    E. Dismounts the database

    F. Closes all sessions

16. What is the primary benefit of using an SPFILE to maintain the parameter file?

    A. The SPFILE can be mirrored across several drives, unlike PFILEs.

    B. Changes to the database configuration can be made persistent across shutdown and startup.

    C. Because the SPFILE is binary, the DBA will be less likely to edit it.

    D. The `ALTER SYSTEM` command cannot modify the contents of an SPFILE.

17. Using SQL*Plus, which two options below will display the value of the parameter `DB_BLOCK_SIZE`?

    A. `SHOW PARAMETER DB_BLOCK_SIZE`

    B. `SHOW PARAMETERS DB_BLOCK_SIZE`

    C. `SHOW ALL`

    D. `DISPLAY PARAMETER DB_BLOCK_SIZE`

18. When you issue the command ALTER SYSTEM ENABLE RESTRICTED SESSION, what happens to the users who are connected to the database?

    A. The users with DBA privilege remain connected, and others are disconnected.

    B. The users with RESTRICTED SESSION remain connected, and others are disconnected.

    C. Nothing happens to the existing users. They can continue working.

    D. The users are allowed to complete their current transaction and are disconnected.

19. Which view has information about users who are granted SYSDBA or SYSOPER privilege?

    A. V$PWFILE_USERS

    B. DBA_PWFILE_USERS

    C. DBA_SYS_GRANTS

    D. None of the above

20. Which of the following initialization parameters is NOT used in OMF operations?

    A. DB_CREATE_FILE_DEST

    B. DB_CREATE_FILE_DEST_2

    C. DB_CREATE_ONLINE_LOG_DEST_1

    D. DB_CREATE_ONLINE_LOG_DEST_5

Answers to Review Questions

1. A. STARTUP NORMAL is an invalid option; to start the database, you issue the STARTUP command without any options or with STARTUP OPEN.

2. A and C. SID and SERIAL# are used to kill a session. You can query the V$SESSION view to obtain these values. The command is ALTER SYSTEM KILL SESSION '<*sid*>, <*serial#*>'.

3. C. The value of the REMOTE_LOGIN_PASSWORDFILE parameter should be set to NONE to use OS authentication. To use password file authentication, the value should be either EXCLUSIVE or SHARED.

4. A. The alert log stores information about block corruption errors, internal errors, and the *non*-default initialization parameters used at instance start-up. The alert log also records information about database start-up, shutdown, archiving, recovery, tablespace modifications, undo segment modifications, and data file modifications.

5. C. The alert log file is written in the BACKGROUND_DUMP_DEST directory. This directory also records the trace files generated by the background processes. The USER_DUMP_DEST directory has the trace files generated by user sessions. The CORE_DUMP_DEST directory is used primarily on Unix platforms to save the core dump files. ALERT_DUMP_DEST is not a valid parameter.

6. D. SHUTDOWN ABORT requires instance recovery when the database is started the next time. Oracle will also roll back uncommitted transactions during start-up. This option shuts down the instance without dismounting the database.

7. B. When SHUTDOWN TRANSACTIONAL is issued, Oracle waits for the users to either commit or roll back their pending transactions. Once all users have either rolled back or committed their transactions, the database is shut down. When using SHUTDOWN IMMEDIATE, the user sessions are disconnected and the changes are rolled back. SHUTDOWN NORMAL waits for the user sessions to disconnect from the database.

8. B. To put a database into read-only mode, you can mount the database and open the database in read-only mode. This can be accomplished in one step by using `STARTUP OPEN READ ONLY`.

9. C. The `DBA` role is created when you create the database and is assigned to the `SYS` and `SYSTEM` users.

10. C. The parameter `ENTRIES` is optional. You must specify a password file name and the `SYS` password. The password file created will be used for authentication.

11. B. The `RESTRICTED SESSION` privilege is required to access a database that is in restricted mode. You start up the database in restricted mode by using `STARTUP RESTRICT`, or you change the database to restricted mode by using `ALTER SYSTEM ENABLE RESTRICTED SESSION`.

12. C. The control file is opened when the instance mounts the database. The data files and redo log files are opened after the database is opened. When the instance is started, the background processes are started.

13. D. When you terminate a session that is `INACTIVE`, the `STATUS` in `V$SESSION` will show as `KILLED`. When `SCOTT` tries to perform any database activity in the SQL*Plus window, he receives an error that his session is terminated. When an `ACTIVE` session is killed, the changes are rolled back and an error message is written to the user's screen.

14. A. `STARTUP FORCE` will terminate the current instance and `start up` the database. It is equivalent to issuing `SHUTDOWN ABORT` and `STARTUP OPEN`.

15. D, F, B, C, E, and A. `SHUTDOWN TRANSACTIONAL` waits for all user transactions to complete. Once no transactions are pending, it disconnects all sessions and proceeds with the normal shutdown process. The normal shutdown process performs a checkpoint, closes data files and redo log files, dismounts the database, and shuts down the instance.

16. B. Using the `ALTER SYSTEM` command, the changes can be made to the current (MEMORY) configuration, to the next restart (SPFILE), or to both (BOTH).

17. A and B. The SHOW PARAMETER command will display the current value of the parameter. If you provide the parameter name, its value is displayed; if you omit the parameter name, all the parameter values are displayed. SHOW ALL in SQL*Plus will display the SQL*Plus environment settings, not the parameters.

18. C. If you enable RESTRICTED SESSION when users are connected, nothing happens to the already connected sessions. Future sessions are started only if the user has the RESTRICTED SESSION privilege.

19. A. The dynamic view V$PWFILE_USERS has the username and a value of TRUE in column SYSDBA if the SYSDBA privilege is granted, or a value of TRUE in column SYSOPER if the SYSOPER privilege is granted.

20. B. Only one file destination is allowed. Control files and redo log files use the same parameter; the parameter DB_CREATE_ONLINE_LOG_DEST_*n* (*n* can have values from 1 to 5).

Creating a Database and Data Dictionary

ORACLE9i DBA FUNDAMENTALS I EXAM OBJECTIVES OFFERED IN THIS CHAPTER:

- ✓ Describe the prerequisites necessary for database creation
- ✓ Create a database using the Oracle Database Configuration Assistant (DBCA)
- ✓ Create a database manually
- ✓ Identify key data dictionary components
- ✓ Identify the contents and uses of the data dictionary
- ✓ Query the data dictionary

Exam objectives are subject to change at any time without prior notice and at Oracle's sole discretion. Please visit Oracle's Training and Certification website (`http://www.oracle.com/education/certification/`) for the most current exam objectives listing.

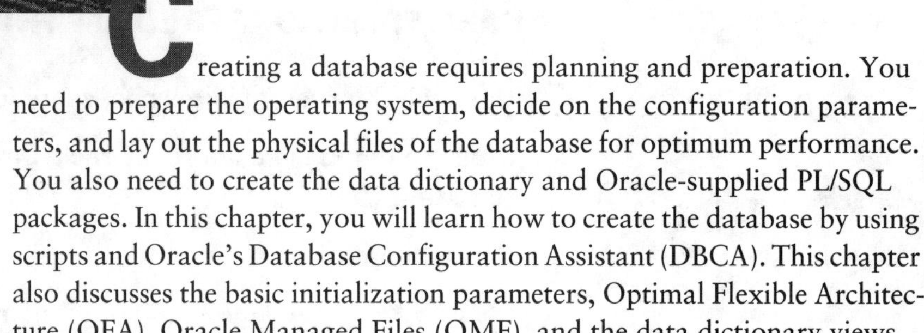

Creating a database requires planning and preparation. You need to prepare the operating system, decide on the configuration parameters, and lay out the physical files of the database for optimum performance. You also need to create the data dictionary and Oracle-supplied PL/SQL packages. In this chapter, you will learn how to create the database by using scripts and Oracle's Database Configuration Assistant (DBCA). This chapter also discusses the basic initialization parameters, Optimal Flexible Architecture (OFA), Oracle Managed Files (OMF), and the data dictionary views.

Creating a Database

Creating an Oracle database requires planning and is done in multiple steps. The database is a collection of physical files that work together with an area of allocated memory and background processes. You create the database only once, but you can change the configuration (except the block size) or add more files to the database. Before creating the database, you must have the following:

- Necessary hardware resources such as memory and disk space
- Operating system and SYSDBA privileges
- A plan to lay out the files and their sizes
- A parameter file
- Defined environment variables
- Oracle software installed
- A backup of existing databases

After you complete these steps, you can create the database using the CREATE DATABASE command. Once the database is created, it is recommended that you create an SPFILE to replace the PFILE parameter file.

Oracle Objective **Describe the prerequisites necessary for database creation**

Preparing Resources

Preparing the operating system resources is an important step. Depending on the operating system, you may have to adjust certain configuration parameters. For example, on Unix platforms, you must configure the shared memory parameters, because Oracle uses a single shared memory segment for the SGA (System Global Area). Since a major share of Oracle databases are created on Unix platforms, we will discuss certain operating system parameters that must be configured before you can create any Oracle database. The following list itemizes the Unix kernel parameters and describes their purposes. The super-user administers these kernel parameters.

SHMMAX The maximum size of a shared memory segment

SHMMNI The maximum number of shared memory identifiers in the system

SHMSEG The maximum number of shared memory segments to which a user process can attach

SEMMNI The maximum number of semaphore identifiers in the system

SHMMAX * SHMSEG The total maximum shared memory that can be allocated

Allocate enough memory for creating the SGA when creating the database and for future database operation. It is better to fit the SGA in real memory, rather than using virtual memory, to avoid paging. Paging will degrade performance.

The Oracle software should be installed on the machine on which you will be creating the database. The user account that installs the software needs certain administrative privileges on Windows NT/2000/XP, but on Unix platforms, the user account that installs the software need not have super-user privileges. The super-user privilege is required only to set up the Oracle account and to complete certain post-installation tasks such as creating the `oratab` file. The `oratab` file lists all the database instance names on that machine, their Oracle home locations, and whether the database should be started automatically at boot time. Certain Oracle scripts and Enterprise Manager discovery services use this file. The `oratab` file resides in the `/etc` directory under AIX, HP-UX, and Tru64 or the `/var/opt/oracle` directory under Solaris and Linux.

The user account that owns the Oracle software should have the necessary privileges to create the data files, redo log files, and control files. You must make sure that enough free space is available to create these files, and you must follow certain Oracle guidelines about where to create the files, which are discussed in the section "*Optimal Flexible Architecture.*"

The parameter file lists the parameters that will be used for creating and configuring the database. The common parameters are discussed in the section "Parameters."

Anyone can make mistakes; before performing any major task, ensure that you have methods to fix the mistakes. If you are already running databases on the server where you want to create the new database, make a full backup of all of them. If you overwrite an existing database file when creating the new database, the existing database will become useless.

Parameters

Oracle uses the parameter file to start up the instance before creating the database. You specify some database configuration values via the parameter file. The purpose and format of the parameter file were discussed in Chapter 3, "Installing and Managing Oracle." The following parameters affect database configuration and creation:

`CONTROL_FILES` Specifies the control file location(s) for the new database with the full pathname. Specify at least two control files on different disks. You can specify a maximum of eight control file names. Oracle creates these control files when the database is created. Be careful when specifying the control file; if you specify the control file name of an existing database, Oracle could overwrite the control file, which will damage the existing database. If you do not use this parameter, Oracle uses the default filename, which is operating system dependent.

DB_BLOCK_SIZE Specifies the database block size as a multiple of the operating system block size—this value cannot be changed after the database is created. The default block size is 4KB on most platforms. Oracle allows block sizes from 2KB to 32KB, depending on the operating system.

DB_NAME Specifies the database name—the name cannot be changed easily after the database is created (you must re-create the control file). The DB_NAME value can be a maximum of eight characters. You can use alphabetic characters, numbers, the underscore (_), the pound symbol (#), and the dollar symbol ($) in the name. No other characters are valid. The first character should be an alphabetic character. Oracle removes double quotation marks before processing the database name. During database creation, the DB_NAME value is recorded in the data files, redo log files, and control file of the database.

Table 4.1 lists and describes the other parameters that can be included in the parameter file. You must at least define the DB_CACHE_SIZE, LOG_BUFFER and SHARED_POOL_SIZE to calculate the SGA, which must fit into real, not virtual, memory.

TABLE 4.1 Initialization Parameters

Parameter Name	Description
OPEN_CURSORS	The maximum number of open cursors a session can have. The default is 50.
MAX_ENABLED_ROLES	The maximum number of database roles that users can enable. The default is 20.
DB_CACHE_SIZE	The size of the default buffer cache, with blocks sized by DB_BLOCK_SIZE. This parameter can be dynamically altered.

TABLE 4.1 Initialization Parameters *(continued)*

Parameter Name	Description
SGA_MAX_SIZE	The maximum size allowed for all components of the SGA. Sets an upper limit to prevent dynamically altered sizes of other parameters to push the total SGA size over this limit.
SHARED_POOL_SIZE	Size of the shared pool. Can be specified in bytes or KB or MB. The default value on most platforms is 16MB.
LARGE_POOL_SIZE	The large pool area of the SGA. Default value is 0.
JAVA_POOL_SIZE	Size of the Java pool; the default value is 20,000KB. If you are not using Java, specify the value as 0.
PROCESSES	The maximum number of processes that can connect to the instance. This includes the background processes.
LOG_BUFFER	Size of the redo log buffer in bytes.
BACKGROUND_DUMP_DEST	Location of the background dump directory. The alert log file is written in this directory.
CORE_DUMP_DEST	Location of the core dump directory.
USER_DUMP_DEST	Location of the user dump directory.
REMOTE_LOGIN_PASSWORDFILE	The authentication method. When creating the database, make sure you have either commented out this parameter or set it to NONE. If you create the password file before creating the database, you can specify a different value such as EXCLUSIVE or SHARED.

TABLE 4.1 Initialization Parameters *(continued)*

Parameter Name	Description
COMPATIBLE	The release with which the database server must maintain compatibility. You can specify values from 9.0 to the current release number.
SORT_AREA_SIZE	Size of the area allocated for temporary sorts.
LICENSE_MAX_SESSIONS	Maximum number of concurrent user sessions. When this limit is reached, only users with RESTRICTED SESSION privilege are allowed to connect. The default is 0—unlimited.
LICENSE_SESSIONS_WARNING	A warning limit on the number of concurrent user sessions. Messages are written to the alert log when new users connect after this limit is reached. The new user is allowed to connect up to the LICENSE_MAX_SESSIONS value. The default value is 0—unlimited.
LICENSE_MAX_USERS	Maximum number of users that can be created in the database. The default is 0—unlimited.

Environment Variables

If you are creating a database on Unix, be sure to set up the appropriate *environment variables*. The examples in the environment variables below conform with Optimal Flexible Architecture (OFA).

ORACLE_BASE The directory at the top of the Oracle tree, for example, /u01/apps/oracle. All versions of Oracle installed on this server are stored under this directory.

ORACLE_HOME The location of the Oracle software, relative to ORACLE_BASE. The OFA-recommended location is $ORACLE_BASE/product/<release>, which in this case would resolve to /u01/apps/oracle/product/901.

ORACLE_SID The instance name for the database. This name must be unique for all other instances, regardless of version, running on this server.

ORA_NLS33 The environment variable that you must set if you want to use a character set other than the default.

PATH The standard Unix pathname that should already exist in the Unix environment; you must add the directory for the Oracle binary executables to this path variable: $ORACLE_HOME/bin.

LD_LIBRARY_PATH Other program libraries, both Oracle and non-Oracle, that reside in this directory.

The *CREATE DATABASE* Command

You create the database using the CREATE DATABASE command. You must start up the instance (with STARTUP NOMOUNT PFILE=) before issuing the command.

Oracle Objective | **Create a database manually**

The following is a sample database creation command:

```
CREATE DATABASE "PROD01"
CONTROLFILE REUSE
LOGFILE GROUP 1
        ('/oradata02/PROD01/redo0101.log',
         '/oradata03/PROD01/redo0102.log) SIZE 5M REUSE,
        GROUP 2
        ('/oradata02/PROD01/redo0201.log',
         '/oradata03/PROD01/redo0202.log) SIZE 5M REUSE
```

```
MAXLOGFILES 4
MAXLOGMEMBERS 2
MAXLOGHISTORY 0
MAXDATAFILES 254
MAXINSTANCES 1
NOARCHIVELOG
CHARACTER SET "WE8MSWIN1252"
NATIONAL CHARACTER SET "AL16UTF16"
DATAFILE '/oradata01/PROD01/system01.dbf' SIZE 80M
         AUTOEXTEND ON NEXT 5M MAXSIZE UNLIMITED
UNDO TABLESPACE UNDOTBS
DATAFILE '/oradata04/PROD01/undo01.dbf' SIZE 35M
DEFAULT TEMPORARY TABLESPACE TEMP
TEMPFILE '/oradata05/PROD01/temp01.dbf' SIZE 20M;
```

Let's look at the clauses used in the CREATE DATABASE command. The only mandatory portion in this command is the CREATE DATABASE clause. If you omit the database name, Oracle takes the default value from the parameter DB_NAME defined in the initialization parameter file. The value specified in the parameter file and the database name in this command should be the same.

The CONTROLFILE REUSE clause overwrites an existing control file. Normally you use this clause only when re-creating a database. If you omit this clause, and any of the files specified by the CONTROL_FILES parameter exist, Oracle returns an error.

The LOGFILE clause specifies the location of the online redo log files. If you omit the GROUP clause, Oracle creates the files specified in separate groups with one member in each. A database must have at least two redo groups. In the example, Oracle creates two redo log groups with two members in each. It is recommended that all redo log groups be the same size. The REUSE clause overwrites an existing file, if any, and applies the new size, if specified; if SIZE is not specified, the original size is retained. REUSE must be used if the file already exists, otherwise an error is returned.

The next five clauses specify limits for the database. The control file size depends on these limits, because Oracle pre-allocates space in the control file. MAXLOGFILES specifies the maximum number of redo log groups that can ever be created in the database. MAXLOGMEMBERS specifies the maximum number or redo log members (copies of redo log files) for each redo log group. The MAXLOGHISTORY is used only for the Real Application

Cluster configuration. It specifies the maximum number of archived redo log files for automatic media recovery. MAXDATAFILES specifies the maximum number of data files that can be created in this database. Data files are created when you create a tablespace or add more space to a tablespace by adding a data file. MAXINSTANCES specifies the maximum number of instances that can simultaneously mount and open this database. If you want to change any of these limits after the database is created, you must re-create the control file.

The initialization parameter DB_FILES specifies the maximum number of data files accessible to the instance. The MAXDATAFILES clause in the CREATE DATABASE command specifies the maximum number of data files allowed for the database. The DB_FILES parameter cannot specify a value larger than MAXDATAFILES.

You can specify NOARCHIVELOG or ARCHIVELOG to configure the redo log archiving. The default is NOARCHIVELOG; you can change the database to ARCHIVELOG mode by using the ALTER DATABASE command after the database is created.

The CHARACTER SET clause specifies the character set used to store data. The default is WE8MSWIN1252 on Windows platforms. The character set cannot be changed after database creation unless the old character set is a proper subset of the new character set. The NATIONAL CHARACTER SET clause specifies the national character set used to store data in columns specifically defined as NCHAR, NCLOB, or NVARCHAR2. If not specified, the national character set defaults to the database character set.

The unqualified DATAFILE clause in this example specifies one or more files created for the SYSTEM tablespace. You can optionally specify the AUTOEXTEND clause, which is discussed in detail in Chapter 6, "Logical and Physical Database Structures."

The UNDO TABLESPACE clause specifies an undo tablespace with one or more associated data files. This tablespace contains undo segments when automatic undo management is enabled with the initialization parameter UNDO_MANAGEMENT=AUTO.

The DEFAULT TEMPORARY TABLESPACE clause defines the tablespace location for all temporary segments. If you create a user without specifying a temporary tablespace, this one is used.

Now that you have seen what is involved in creating a database, let's put this all together:

1. Be sure you have enough resources available and the necessary privileges.
2. Decide on a database name, control file locations, and a database block size, and prepare a parameter file including other necessary parameters.
3. Decide on the locations for control files, data files, and redo log files. If at all possible, spread out data files that may compete for the same resources to different physical volumes. For example, updates to a table will generate I/O against both the table and the index. Therefore, placing the indexes in a different tablespace on a different physical volume may improve performance.
4. Decide on the version of the database and the instance name. Set the environment variables *ORACLE_HOME* with the directory name of the Oracle software installation and *ORACLE_SID* with the instance name. Normally the instance name and database name are the same. Set up the *ORA_NLS33* environment variable if you are using a character set other than the default.
5. Start the instance. Using SQL*Plus, connect using a SYSDBA account and issue STARTUP NOMOUNT.
6. Create the database by using the CREATE DATABASE command.

Using OMF to Create a Database

In contrast to using the CREATE DATABASE command, using *Oracle Managed Files (OMF)* can make the process of creating a database much simpler. As discussed in Chapter 3, if the initialization parameters DB_CREATE_FILE_DEST and DB_CREATE_ONLINE_DEST_*n* are defined with the desired operating system locations for the data files and online redo log files, creating a database can be as simple as the following:

```
CREATE DATABASE DEFAULT TEMPORARY TABLESPACE TMP;
```

Creating an SPFILE

As discussed in Chapter 3, using an SPFILE instead of a PFILE for database initialization has many distinct benefits for the DBA, including but not limited to "on-the-fly" modifications to SPFILE contents, with the effect of any parameter change taking place immediately or after the next instance restart. After you configure the `init.ora` file correctly, create the SPFILE when connected as SYSDBA:

```
SQL> CREATE SPFILE FROM PFILE;
```

By default, both the PFILE and SPFILE reside in the same location. At instance startup, the Oracle Server looks for a file named `spfileSID.ora` first. If it doesn't exist, the file `spfile.ora` is used next. If that file does not exist, `initSID.ora` (a PFILE) is used.

The Data Dictionary

The most important part of the Oracle database is the data dictionary. The *data dictionary* is a set of tables and views that hold the database's metadata information. You cannot update the dictionary directly; Oracle updates the dictionary when you issue any Data Definition Language (DDL) commands. The dictionary is provided as read-only for users and administrators. The contents of the data dictionary and obtaining information from the dictionary are discussed in the section "Querying the Dictionary."

Oracle Objective **Identify key data dictionary components**

The data dictionary consists of *base tables* and user-accessible views. The base tables are normalized and contain cryptic, version-specific information. You use the views to query the dictionary and extract meaningful information. To create the views, install the additional Oracle-supplied scripts after the database is created.

The base tables contain information such as the users of the database and their permissions, the amount of the used and unused space for database objects, constraint information, and so on. Users and administrators rarely, if ever, need to access the base tables, with the exception of tables such as AUD$, which contains auditing information for objects in the database.

When the database is created, Oracle creates two users, SYS and SYSTEM. SYS is the owner of the data dictionary, and SYSTEM is a DBA account. The initial password for SYS is CHANGE_ON_INSTALL; the initial password for SYSTEM is MANAGER. Change these passwords once the database is created.

Never change the definition or contents of the data dictionary base tables. Oracle uses the dictionary information for proper functioning of the database.

Creating the Dictionary

The Oracle database is functional only when you create the dictionary views and additional tablespaces, rollback segments, users, and so on. Creating the dictionary views is the next step after you create the database by using the CREATE DATABASE command. Running certain Oracle-supplied scripts creates the dictionary views. We'll discuss all these topics in this section as well as give you some basics of how PL/SQL packages are created and maintained in the data dictionary.

Data Dictionary Scripts

The data dictionary base tables are created under the SYS schema in the SYSTEM tablespace when you issue the CREATE DATABASE command. Oracle automatically creates the tablespace and tables using the *sql.bsq* script found under the $ORACLE_HOME/rdbms/admin directory. This script creates the following:

- The SYSTEM tablespace by using the data file(s) specified in the CREATE DATABASE command
- A rollback segment named SYSTEM in the SYSTEM tablespace
- The SYS and SYSTEM user accounts
- The dictionary base tables and clusters

- Indexes on dictionary tables and sequences for dictionary use
- The roles PUBLIC, CONNECT, RESOURCE, DBA, DELETE_CATALOG_ROLE, EXECUTE_CATALOG_ROLE, and SELECT_CATALOG_ROLE
- The DUAL table

Don't modify the definitions in the `sql.bsq` script—for example, by adding columns, removing columns, or changing the data types or width. You can change these storage parameters: INITIAL, NEXT, MINEXTENTS, MAXEXTENTS, PCTINCREASE, FREELISTS, FREELIST GROUPS, and OPTIMAL.

The *DUAL* table is a dummy table owned by SYS and accessible to all users of the database. The table has only one column, named DUMMY, and only one row. Do not add more rows to this table.

Running the script `catalog.sql` creates the data dictionary views. This script creates synonyms on the views to allow users easy access to the views. Before running any data dictionary script, connect to the database as SYS. The dictionary creation scripts are under the `$ORACLE_HOME/rdbms/admin` directory on most platforms.

The script `catproc.sql` creates the dictionary items necessary for PL/SQL functionality. The other scripts necessary for creating dictionary objects depend on the operating system and the functionality you want in the database. For example, if you are not using Real Application Clusters (RACs), you need not install any RAC-related dictionary items. At a minimum, run the `catalog.sql` and `catproc.sql` scripts after creating the database.

Oracle Objective

Identify the contents and uses of the data dictionary

The dictionary creation scripts all begin with `cat`. Many of the scripts call other scripts. For example, when you execute `catalog.sql`, it calls the following scripts:

`standard.sql` Creates a package called STANDARD, which contains the SQL functions to implement basic language features

`cataudit.sql` Creates data dictionary views to support auditing

catexp.sql Creates data dictionary views to support import/export

catldr.sql Creates data dictionary views to support direct-path load of SQL*Loader

catpart.sql Creates data dictionary views to support partitioning

catadt.sql Creates data dictionary views to support Oracle objects and types

catsum.sql Creates data dictionary views to support Oracle summary management

From the name of a script, you can sometimes identify its purpose. The following list indicates the categories of scripts.

cat*.sql Catalog and data dictionary scripts

dbms*.sql PL/SQL administrative package definitions

prvt*.plb PL/SQL administrative package code, in wrapped (encrypted) form

uNNNNNN.sql Database upgrade/migration scripts

dNNNNNN.sql Database downgrade scripts

utl*.sql Additional tables and views needed for database utilities

Administering Stored Procedures and Packages

The PL/SQL stored programs are stored in the data dictionary. They are treated like any other database object. The code used to create the *procedure*, *package*, or *function* is available in the dictionary views DBA_SOURCE, ALL_SOURCE, and USER_SOURCE–except when you create them with the WRAP utility. The WRAP utility generates encrypted code, which only the Oracle server can interpret.

You manage the privileges on these stored programs by using regular GRANT and REVOKE statements. You can GRANT and REVOKE execute privileges on these objects to other users of the database.

The DBA_OBJECTS, ALL_OBJECTS, and USER_OBJECTS views give information about the status of the stored program. If a procedure is invalid, you can recompile it by using the following statement:

```
ALTER PROCEDURE <procedure_name> COMPILE;
```

To recompile a package, compile the package definition and then the package body as in the following statements:

```
ALTER PACKAGE <package_name> COMPILE;
ALTER PACKAGE <package_name> COMPILE BODY;
```

To compile the package, procedure, or function owned by any other schema, you must have the ALTER ANY PROCEDURE privilege.

Completing the Database Creation

After creating the database and creating the dictionary views, you must create additional tablespaces to complete the database creation process. Oracle recommends creating the following tablespaces if they were not created in the CREATE DATABASE script or with DBCA (Database Configuration Assistant), discussed later in this chapter. You can create additional tablespaces depending on the requirements of your application.

UNDOTBS Holds the undo segments for automatic undo management. When you create the database, Oracle creates a SYSTEM undo segment in the SYSTEM tablespace. For the database that has multiple tablespaces, you must have at least one undo segment that is not in the SYSTEM tablespace for manual undo management or one undo tablespace for automatic undo management.

TEMP Holds the temporary segments. Oracle uses temporary segments for sorting and for any intermediate operation. Oracle uses these segments when the information to be sorted will not fit in the SORT_AREA_SIZE parameter specified in the initialization file.

USERS Contains the user tables.

INDX Contains the user indexes.

TOOLS Holds the tables and indexes created by the Oracle administrative tools.

After creating these tablespaces, you must create additional users for the database. As soon as the database is created, back it up, and then immediately change the passwords for SYS and SYSTEM.

Querying the Dictionary

You can query the data dictionary views and tables in the same way that you query any other table or view. From the prefix of the data dictionary views, you can determine for whom the view is intended. Some views are accessible to all Oracle users; others are intended for database administrators only.

Oracle Objective **Query the data dictionary**

The data dictionary views can be classified into the following categories based on their prefix:

DBA_ These views contain information about all structures in the database—they show what is in all users' schemas. Accessible to the DBA or anyone with the SELECT_CATALOG_ROLE privilege, they provide information on all the objects in the database and have an OWNER column.

ALL_ These views show information about all objects that the user has access to. They are accessible to all users. Each view has an OWNER column, providing information about objects accessible by the user.

USER_ These views show information about the structures owned by the user (in the user's schema). They are accessible to all users and do not have an OWNER column.

V$ These views are known as *dynamic performance views*, because they are continuously updated while a database is open and in use, and their contents relate primarily to performance. The actual dynamic performance views are identified by the prefix V_$. Public synonyms for these views have the prefix V$.

**GV$** For almost all V$ views, Oracle has a corresponding GV$ view. These are the global dynamic performance views and are useful if you are running Oracle Real Application Clusters. The corresponding GV$ view has an additional column identifying the instance number called INST_ID.

The ALL_ views and USER_ views contain almost identical information except for the OWNER column, but the DBA_ views often contain more information useful for administrators.

In Oracle9i, the initialization parameter 07_DICTIONARY_ACCESSIBILITY now defaults to FALSE. Therefore, even users with the SELECT ANY TABLE privilege cannot access the dictionary views unless they have either explicit object permissions or the role SELECT_CATALOG_ROLE.

You can use the data dictionary information to generate the source code for all the objects created in the database. For example, the information on tables is available in the dictionary views DBA_TABLES, DBA_TAB_COLUMNS, or ALL_TABLES, ALL_TAB_COLUMNS, or USER_TABLES, USER_TAB_COLUMNS.

The dictionary view *DICTIONARY* contains names and descriptions of all the data dictionary views in the database. DICT is a synonym for DICTIONARY view; the dynamic performance view V$FIXED_TABLE contains similar information to that found in DICTIONARY. The DICT_COLUMNS dictionary view contains the description of all columns in the dictionary views. If you want to know all the dictionary views that provide information about tables, you can run a query similar to the following.

```
SQL> COL TABLE_NAME FORMAT A25
SQL> COL COMMENTS FORMAT A40
SQL> SELECT * FROM DICT
WHERE  TABLE_NAME LIKE '%TAB%';
```

The dictionary views ALL_OBJECTS, DBA_OBJECTS, and USER_OBJECTS provide information about the objects in the database. These views contain the timestamp of object creation and the last DDL timestamp. The STATUS column shows whether the object is invalid; this information is especially useful for PL/SQL–stored programs and views.

Query the data dictionary view PRODUCT_COMPONENT_VERSION or V$VERSION to see the version of the database and installed components. Oracle product versions have five numbers. For example, in the version number 9.0.1.0.1, 9 is the version, the first zero is the new features' release, the first 1 is the maintenance release, the second zero is the generic patch set number, and the last 1 is the platform-specific patch set number.

Real World Scenario

Data Dictionary Views vs. Dynamic Performance Tables

The usual distinction between data dictionary views and dynamic performance views is that data dictionary views are relatively static and that dynamic performance tables are primarily related to performance.

In reality, though, there are exceptions to this rule! The dynamic performance view V$VERSION may not change for months, and the data dictionary view DBA_PENDING_TRANSACTIONS may change constantly in a distributed environment.

The experienced DBA, therefore, cannot always rely on view prefixes and sometimes just has to know where to look for information about the running database.

The Database Configuration Assistant

The Database Configuration Assistant (DBCA) is Oracle's GUI DBA tool for creating, modifying, or deleting a database. After you answer a few questions, this tool can create a database, save a template for future use, or give you the scripts to create the database. It is a good idea to generate the scripts by using this tool and then customize the script files, if needed, and create the database. You can create the database with a Shared Server configuration (MTS) or a dedicated server configuration. You can also choose the additional options you want to install in the database, such as Oracle InterMedia and Oracle JVM.

Oracle Objective

Create a database using the Oracle Database Configuration Assistant (DBCA)

You can run the DBCA as part of the Oracle Universal Installer (OUI) or as a stand-alone application. As with the manual creation of the database, be sure to define the environment variables before creating the database.

If you choose the typical installation option, you have only a few questions to answer. You also have the option of copying a preconfigured database (template) or creating a new database. The tool generates the initialization parameters based on the type of database you create; the options are Online Transaction Processing (OLTP), Data Warehousing, or Multipurpose.

If you choose the custom installation option, you have full control of the SGA sizing. Figure 4.1 shows the SGA memory configuration screen of the DBCA.

FIGURE 4.1 DBCA SGA Sizing

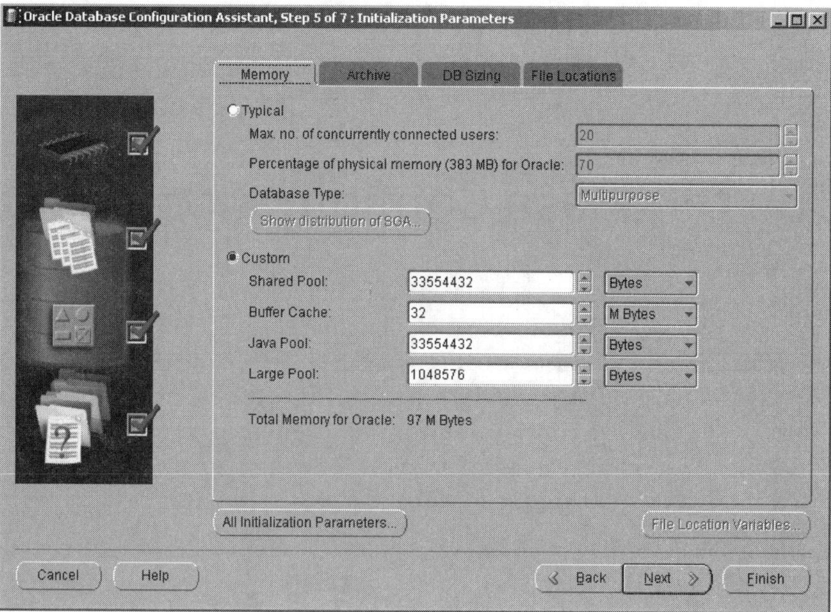

To run the DBCA, use the `dbca` command under Unix, or find DBCA in the Windows Start menu under Oracle/Configuration and Migration Tools/ Database Configuration Assistant.

You can easily configure many, if not all, of the other initialization parameters from within the DBCA. Following are some typical parameters:

- File locations: pathname for parameter and trace files
- Character set values: NLS-related
- Archiving: location and format of the archived log files
- Trace files: location of the user and system trace files
- Storage: block size, sizing control files, datafiles and tablespaces, redo log groups
- Sorting: `SORT_AREA_SIZE`

Figure 4.2 shows a sample DBCA screen in which the character set options and sort area size can be adjusted. If you are an advanced DBA, you can modify virtually every initialization parameter, as shown in Figure 4.3.

FIGURE 4.2 DBCA Sort Area Sizing

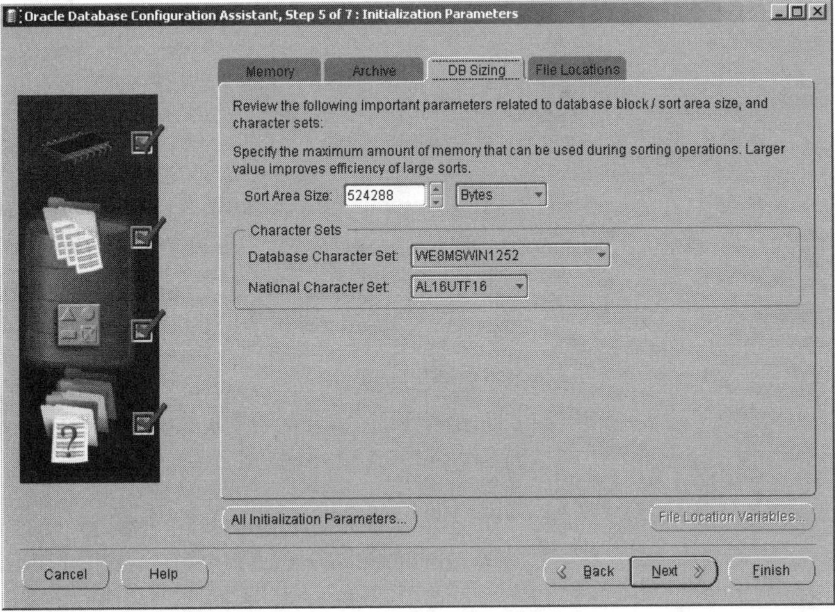

FIGURE 4.3 DBCA Initialization Parameter Editing

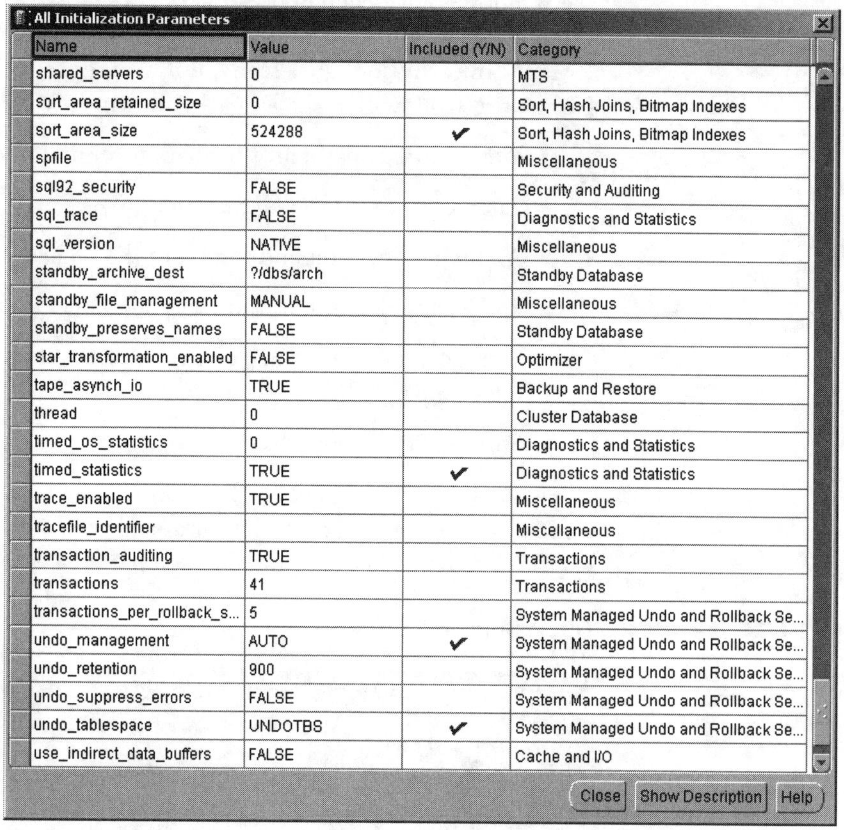

All Initialization Parameters

Name	Value	Included (Y/N)	Category
shared_servers	0		MTS
sort_area_retained_size	0		Sort, Hash Joins, Bitmap Indexes
sort_area_size	524288	✔	Sort, Hash Joins, Bitmap Indexes
spfile			Miscellaneous
sql92_security	FALSE		Security and Auditing
sql_trace	FALSE		Diagnostics and Statistics
sql_version	NATIVE		Miscellaneous
standby_archive_dest	?/dbs/arch		Standby Database
standby_file_management	MANUAL		Miscellaneous
standby_preserves_names	FALSE		Standby Database
star_transformation_enabled	FALSE		Optimizer
tape_asynch_io	TRUE		Backup and Restore
thread	0		Cluster Database
timed_os_statistics	0		Diagnostics and Statistics
timed_statistics	TRUE	✔	Diagnostics and Statistics
trace_enabled	TRUE		Miscellaneous
tracefile_identifier			Miscellaneous
transaction_auditing	TRUE		Transactions
transactions	41		Transactions
transactions_per_rollback_s...	5		System Managed Undo and Rollback Se...
undo_management	AUTO	✔	System Managed Undo and Rollback Se...
undo_retention	900		System Managed Undo and Rollback Se...
undo_suppress_errors	FALSE		System Managed Undo and Rollback Se...
undo_tablespace	UNDOTBS	✔	System Managed Undo and Rollback Se...
use_indirect_data_buffers	FALSE		Cache and I/O

Close | Show Description | Help

The script generated by the DBCA does the following (this is a good template for you to use when creating new databases):

1. Creates a parameter file, starts up the database in `NOMOUNT` mode, and creates the database by using the `CREATE DATABASE` command.
2. Runs `catalog.sql`.
3. Creates tablespaces for tools (`TOOLS`), undo (`UNDOTBS`), temporary (`TEMP`), user (`USERS`), and index (`INDX`).
4. Runs the following scripts:
   a. **catproc.sql**—sets up PL/SQL and installs the heterogeneous services (HS) data dictionary, providing the ability to access non-Oracle databases from the Oracle database. HS is an integrated component in the 9i database.

   b. **dbmsotrc.sql**—sets up Oracle Trace server stored procedures. It is run by the installer.

   c. **utlsampl.sql**—sets up sample user SCOTT and creates demo tables.

   d. **pupbld.sql**—creates product and user profile tables. This script is run as SYSTEM.

5. Runs the scripts necessary to install the other options chosen.

You can also use the DBCA to manage *templates*, which makes it easier to create a similar database on the same or a different server. You can create the template from scratch, or generate it from an existing database. You can create these derived templates with or without the data from the original database. In essence, this template management feature let you easily clone a database.

When you create a template that contains both the structure and the data from an existing database, any database you create with this template must contain all datafiles, tablespaces and undo segments in the template. You cannot add or remove any datafiles, tablespaces or undo segments before the database is created, nor can you change any initialization parameters. You *can* change control files, log groups and data file destinations.

Summary

In this chapter, you learned how to create a database. The Oracle database is created by using the command CREATE DATABASE. This command runs the sql.bsq script, which in turn creates the data dictionary tables. The three parameters that you should pay particular attention to before creating a database are CONTROL_FILES, DB_NAME, and DB_BLOCK_SIZE. You cannot change the block size of the database once it is created.

Running the script catalog.sql creates the data dictionary views. DBAs and users use these views to query the information from the data dictionary. The data dictionary is a set of tables and views that hold the metadata. The views prefixed with DBA_ are accessible only to the DBA or user with the SELECT_CATALOG_ROLE privilege. The views prefixed with ALL_ have information about all objects in the database that the user has any privilege on. The USER_ views show information about the objects that the user owns.

Before creating the database, be sure that you have enough resources, such as disk space and memory. You also need to prepare the operating system by setting the resource parameters, if any, and making sure that you have enough privileges. Oracle Managed Files (OMF) aids in the database creation by centralizing default operating system file locations.

PL/SQL has several administrative packages that are useful to the DBA as well as developers. To install these packages you run the script `catproc.sql`. Most of the administrative scripts are located under the directory `$ORACLE_HOME/rdbms/admin`.

Oracle has a graphical database creation tool, DBCA, designed to ease the administrative burden of creating scripts manually. DBCA also allows the DBA to create database templates, with and without data files.

Exam Essentials

Understand the preparation and planning steps for creating a database. Important items to verify include sufficient memory and disk space, along with a sufficient number of physical destinations to ensure recoverability.

Identify the environment variables and their purpose. Enumerate the minimum subset of environment variables needed to create or start a database.

Use the Database Configuration Assistant to create and maintain templates. Understand the different types of templates that can be created and modified; differentiate between the database objects that can and cannot be adjusted when using a template with datafiles.

Be able to manually construct a `CREATE DATABASE` statement. Understand the minimum set of parameters that need to be defined in `init.ora`; be able to use OMF to simplify the construction of the `CREATE DATABASE` statement, and understand how to create an SPFILE from an existing PFILE.

Understand how the base tables and data dictionary views are built during database creation. Identify the key script names that create the base tables, views, and packages.

Identify and describe the three categories of data dictionary views. Be able to describe the difference between the three types of views and how the contents differ based on the user rights and permissions in the database.

Differentiate the content and purpose of the dynamic performance views vs. the data dictionary views. Describe the conditions under which database information can be retrieved from one type of view instead of another, in addition to the database states under which some views are not available.

Key Terms

Before you take the exam, make sure you're familiar with the following terms:

base tables

data dictionary

DICTIONARY

DUAL

dynamic performance views

environment variables

function

ORA_NLS33

Oracle Managed Files (OMF)

ORACLE_HOME

ORACLE_SID

package

procedure

sql.bsq

templates

Review Questions

1. How many control files are required to create a database?

   A. One

   B. Two

   C. Three

   D. None

2. Which environment variable or registry entry variable represents the instance name?

   A. ORA_SID

   B. INSTANCE_NAME

   C. ORACLE_INSTANCE

   D. ORACLE_SID

3. Complete the following sentence: The recommended configuration for control files is

   A. One control file per database

   B. One control file per disk

   C. Two control files on two disks

   D. Two control files on one disk

4. You have specified the LOGFILE clause in the CREATE DATABASE command as follows. What happens if the size of the log file redo0101.log, which already exists, is 10MB?

```
LOGFILE GROUP 1
        ('/oradata02/PROD01/redo0101.log',
         '/oradata03/PROD01/redo0102.log) SIZE 5M
REUSE,
        GROUP 2
        ('/oradata02/PROD01/redo0201.log',
         '/oradata03/PROD01/redo0202.log) SIZE 5M REUSE
```

A. Oracle adjusts the size of all the redo log files to 10MB.

B. Oracle creates all the redo log files as 5MB.

C. Oracle creates all the redo log files as 5MB except `redo0101.log`, which is created as 10MB.

D. The command fails.

5. Which command must you issue before you can execute the `CREATE DATABASE` command?

A. `STARTUP INSTANCE`

B. `STARTUP NOMOUNT`

C. `STARTUP MOUNT`

D. None of the above

6. Which initialization parameter cannot be changed after creating the database?

A. `DB_BLOCK_SIZE`

B. `DB_NAME`

C. `CONTROL_FILES`

D. None; all the initialization parameters can be changed as and when required.

7. Which of the following objects or structures can be added or removed from a DBCA template? (Choose three.)

A. Tablespaces

B. File destinations

C. Datafiles

D. Control files

E. Log file groups

8. When you are creating a database, where does Oracle find information about the control files that need to be created?

A. From the initialization parameter file

B. From the CREATE DATABASE command line

C. From the environment variable

D. Files created under $ORACLE_HOME and name derived from *<db_name>.ctl*

9. Which script creates the data dictionary views?

A. catalog.sql

B. catproc.sql

C. sql.bsq

D. dictionary.sql

10. Which prefix for the data dictionary views indicates that the contents of the view belong to the current user?

A. ALL_

B. DBA_

C. USR_

D. USER_

11. Which data dictionary view shows information about the status of a procedure?

A. DBA_SOURCE

B. DBA_OBJECTS

C. DBA_PROCEDURES

D. DBA_STATUS

12. How do you correct a procedure that has become invalid when one of the tables it is referring to was altered to drop a constraint?

A. Re-create the procedure

B. ALTER PROCEDURE *<procedure_name>* RECOMPILE

C. ALTER PROCEDURE *<procedure_name>* COMPILE

D. VALIDATE PROCEDURE *<procedure_name>*

13. Which of the following views does *not* have information about the operating system locations of the components?

A. V$CONTROLFILE

B. V$DATAFILE

C. V$PWFILE_USERS

D. V$LOGFILE

E. V$TEMPFILE

14. How many data files can be specified in the DATAFILE clause when creating a database?

A. One.

B. Two.

C. More than one; only one will be used for the SYSTEM tablespace.

D. More than one; all will be used for the SYSTEM tablespace.

15. Who owns the data dictionary?

A. SYS

B. SYSTEM

C. DBA

D. ORACLE

16. What is the default password for the SYS user?

A. MANAGER

B. CHANGE_ON_INSTALL

C. SYS

D. There is no default password.

17. Which data dictionary view provides information about the version of the database and installed components?

    A. DBA_VERSIONS

    B. PRODUCT_COMPONENT_VERSION

    C. PRODUCT_VERSIONS

    D. ALL_VERSION

18. What is the prefix for dynamic performance views?

    A. DBA_

    B. X$

    C. V$

    D. X#

19. Which is an invalid clause in the CREATE DATABASE command?

    A. MAXLOGMEMBERS

    B. MAXLOGGROUPS

    C. MAXDATAFILES

    D. MAXLOGHISTORY

20. Which database underlying table can be updated directly by the DBA without severe consequences to the operation of the database?

    A. AUD$

    B. LINK$

    C. sql.bsq

    D. DICT

    E. HELP

Answers to Review Questions

1. D. You do not need any control files to create a database; the control files are created when you create the database, based on the filenames specified in the CONTROL_FILES parameter of the parameter file.

2. D. The ORACLE_SID environment variable represents the instance name. When you connect to the database without specifying a connect string, Oracle connects you to this instance.

3. C. Oracle allows multiplexing of control files. If you have two control files on two disks, one disk failure will not damage both control files.

4. B. The CREATE DATABASE command succeeds, and sets all log files to a size of 5M, including the log file that already exists. If a particular log file does not exist, the REUSE clause is ignored and a new file with a size of 5M is created. If a file already exists, you must specify REUSE.

5. B. You must start up the instance to create the database. Connect to the database by using the SYSDBA privilege, and start up the instance by using the command STARTUP NOMOUNT.

6. A. The block size of the database cannot be changed after database creation. The database name can be changed after re-creating the control file with the new name, and the CONTROL_FILES parameter can be changed if the files are copied to a new location.

7. B, D, E. In addition to tablespaces and data files, undo segments and initialization parameters must also remain exactly the same as defined in the template.

8. A. The control file names and locations are obtained from the initialization parameter file. The parameter name is CONTROL_FILES. If this parameter is not specified, Oracle creates a control file; the location and name depend on the operating system platform.

9. A. The catalog.sql script creates the data dictionary views. The base tables for these views are created by the script sql.bsq, which is executed when you issue the CREATE DATABASE command.

10. D. DBA_ prefixed views are accessible to the DBA or anyone with the SELECT_CATALOG_ROLE privilege; these views provide information on all the objects in the database and have an OWNER column. The ALL_ views show information about the structures that the user has access to. USER_ views show information about the structures owned by the user.

11. B. The DBA_OBJECTS dictionary view contains information on the objects, their creation, and modification timestamp and status.

12. C. The invalid procedure, trigger, package, or view can be recompiled by using the ALTER *<object>* COMPILE command.

13. C. The view V$PWFILE_USERS contains the list of users that have SYSDBA and SYSOPER rights; however, the password file is not a part of the database. The database consists of data files, log files, and control files.

14. D. You can specify more than one data file; the files will be used for the SYSTEM tablespace. The files specified cannot exceed the number of data files specified in the MAXDATAFILES clause.

15. A. The SYS user owns the data dictionary. The SYS and SYSTEM users are created when the database is created.

16. B. The default password for SYS is CHANGE_ON_INSTALL, and for SYSTEM it is MANAGER. You should change these passwords once the database is created.

17. B. The dictionary view PRODUCT_COMPONENT_VERSION shows information about the database version. The view V$VERSION has the same information.

18. C. The dynamic performance views have a prefix of V$. The actual views have the prefix of V_$, and the synonyms have a V$ prefix. The views are called dynamic performance views because they are continuously updated while the database is open and in use, and their contents relate primarily to performance.

19. B. MAXLOGGROUPS is an invalid clause; the maximum log file groups are specified using the clause MAXLOGFILES.

20. A. AUD$ contains records that audit DML operations against the database. No other base tables should be modified directly and should rarely be accessed read-only other than through a data dictionary view. sql.bsq is a script, not a table; DICT is a synonym for the DICTIONARY view. LINK$ and HELP are base tables.

Control and Redo Log Files

ORACLE9i DBA FUNDAMENTALS I EXAM OBJECTIVES OFFERED IN THIS CHAPTER:

- ✓ Explain the uses of the control file
- ✓ Describe the contents of the control file
- ✓ Multiplex and manage the control file
- ✓ Manage the control file with Oracle Managed Files (OMF)
- ✓ Obtain control file information
- ✓ Explain the purpose of online redo log files
- ✓ Describe the structure of online redo log files
- ✓ Control log switches and checkpoints
- ✓ Multiplex and maintain online redo log files
- ✓ Manage online redo log files with Oracle Managed Files (OMF)

Exam objectives are subject to change at any time without prior notice and at Oracle's sole discretion. Please visit Oracle's Training and Certification website (`http://www.oracle.com/education/certification/`) for the most current exam objectives listing.

This chapter discusses two important components of the Oracle database: the control file and the redo log files. The control file keeps information about the physical structure of the database. The redo log files record all changes made to data. These two files are critical for database recovery in case of a failure. You can multiplex both the control and the redo log files. You will learn more about control files, putting the database in ARCHIVELOG mode, controlling checkpoints, and managing redo logs and control files with Oracle Managed Files (OMF).

Maintaining the Control File

You can think of the *control file* as a metadata repository for the physical database. It has the structure of the database—the data files and redo log files that constitute a database. The control file is a binary file, created when the database is created, and is updated with the physical changes whenever you add or rename a file.

Oracle Objective

Explain the uses of the control file

Describe the contents of the control file

The control file is updated continuously and should be available at all times. Don't edit the contents of the control file; only Oracle processes should update its contents. When you start up the database, Oracle uses the control file to identify the data files, redo log files, and open them. Control files play a major role when recovering a database.

The contents of the control file include the following:

- Database name to which the control file belongs. A control file can belong to only one database.
- Database creation timestamp.
- Data files—name, location, and online/offline status information.
- Redo log files—name and location.
- Redo log archive information.
- Tablespace names.
- Current *log sequence number*, a unique identifier that is incremented and recorded when an online redo log file is switched.
- Most recent checkpoint information. A *checkpoint* occurs when all the modified database buffers in the SGA are written to the data files. The *system change number (SCN)*, a number sequentially assigned to each transaction in the database, is also recorded in the control file against the data file name that is taken offline or made read-only.
- Begin and end of undo segments.
- Recovery Manager's (RMAN's) backup information. RMAN is the Oracle utility you use to back up and recover databases.

The control file size is determined by the `MAX` clauses you provide when you create the database—`MAXLOGFILES`, `MAXLOGMEMBERS`, `MAXLOGHISTORY`, `MAXDATAFILES`, and `MAXINSTANCES`. Oracle pre-allocates space for these maximums in the control file. Therefore, when you add or rename a file in the database, the control file size does not change.

When you add a new file to the database or relocate a file, an Oracle server process immediately updates the information in the control file. Back up the control file after any structural changes. The log writer process (LGWR) updates the control file with the current log sequence number. The checkpoint process (CKPT) updates the control file with the recent checkpoint information. When the database is in `ARCHIVELOG` mode, the archiver process (`ARCn`) updates the control file with archiving information such as the archive log file name and log sequence number.

The control file contains two types of *record sections*: reusable and not reusable. Recovery Manager information is kept in the reusable section. Items such as the names of the backup data files are kept in this section, and once this section fills up, the entries are re-used in a circular fashion.

Multiplexing Control Files

Since the control file is critical for the database operation, Oracle recommends a minimum of two control files. You duplicate the control file on different disks either by using the multiplexing feature of Oracle or by using the mirroring feature of your operating system. The next two sections discuss the two ways you can implement the multiplexing feature: using `init.ora` and using an SPFILE.

Oracle Objective — **Multiplex and manage the control file**

Multiplexing Control Files Using *init.ora*

Multiplexing is defined as keeping a copy of the same control file in different locations. Copying the control file to multiple locations and changing the `CONTROL_FILES` parameter in the initialization file `init.ora` to include all control file names specifies the multiplexing of the control file. The following syntax shows three multiplexed control files.

```
CONTROL_FILES = ('/ora01/oradata/MYDB/ctrlMYDB01.ctl',
                 '/ora02/oradata/MYDB/ctrlMYDB02.ctl',
                 '/ora03/oradata/MYDB/ctrlMYDB03.ctl')
```

By storing the control file on multiple disks, you avoid the risk of a single point of failure. When multiplexing control files, updates to the control file can take a little longer, but that is insignificant when compared with the benefits. If you lose one control file, you can restart the database after copying one of the other control files or after changing the `CONTROL_FILES` parameter in the initialization file.

When multiplexing control files, Oracle updates all the control files at the same time, but uses only the first control file listed in the `CONTROL_FILES` parameter for reading.

When creating a database, you can list the control file names in the CONTROL_FILES parameter, and Oracle creates as many control files as are listed. You can have a maximum of eight multiplexed control file copies.

If you need to add more control file copies, do the following:

1. Shut down the database.
2. Copy the control file to more locations by using an operating system command.
3. Change the initialization parameter file to include the new control file name(s) in the parameter CONTROL_FILES.
4. Start up the database.

After creating the database, you can change the location of the control files, rename the control files, or drop certain control files. You must have at least one control file for each database. To add, rename, or delete control files, you need to follow the preceding steps. Basically, you shut down the database, use the operating system copy command (copy, rename, or drop the control files accordingly), edit the CONTROL_FILES parameter in init.ora and start up the database.

Multiplexing Control Files Using an SPFILE

Multiplexing using an SPFILE is similar to multiplexing using init.ora; the major difference being how the CONTROL_FILES parameter is changed. Follow these steps:

1. Alter the SPFILE while the database is still open:

   ```
   SQL> ALTER SYSTEM SET CONTROL_FILES =
         '/ora01/oradata/MYDB/ctrlMYDB01.ctl',
         '/ora02/oradata/MYDB/ctrlMYDB02.ctl',
         '/ora03/oradata/MYDB/ctrlMYDB03.ctl',
         '/ora04/oradata/MYDB/ctrlMYDB04.ctl' SCOPE=SPFILE;
   ```

   This parameter change will only take effect after the next instance restart by using the SCOPE=SPFILE qualifier. The contents of the binary SPFILE are changed immediately, but the old specification of CONTROL_FILES will be used until the instance is restarted.

2. Shut down the database.

   ```
   SQL> SHUTDOWN NORMAL
   ```

3. Copy an existing control file to the new location:

```
$ cp /ora01/oradata/MYDB/ctrlMYDB01.ctl
↳   /ora04/oradata/MYDB/ctrlMYDB04.ctl
```

4. Start the instance.

```
SQL> STARTUP
```

If you lose one of the control files, you can shut down the database, copy a control file, or change the CONTROL_FILES parameter and restart the database.

Using OMF to Manage Control Files

Using OMF can make the creation and maintenance of control files much easier. To use OMF-created control files, do not specify the CONTROL_FILES parameter in init.ora, but instead make sure that the parameter DB_CREATE_ONLINE_LOG_DEST_n is specified *n* times starting with 1. Therefore, *n* is the number of desired control files to be created. The actual names of the control files are system generated and can be found in the alert logs located in $ORACLE_HOME/admin/bdump.

Oracle Objective

Manage the control file with Oracle Managed Files (OMF)

To add more copies of the control file later, use the method described in the previous section, "Multiplexing Control Files Using an SPFILE."

The initialization parameter DB_CREATE_ONLINE_LOG_DEST_n is used to create both control files and online redo logs.

Creating New Control Files

You can create a new control file by using the CREATE CONTROLFILE command. You will need to create a new control file if you lose all the control files that belong to the database, if you want to change any of the MAX clauses in the CREATE DATABASE command, or if you want to change the database name. You must know the data file names and redo log file names to create the control file. Follow these steps to create the new control file:

1. Prepare the CREATE CONTROLFILE command. You should have the complete list of data files and redo log files. If you omit any data files, they can no longer be a part of the database. The following is an example of the CREATE CONTROLFILE command.

```
CREATE CONTROLFILE SET DATABASE "ORACLE"
    NORESETLOGS NOARCHIVELOG
    MAXLOGFILES 32
    MAXLOGMEMBERS 2
    MAXDATAFILES 32
    MAXINSTANCES 1
    MAXLOGHISTORY 1630
LOGFILE
  GROUP 1 'C:\ORACLE\DATABASE\LOG2ORCL.ORA' SIZE 500K,
  GROUP 2 'C:\ORACLE\DATABASE\LOG1ORCL.ORA' SIZE 500K
DATAFILE
  'C:\ORACLE\DATABASE\SYS1ORCL.ORA',
  'C:\ORACLE\DATABASE\USR1ORCL.ORA',
  'C:\ORACLE\DATABASE\RBS1ORCL.ORA',
  'C:\ORACLE\DATABASE\TMP1ORCL.ORA',
  'C:\ORACLE\DATABASE\APPDATA1.ORA',
  'C:\ORACLE\DATABASE\APPINDX1.ORA'
;
```

   The options in this command are similar to the CREATE DATABASE command, discussed in Chapter 4, "Creating a Database and Data Dictionary." The NORESETLOGS option specifies that the online redo log files should not be reset.

2. Shut down the database.

3. Start up the database with the NOMOUNT option. Remember, to mount the database, Oracle needs to open the control file.

4. Create the new control file with a command similar to the preceding example. The control files will be created using the names and locations specified in the initialization parameter CONTROL_FILES.

5. Open the database by using the ALTER DATABASE OPEN command.
6. Shut down the database and back up the database.

The steps provided here are very basic. Depending on the situation, you might have to perform additional steps. Detailing all the steps that might be required to create a control file and the options in opening a database are beyond the scope of this book.

You can generate the CREATE CONTROLFILE command from the current database by using the command ALTER DATABASE BACKUP CONTROLFILE TO TRACE. The control file creation script is written to the USER_DUMP_DEST directory.

After creating the control file, determine whether any of the data files listed in the dictionary are missing in the control file. If you query the V$DATAFILE view, the missing files will have the name MISSING*nnnn*. If you created the control file by using the RESETLOGS option, the missing data files cannot be added back to the database. If you created the control file with the NORESETLOGS option, the missing data file can be included in the database by performing a media recovery.

You can back up the control file when the database is up by using the command

```
ALTER DATABASE BACKUP CONTROLFILE TO '<filename>' REUSE;
```

Another way to back up a control file is by using the command

```
ALTER DATABASE BACKUP CONTROLFILE TO TRACE;
```

This command places the contents of the control file into a text-format trace file, located in USER_DUMP_DEST, albeit with some extraneous information that must be edited out before using it to re-create the control file:

```
Dump file H:\Oracle9i\admin\or90\udump\ORA01568.TRC
Wed Oct 10 22:00:05 2001
ORACLE V9.0.1.1.1 - Production vsnsta=0
vsnsql=10 vsnxtr=3
Windows 2000 Version 5.0 Service Pack 2, CPU type 586
Oracle9i Enterprise Edition Release 9.0.1.1.1 - Production
With the Partitioning option
JServer Release 9.0.1.1.1 - Production
Windows 2000 Version 5.0 Service Pack 2, CPU type 586
Instance name: or90
```

```
Redo thread mounted by this instance: 1

Oracle process number: 13

Windows thread id: 1568, image: ORACLE.EXE


*** SESSION ID:(8.39) 2001-10-10 22:00:05.000
*** 2001-10-10 22:00:05.000
# The following commands will create a new control file and use it
# to open the database.
# Data used by the recovery manager will be lost. Additional logs may
# be required for media recovery of offline data files. Use this
# only if the current version of all online logs are available.
STARTUP NOMOUNT
CREATE CONTROLFILE REUSE DATABASE "OR90" NORESETLOGS NOARCHIVELOG
    MAXLOGFILES 50
    MAXLOGMEMBERS 5
    MAXDATAFILES 100
    MAXINSTANCES 1
    MAXLOGHISTORY 113
LOGFILE
  GROUP 1 'H:\ORACLE9I\ORADATA\OR90\REDO01.LOG'  SIZE 100M,
  GROUP 2 'H:\ORACLE9I\ORADATA\OR90\REDO02.LOG'  SIZE 100M,
  GROUP 3 'H:\ORACLE9I\ORADATA\OR90\REDO03.LOG'  SIZE 100M
# STANDBY LOGFILE
DATAFILE
  'H:\ORACLE9I\ORADATA\OR90\SYSTEM01.DBF',
  'H:\ORACLE9I\ORADATA\OR90\UNDOTBS01.DBF',
  'H:\ORACLE9I\ORADATA\OR90\CWMLITE01.DBF',
  'H:\ORACLE9I\ORADATA\OR90\DRSYS01.DBF',
  'H:\ORACLE9I\ORADATA\OR90\EXAMPLE01.DBF',
  'H:\ORACLE9I\ORADATA\OR90\INDX01.DBF',
  'H:\ORACLE9I\ORADATA\OR90\TOOLS01.DBF',
  'H:\ORACLE9I\ORADATA\OR90\USERS01.DBF',
  'H:\ORACLE9I\ORADATA\OR90\OEM_REPOSITORY.DBF'
CHARACTER SET WE8MSWIN1252
;
```

```
# Recovery is required if any of the datafiles are restored backups,
# or if the last shutdown was not normal or immediate.
RECOVER DATABASE
# Database can now be opened normally.
ALTER DATABASE OPEN;
# Commands to add tempfiles to temporary tablespaces.
# Online tempfiles have complete space information.
# Other tempfiles may require adjustment.
ALTER TABLESPACE TEMP ADD TEMPFILE
'H:\ORACLE9I\ORADATA\OR90\TEMP01.DBF' REUSE;
# End of tempfile additions.
#
```

Oracle recommends backing up the control file whenever you make a change to the database structure, such as adding data files, renaming files, or dropping redo log files.

Querying Control File Information

The Oracle data dictionary holds all the information about the control file. The view *V$CONTROLFILE* lists the names of the control files for the database. The STATUS column should always be NULL; when a control file is missing, the STATUS would be INVALID, but that should never occur because when Oracle cannot update one of the control files, the instance crashes—you can start up the database only after copying a good control file.

Oracle Objective **Obtain control file information**

```
SQL> SELECT * FROM V$CONTROLFILE;
STATUS  NAME
------  ---------------------------------------
        /ora01/oradata/MYDB/ctrlMYDB01.ctl
        /ora02/oradata/MYDB/ctrlMYDB02.ctl
        /ora03/oradata/MYDB/ctrlMYDB03.ctl

3 rows selected.
SQL>
```

You can also use the SHOW PARAMETER command to retrieve the names of the control files.

```
SQL> show parameter control_files
NAME             TYPE        VALUE
---------------- ----------- ------------------------------
control_files    string      H:\Oracle9i\oradata\or90\CONTR
                             OL01.CTL, H:\Oracle9i\oradata\
                             or90\CONTROL02.CTL, H:\Oracle9i\
                             oradata\or90\CONTROL03.CTL
```

The other data dictionary view that gives information about the control file is V$CONTROLFILE_RECORD_SECTION, which displays the control file record sections. The record type, record size, total records allocated, number of records used, and the index position of the first and last records are in this view. For a listing of the record types, record sizes, and usage, run the following query.

```
SQL> SELECT TYPE, RECORD_SIZE, RECORDS_TOTAL, RECORDS_USED
  2  FROM   V$CONTROLFILE_RECORD_SECTION;
TYPE              RECORD_SIZE RECORDS_TOTAL RECORDS_USED
--------------- ----------- ------------- ------------
DATABASE                  192             1            1
CKPT PROGRESS            4084             1            0
REDO THREAD               104             1            1
REDO LOG                   72            32            3
DATAFILE                  180           254            8
FILENAME                  524           319           11
TABLESPACE                 68           254            8
TEMPORARY FILENAME         56           254            0
RMAN CONFIGURATION          1             1            0
LOG HISTORY                36          1815         1217
OFFLINE RANGE              56           291            0
ARCHIVED LOG              584            13            0
BACKUP SET                 40           408            0
BACKUP PIECE              736           510            0
BACKUP DATAFILE           116           563            0
BACKUP REDOLOG             76           107            0
DATAFILE COPY             660           519            0
BACKUP CORRUPTION          44           371            0
COPY CORRUPTION            40           408            0
DELETED OBJECT             20           408            0
```

```
PROXY COPY                852          575            0
RESERVED4                   1         8168            0

22 rows selected.

SQL>
```

Other data dictionary views read information from the control file. Table 5.1 lists and describes these dynamic performance views. You can access these views when the database is mounted, that is, before opening the database.

TABLE 5.1 Dictionary Views That Read from the Control File

View Name	Description
V$ARCHIVED_LOG	Archive log information such as size, SCN, timestamp, etc.
V$BACKUP	Backup status for individual datafiles that constitute the database.
V$BACKUP_DATAFILE	Contains filename, timestamp, etc. of the data files backed up using RMAN.
V$BACKUP_PIECE	Information about backup pieces, updated when using RMAN.
V$BACKUP_REDOLOG	Information about the archived log files backed up using RMAN.
V$BACKUP_SET	Information about complete, successful backups using RMAN.
V$DATABASE	Database information such as name, creation timestamp, archive log mode, SCN, log sequence number, etc.
V$DATAFILE	Information about the data files associated with the database.
V$DATAFILE_COPY	Information about data files copied during a hot backup or using RMAN.

TABLE 5.1 Dictionary Views That Read from the Control File *(continued)*

View Name	Description
V$DATAFILE_HEADER	Data file header information; the filename and status are obtained from the control file.
V$LOG	Online redo log group information.
V$LOGFILE	Files or members of the online redo log group.
V$THREAD	Information about the log files assigned to each instance.

Maintaining and Monitoring Redo Log Files

Redo logs record all changes to the database. The redo log buffer in the SGA is written to the redo log file periodically by the LGWR process. The redo log files are accessed and are open during normal database operation; hence they are called the online redo log files. Every Oracle database must have at least two redo log files. The LGWR process writes to these files in a circular fashion. For example, say there are three online redo log files. The LGWR process writes to the first file, and when this file is full, it starts writing to the second file, and then to the third file, and then again to the first file (overwriting the contents).

Oracle Objective

Explain the purpose of online redo log files

Describe the structure of online redo log files

Online redo log files are filled with redo records. A *redo record*, also called a *redo entry*, is made up of a group of *change vectors*, each of which is a description of a change made to a single block in the database. Redo entries record data that you can use to reconstruct all changes made to the database, including the undo segments. When you recover the database by using redo log files, Oracle reads the change vectors in the redo records and applies the changes to the relevant blocks.

LGWR writes redo information from the redo log buffer to the online redo log files under a variety of circumstances:

- A user commits a transaction, even if this is the only transaction in the log buffer.
- The redo log buffer becomes one-third full.
- When there is approximately 1MB of *changed* records in the buffer. This total does not include deleted or inserted records.

LGWR always writes its records to the online redo log file *before* DBW*n* writes new or modified database buffer cache records to the datafiles.

Each database has its own online *redo log groups*. A log group can have one or more *redo log members* (each member is a single operating system file). If you have a Real Application Cluster configuration, in which multiple instances are mounted to one database, each instance will have one online redo thread. That is, the LGWR process of each instance writes to the same online redo log files, and hence Oracle has to keep track of the instance from where the database changes are coming. For single instance configurations, there will be only one thread, and that thread number is 1. The redo log file contains both committed and uncommitted transactions. Whenever a transaction is committed, a system change number is assigned to the redo records to identify the committed transaction.

The redo log group is referenced by an integer; you can specify the group number when you create the redo log files, either when you create the database or when you create the control file. You can also change the redo log configuration (add/drop/rename files) by using database commands. The following example shows a `CREATE DATABASE` command.

```
CREATE DATABASE "MYDB01"
LOGFILE '/ora02/oradata/MYDB01/redo01.log' SIZE 10M,
        '/ora03/oradata/MYDB01/redo02.log' SIZE 10M;
```

Two *log file groups* are created here; the first file will be assigned to group 1, and the second file will be assigned to group 2. You can have more files in each group; this practice is known as the multiplexing of redo log files, which we'll discuss later in the chapter. You can specify any group number—the range will be between 1 and MAXLOGFILES. Oracle recommends that all redo log groups be the same size. The following is an example of creating the log files by specifying the groups.

```
CREATE DATABASE "MYDB01"
LOGFILE GROUP 1 '/ora02/oradata/MYDB01/redo01.log' SIZE 10M,
        GROUP 2 '/ora03/oradata/MYDB01/redo02.log' SIZE 10M;
```

Log Switch Operations

The LGWR process writes to only one redo log file group at any time. The file that is actively being written to is known as the *current* log file. The log files that are required for instance recovery are known as the *active* log files. The other log files are known as *inactive*. Oracle automatically recovers an instance when starting up the instance by using the online redo log files. Instance recovery may be needed if you do not shut down the database properly or if your computer crashes.

Oracle Objective

Control log switches and checkpoints

The log files are written in a circular fashion. A log switch occurs when Oracle finishes writing to one file and starts writing to the next file. A log switch always occurs when the current redo log file is completely full and log writing must continue. You can force a log switch by using the ALTER SYSTEM command. A manual log switch may be necessary when performing maintenance on the redo log files by using the ALTER SYSTEM SWITCH LOGFILE command. Figure 5.1 shows how LGWR writes to the redo log groups in a circular fashion.

Whenever a log switch occurs, Oracle allocates a sequence number to the new redo log file before writing to it. As stated earlier, this number is known as the log sequence number. If there are lots of transactions or changes to the database, the log switches can occur too frequently. Size the redo log file appropriately to avoid frequent log switches. Oracle writes to the alert log file whenever a log switch occurs.

FIGURE 5.1 Redo log file usage

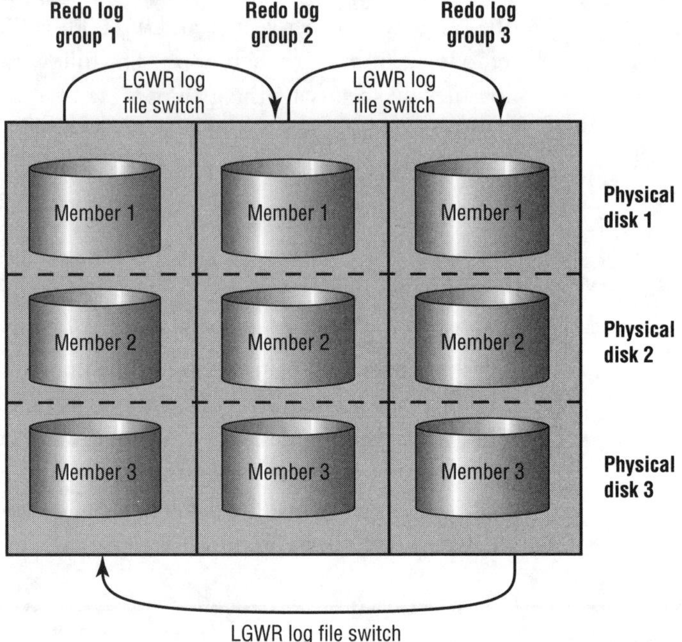

Redo log files are written sequentially on the disk, so the I/O will be fast if there is no other activity on the disk (the disk head is always properly positioned). Keep the redo log files on a separate disk for better performance. If you have to store a data file on the same disk as the redo log file, do not put the SYSTEM, UNDOTBS, or any very active data or index tablespace file on this disk.

Database checkpoints are closely tied to redo log file switches. A *checkpoint* is an event that flushes the modified data from the buffer cache to the disk and updates the control file and data files. The CKPT process updates the headers of data files and control files; the actual blocks are written to the file by the DBW*n* process. A checkpoint is initiated when the redo log file is filled and a log switch occurs, when the instance is shut down with NORMAL, TRANSACTIONAL, or IMMEDIATE, when a tablespace status is changed to read-only or put into BACKUP mode, when a tablespace or datafile is taken offline, or when other values specified by certain parameters (discussed later in this section) are reached.

You can force a checkpoint if needed. Forcing a checkpoint ensures that all changes to the database buffers are written to the data files on disk.

```
ALTER SYSTEM CHECKPOINT;
```

Another way to force a checkpoint is by forcing a log file switch.

```
ALTER SYSTEM SWITCH LOGFILE;
```

The size of the redo log affects the checkpoint performance. If the size of the redo log is smaller compared with the number of transactions, a log switch occurs often and so does the checkpoint. The DBW*n* process writes the dirty buffer blocks whenever a checkpoint occurs. This situation might reduce the time required for instance recovery, but it might also affect the runtime performance. You can adjust checkpoints primarily by using the initialization parameter `FAST_START_MTTR_TARGET`. This parameter replaces the deprecated parameters `FAST_START_IO_TARGET` and `LOG_CHECKPOINT_TIMEOUT` in previous versions of the Oracle database. It is used to ensure that recovery time at instance startup (if required) will not exceed a certain number of seconds.

For example, setting `FAST_START_MTTR_TARGET` to 600 ensures that system recovery will not take more than 600 seconds, by writing redo log buffer blocks more often, writing dirty database buffer cache entries more often, and so on.

Setting the parameter `LOG_CHECKPOINTS_TO_ALERT` to `TRUE` logs each checkpoint activity to the alert log file, which is useful for determining if checkpoints are occurring at the desired frequency.

Real World Scenario

Redo Log Troubleshooting

In the case of redo log groups, it's best to be generous with the number of groups and the number of members for each group. After estimating the number of groups that would be appropriate for your installation, add one more. I can remember many database installations in which I was trying to be overly cautious about disk space usage, not putting things into perspective, and realizing that the slight additional work involved in maintaining either additional or larger redo logs is small in relation to the time needed to fix a problem when the number of users and concurrent active transactions increase.

> The space needed for additional log file groups is minimal and is well worth the effort up front to avoid the dreaded "Checkpoint not complete" message in the alert log and potentially increasing the recovery time in the event of an instance failure.

Multiplexing Log Files

You can keep multiple copies of the online redo log file to safeguard against damage to these files. When multiplexing online redo log files, LGWR concurrently writes the same redo log information to multiple identical online redo log files, thereby eliminating a single point of redo log failure. All copies of the redo file are the same size and are known as a *group*, which is identified by an integer. Each redo log file in the group is known as a *member*. You must have at least two redo log groups for normal database operation.

Oracle Objective — **Multiplex and maintain online redo log files**

When multiplexing redo log files, it is preferable to keep the members of a group on different disks, so that one disk failure will not affect the continuing operation of the database. If LGWR can write to at least one member of the group, database operation proceeds as normal; an entry is written to the alert log file. If all members of the redo log file group are not available for writing, Oracle shuts down the instance. An instance recovery or media recovery may be needed to bring up the database.

You can create multiple copies of the online redo log files when you create the database. For example, the following statement creates two redo log file groups with two members in each.

```
CREATE DATABASE "MYDB01"
LOGFILE
  GROUP 1 ('/ora02/oradata/MYDB01/redo0101.log',
           '/ora03/oradata/MYDB01/redo0102.log') SIZE 10M,
  GROUP 2 ('/ora02/oradata/MYDB01/redo0201.log',
           '/ora03/oradata/MYDB01/redo0202.log') SIZE 10M;
```

The maximum number of log file groups is specified in the clause MAXLOGFILES, and the maximum number of members is specified in the clause MAXLOGMEMBERS. You can separate the filenames (members) by using a space or a comma.

Creating New Groups

You can create and add more redo log groups to the database by using the ALTER DATABASE command. The following statement creates a new log file group with two members.

```
ALTER DATABASE ADD LOGFILE
  GROUP 3 ('/ora02/oradata/MYDB01/redo0301.log',
           '/ora03/oradata/MYDB01/redo0402.log') SIZE 10M;
```

If you omit the GROUP clause, Oracle assigns the next available number. For example, the following statement also creates a multiplexed group.

```
ALTER DATABASE ADD LOGFILE
     ('/ora02/oradata/MYDB01/redo0301.log'
      '/ora03/oradata/MYDB01/redo0402.log') SIZE 10M;
```

To create a new group without multiplexing, use the following statement.

```
ALTER DATABASE ADD LOGFILE
     '/ora02/oradata/MYDB01/redo0301.log' REUSE;
```

You can add more than one redo log group by using the ALTER DATABASE command—just use a comma to separate the groups.

If the redo log files you create already exist, use the REUSE option and don't specify the size. The new redo log size will be same as that of the existing file.

Adding New Members

If you forgot to multiplex the redo log files when creating the database or if you need to add more redo log members, you can do so by using the ALTER DATABASE command. When adding new members, you do not specify the file size, because all group members will have the same size.

If you know the group number, using the following statement will add a member to group 2.

```
ALTER DATABASE ADD LOGFILE MEMBER
'/ora04/oradata/MYDB01/redo0203.log' TO GROUP 2;
```

You can also add group members by specifying the names of other members in the group, instead of specifying the group number. Specify all the existing group members with this syntax.

```
ALTER DATABASE ADD LOGFILE MEMBER
'/ora04/oradata/MYDB01/redo0203.log' TO
('/ora02/oradata/MYDB01/redo0201.log',
 '/ora03/oradata/MYDB01/redo0202.log');
```

Adding New Members Using Storage Manager

Adding redo log members is even easier with Storage Manager. Figure 5.2 shows the screen from Storage Manager that you can use to add new redo log members to a redo log group.

FIGURE 5.2 Storage Manager

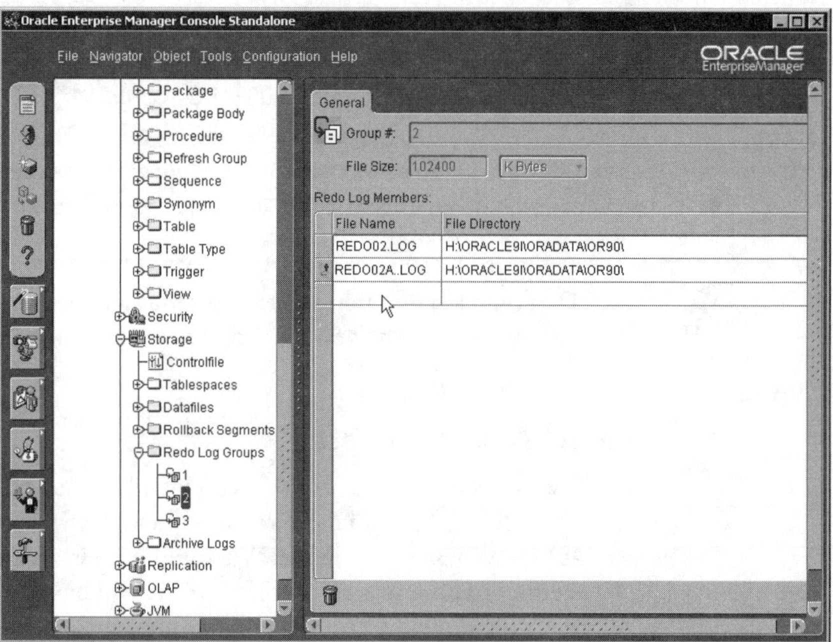

Renaming Log Members

If you want to move the log file member from one disk to another or just want a more meaningful name, you can rename a redo log member. Before renaming the online redo log members, the new (target) online redo files should exist. The SQL commands in Oracle change only the internal pointer in the control file to a new log file; they do not change or rename the operating system file. You must use an operating system command to rename or move the file. Follow these steps to rename a log member:

1. Shut down the database (a complete backup is recommended).
2. Copy/rename the redo log file member to the new location by using an operating system command.
3. Start up the instance and mount the database (`STARTUP MOUNT`).
4. Rename the log file member in the control file. Use `ALTER DATABASE RENAME FILE` '*<old_redo_file_name>*' `TO` '*<new_redo_file_name>*';
5. Open the database (`ALTER DATABASE OPEN`).
6. Back up the control file.

Dropping Redo Log Groups

You can drop a redo log group and its members by using the `ALTER DATABASE` command. Remember that you should have at least two redo log groups for the database to function normally. The group that is to be dropped should not be the active group or the current group—that is, you can drop only an inactive log file group. If the log file to be dropped is not inactive, use the `ALTER SYSTEM SWITCH LOGFILE` command.

To drop the log file group 3, use the following SQL statement.

```
ALTER DATABASE DROP LOGFILE GROUP 3;
```

When an online redo log group is dropped from the database, the operating system files are not deleted from disk. The control files of the associated database are updated to drop the members of the group from the database structure. After dropping an online redo log group, make sure that the drop is completed successfully, and then use the appropriate operating system command to delete the dropped online redo log files.

Dropping Redo Log Members

Similar to conditions for dropping a redo log group, you can drop only the members of an inactive redo log group. Also, if there are only two groups, the log member to be dropped should not be the last member of a group. You can have a different number of members for each redo log group, though it is not advised. For example, say you have three log groups, each with two members. If you drop a log member from group 2, and a failure occurs to the sole member of group 2, the instance crashes. So even if you drop a member for maintenance reasons, ensure that all redo log groups have the same number of members.

To drop the log member, use the `DROP LOGFILE MEMBER` clause of the `ALTER DATABASE` command.

```
ALTER DATABASE DROP LOGFILE MEMBER
'/ora04/oradata/MYDB01/redo0203.log';
```

The operating system file is not removed from the disk; only the control file is updated. Use an operating system command to delete the redo log file member from disk.

If a database is running in `ARCHIVELOG` mode, redo log members cannot be deleted unless the redo log group has been archived.

Clearing Online Redo Log Files

Under certain circumstances, a redo log group member (or all members of a log group) may become corrupted. To solve this problem, you can drop and re-add the log file group or group member. It is much easier, however, to use the `ALTER DATABASE CLEAR LOGFILE` command. The following example clears the contents of redo log group 3 in the database:

```
ALTER DATABASE CLEAR LOGFILE GROUP 3;
```

Another distinct advantage of this command is that you can clear a log group even if the database has only two log groups, and only one member in each group. You can also clear a log group member even if it has not been archived yet by using the `UNARCHIVED` keyword. In this case, it is advisable to do a full database backup at the earliest convenience, because the unarchived redo log file is no longer usable for database recovery.

Managing Online Redo Log Files with OMF

OMF simplifies online redo log management. As with all OMF-related operations, be sure that the proper initialization parameters are set. If you are multiplexing redo logs in three locations, be sure to set the parameters `DB_CREATE_ONLINE_LOG_DEST_1` through `_3`.

Oracle Objective	**Manage online redo log files with Oracle Managed Files (OMF)**

To add a new log file group, use the following command:

```
ALTER DATABASE ADD LOGFILE;
```

The filenames for the three new operating systems files are generated automatically. Be sure to set each `DB_CREATE_ONLINE_LOG_DEST_`*n* parameter to path names on different physical volumes.

Archiving Log Files

You know that online redo log files record all changes to the database. Oracle lets you copy these log files to a different location or to an offline storage medium. The process of copying is called *archiving*. The archiver process (ARC*n*) does this archiving. By archiving the redo log files, you can use them later to recover a database, update the standby database, or use the LogMiner utility to audit the database activities.

When an online redo log file is full, and LGWR starts writing to the next redo log file, ARC*n* copies the completed redo log file to the archive destination. It is possible to specify more than one archive destination. The LGWR process waits for the ARC*n* process to complete the copy operation before overwriting any online redo log file.

When the archiver process is copying the redo log files to another destination, the database is said to be in *ARCHIVELOG* mode. If archiving is not enabled, the database is said to be in *NOARCHIVELOG* mode. For production systems, for which you cannot afford to lose data, you must run the database in ARCHIVELOG mode so that in the event of a failure, you can recover the database to the time of failure or to a point in time. You can achieve this ability to recover by restoring the database backup and applying the database changes by using the archived log files.

Setting the Archive Destination

You specify the archive destination in the initialization parameter file. To change the archive destination parameters during normal database operation, you use the ALTER SYSTEM command. The following parameters are associated with archive log destinations and the archiver process:

LOG_ARCHIVE_DEST Specifies the destination to write archive log files. This location should be a valid directory on the server where the database is located. You can change the archiving location specified by this parameter by using ALTER SYSTEM SET LOG_ARCHIVE_DEST = '<*new_location*>';

LOG_ARCHIVE_DUPLEX_DEST Specifies a second destination to write the archive log files. This destination must be a location on the server where the database is located. This destination can be either a must-succeed or a best-effort archive destination, depending on how many archive destinations must succeed. You specify the minimum successful number of archive destinations in the parameter LOG_ARCHIVE_MIN_SUCCEED_DEST. You can change the archiving location specified by this parameter by using ALTER SYSTEM SET LOG_ARCHIVE_DUPLEX_DEST = '<*new_location*>';

LOG_ARCHIVE_DEST_*n* Using this parameter, you can specify as many as ten archiving destinations. These archive locations can be either on the local machine or on a remote machine where the standby database is located. When these parameters are used, you cannot use the LOG_ARCHIVE_DEST or LOG_ARCHIVE_DUPLEX_DEST parameters to specify the archiving location. The syntax for specifying this parameter in the initialization file is as follows:

```
LOG_ARCHIVE_DEST_n =  "null_string" |
((SERVICE = <tnsnames_name> |
  LOCATION = '<directory_name>')
 [MANDATORY | OPTIONAL]
 [REOPEN [= <integer>]])
```

For example, LOG_ARCHIVE_DEST_1 = ((LOCATION='/archive/MYDB01') MANDATORY REOPEN = 60) specifies a location for the archive log files on the local machine at /archive/MYDB01. The MANDATORY clause specifies that writing to this location must succeed. The REOPEN clause specifies when the next attempt to write to this location should be made, when the first attempt did not succeed. The default value is 300 seconds.

Here is another example, which applies the archive logs to a standby database on a remote computer.

```
LOG_ARCHIVE_DEST_2 = (SERVICE=STDBY01) OPTIONAL REOPEN;
```

Here `STDBY01` is the Oracle Net connect string used to connect to the remote database. Since writing is optional, the database activity continues even if ARC*n* could not write the archive log file. It tries the writing operation again since the `REOPEN` clause is specified.

`LOG_ARCHIVE_MIN_SUCCEED_DEST` Specifies the number of destinations the ARC*n* process should successfully write at a minimum to proceed with overwriting the online redo log files. The default value of this parameter is 1. If you are using the `LOG_ARCHIVE_DEST` and `LOG_ARCHIVE_DUPLEX_DEST` parameters, setting this value to 1 makes `LOG_ARCHIVE_DEST` mandatory and `LOG_ARCHIVE_DUPLEX_DEST` optional. If you set the parameter to 2, writing to both destinations must be successful. If you are using the `LOG_ARCHIVE_DEST_`*`n`* parameter, the `LOG_ARCHIVE_MIN_SUCCEED_DEST` parameter cannot exceed the total number of enabled destinations. If this parameter value is less than the number of `MANDATORY` destinations, the parameter is ignored.

`LOG_ARCHIVE_FORMAT` Specifies the format in which to write the filename of the archived redo log files. You can provide a text string and any of the predefined variables. The variables are as follows:

- **%s** Log sequence number
- **%S** Log sequence number, zero filled
- **%t** Thread number
- **%T** Thread number, zero filled

For example, specifying the `LOG_ARCHIVE_FORMAT = 'arch_%t_%s'` generates the archive log file names as `arch_1_101`, `arch_1_102`, `arch_1_103`, and so on; 1 is the thread number, and 101, 102, and 103 are log sequence numbers. Specifying the format as `arch_%S` generates filenames such as `arch_00000101`, `arch_00000102`, and so on; the number of leading zeros depends on the operating system.

`LOG_ARCHIVE_MAX_PROCESSES` Specifies the maximum number of ARC*n* processes Oracle should start when starting up the database. By default the value is 1.

LOG_ARCHIVE_START Specifies whether Oracle should enable automatic archiving. If this parameter is set to FALSE, none of the ARC*n* processes are started. You can override this parameter by using the command ARCHIVE LOG START or ARCHIVE LOG STOP.

Setting *ARCHIVELOG*

Specifying these parameters does not start writing the archive log files; you should place the database in ARCHIVELOG mode to enable archiving of the redo log files. You can specify the ARCHIVELOG clause while creating the database. However, most DBAs prefer to create the database first and then enable ARCHIVELOG mode. To enable ARCHIVELOG mode, follow these steps:

1. Shut down the database. Set up the appropriate initialization parameters.
2. Start up and mount the database.
3. Enable ARCHIVELOG mode by using the command ALTER DATABASE ARCHIVELOG.
4. Open the database by using ALTER DATABASE OPEN.

To disable ARCHIVELOG mode, follow these steps:

1. Shut down the database.
2. Start up and mount the database.
3. Disable ARCHIVELOG mode by using the command ALTER DATABASE NOARCHIVELOG.
4. Open the database by using ALTER DATABASE OPEN.

You can enable automatic archiving by setting the parameter LOG_ARCHIVE_START = TRUE. If you set the parameter to FALSE, Oracle does not start the ARC*n* process. Therefore, when the redo log files are full, the database will hang, waiting for the redo log files to be archived. You can initiate the automatic archive process by using the command ALTER SYSTEM ARCHIVE LOG START, which starts the ARC*n* processes; to manually archive all unarchived logs, use the command ALTER SYSTEM ARCHIVE LOG ALL.

Querying Log and Archive Information

You can query the redo log file information from the SQL command ARCHIVE LOG LIST or by querying the dynamic performance views. The ARCHIVE LOG LIST command shows whether the database is in ARCHIVELOG mode, whether automatic archiving is enabled, the archival destination, and the oldest, next, and current log sequence numbers.

```
SQL> archive log list
Database log mode              Archive Mode
Automatic archival             Enabled
Archive destination            C:\Oracle\oradata\ORADB02\archive
Oldest online log sequence     194
Next log sequence to archive   196
Current log sequence           196
SQL>
```

The view V$DATABASE shows whether the database is in ARCHIVELOG mode or in NOARCHIVELOG mode.

V$LOG

This dynamic performance view contains information about the log file groups and sizes and its status. The valid status codes in this view and their meanings are as follows:

UNUSED New log group, never used.

CURRENT Current log group.

ACTIVE Log group that may be required for instance recovery.

CLEARING You issued an ALTER DATABASE CLEAR LOGFILE command.

CLEARING_CURRENT Empty log file after issuing the ALTER DATABASE CLEAR LOGFILE command.

INACTIVE The log group is not needed for instance recovery.

Here is a query from V$LOG:

```
SQL> SELECT * FROM V$LOG;

    GROUP#    THREAD#  SEQUENCE#      BYTES    MEMBERS
---------- ---------- ---------- ---------- ----------
ARCHIVED STATUS           FIRST_CHANGE# FIRST_TIM
-------- ---------------- ------------- ---------
         1          1        196    1048576          2
NO       CURRENT                  56686 30-JUL-01

         2          1        194    1048576          2
YES      INACTIVE                 36658 28-JUL-01

         3          1        195    1048576          2
YES      INACTIVE                 36684 28-JUL-01


SQL>
```

V$LOGFILE

The *V$LOGFILE* view has information about the log group members. The filenames and group numbers are in this view. The STATUS column can have the value INVALID (file is not accessible), STALE (file's contents are incomplete), DELETED (file is no longer used), or blank (file is in use).

```
SQL> SELECT * FROM V$LOGFILE
  2  ORDER BY GROUP#;

    GROUP# STATUS  TYPE    MEMBER
--------- ------- ------- -----------------------------------
        1         ONLINE  C:\ORACLE\ORADATA\ORADB02\REDO11.LOG
        1         ONLINE  D:\ORACLE\ORADATA\ORADB02\REDO12.LOG
        2 STALE   ONLINE  C:\ORACLE\ORADATA\ORADB02\REDO21.LOG
        2         ONLINE  D:\ORACLE\ORADATA\ORADB02\REDO22.LOG
        3         ONLINE  C:\ORACLE\ORADATA\ORADB02\REDO31.LOG
        3         ONLINE  D:\ORACLE\ORADATA\ORADB02\REDO32.LOG
6 rows selected.
SQL>
```

V$THREAD

This view shows information about the threads in the database. A single instance database will have only one thread. This view shows the instance name, thread status, SCN status, log sequence numbers, timestamp of checkpoint, and so on.

```
SQL> SELECT THREAD#, GROUPS, CURRENT_GROUP#, SEQUENCE#
  2  FROM V$THREAD;

   THREAD#     GROUPS CURRENT_GROUP#  SEQUENCE#
---------- ---------- -------------- ----------
         1          3              1        199
SQL>
```

V$LOG_HISTORY

This view contains the history of the log information. It has the log sequence number, first and highest SCN for each log change, control file ID, and so on.

```
SQL> SELECT SEQUENCE#, FIRST_CHANGE#, NEXT_CHANGE#,
  2  TO_CHAR(FIRST_TIME,'DD-MM-YY HH24:MI:SS') TIME
  3  FROM V$LOG_HISTORY
  4  WHERE SEQUENCE# BETWEEN 50 AND 53;

 SEQUENCE# FIRST_CHANGE# NEXT_CHANGE# TIME
---------- ------------- ----------- -----------------
        50         22622       22709 28-07-01 19:15:22
        51         22709       23464 28-07-01 19:15:26
        52         23464       23598 28-07-01 19:15:33
        53         23598       23685 28-07-01 19:15:39
SQL>
```

V$ARCHIVED_LOG

This view displays archive log information, including archive filenames, size of the file, redo log block size, SCNs, timestamp, and so on.

```
SQL> SELECT NAME, SEQUENCE#, FIRST_CHANGE#, NEXT_CHANGE#,
     BLOCKS, BLOCK_SIZE
     FROM V$ARCHIVED_LOG
     WHERE SEQUENCE# BETWEEN 193 AND 194;

NAME
-----------------------------------------------------------
SEQUENCE# FIRST_CHANGE# NEXT_CHANGE# BLOCKS BLOCK_SIZE
--------- ------------- ------------ ------ ----------
C:\ORACLE\ORADATA\ORADB02\ARCHIVE\ARCH_00193.ARC
      193         36549        36658    722        512
C:\ORACLE\ORADATA\ORADB02\ARCHIVE\ARCH_00194.ARC
      194         36658        36684     39        512
SQL>
```

V$ARCHIVE_DEST

This view has information about the ten archive destinations, their status, any failures, and so on. The STATUS column can have six values: INACTIVE (not initialized), VALID (initialized), DEFERRED (manually disabled by the DBA), ERROR (error during copy), DISABLED (disabled after error), and BAD PARAM (bad parameter value specified). The BINDING column shows whether the target is OPTIONAL or MANDATORY, and the TARGET column indicates whether the copy is to a PRIMARY or STANDBY database.

```
SQL> SELECT DESTINATION, BINDING, TARGET, REOPEN_SECS
     FROM V$ARCHIVE_DEST
     WHERE STATUS = 'VALID';

DESTINATION                    BINDING   TARGET
  REOPEN_SECS
------------------------------ --------- -------
C:\ARCHIVE\ORADB02\archive     MANDATORY PRIMARY
          0
D:\ARCHIVE\ORADB02\archive     OPTIONAL  PRIMARY
        180
SQL>
```

V$ARCHIVE_PROCESSES

This view displays information about the state of the 10 archive processes (ARC*n*). The LOG_SEQUENCE is available only if the STATE is BUSY.

```
SQL> SELECT * FROM V$ARCHIVE_PROCESSES;

PROCESS STATUS     LOG_SEQUENCE STATE
------- ---------- ------------ -----
      0 ACTIVE                0 IDLE
      1 STOPPED               0 IDLE
      2 STOPPED               0 IDLE
      3 STOPPED               0 IDLE
      4 STOPPED               0 IDLE
      5 STOPPED               0 IDLE
      6 STOPPED               0 IDLE
      7 STOPPED               0 IDLE
      8 STOPPED               0 IDLE
      9 STOPPED               0 IDLE
10 rows selected.
SQL>
```

Summary

In this chapter, we discussed two important components of the Oracle database—the control file and the redo log files. The control file records information about the physical structure of the database along with the database name, tablespace names, log sequence number, checkpoint, and RMAN information. The size of the control file depends on the five MAX clauses you specify at the time of database creation: MAXLOGFILES, MAXLOGMEMBERS, MAXLOGHISTORY, MAXDATAFILES, and MAXINSTANCES.

Oracle provides a mechanism to multiplex the control file. The information is concurrently updated to all the control files. The parameter CONTROL_FILES in the parameter file specifies the control files at the time of database creation and afterward at database start-up. You can re-create the control files by specifying all the redo log files and data files. The V$CONTROLFILE view provides the names of the control files.

Redo log files record all changes to the database. The LGWR process writes the redo log buffer information from the SGA to the redo log files. The redo log file is treated as a group. The group can have more than one member. If more than one member is present in a group, the group is known as a multiplexed group, and the LGWR process writes to all the members of the group at the same time. Even if you lose one member, LGWR continues writing with the remaining members. You can use OMF to simplify the creation and maintenance of online redo log files.

The LGWR process writes to only one redo log file group at any time. The file that is actively being written to is known as the current log file. The log files that are required for instance recovery are known as active log files. The other log files are known as inactive. A log switch occurs when Oracle finishes writing one file and starts the next file. A log switch always occurs when the current redo log file is completely full and writing must continue.

A checkpoint is an event that flushes the modified data from the buffer cache to the disk and updates the control file and data files. The checkpoint process (CKPT) updates the headers of data files and control files; the DBW*n* process writes the *actual* blocks to the file. You can manually initiate a checkpoint or a log switch by using the `ALTER SYSTEM SWITCH LOGFILE` command.

By saving the redo log files to a different (or offline storage) location, you can recover a database or audit the redo log files. The ARC*n* process does the archiving when the database is in `ARCHIVELOG` mode. You specify the archive destination in the initialization parameter file. The dictionary views `V$LOG` and `V$LOGFILE` provide information about the redo log files.

Exam Essentials

Be able to define the characteristics of the control file. Identify when the control file is accessed, the relationship between a control file and a database, and how it is sized. List the initialization parameters that define the size of the control file and the two types of sections in the control file with their contents.

Be able to multiplex a control file. List the steps required to create additional copies of the control file, for both a PFILE and an SPFILE. Create new control file copies using OMF.

Use dynamic performance views to obtain information about the control file. Identify the views that contain the control file locations, and identify other views that use the control file as their source of information.

Understand the structure of the redo log files. Be able to clearly differentiate log file groups and log file group members. Describe how these logs are filled and re-used.

Describe the purpose and operation of the LGWR and CKPT processes. Enumerate the conditions under which LGWR is active, and describe how the CKPT process is dependent on the LGWR process.

List the primary maintenance operations for redo log groups. Be able to add and delete log file groups and group members, using both the command-line and GUI interfaces. Identify the conditions under which log files are cleared, and describe how to accomplish this task in various scenarios. Be able to use OMF to maintain the redo log files.

Become familiar with the dynamic performance views that contain log file information. Use the V$LOG view to extract status and error information about individual log file members.

Describe the basic differences between operating a database in `ARCHIVELOG` mode and operating it in `NOARCHIVELOG` mode. Identify the initialization parameters and commands that control the archive process. Briefly describe how archive log information is recorded in the control file.

Key Terms

Before you take the exam, be sure you're familiar with the following terms:

ARCHIVELOG

ARC*n*

change vectors

checkpoint

control file

log file groups

log sequence number

multiplexing

NOARCHIVELOG

record sections

redo entry

redo log groups

redo log members

redo record

system change number (SCN)

V$CONTROLFILE

V$LOG

V$LOGFILE

Review Questions

1. Which method is best for renaming a control file?
   A. Use the `ALTER DATABASE RENAME FILE` command.
   B. Shut down the database, rename the control file by using an operating system command, and restart the database after changing the `CONTROL_FILES` parameter in the initialization parameter file.
   C. Put the database in `RESTRICTED` mode and issue the `ALTER DATABASE RENAME` FILE command.
   D. Shut down the database, change the `CONTROL_FILES` parameter, and start up the database.
   E. Re-create the control file using the new name.

2. Which piece of information is not available in the control file?
   A. Instance name
   B. Database name
   C. Datafile names
   D. Log sequence number

3. When you create a control file, the database has to be:
   A. Mounted
   B. Not mounted
   C. Open
   D. Restricted

4. Which data dictionary view provides the names of the control files?
   A. `V$DATABASE`
   B. `V$INSTANCE`
   C. `V$CONTROLFILESTATUS`
   D. None of the above

5. The initialization parameter FAST_START_MTTR_TARGET has been set to 500. What does this mean?

   A. A checkpoint will occur every 500 seconds regardless of database activity.

   B. A checkpoint will occur after writing 500 blocks to the redo log file.

   C. Upon instance startup, the database will not be ready for connections for at least 500 seconds while instance recovery is performed by SMON.

   D. Recovery from an instance failure should not take more than 500 seconds.

6. Which data dictionary view shows that the database is in ARCHIVELOG mode?

   A. V$INSTANCE

   B. V$LOG

   C. V$DATABASE

   D. V$THREAD

7. What is the biggest advantage of having the control files on different disks?

   A. Database performance.

   B. Guards against failure.

   C. Faster archiving.

   D. Writes are concurrent, so having control files on different disks speeds up control file writes.

8. Which file records all changes made to the database and is used only when recovering an instance?

   A. Archive log file

   B. Redo log file

   C. Control file

   D. Alert log file

9. What will happen if ARC*n* could not write to a mandatory archive destination?

   A. The database will hang.

   B. The instance will shut down.

   C. ARC*n* starts writing to LOG_ARCHIVE_DUPLEX_DEST if it is specified.

   D. Oracle stops writing the archived log files.

10. How many ARC*n* processes can be associated with an instance?

    A. Five

    B. Four

    C. Ten

    D. Operating system dependent

11. Which of the following is an invalid status code in the V$LOGFILE view?

    A. STALE

    B. Blank

    C. ACTIVE

    D. INVALID

12. If you have two redo log groups with four members each, how many disks does Oracle recommend to keep the redo log files?

    A. Eight

    B. Two

    C. One

    D. Four

13. What will happen if you issue the following command?

```
ALTER DATABASE ADD LOGFILE
    ('/logs/file1', '/logs/file2' REUSE);
```

A. Statement will fail, because the group number is missing

B. Statement will fail, because log file size is missing

C. Creates a new redo log group, with two members

D. Adds two members to the current redo log group

14. Which two parameters cannot be used together to specify the archive destination?

A. LOG_ARCHIVE_DEST and LOG_ARCHIVE_DUPLEX_DEST

B. LOG_ARCHIVE_DEST and LOG_ARCHIVE_DEST_1

C. LOG_ARCHIVE_DEST_1 and LOG_ARCHIVE_DEST_2

D. None of the above; you can specify all the archive destination parameters with valid destination names.

15. Which of the following statements is NOT true regarding the use of OMF for redo logs?

A. Dropping log files with OMF automatically drops the related operating system file.

B. OMF manages archived redo log files using the initialization parameter DB_CREATE_ARCHIVE_LOG_DEST_n.

C. A new log file group can be added without specifying a filename in the ALTER DATABASE statement.

D. A log file group managed with OMF can be dropped by specifying only the log group number.

16. Querying which view will show whether automatic archiving is enabled?

A. `V$ARCHIVE_LOG`

B. `V$DATABASE`

C. `V$PARAMETER`

D. `V$LOG`

17. If you need to have your archive log files named with the log sequence numbers as `arch_0000001`, `arch_0000002`, and so on (zero filled, fixed width), what should be the value of the `LOG_ARCHIVE_FORMAT` parameter?

A. `arch_%S`

B. `arch_%s`

C. `arch_000000%s`

D. `arch_%0%s`

18. Following are the steps needed to rename a redo log file. Order them in the proper sequence.

A. Use an operating system command to rename the redo log file.

B. Shut down the database.

C. `ALTER DATABASE RENAME FILE 'oldfile' TO 'newfile'`

D. `STARTUP MOUNT`

E. `ALTER DATABASE OPEN`

F. Backup the control file.

19. Which of the following commands is a key step in multiplexing control files using an SPFILE?

    A. `ALTER SYSTEM SET CONTROL_FILES=`
    `'/u01/oradata/PRD/cntrl01.ctl',`
    `'/u01/oradata/PRD/cntrl02.ctl' SCOPE=SPFILE;`

    B. `ALTER SYSTEM SET CONTROL_FILES=`
    `'/u01/oradata/PRD/cntrl01.ctl',`
    `'/u01/oradata/PRD/cntrl02.ctl' SCOPE=MEMORY;`

    C. `ALTER SYSTEM SET CONTROL_FILES=`
    `'/u01/oradata/PRD/cntrl01.ctl',`
    `'/u01/oradata/PRD/cntrl02.ctl' SCOPE=BOTH;`

    D. The number of control files is fixed when the database is created.

20. Which statement will add a member `/logs/redo22.log` to log file group 2?

    A. `ALTER DATABASE ADD LOGFILE '/logs/redo22.log' TO GROUP 2;`

    B. `ALTER DATABASE ADD LOGFILE MEMBER '/logs/redo22.log' TO GROUP 2;`

    C. `ALTER DATABASE ADD MEMBER '/logs/redo22.log' TO GROUP 2;`

    D. `ALTER DATABASE ADD LOGFILE '/logs/redo22.log';`

Answers to Review Questions

1. B. To rename (or multiplex, or drop) a control file, you shut down the database, rename (or copy, or delete) the control file by using operating systems commands, change the parameter CONTROL_FILES in the initialization parameter file, and start up the database.
2. A. The instance name is not in the control file. The control file has information about the physical database structure.
3. B. The database should be in the NOMOUNT state to create a control file. When you mount the database, Oracle tries to open the control file to read the physical database structure.
4. D. The V$CONTROLFILE view shows the names of the control files in the database.
5. D. Oracle will automatically adjust other parameters (buffer sizes, intervals, and so on) to ensure that instance recovery will not exceed a specified number of seconds.
6. C. The V$DATABASE view shows whether the database is in ARCHIVELOG mode or in NOARCHIVELOG mode.
7. B. Having the control files on different disks ensures that even if you lose one disk, you lose only one control file. If you lose one of the control files, you can shut down the database, copy a control file, or change the CONTROL_FILES parameter and restart the database.
8. B. The redo log file records all changes made to the database. The LGWR process writes the redo log buffer entries to the redo log files. These entries are used to roll forward, or to update, the data files during an instance recovery. Archive log files are used for media recovery.
9. A. Oracle will write a message to the alert file, and all database operations will be stopped. Database operation resumes automatically after successfully writing the archived log file. If the archive destination becomes full, you can make room for archives either by deleting the archive log files after copying them to a different location or by changing the parameter to point to a different archive location.

10. C. You can have a maximum of ten archiver processes.

11. C. The STATUS column in V$LOGFILE can have the values INVALID (file is not accessible), STALE (file's contents are incomplete), DELETED (file is no longer used), or blank (file is in use).

12. D. Oracle recommends that you keep each member of a redo log group on a different disk. You should have a minimum of two redo log groups, and it is recommended that you have two members in each group. The maximum number of redo log groups is determined by the MAXLOGFILES database parameter. The MAXLOGMEMBERS database parameter specifies the maximum number of members per group.

13. C. The statement creates a new redo log group with two members. When you specify the GROUP option, you must use an integer value. Oracle will automatically generate a group number if the GROUP option is not specified. Use the SIZE option if you are creating a new file. Use the REUSE option if the file already exists.

14. B. When using a LOG_ARCHIVE_DEST_*n* parameter, you cannot use the LOG_ARCHIVE_DEST or LOG_ARCHIVE_DUPLEX_DEST parameters to specify other archive locations. Using a LOG_ARCHIVE_DEST_*n* parameter, you can specify as many as five archiving locations.

15. B. You canot manage archived redo logs with OMF.

16. C. You enable automatic archiving by setting the initialization parameter LOG_ARCHIVE_START = TRUE. All the parameter values can be queried using the V$PARAMETER view. The ARCHIVE LOG LIST command will also show whether automatic archiving is enabled.

17. A. Four formatting variables are available to use with archive log file names: %s specifies the log sequence number; %S specifies the log sequence number, leading zero filled; %t specifies the thread; and %T specifies the thread, leading zero filled.

18. B, A, D, C, E, and F. The correct order is:

   1. Shut down the database.

   2. Use an operating system command to rename the redo log file.

   3. `STARTUP MOUNT`

   4. `ALTER DATABASE RENAME FILE 'oldfile' TO 'newfile'`

   5. `ALTER DATABASE OPEN`

   6. Back up the control file.

19. A. The location of the new control files is not valid until an operating system copy is made of the current control file to the new location(s), and the instance is restarted. The `SCOPE=SPFILE` option specifies that the parameter change will not take place until a restart. Specifying either `MEMORY` or `BOTH` will cause an error, since the new control file does not exist yet.

20. B. When adding log file members, specify the group number or specify all the existing group members. Option D would create a new group with one member.

Logical and Physical Database Structures

ORACLE9i DBA FUNDAMENTALS I EXAM OBJECTIVES OFFERED IN THIS CHAPTER:

- ✓ Describe the logical structure of tablespaces within the database
- ✓ Create tablespaces
- ✓ Change the size of the tablespace
- ✓ Allocate space for temporary segments
- ✓ Change the status of tablespaces
- ✓ Change the storage settings of tablespaces
- ✓ Implement Oracle Managed Files

Exam objectives are subject to change at any time without prior notice and at Oracle's sole discretion. Please visit Oracle's Training and Certification website (`http://www.oracle.com/education/certification/`) for the most current exam objectives listing.

This chapter covers the physical and logical data storage. Chapter 2 briefly discussed the physical and logical structures, and Chapter 5 discussed two of the three components of the physical database structure—control files and redo log files. The third component of the physical structure is data files. Data files belong to logical units called tablespaces. In this chapter, you will learn to manage data files and tablespaces.

Tablespaces and Data Files

The database's data is stored logically in *tablespaces* and physically in the *data files* corresponding to the tablespaces. The logical storage management is independent of the physical storage of the data files. A tablespace can have more than one data file associated with it. One data file belongs to only one tablespace. A database can have one or more tablespaces. Figure 6.1 shows the relationship between the database, tablespaces, data files, and the objects in the database. Any object (such as a non-partitioned table, an index, and so on) created in the database is stored in a single tablespace. But the object's physical storage can be on multiple data files belonging to that tablespace. A segment cannot be stored in multiple tablespaces.

Oracle Exam Objective

Describe the logical structure of tablespaces within the database

FIGURE 6.1 Tablespaces and data files

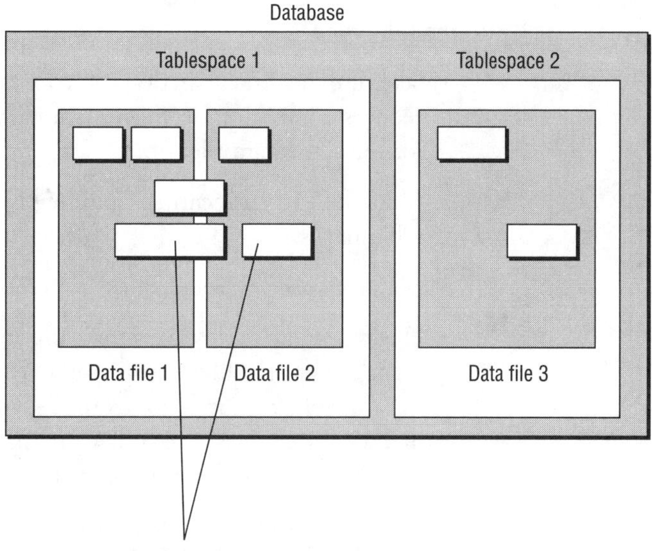

The size of the tablespace is the total size of all the data files belonging to that tablespace. The size of the database is the total size of all tablespaces in the database, which is the total size of all data files in the database. The smallest logical unit of storage in a database is a database block. You define the size of the block when you create the database, and you cannot alter it. The database block size is a multiple of the operating system block size.

Changing the size of the data files belonging to a tablespace can change the size of that tablespace. You can add more space to a tablespace by adding more data files to the tablespace. You can add more space to the database by adding more tablespaces, by adding more data files to the existing tablespaces, or by increasing the size of the existing data files.

When you create a database, Oracle creates the SYSTEM tablespace. All the dictionary objects are stored in this tablespace. The data files you specify when you create the database are assigned to the SYSTEM tablespace. You can add more space to the SYSTEM tablespace after you create the database by adding more data files or by increasing the size of the data files. The PL/SQL program units (such as procedures, functions, packages, or triggers) created in the database are also stored in the SYSTEM tablespace.

Oracle recommends not creating any objects other than the Oracle data dictionary in the SYSTEM tablespace. By having multiple tablespaces, you can do the following:

- Separate the Oracle dictionary from other database objects. Doing so reduces contention between dictionary objects and database objects for the same data file.
- Control I/O by allocating separate physical storage disks for different tablespaces.
- Manage space quotas for users on tablespaces.
- Have separate tablespaces for temporary segments (TEMP) and undo management (Rollback segments). You can also create a tablespace for a specific activity—for example, you can place high-update tables in a separate tablespace. When creating the database, you can specify tablespace names for temporary tablespace and undo tablespace.
- Group application-related or module-related data together, so that when maintenance is required for the application's tablespace, only that tablespace need be taken offline, and the rest of the database is available for users.
- Back up the database one tablespace at a time.
- Make part of the database read-only.

When you create a tablespace, Oracle creates the data files with the size specified. The space reserved for the data file is formatted but does not contain any user data. Whenever spaces for objects are needed, extents are allocated from this free space.

Managing Tablespaces

When Oracle allocates space to an object in a tablespace, it is allocated in chunks of contiguous database blocks known as extents. Each object is allocated a segment, which has one or more extents.

If the object is partitioned, each partition will have a segment allocated. Partitions are discussed in Chapter 8, "Managing Tables, Indexes, and Constraints."

Oracle maintains the extent information such as extents free, extent size, extents allocated, and so on either in the data dictionary or in the tablespace itself.

If you store the *extent management* information in the dictionary for a tablespace, that tablespace is called a *dictionary-managed tablespace*. Whenever an extent is allocated or freed, the information is updated in the corresponding dictionary tables. Such updates also generate undo information.

If you store the management information in a tablespace itself, by using bitmaps in each data file, such a tablespace is known as a *locally managed tablespace*. Each bit in the bitmap corresponds to a block or a group of blocks. When an extent is allocated or freed for reuse, Oracle changes the bitmap values to show the new status of the blocks. These changes do not generate rollback information because they do not update tables in the data dictionary.

To create the tablespace, you use the `CREATE TABLESPACE` statement. You can modify the characteristics of the tablespace using the `ALTER TABLESPACE` statement. In the following sections, we'll create, modify, and drop a tablespace, and we'll query the tablespace information from the data dictionary.

Creating a Tablespace

As the database grows bigger, managing database objects is easier if you have multiple tablespaces. Using the `CREATE TABLESPACE` statement creates a tablespace. In Oracle9i, the only mandatory clause in the CREATE TABLESPACE statement is the tablespace name. For example, when you specify the statement `CREATE TABLESPACE APPLICATION_DATA`, Oracle9i creates a locally managed tablespace with system allocated extent sizes. The data file for this tablespace is created at the location you specify in the `DB_CREATE_FILE_DEST` parameter, and its size is 100MB. The file is auto extensible with no maximum size and has a name similar to `ora_applicat_zyykpt00.dbf`. In the following sections, we will discuss the default values for a CREATE TABLESPACE statement and the various types of tablespaces.

Oracle Exam Objective

Create tablespaces

The tablespace name cannot exceed 30 characters. The name should begin with an alphabetic character and can contain alphabetic characters, numeric characters, and the special characters #, _, and $.

Optionally, you can specify file names, file sizes, and default storage parameters when creating tablespaces. The default storage parameters are used whenever a new object is created (whenever a new segment is allocated) in the tablespace. The storage parameters you specify when you create an object override the default storage parameters of the tablespace containing the object. The default storage parameters for the tablespace are used only when you create an object without specifying any storage parameters.

In Oracle9i, you can create tablespaces without specifying a file name by setting the parameter `DB_CREATE_FILE_DEST` to a valid directory on the server where you want to create the file. Files created in such manner are called *Oracle Managed Files (OMF)*.

We will discuss OMF in the "Managing Data Files" section later in this chapter.

You can specify the extent management clause when creating a tablespace. If you do not specify the extent management clause, Oracle creates a locally managed tablespace. You can have both dictionary-managed and locally managed tablespaces in the same database. A temporary tablespace can be either dictionary-managed or locally managed.

Dictionary-Managed Tablespaces

In dictionary-managed tablespaces, all extent information is stored in the data dictionary. A simple example of a dictionary-managed tablespace creation command is as follows:

```
CREATE TABLESPACE APPL_DATA
DATAFILE '/disk3/oradata/DB01/appl_data01.dbf' SIZE 100M
EXTENT MANAGEMENT DICTIONARY;
```

This statement creates a tablespace named APPL_DATA; the data file specified is created with a size of 100MB. You can specify more than one file under the DATAFILE clause separated by commas; you may need to create more files if there are any operating system limits on the file size. For example, if you need to allocate 6GB for the tablespace, and the operating system allows only a 2GB maximum, you need three data files for the tablespace. The statement is as follows:

```
CREATE TABLESPACE APPL_DATA
DATAFILE '/disk3/oradata/DB01/appl_data01.dbf' SIZE 2000M,
         '/disk3/oradata/DB01/appl_data02.dbf' SIZE 2000M,
         '/disk4/oradata/DB01/appl_data03.dbf' SIZE 2000M;
```

The options available when creating and reusing a data file are discussed in the "Managing Data Files" section later in this chapter.

The following statement creates a tablespace using all optional clauses.

```
CREATE TABLESPACE APPL_DATA
   DATAFILE '/disk3/oradata/DB-1/appl_data01.dbf' SIZE 100M
   DEFAULT STORAGE (
                  INITIAL 256K
                  NEXT 256K
                  MINEXTENTS 2
                  PCTINCREASE 0
                  MAXEXTENTS 4096)
   BLOCKSIZE 4K
   MINIMUM EXTENT 256K
```

```
LOGGING
ONLINE
PERMANENT
EXTENT MANAGEMENT DICTIONARY
SEGMENT SPACE MANAGEMENT MANUAL;
```

The clauses in the CREATE TABLESPACE command specify the following:

DEFAULT STORAGE Specifies the default storage parameters for new objects that are created in the tablespace. If you specify an explicit storage clause when creating an object, the tablespace defaults are not used for the specified storage parameters. You specify storage parameters within parentheses; no parameter is mandatory, but if you specify the DEFAULT STORAGE clause, you must specify at least one parameter inside the parentheses.

BLOCKSIZE Specifies the block size that is used for the objects created in the tablespace. By default, this block size is the database block size, which you define using the DB_BLOCK_SIZE parameter when creating the database. In Oracle9i, a database can have multiple block sizes. The database block size specified by DB_BLOCK_SIZE parameter is used for the SYSTEM tablespace and is known as the *standard block size*. The valid sizes of non-standard block size are 2KB, 4KB, 8KB, 16KB, and 32KB. If you do not specify a block size for the tablespace, the database block size is assumed. Multiple block sizes in the database are beneficial for large databases with OLTP (Online Transaction Processing) and DSS (Decision Support System) data stored together or for storing large tables. In the "Using Non-standard Block Sizes" section later in this chapter, we'll discuss the restrictions on specifying non-standard block sizes when you create the tablespace.

INITIAL Specifies the size of the object's (segment's) first extent. NEXT specifies the size of the segment's next and successive extents. The size is specified in bytes. You can also specify the size in KB by post-fixing the size with K, or you can specify MB by post-fixing the size with M. The default value of INITIAL and NEXT is 5 database blocks. The minimum value of INITIAL is 3 database blocks for locally managed tablespaces (for manual segment space management, it is 2 blocks plus 1 block for each free list group in the segment) and 2 blocks for dictionary-managed tablespaces; NEXT is 1 database block. Even if you specify sizes smaller than these values, Oracle allocates the minimum sizes when creating segments in the tablespace.

PCTINCREASE Specifies how much the third and subsequent extents grow over the preceding extent. The default value is 50, meaning that each subsequent extent is 50 percent larger than the preceding extent. The minimum value is 0, meaning all extents after the first are the same size. For example, if you specify storage parameters as (INITIAL 1M NEXT 2M PCTINCREASE 0), the extent sizes are 1MB, 2MB, 2MB, 2MB, and so on. If you specify the PCTINCREASE as 50, the extent sizes are 1MB, 2MB, 3MB, 4.5MB, 6.75MB, and so on. The actual NEXT extent size is rounded to a multiple of the block size.

MINEXTENTS Specifies the total number of extents allocated to the segment at the time of creation. Using this parameter, you can allocate a large amount of space when you create an object, even if the space available is not contiguous. The default and minimum value is 1. When you specify MINEXTENTS as more than 1, the extent sizes are calculated based on NEXT and PCTINCREASE. MAXEXTENTS specifies the maximum number of extents that can be allocated to a segment. You can specify an integer or UNLIMITED. The minimum value is 1, and the default value depends on the database block size.

MINIMUM EXTENT Specifies that the extent sizes are a multiple of the size specified. You can use this clause to control fragmentation in the tablespace by allocating extents of at least the size specified and as always a multiple of the size specified. In the CREATE TABLESPACE example earlier in this chapter, all the extents allocated in the tablespace are a multiple of 256KB. The INITIAL and NEXT extent sizes you specify should be a multiple of MINIMUM EXTENT.

LOGGING Specifies that the DDL operations and direct-load INSERT are recorded in the redo log files. LOGGING is the default, and you can omit the clause. When you specify NOLOGGING, data is modified with minimal logging and hence the commands complete faster. Since the changes are not recorded in the redo log files, you need to apply the commands again if you have to recover media. Specifying LOGGING or NOLOGGING in the individual object creation statement overrides the tablespace default.

ONLINE Specifies that the tablespace be created online or available as soon as it is created. ONLINE is the default, and hence you can omit the clause. If you do not want the tablespace to be available, you can specify `OFFLINE`.

`PERMANENT` Specifies whether the tablespace is to be used to create permanent objects such as tables, indexes, and so on. `PERMANENT` is the default, and hence you can omit it. If you plan to use the tablespace for temporary segments (such as to handle sorts in SQL), you can mark the tablespace as `TEMPORARY`. You cannot create permanent objects such as tables or indexes in a `TEMPORARY` tablespace. We'll discuss temporary tablespaces later in this chapter.

`EXTENT MANAGEMENT` Until Oracle9i, dictionary managed tablespaces were the default. That is, if you did not specify the `EXTENT MANAGEMENT` clause, Oracle created a dictionary-managed tablespace. In Oracle9i, to create a dictionary-managed tablespace, you need to explicitly specify the `EXTENT MANAGEMENT DICTIONARY` clause. If you omit this clause, Oracle creates the tablespace as locally managed.

`SEGMENT SPACE MANAGEMENT` This clause is applicable only to locally managed tablespaces. The valid values are `MANUAL` and `AUTO`. `MANUAL` is the default. If you specify `AUTO`, Oracle manages the free space in the segments using bit maps rather than free lists. For `AUTO`, Oracle ignores the storage parameters `PCTUSED`, `FREELISTS`, and `FREELIST GROUPS` when creating objects.

Using Non-standard Block Sizes

When creating the database, you specify the block size in the initialization parameter using the `DB_BLOCK_SIZE` parameter. This specification is known as the standard block size for the database. You must choose a block size that suits most of your tables. In most databases, will never need another block size. Oracle9i gives you option of using multiple block sizes, which is especially useful when you're transporting tablespaces from another database with a different block size. When creating a tablespace with a non-standard block size, you must specify the `BLOCKSIZE` clause in the `CREATE TABLESPACE` statement. You cannot alter this block size.

The `DB_CACHE_SIZE` parameter defines the buffer cache size associated with the standard block size. To create tablespaces with non-standard block size, you must set the appropriate initialization parameter to define a buffer cache size for the block size. The initialization parameter is

DB_*n*K_CACHE_SIZE; *n* is the non-standard block size. It can have the values 2, 4, 8, 16, or 32, but cannot have the size of the standard block size. For example, if your standard block size is 8KB, you cannot set the parameter DB_8K_CACHE_SIZE. If you need to create a tablespace that uses a different block size, say 16KB, you must set the DB_16K_CACHE_SIZE parameter. By default, the value for DB_*n*K_CACHE_SIZE parameters is 0MB.

Temporary tablespaces should have standard block size.

The DB_*n*K_CACHE_SIZE The parameter is dynamic; you can alter its value using the ALTER SYSTEM statement.

Locally Managed Tablespace

Using the CREATE TABLESPACE command with the EXTENT MANAGEMENT LOCAL clause creates a locally managed tablespace. Locally managed tablespaces manage space more efficiently, provide better methods to reduce fragmentation, and increase reliability. The extent allocation information is stored as bitmaps in the file headers, and hence it improves the speed of allocation and deallocation operations. You cannot specify the DEFAULT STORAGE, TEMPORARY, and MINIMUM EXTENT clauses of the CREATE TABLESPACE in a locally managed tablespace.

You can specify that Oracle manage extents automatically by using the AUTOALLOCATE option. When using this option, you cannot specify sizes for the objects created in the tablespace. Oracle manages the extent sizes; you have no control over the extent sizes or the extent's allocation and deallocation. Following is an example of creating a locally managed tablespace with Oracle managing the extent allocation (since EXTENT MANAGEMENT LOCAL AUTOALLOCATE is the default, it is omitted from the statement):

```
CREATE TABLESPACE USER_DATA
DATAFILE '/disk1/oradata/MYDB01/user_data01.dbf' SIZE 300M;
```

You can specify that the tablespace be managed with uniform extents of a specific size by using the UNIFORM SIZE clause. All the extents will be created with the size you specify. You cannot specify extent sizes (STORAGE clause) when creating the tablespace. The following is an example of creating a locally managed tablespace with uniform extent sizes of 512KB.

```
CREATE TABLESPACE USER_DATA
DATAFILE '/disk1/oradata/MYDB01/user_data01.dbf' SIZE 300M
EXTENT MANAGEMENT LOCAL UNIFORM SIZE 512K;
```

If you set the DB_CREATE_FILE_DEST parameter to a valid directory on the server and execute the statement CREATE TABLESPACE MYTS, a new tablespace MYTS is created as locally managed with auto allocated extent sizes, standard block size, and manual segment space management.

You manage the free space in the tablespace's segment using free lists. In Oracle9i, the database can manage the free space by using bitmaps. If you want a locally managed tablespace to have the segment's free space managed by Oracle, you must specify the SEGMENT SPACE MANAGEMENT AUTO clause in the CREATE TABLESPACE statement.

Free Space Management

When creating locally managed permanent tablespaces, you can specify the SEGMENT SPACE MANAGEMENT clause to AUTO or MANUAL. MANUAL is the default and is the only behavior available in pre-Oracle9i databases. In pre-Oracle9i databases, you managed the free space in the segments by using free lists.

In Oracle9i, Oracle can manage the free space in blocks using bitmaps if you specify the SEGMENT SPACE MANAGEMT AUTO clause while creating a tablespace. A bitmap that shows the status of the block is maintained—the status shows whether a block is available for insert. Thus, performance improves when multiple sessions are doing inserts to the same block. Space is also used effectively for objects with varying size rows.

When you set SEGMENT SPACE MANAGEMENT to AUTO, for all segments created in the tablespace Oracle ignores the storage parameters FREELISTS, FREELIST GROUPS, and PCTUSED. Therefore, you need not worry about tuning these parameters!

Undo Tablespace

Oracle9i can manage undo information automatically. You need not create rollback segments and worry about their sizes and number. For automatic undo management, you must have one *undo tablespace*. You create the undo tablespace using the CREATE UNDO TABLESPACE statement.

When creating undo tablespace, you can specify only the EXTENT MANAGEMENT LOCAL and DATAFILE clauses. Oracle creates a locally managed permanent tablespace. (Chapter 7 discusses undo management.) The following statement creates an undo tablespace:

```
CREATE UNDO TABLESPACE UNDO_TBS
DATAFILE '/ora1/oradata/MYDB/undo_tbs01.dbf' SIZE 500M;
```

You can create an undo tablespace when creating a database using the UNDO TABLESPACE clause of the CREATE DATABASE statement.

Temporary Tablespace

Oracle Exam Objective

Allocate space for temporary segments

Oracle can manage space for sort operations more efficiently by using *temporary tablespaces*. By exclusively designating a tablespace for temporary segments, Oracle eliminates allocation and deallocation of temporary segments. A temporary tablespace can be used only for sort segments. Only one sort segment is allocated for an instance in a temporary tablespace, and all sort operations use this sort segment. More than one transaction can use the same sort segment, but each extent can be used by only one transaction. The sort segment for a given temporary tablespace is created at the time of the first sort operation on that tablespace. The sort segment expands by allocating extents until the segment size is sufficient for the total storage demands of all the active sorts running on that instance.

A temporary tablespace can be dictionary-managed or locally managed. Using the CREATE TABLESPACE command with the TEMPORARY clause creates a dictionary-managed temporary tablespace. Here is an example:

```
CREATE TABLESPACE TEMP
DATAFILE '/disk5/oradata/MYDB01/temp01.dbf' SIZE 300M
DEFAULT STORAGE (INITIAL 2M NEXT 2M PCTINCREASE 0
                 MAXEXTENTS UNLIMITED)
TEMPORARY;
```

When the first sort operation is performed on disk, a temporary segment is allocated with a 2MB initial extent size and 2MB subsequent extent sizes. The extents, once allocated, are freed only when the instance is shut down.

Temporary segments are based on the default storage parameters of the tablespace. For a TEMPORARY tablespace, the recommended INITIAL and NEXT parameters should be equal, and the extent size should be a multiple of SORT_AREA_SIZE plus DB_BLOCK_SIZE to reduce the possibility of fragmentation. Keep PCTINCREASE equal to zero. For example, if your sort area size is 64KB and database block size is 8KB, provide the default storage of the temporary tablespace as (INITIAL 136K NEXT 136K PCTINCREASE 0 MAXEXTENTS UNLIMITED).

If you are using a PERMANENT tablespace for sort operations, temporary segments are created in the tablespace when the sort is performed and are freed when the sort operation completes. There will be one sort segment for each sort operation, which requires a lot of extent and segment management operations.

To create a locally managed temporary tablespace, use the CREATE TEMPORARY TABLESPACE command. The following statement creates a locally managed temporary tablespace:

```
CREATE TEMPORARY TABLESPACE TEMP
TEMPFILE '/disk5/oradata/MYDB01/temp01.tmp' SIZE 500M
EXTENT MANAGEMENT LOCAL
UNIFORM SIZE 5M;
```

Notice that the DATAFILE clause of the CREATE TABLESPACE command is replaced with the TEMPFILE clause. Temporary files are always in NOLOGGING mode and are not recoverable. They cannot be made read-only, cannot be renamed, cannot be created with the ALTER DATABASE command, do not generate any information during the BACKUP CONTROLFILE command, and are not included during a CREATE CONTROLFILE command. The EXTENT MANAGEMENT LOCAL clause is optional and can be omitted; it is provided to improve readability. If you do not specify the extent size by using the UNIFORM SIZE clause, the default size used is 1MB.

An Oracle temporary file (called a *tempfile*) is not a temporary file in the traditional operating system sense; only the objects within a temporary tablespace consisting of one or more tempfiles are temporary.

When you create a user, that user is assigned a temporary tablespace. By default, the default tablespace (where the user creates objects) and the temporary tablespace (where the user's sort operations are performed) are both the SYSTEM tablespace. No user should have SYSTEM as their default or temporary tablespace. This unnecessarily increases fragmentation in the SYSTEM tablespace.

When creating a database, you can also create a temporary tablespace using the DEFAULT TEMPORARY TABLESPACE clause of the CREATE DATABASE statement. If the default temporary tablespace is defined in the database, all new users will have that tablespace assigned as the temporary tablespace by default, if you do not specify another tablespace for the user's temporary tablespace.

Altering a Tablespace

You can alter a tablespace using the ALTER TABLESPACE command. This command allow you to do the following:

- Change the default storage parameters of a dictionary-managed tablespace
- Change the extent allocation and LOGGING/NOLOGGING modes
- Change the tablespace from PERMANENT to TEMPORARY or vice versa
- Change the availability of the tablespace
- Make the tablespace read-only or read-write
- Coalesce the contiguous free space
- Add more space by adding new data files or temporary files
- Rename files belonging to the tablespace
- Begin and end a backup

Oracle Exam Objective

Change the storage settings of tablespaces

Changing the default storage, extent allocation, or LOGGING/NOLOGGING does not affect the existing objects in the tablespace. The DEFAULT STORAGE and LOGGING/NOLOGGING clauses are applied to the newly created segments if you do not explicitly define such a clause when creating new objects. For example, to change the storage parameters, use the following statement:

```
ALTER TABLESPACE APPL_DATA
DEFAULT STORAGE (INITIAL 2M NEXT 2M);
```

Only the INITIAL and NEXT values of the storage clause are changed; the other storage parameters such as PCTINCREASE or MINEXTENTS remain unaltered.

You can change a dictionary-managed temporary tablespace to permanent or vice versa by using the ALTER TABLESPACE command, if the tablespace is empty and the permanent tablespace uses standard block size. You cannot use the ALTER TABLESPACE command, with the TEMPORARY keyword, to change a locally managed permanent tablespace into a locally managed temporary tablespace. You must use the CREATE TEMPORARY TABLESPACE statement to create a locally managed temporary tablespace. You can not use the ALTER TABLESPACE command to change a locally managed temporary tablespace to a locally managed permanent tablespace. The following statement changes a dictionary managed permanent tablespace to temporary:

```
ALTER TABLESPACE TEMP TEMPORARY;
```

The clauses in the ALTER TABLESPACE command are all mutually exclusive; you can specify only one clause at a time.

You cannot use the ALTER TABLESPACE statement to change the tablespace's extent allocation to DICTIONARY or LOCAL.

Tablespace Availability

Oracle Exam Objective

Change the status of tablespaces

You can control the availability of certain tablespaces by placing them offline or online. When you make a tablespace offline, the segments in that tablespace are not accessible. The data stored in other tablespaces is available for use. When making a tablespace unavailable, you can use the following four options:

NORMAL This option is the default. Oracle writes all the dirty buffer blocks in the SGA (System Global Area) to the data files of the tablespace and closes the data files. All data files belonging to the tablespace must be online. You need not do a media recovery when bringing the tablespace online. For example:

```
ALTER TABLESPACE USER_DATA OFFLINE NORMAL
```

TEMPORARY Oracle performs a checkpoint on all online data files. It does not ensure that the data files are available. You might need to perform a media recovery on the offline data files when the tablespace is brought online. For example:

```
ALTER TABLESPACE USER_DATA OFFLINE TEMPORARY;
```

IMMEDIATE Oracle does not perform a checkpoint and does not make sure that all data files are available. You must perform a media recovery when the tablespace is brought back online. For example:

```
ALTER TABLESPACE USER_DATA OFFLINE IMMEDIATE;
```

FOR RECOVER This option places the tablespace offline for point-in-time recovery. You can copy the data files belonging to the tablespace from a backup and apply the archive log files. For example:

```
ALTER TABLESPACE USER_DATA OFFLINE FOR RECOVER;
```

This option is deprecated in Oracle9i, and is available only for backward compatibility.

You cannot place the SYSTEM tablespace offline because the data dictionary must always be available for the database to function. If a tablespace is offline when you shut down the database, it remains offline when you start up the database. You can place a tablespace back on line by using the statement ALTER TABLESPACE USER_DATA ONLINE.

When you take a tablespace offline, SQL statements cannot reference any objects contained in that tablespace. If there are unsaved changes when you take the tablespace offline, Oracle saves rollback data corresponding to those changes in a deferred rollback segment in the SYSTEM tablespace. When you bring the tablespace back online, Oracle applies the rollback data to the tablespace, if needed.

Coalescing Free Space

You can use the ALTER TABLESPACE command with the COALESCE clause to *coalesce* the adjacent free extents. When you free up the extents used by an object, either by altering the object storage or by dropping the object, Oracle does not combine the adjacent free extents. When coalescing tablespaces, Oracle does not combine all free space into one big extent; Oracle combines only the adjacent extents. For example, Figure 6.2 shows the extent allocation in a tablespace before and after coalescing.

FIGURE 6.2 Coalescing a tablespace

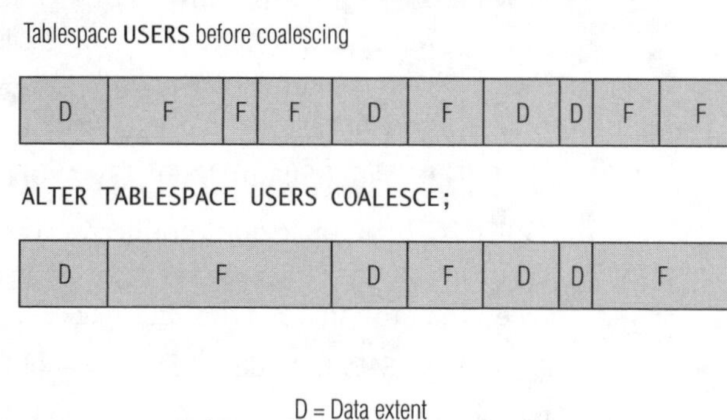

The SMON (system monitor) process coalesces the tablespace. If you set the PCTINCREASE storage parameter for the tablespace to a nonzero value, the SMON process automatically coalesces the tablespace's unused extents. Even if you set PCTINCREASE to zero, Oracle coalesces the tablespace when it does not find a free extent that is big enough. Oracle also does a limited amount of coalescing if the PCTINCREASE value of the object dropped is not zero. If the extent sizes of the tablespace are all uniform, there is no need to coalesce.

Read-Only Tablespace

If you do not want users to change any data in the tablespace, you can specify that it is read-only. All objects in the tablespace are available for queries. INSERT, UPDATE, and DELETE operations on the data are not allowed. When the tablespace is made read-only, the data file headers are no longer updated when the checkpoint occurs. You need to back up the *read-only tablespaces* only once. You cannot make the SYSTEM tablespace read-only. When you make a tablespace read-only, all the data files must be online, and the tablespace can have no pending transactions.

You can drop objects such as tables or indexes from a read-only tablespace, but you cannot create new objects in a read-only tablespace.

To make the USERS tablespace read-only, use the following statement:

```
ALTER TABLESPACE USERS READ ONLY;
```

If you issue the ALTER TABLESPACE *<tablespace name>* READ ONLY statement when there are active transactions in the tablespace, the tablespace goes into a transitional read-only mode in which no further DML (Data Manipulation Language) statements are allowed, although existing transactions that are modifying the tablespace are allowed to commit or roll back.

To change a tablespace to read-write mode, use the following command:

```
ALTER TABLESPACE USERS READ WRITE;
```

Oracle normally checks the availability of all data files belonging to the database when starting up the database. If you are storing your read-only tablespace on an offline storage medium or on a CD-ROM, you might want to skip the data file availability checking when starting up the database. To do so, set the parameter READ_ONLY_OPEN_DELAYED to TRUE. Oracle checks the availability of data files belonging to read-only tablespaces only at the time of access to an object in the tablespace. A missing or bad read-only file will not be detected at database start-up time.

Adding Space to a Tablespace

Oracle Exam Objective

Change the size of the tablespace

You can add more space to a tablespace by adding more data files to it or by changing the size of the existing data files. To add more data files or temporary files to the tablespace, use the ALTER TABLESPACE command with the ADD [DATAFILE/TEMPFILE] clause. For example, to add a file to a tablespace, run the following command:

```
ALTER TABLESPACE USERS ADD DATAFILE
'/disk5/oradata/DB01/users02.dbf' SIZE 25M;
```

If you are modifying a locally managed temporary tablespace to add more files, use the following statement:

```
ALTER TABLESPACE USER_TEMP ADD TEMPFILE
'/disk4/oradata/DB01/user_temp01.dbf' SIZE 100M;
```

For locally managed temporary tablespaces, you can use only the ADD TEMPFILE clause with the ALTER TABLESPACE command.

Dropping a Tablespace

You use the DROP TABLESPACE statement to drop a tablespace from the database. If the tablespace to be dropped is not empty, use the INCLUDING CONTENTS clause. For example, to drop the USER_DATA tablespace, use the following statement:

```
DROP TABLESPACE USER_DATA;
```

If the tablespace is not empty, specify the following:

```
DROP TABLESPACE USER_DATA INCLUDING CONTENTS;
```

If there are referential integrity constraints from the objects on other tablespaces referring to the objects in the tablespace that is being dropped, you must specify the CASCADE CONSTRAINTS clause:

```
DROP TABLESPACE USER_DATA INCLUDING CONTENTS CASCADE
CONSTRAINTS;
```

When you drop a tablespace, the control file is updated with the tablespace and data file information. The actual data files belonging to the tablespace are removed only if the data files are Oracle Managed Files.

If the files are not Oracle managed, you can either use operating system commands to remove the data files belonging to the dropped tablespace or use the AND DATAFILES clause to free up the disk space. The following statement drops the tablespace and removes all data files belonging to the tablespace from the disk.

```
DROP TABLESPACE USER_DATA INCLUDING CONTENTS AND
DATAFILES;
```

You cannot drop the SYSTEM tablespace.

Querying Tablespace Information

You query tablespace information from the following data dictionary views.

DBA_TABLESPACES

The DBA_TABLESPACES view shows information about all tablespaces in the database. (USER_TABLESPACES shows tablespaces that are accessible to the user.) This view contains default storage parameters and specifies the type of tablespace, the status, and so on

```
SQL> SELECT TABLESPACE_NAME, EXTENT_MANAGEMENT,
  2         ALLOCATION_TYPE, CONTENTS,
  3         SEGMENT_SPACE_MANAGEMENT
  4  FROM DBA_TABLESPACES;

TABLESPACE_NAME  EXTENT_MAN ALLOCATIO CONTENTS  SEGMEN
---------------- ---------- --------- --------- ------
SYSTEM           DICTIONARY USER      PERMANENT MANUAL
UNDOTBS          LOCAL      SYSTEM    UNDO      MANUAL
CWMLITE          LOCAL      SYSTEM    PERMANENT MANUAL
DRSYS            LOCAL      SYSTEM    PERMANENT MANUAL
EXAMPLE          LOCAL      SYSTEM    PERMANENT MANUAL
TEMP             LOCAL      UNIFORM   TEMPORARY MANUAL
TOOLS            LOCAL      SYSTEM    PERMANENT MANUAL
USERS            LOCAL      SYSTEM    PERMANENT MANUAL
APP_DATA         DICTIONARY USER      PERMANENT MANUAL
APP_INDEX        LOCAL      UNIFORM   PERMANENT AUTO

10 rows selected.
SQL>
```

The following columns are displayed in DBA_TABLESPACES view:

TABLESPACE_NAME

BLOCK_SIZE

INITIAL_EXTENT

NEXT_EXTENT

MIN_EXTENTS

MAX_EXTENTS

```
PCT_INCREASE
MIN_EXTLEN
STATUS
CONTENTS
LOGGING
EXTENT_MANAGEMENT
ALLOCATION_TYPE
PLUGGED_IN
SEGMENT_SPACE_MANAGEMENT
```

V$TABLESPACE

V$TABLESPACE shows the tablespace number, the name, and the backup status from the control file.

```
SQL> SELECT * FROM V$TABLESPACE;

       TS# NAME                           INC
---------- ------------------------------ ---
         2 CWMLITE                        YES
         3 DRSYS                          YES
         4 EXAMPLE                        YES
        11 APP_INDEX                      YES
         0 SYSTEM                         YES
         7 TOOLS                          YES
         1 UNDOTBS                        YES
         8 USERS                          YES
         6 TEMP                           YES
        10 APP_DATA                       YES

10 rows selected.
SQL>
```

DBA_FREE_SPACE

This view shows the free extents available in all tablespaces. You use this view to find the total free space available in a tablespace. USER_FREE_SPACE shows the free extents in tablespaces accessible to the current user. Locally managed temporary tablespaces are not shown in this view.

```
SQL> SELECT TABLESPACE_NAME, SUM(BYTES) FREE_SPACE
  2  FROM   DBA_FREE_SPACE
  3  GROUP BY TABLESPACE_NAME;

TABLESPACE_NAME  FREE_SPACE
---------------- ----------
APP_DATA           10481664
APP_INDEX          10223616
CWMLITE            14680064
DRSYS              12845056
EXAMPLE              196608
SYSTEM             88281088
TOOLS               4390912
UNDOTBS           208338944
USERS              24051712

9 rows selected.
SQL>
```

The following columns are displayed in DBA_FREE_SPACE view:

TABLESPACE_NAME

FILE_ID

BLOCK_ID

BYTES

BLOCKS

RELATIVE_FNO

V$SORT_USAGE

This view shows information about the active sorts in the database; it shows the space used, the username, the SQL address, and the hash value. You can join this view with V$SESSION or V$SQL to get more information about the session.

```
SQL> SELECT USER, SESSION_ADDR, SESSION_NUM, SQLADDR,
  2         SQLHASH, TABLESPACE, EXTENTS, BLOCKS
  3  FROM V$SORT_USAGE;

USER                 SESSION_ SESSION_NUM SQLADDR
-------------------- -------- ----------- --------
   SQLHASH TABLESPACE                 EXTENTS     BLOCKS
---------- -------------------- ---------- ----------
SCOTT                030539F4           24 0343E200
1877781575 TEMP                         45        360
```

The following columns are displayed in V$SORT_USAGE view:

USERNAME

USER

SESSION_ADDR

SESSION_NUM

SQLADDR

SQLHASH

TABLESPACE

CONTENTS

SEGTYPE

SEGFILE#

SEGBLK#

EXTENTS

BLOCKS

SEGRFNO#

Other Views

The following views also show information related to tablespaces:

DBA_SEGMENTS, USER_SEGMENTS Shows information about the segments, segment types, size, and storage parameter values associated with tablespaces. This example shows the tablespace and total space occupied by each type of segment owned by PM schema.

```
SQL> SELECT TABLESPACE_NAME, SEGMENT_TYPE, SUM(BYTES)
  2  FROM   DBA_SEGMENTS
  3  WHERE  OWNER = 'PM'
  4  GROUP BY ROLLUP(TABLESPACE_NAME, SEGMENT_TYPE);

TABLESPACE_NAME SEGMENT_TYPE       SUM(BYTES)
--------------- ------------------ ----------
EXAMPLE         INDEX                  196608
EXAMPLE         LOBINDEX              1114112
EXAMPLE         LOBSEGMENT            1572864
EXAMPLE         NESTED TABLE            65536
EXAMPLE         TABLE                  131072
EXAMPLE                               3080192
                                      3080192

7 rows selected.
SQL>
```

DBA_EXTENTS, USER_EXTENTS Shows information about the extents, extent sizes, associated segment, and tablespace.

DBA_DATA_FILES Shows data files belonging to tablespaces.

DBA_TEMP_FILES Shows temporary files belonging to locally managed temporary tablespaces.

V$TEMP_EXTENT_MAP Shows all extents of a locally managed temporary tablespace.

V$TEMP_EXTENT_POOL Shows the temporary space used and cached for the current instance, for locally managed temporary tablespaces.

V$TEMP_SPACE_HEADER Shows the space used and free in each temporary tablespace files.

V$SORT_SEGMENT Shows information about sort segments.

DBA_USERS Shows information about the default and temporary tablespace assignments to users. The following query shows the default tablespace assignments of user HR.

```
SQL> SELECT DEFAULT_TABLESPACE, TEMPORARY_TABLESPACE
  2  FROM   DBA_USERS
  3  WHERE  USERNAME = 'HR';

DEFAULT_TABLESPACE              TEMPORARY_TABLESPACE
------------------------------ -----------------------
EXAMPLE                         TEMP
SQL>
```

Managing Data Files

Data files (or temporary files) are created when you create a tablespace or when you alter a tablespace to add files. Before Oracle9i, you had to specify a file name and size to create files. In Oracle9i, Oracle can create files and remove them when the tablespace is removed. Such files are known as Oracle Managed Files. We briefly discussed Oracle Managed Files for creating control files and redo log files in Chapter 5, and we'll look at how you can use OMF to specify data files later in this chapter.

You can specify the size of the file when you create a file or reuse an existing file. When you reuse an existing file, that file should not belong to any Oracle database—the contents of the file are overwritten. Use the REUSE clause to specify an existing file. If you omit the REUSE clause and the data file being created exists, Oracle returns an error. For example:

```
CREATE TABLESPACE APPL_DATA
DATAFILE '/disk2/oradata/DB01/appl_data01.dbf' REUSE;
```

When you specify REUSE, you can omit the SIZE clause. If you specify the SIZE clause, the size of the file should be the same as the existing file. If the file to be created does not exist, Oracle creates a new file even if you specify the REUSE clause.

Always specify the fully qualified directory name for the file being created. If you omit the directory, Oracle creates the file under the default database directory or in the current directory, depending on the operating system.

In the following sections we will discuss how to specify file sizes, resize data files, relocate tablespaces by renaming the data files, and display the dictionary views that contain information about data files and temporary files.

Sizing Files

Oracle Exam Objective

Change the size of the tablespace

You can specify that the data file (or temporary file) grow automatically whenever space is needed in the tablespace. To do so, specify the AUTOEXTEND clause for the file. This functionality enables you to have fewer data files per tablespace and can simplify the administration of data files. You can turn the AUTOEXTEND clause ON and OFF; you can also specify file size increments. You can set a maximum limit for the file size; by default the file size limit is UNLIMITED. You can specify the AUTOEXTEND clause for files when you run the CREATE DATABASE, CREATE TABLESPACE, ALTER TABLESPACE, or ALTER DATAFILE commands. For example:

```
CREATE TABLESPACE APPL_DATA
DATAFILE '/disk2/oradata/DB01/appl_data01.dbf'
SIZE 500M
AUTOEXTEND ON NEXT 100M MAXSIZE 2000M;
```

The AUTOEXTEND ON clause specifies that the automatic file resize feature be enabled for the specified file; NEXT specifies the size by which the file should be incremented; and MAXSIZE specifies the maximum size for the file. When Oracle tries to allocate an extent in the tablespace, it looks for a free extent. If Oracle cannot locate a large enough free extent (even after coalescing), Oracle increases the data file size by 100MB and tries to allocate the new extent.

The following statement disables the automatic file extension feature:

```
ALTER DATABASE
DATAFILE '/disk2/oradata/DB01/appl_data01.dbf'
AUTOEXTEND OFF;
```

If the file already exists in the database, and you want to enable the auto extension feature, use the ALTER DATABASE command. For example, you can use the following statement:

```
ALTER DATABASE
DATAFILE '/disk2/oradata/DB01/appl_data01.dbf'
AUTOEXTEND ON NEXT 100M MAXSIZE 2000M;
```

You can increase or decrease the size of a data file or temporary file (thus increasing or decreasing the size of the tablespace) by using the RESIZE clause of the ALTER DATABASE DATAFILE command. For example, to redefine the size of a file, use the following statement:

```
ALTER DATABASE
DATAFILE '/disk2/oradata/DB01/appl_data01.dbf'
RESIZE 1500M;
```

When decreasing the file size, Oracle returns an error if it finds data beyond the new file size. You cannot reduce the file size below the high-water mark in the file. Reducing the file size helps to reclaim unused space.

Oracle Managed Files

Oracle Exam Objective

Implement Oracle Managed Files

Oracle managed files are appropriate for smaller non-production databases or databases on disks that use the logical volume manager (LVM). LVM is software available with most disk systems to combine partitions of multiple physical disks to one logical volume. LVM can use mirroring, striping, RAID 5, and so on. The following benefits are associated with using the OMF:

Prevention of errors Because Oracle removes the files associated with the tablespace, you cannot make a mistake by removing a file that belongs to an active tablespace.

Standard naming convention The files you create using OMF have unique and standard file names.

Space retrieval When tablespaces are removed, Oracle removes the files associated with the tablespace, thus freeing up space immediately on the disk. The DBA might forget to remove the file from disk.

Easy script writing Application vendors need not worry about the syntax of specifying directory names in the scripts when porting an application to multiple platforms. The same script can be used to create tablespaces on different operating system platforms.

You can use OMF to create files and to remove them when the corresponding object (redo log group or tablespace) is dropped from the database. You manage OMF-created files, using the traditional methods for renaming or resizing files.

Creating Files

Before you can create Oracle Managed Files, you must set the parameter `DB_CREATE_FILE_DEST`. You can specify this parameter in the initialization parameter file or set/change it using the `ALTER SYSTEM` or `ALTER SESSION` statement. The `DB_CREATE_FILE_DEST` parameter defines the directory where Oracle can create data files. Oracle must have read/write permission on this directory, and the directory must exist on the server where the database is located. Oracle will not create the directory; it will create only create the data file.

You can use OMF to create data files when using the `CREATE DATABASE`, `CREATE TABLESPACE`, or `ALTER TABLESPACE` statements. In the `CREATE DATABASE` statement, you need not specify the data file names for `SYSTEM` or `UNDO` or `TEMPORARY` tablespaces. You can omit the `DATAFILE` clause in the `CREATE TABLESPACE` statement. In the `ALTER TABLESPACE ADD DATAFILE` statement, you can omit the file name.

The data files you create using OMF will have a standard format. For a data file the format is `ora_%t_%u.dbf`. The format for a temp file is `ora_%t_%u.tmp`; `%t` is the tablespace name, and `%u` is a unique 8-character string that Oracle derives. If the tablespace name is more than 8 characters, only the first 8 characters are used. The file names that Oracle generates are reported in the alert log file.

You can also use the OMF feature to create control files and redo log files of the database. Since these two types of files can be multiplexed, Oracle provides another parameter to specify the location of files—DB_CREATE_ONLINE_LOG_DEST_*n*, in which *n* can be 1, 2, 3, 4, or 5. You can also alter these initialization parameters using ALTER SYSTEM or ALTER SESSION. If you set the parameters DB_CREATE_ONLINE_LOG_DEST_1 and DB_CREATE_ONLINE_LOG_DEST_2 in the parameter file when creating a database, Oracle creates two control files (one in each directory) and creates two online redo log groups with two members each (one member each in both directories).

The redo log file names will have the format ora_%g_%u.log, in which %g is the log group number and %u is an 8-character string unique to the database. The control file name will have the format ora_%u.ctl, in which %u is an 8-character string.

Let's consider an example of creating a database. The following parameters are set in the initialization parameter file.

```
UNDO_MANAGEMENT = AUTO
DB_CREATE_ONLINE_LOG_DEST_1 = '/ora1/oradata/MYDB'
DB_CREATE_ONLINE_LOG_DEST_2 = '/ora2/oradata/MYDB'
DB_CREATE_FILE_DEST = '/ora1/oradata/MYDB'
```

The CONTROL_FILES parameter is not set. Create the database using the following statement:

```
CREATE DATABASE MYDB
DEFAULT TEMPORARY TABLESPACE TEMP;
```

The following files will be created.:

- The SYSTEM tablespace data file in /ora1/oradata/MYDB
- The TEMP tablespace temp file in /ora1/oradata/MYDB
- A control file in /ora1/oradata/MYDB
- A control file in /ora2/oradata/MYDB
- One member of the first redo log group in /ora1/oradata/MYDB and a second member in /ora2/oradata/MYDB
- One member of the second redo log group in /ora1/oradata/MYDB and a second member in /ora2/oradata/MYDB

Because we specified the UNDO_MANAGEMENT clause and did not specify a name for the undo tablespace, Oracle creates SYS_UNDOTBS tablespace as undo tablespace and creates its data file under /ora1/oradata/MYDB. If you omit the DEFAULT TEMPORARY TABLESPACE clause, Oracle will not create a temporary tablespace.

When using OMF to create control files, you must get the names of control files from the alert log and add them to the initialization parameter file using the CONTROL_FILES parameter, for the instance to start again.

If you do not specify the DB_CREATE_ONLINE_LOG_DEST_*n* parameter when creating a database or when adding a redo log group, OMF creates one control file and two groups with one member each for redo log files in the DB_CREATE_FILE_DEST directory. If you also do not set the DB_CREATE_FILE_DEST parameter and you did not provide data file names and redo log file names, Oracle creates the files under a default directory (usually $ORACLE_HOME/dbs), but these files will not be Oracle managed. This is the default behavior of the database.

The data files and temp files that OMF creates will have a default size of 100MB, which is auto extensible with no maximum file size. Each redo log member will be 100MB in size by default.

Let's look at another example that creates two tablespaces. The data file for the APP_DATA tablespace will be stored in the /ora5/oradata/MYDB directory. The data file for the APP_INDEX tablespace will be stored in the /ora6/oradata/MYDB directory.

```
ALTER SESSION SET DB_CREATE_FILE_DEST = '/ora5/oradata/MYDB';
CREATE TABLESPACE APP_DATA
EXTENT MANAGEMENT DICTIONARY;
ALTER SESSION SET DB_CREATE_FILE_DEST = '/ora6/oradata/MYDB';
CREATE TABLESPACE APP_INDEX;
```

Overriding the Default File Size

If you want a different size for the files created by OMF, you can specify the DATAFILE clause without a file name. You can also turn off the auto-extensible feature of the data file. The following statement creates a tablespace of 10MB and turns off the auto-extensible feature:

```
CREATE TABLESPACE PAY_DATA DATAFILE SIZE 10M
AUTOEXTEND OFF;
```

Here is another example, which creates multiple data files for the tablespace. The second and third data files are auto-extensible.

```
CREATE TABLESPACE PAY_INDEX
DATAFILE SIZE 20M AUTOEXTEND OFF,
SIZE 30M AUTOEXTEND ON MAXSIZE 1000M,
SIZE 1M;
```

The following example adds files to an existing tablespace.

```
ALTER SYSTEM SET DB_CREATE_FILE_DEST = '/ora5/oradata/MYDB';
ALTER TABLESPACE USERS ADD DATAFILE;
ALTER SYSTEM SET DB_CREATE_FILE_DEST = '/ora8/oradata/MYDB';
ALTER TABLESPACE APP_DATA
ADD DATAFILE SIZE 200M AUTOEXTEND OFF;
```

Once created, Oracle-managed files are treated as other database files. You can rename and resize them, and you must back them up. Archive log files are not OMF.

Real World Scenario

How Do You Create a Database and Tablespaces with OMF?

Your manager has asked you to create a test database for a new application your company just bought. The database is for testing the functionality of the application. The vendor told you that you need four tablespaces: SJC_DATA, SJC_INDEX, WKW_DATA, and WKW_INDEX. The index tablespaces must have uniform extent sizes of 512KB and should have minimum size of 500MB. The SJC_DATA tablespace is to be dictionary managed with the minimum and extent size multiple to be 128K and a tablespace size of 1GB. The SJC_DATA tablespace should be 250MB.

Since this is a database for testing the functionality of the application, you decide to use Oracle Managed Files, which makes your life easier by creating and cleaning the files in the database.

Let's create the database. Your systems administrator has given you four disks: /ora1, /ora2, /ora3, and /ora4, each with 900MB of space.

Be sure to include the following in the parameter file:

```
UNDO_MANAGEMENT = AUTO

DB_CREATE_FILE_DEST = /ora1

DB_CREATE_ONLINE_LOG_DEST_1 = /ora1

DB_CREATE_ONLINE_LOG_DEST_2 = /ora2
```

Create the database using the following statement:

```
CREATE DATABASE SJCTEST

LOGFILE SIZE 20M

DEFAULT TEMPORARY TABLESPACE TEMP

TEMPFILE SIZE 200M

EXTENT MANAGEMENT LOCAL UNIFORM SIZE 2M

UNDO TABLESPACE UNDO_TBS SIZE 200M;
```

This statement creates a database named SJCTEST. The system tablespace, undo tablespace, and temporary tablespace are created in /ora1. System tablespace has the default size of 100M; undo tablespace and temporary tablespace have the size of 200MB. Since we did not want each log file member to be 100MB, we specified a smaller size for online redo log members.

Two control files and redo log files with two members are created. Each member is stored in /ora1 and /ora2.

After running the necessary scripts to create the catalog and packages, we'll create the tablespaces for the application.

```
ALTER SYSTEM SET DB_CREATE_FILE_DEST = "/ora2";
```

```
CREATE TABLESPACE SJC_DATA
EXTENT MANAGEMENT DICTIONARY
MINIMUM EXTENT 128K
DATAFILE SIZE 800M;
ALTER SYSTEM SET DB_CREATE_FILE_DEST = "/ora3";
ALTER TABLESPACE SJC_DATA ADD DATAFILE SIZE 200M;
CREATE TABLESAPCE WKW_INDEX
EXTENT MANAGEMENT LOCAL UNIFORM SIZE 512K
DATAFILE SIZE 500M;
ALTER SYSTEM SET DB_CREATE_FILE_DEST = "/ora4";
CREATE TABLESPACE WKW_DATA;
CREATE TABLESPACE SJC_INDEX
EXTENT MANAGEMENT LOCAL UNIFORM SIZE 512K
DATAFILE SIZE 500M;
```

Since we have only 900MB in each file system, we need two data files to allocate 1GB to the SJC_DATA tablespace. This is accomplished in two steps.

Renaming and Relocating Files

You rename data files using the RENAME FILE clause of the ALTER DATABASE command. You can also rename data files by using the RENAME DATAFILE clause of the ALTER TABLESPACE command. You use the RENAME functionality to logically move tablespaces from one location to another. Consider the following example.

The tablespace USER_DATA has three data files:

- /disk1/oradata/DB01/user_data01.dbf
- /disk1/oradata/DB01/userdata2.dbf
- /disk1/oradata/DB01/user_data03.dbf

You'll notice that the second file does not follow the naming standard set for your company, so you need to rename the file. Follow these steps:

1. Take the tablespace offline.

   ```
   ALTER TABLESPACE USER_DATA OFFLINE;
   ```

2. Copy or move the file to the new location, or rename the file by using operating system commands.

3. Rename the file in the database by using one of the following two commands:

   ```
   ALTER DATABASE RENAME FILE
   '/disk1/oradata/DB01/userdata2.dbf' TO
   '/disk1/oradata/DB01/user_data02.dbf';
   ```

   or

   ```
   ALTER TABLESPACE USER_DATA RENAME DATAFILE
   '/disk1/oradata/DB01/userdata2.dbf' TO
   '/disk1/oradata/DB01/user_data02.dbf';
   ```

4. Bring the tablespace online.

   ```
   ALTER TABLESPACE USER_DATA ONLINE;
   ```

If you need to relocate the tablespace from disk 1 to disk 2, follow the same steps. You can rename all the files in the tablespace by using a single command. The steps are as follows:

1. Take the tablespace offline.

   ```
   ALTER TABLESPACE USER_DATA OFFLINE;
   ```

2. Copy the file to the new location by using operating system commands on the disk.

3. Rename the files in the database by using one of the following two commands. The number of data files specified before the keyword `TO` should equal the number of files specified after the keyword.

   ```
   ALTER DATABASE RENAME FILE
   '/disk1/oradata/DB01/user_data01.dbf',
   '/disk1/oradata/DB01/userdata2.dbf',
   '/disk1/oradata/DB01/user_data03.dbf'
   ```

```
'/disk1/oradata/DB01/user_data03.dbf'
 TO
'/disk2/oradata/DB01/user_data01.dbf',
'/disk2/oradata/DB01/user_data02.dbf',
'/disk2/oradata/DB01/user_data03.dbf';
```

or

```
ALTER TABLESPACE USER_DATA RENAME DATAFILE
'/disk1/oradata/DB01/user_data01.dbf',
'/disk1/oradata/DB01/userdata2.dbf',
'/disk1/oradata/DB01/user_data03.dbf'
 TO
'/disk2/oradata/DB01/user_data01.dbf',
'/disk2/oradata/DB01/user_data02.dbf',
'/disk2/oradata/DB01/user_data03.dbf';
```

4. Bring the tablespace online.

```
ALTER TABLESPACE USER_DATA ONLINE;
```

If more than one tablespace needs its files moved or renamed, or if a file belonging to the SYSTEM tablespace must be moved or renamed, follow these steps:

1. Shut down the database. A complete backup is recommended before making any structural changes.
2. Copy or rename the files on the disk by using operating system commands.
3. Start up and mount the database (STARTUP MOUNT).
4. Rename the files in the database by using the ALTER DATABASE RENAME FILE command.
5. Open the database by using ALTER DATABASE OPEN.

If you need to move read-only tablespaces to CD-ROM or to any write-once read-many device, follow these steps:

1. Make the tablespace read-only.
2. Copy the data files that belong to the tablespace to the device.
3. Rename the files in the database by using the ALTER DATABASE RENAME FILE command.

Querying Data File Information

You can query data file and temporary file information by using the following views.

V$DATAFILE

This view shows data file information from the control file.

```
SQL> SELECT FILE#, RFILE#, STATUS, BYTES, BLOCK_SIZE
  2  FROM V$DATAFILE;

     FILE#     RFILE# STATUS       BYTES BLOCK_SIZE
---------- ---------- ------- ---------- ----------
         1          1 SYSTEM   267386880       8192
         2          2 ONLINE   545259520       8192
         3          3 ONLINE    17039360       8192
         4          4 ONLINE    75497472       8192
         5          5 ONLINE    17825792       8192
         6          6 ONLINE    26214400       8192
         7          7 ONLINE    92274688       8192
         8          8 ONLINE    31465472       8192
```

The following columns are displayed in V$DATAFILE view:

FILE#

CREATION_CHANGE#

CREATION_TIME

TS#

RFILE#

STATUS

ENABLED

CHECKPOINT_CHANGE#

CHECKPOINT_TIME

UNRECOVERABLE_CHANGE#

UNRECOVERABLE_TIME

LAST_CHANGE#

LAST_TIME

OFFLINE_CHANGE#

ONLINE_CHANGE#

ONLINE_TIME

BYTES

BLOCKS

CREATE_BYTES

BLOCK_SIZE

NAME

PLUGGED_IN

BLOCK1_OFFSET

AUX_NAME

V$TEMPFILE

Similar to the V$DATAFILE view, this view shows information about the temporary files.

```
SQL> SELECT FILE#, RFILE#, STATUS, BYTES, BLOCK_SIZE
  2  FROM V$TEMPFILE;

     FILE#     RFILE# STATUS       BYTES BLOCK_SIZE
---------- ---------- ------- ---------- ----------
         1          1 ONLINE    10485760       8192
```

DBA_DATA_FILES

This view shows information about the data file names, associated tablespace names, size, status, and so on.

```
SQL> SELECT TABLESPACE_NAME, FILE_NAME, BYTES,
  2         AUTOEXTENSIBLE
  3  FROM DBA_DATA_FILES;
```

```
TABLESPACE_NAME  FILE_NAME                             BYTES AUT
---------------- -------------------------------- ---------- ---
SYSTEM           C:\ORACLE\BTWIN01\SYSTEM01.DBF    340787200 YES
APP_DATA         C:\ORACLE\ORA_APP_DATA_ZZPSNR00.   10485760 YES
                 DBF
UNDOTBS          C:\ORACLE\BTWIN01\UNDOTBS01.DBF   209715200 YES
CWMLITE          C:\ORACLE\BTWIN01\CWMLITE01.DBF    20971520 YES
DRSYS            C:\ORACLE\BTWIN01\DRSYS01.DBF      20971520 YES
EXAMPLE          C:\ORACLE\BTWIN01\EXAMPLE01.DBF   160563200 YES
APP_INDEX        C:\ORACLE\ORA_APP_INDE_ZZPT8F00.   10485760 YES
                 DBF
TOOLS            C:\ORACLE\BTWIN01\TOOLS01.DBF      10485760 YES
USERS            C:\ORACLE\BTWIN01\USERS01.DBF      26214400 YES
PAY_DATA         C:\ORACLE\ORA_PAY_DATA_ZZQBLZ00.   10485760 NO
                 DBF
PAY_INDEX        C:\ORACLE\ORA_PAY_INDE_ZZQBPF00.   20971520 NO
                 DBF
PAY_INDEX        C:\ORACLE\ORA_PAY_INDE_ZZQBPG00.   31457280 NO
                 DBF
```

The following columns are displayed in DBA_DATA_FILES view:

FILE_NAME

FILE_ID

TABLESPACE_NAME

BYTES

BLOCKS

STATUS

RELATIVE_FNO

AUTOEXTENSIBLE

MAXBYTES

MAXBLOCKS

INCREMENT_BY

USER_BYTES

USER_BLOCKS

DBA_TEMP_FILES

This view shows information similar to that of the DBA_DATA_FILES view for the temporary files in the database.

```
SQL> SELECT TABLESPACE_NAME, FILE_NAME, BYTES,
  2         AUTOEXTENSIBLE
  3  FROM DBA_TEMP_FILES;

TABLESPACE FILE_NAME                             BYTES AUT
---------- ----------------------------------  ---------- ---
TEMP_LOCAL C:\ORACLE\DB01\TEMP_LOCAL01.DBF    10485760 NO
```

The maximum number of data files per tablespace is depends on the operating system, but on most operating systems, it is 1022. The maximum number of data files per database is 65,533. The MAXDATAFILES clause in the CREATE DATABASE or CREATE CONTROLFILE statements also limits the number of data files per database. The maximum data file size is also depends on the operating system. There is no limit on the number of tablespaces per database. Because only 65,533 data files are allowed per database, you cannot have more than 65,533 tablespaces, because each tablespace needs at least one data file.

Summary

This chapter discussed the tablespaces and data files—the logical storage structures and physical storage elements of the database. A data file belongs to one tablespace, and a tablespace can have one or more data files. The size of the tablespace is the total size of all the data files belonging to that tablespace. The size of the database is the total size of all tablespaces in the database, which is the same as the total size of all data files in the database. Tablespaces are logical storage units used to group data by their type or category.

You create tablespaces using the CREATE TABLESPACE command. Oracle always allocates space to an object in chunks of blocks known as extents. Tablespaces can handle the extent management through the Oracle dictionary or locally in the data files that belong to the tablespace. When creating tablespaces, you can specify default storage parameters for the objects that will be created in the tablespace. If you do not specify any storage parameters when creating an object, the storage parameters for the tablespace are used for the new object.

Locally managed tablespaces can have uniform extent sizes, which reduces fragmentation and wasted space. You can also specify that Oracle do the entire extent sizing for locally managed tablespaces.

A temporary tablespace is used only for sorting; you can't create permanent objects in a temporary tablespace. Only one sort segment is created for each instance in the temporary tablespace. Multiple transactions can use the same sort segment, but one transaction can use only one extent. To create locally managed temporary tablespaces, you use the CREATE TEMPORARY TABLESPACE command. Temporary files (instead of data files) are created when you use this command. Although these files are part of the database, they do not appear in the control file, and the block changes do not generate any redo information because all the segments created on locally managed temporary tablespaces are temporary segments.

You can alter a tablespace to change its availability or to make it read-only. Data in an offline tablespace is not accessible, whereas data in the read-only tablespaces cannot be modified or deleted. You can drop objects from a read-only tablespace.

Space is added to the tablespace by adding new data files to the tablespace or by increasing the size of the data files. You can obtain tablespace information from the dictionary using the DBA_TABLESPACES and V$TABLESPACE views. The data files can be renamed through Oracle. This feature is useful to relocate a tablespace.

Oracle9i can manage the physical files belonging to the database using the Oracle Managed Files feature. OMF is good for non-production databases and databases on Logical Volume Manager. The V$DATAFILE, V$TEMPFILE, DBA_DATA_FILES, and DBA_TEMP_FILES views provide information on the data files.

Exam Essentials

Understand the syntax of the CREATE TABLESPACE statement. Learn to create locally managed and dictionary-managed tablespaces. Remember that locally managed tablespace is the default. You can create the tablespace without specifying a file name, when using the OMF option.

Know the options of the ALTER TABLESPACE statement. The options of the ALTER TABLESPACE statement are mutually exclusive, and you can use them to change the storage settings, change the status, relocate files, and alter the default storage settings.

Know the options you can use to take a tablespace offline. You can take a tablespace offline using the NORMAL, TEMPORARY, IMMEDIATE, or FOR RECOVER clause. Understand the difference between each state of the tablespace.

Understand the dictionary views. Query the DBA_TABLESPACES, DBA_DATA_FILES, V$SORT_SEGMENT, V$DATAFILE, and DBA_FREE_SPACE dictionary views. The tablespace name is available in most of the views.

Note the parameters associated with creating non-standard block sizes. Non-standard block size is new to Oracle9i. You can specify a different block size for the tablespace by using the BLOCKSIZE clause in the CREATE TABLESPACE statement. You must set the DB_*n*K_CACHE_SIZE parameter, in which *n* is the non-standard block size.

Learn to create tablespaces and add files to tablespaces using OMF. OMF is new to Oracle9i. Learn to set up the OMF parameters using ALTER SESSION and ALTER SYSTEM and create tablespaces and add data files. Understand the format of file names generated by Oracle.

Know how to change the size of the tablespace. You can change the size of the tablespace by two ways. Use the ALTER TABLESPACE statement to add a new file to the tablespace, or use the ALTER DATABASE or ALTER TABLESPACE statement to resize an existing file.

Key Terms

Before you take the exam, be sure you're familiar with the following terms:

- coalesce
- data file
- dictionary-managed tablespace
- extent management
- locally managed tablespace
- Oracle Managed Files (OMF)
- read-only tablespace
- standard block size
- tablespace
- tempfile
- temporary tablespace
- undo tablespace

Review Questions

1. Which two of the following statements do you execute to make the USERS tablespace read-only, if the tablespace is offline?

   A. ALTER TABLESPACE USERS READ ONLY

   B. ALTER DATABASE MAKE TABLESPACE USERS READ ONLY

   C. ALTER TABLESPACE USERS ONLINE

   D. ALTER TABLESPACE USERS TEMPORARY

2. When is a sort segment that is allocated in a temporary tablespace released?

   A. When the sort operation completes

   B. When the instance is shut down

   C. When you issue ALTER TABLESPACE COALESCE

   D. When SMON clears up inactive sort segments

3. You created a tablespace using the following statement:

   ```
   CREATE TABLESPACE MYTS
   DATAFILE SIZE 200M AUTOEXTEND ON MAXSIZE 2G
   EXTENT MANAGEMENT LOCAL UNIFORM SIZE 5M
   SEGMENT SPACE MANAGEMENT AUTO;
   ```

   Which three parameters does Oracle ignore when you create a table in the MYTS tablespace?

   A. PCTFREE

   B. PCTUSED

   C. FREELISTS

   D. FREELIST GROUPS

   E. INITIAL

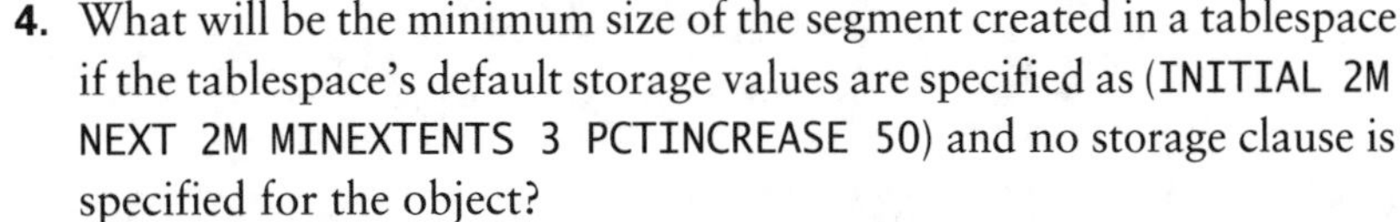

4. What will be the minimum size of the segment created in a tablespace if the tablespace's default storage values are specified as (`INITIAL 2M NEXT 2M MINEXTENTS 3 PCTINCREASE 50`) and no storage clause is specified for the object?

A. 2MB

B. 4MB

C. 5MB

D. 7MB

E. 8MB

5. Which of the following would you use to add more space to a tablespace? (Choose two.)

A. `ALTER TABLESPACE` *<TABLESPACE NAME> ADD DATAFILE SIZE <N>*

B. `ALTER DATABASE DATAFILE` *<FILENAME> RESIZE <N>*

C. `ALTER DATAFILE` *<FILENAME>* `RESIZE` *<N>*

D. `ALTER TABLESPACE` *<TABLESPACE NAME>* `DATAFILE` *<FILENAME>* `RESIZE` *<N>*

6. If the `DB_BLOCK_SIZE` of the database is 8KB, what will be the size of the third extent when you specify the storage parameters as (`INITIAL 8K NEXT 8K PCTINCREASE 50 MINEXTENTS 3`)?

A. 16KB

B. 24KB

C. 12KB

D. 40KB

7. The standard block size for the database is 8KB. You need to create a tablespace with block size of 16KB. Which initialization parameters should be set? (Choose two.)

A. DB_8K_CACHE_SIZE

B. DB_16K_CACHE_SIZE

C. DB_CACHE_SIZE

D. UNDO_MANAGEMENT

E. DB_CREATE_FILE_DEST

8. Which data dictionary view can you query to obtain information about the files that belong to locally managed temporary tablespaces?

   A. DBA_DATA_FILES

   B. DBA_TABLESPACES

   C. DBA_TEMP_FILES

   D. DBA_LOCAL_FILES

9. When does the SMON process automatically coalesce the tablespaces?

   A. When the initialization parameter COALESCE_TABLESPACES is set to TRUE

   B. When the PCTINCREASE default storage of the tablespace is set to 0

   C. When the PCTINCREASE default storage of the tablespace is set to 50

   D. Whenever the tablespace has more than one free extent

10. Which operation is permitted on a read-only tablespace?

   A. Delete data from table

   B. Drop table

   C. Create new table

   D. None of the above

11. How would you drop a tablespace if the tablespace were not empty?

A. Rename all the objects in the tablespace and then drop the tablespace

B. Remove the data files belonging to the tablespace from the disk

C. Use `ALTER DATABASE DROP` *<TABLESPACE NAME> CASCADE*

D. Use `DROP TABLESPACE` *<TABLESPACE NAME> INCLUDING CONTENTS*

12. Which command is used to enable the auto-extensible feature for a file, if the file is already part of a tablespace?

A. `ALTER DATABASE.`

B. `ALTER TABLESPACE.`

C. `ALTER DATA FILE.`

D. You cannot change the auto-extensible feature once the data file created.

13. The database block size is 4KB. You created a tablespace using the following command.

```
CREATE TABLESPACE USER_DATA DATAFILE 'C:/DATA01.DBF'
EXTENT MANAGEMENT DICTIONARY;
```

If you create an object in the database without specifying any storage parameters, what will be the size of the third extent that belongs to the object?

A. 6KB

B. 20KB

C. 50KB

D. 32KB

14. Which of the following statements is false?

    A. You can make a dictionary-managed temporary tablespace permanent.

    B. You cannot change the size of the locally managed temporary tablespace file.

    C. Once it is created, you cannot alter the extent management of a tablespace using ALTER TABLESPACE.

    D. You cannot make a locally managed permanent tablespace temporary.

    E. If you do not specify an extent management clause when creating a tablespace, Oracle creates a locally managed tablespace.

15. Which of the following statements is true regarding the SYSTEM tablespace?

    A. Can be made read-only.

    B. Can be offline.

    C. Data files can be renamed.

    D. Data files cannot be resized.

16. What are the recommended INITIAL and NEXT values for a temporary tablespace, to reduce fragmentation?

    A. INITIAL = 1MB; NEXT = 2MB

    B. INITIAL = multiple of SORT_AREA_SIZE + 1; NEXT = INITIAL

    C. INITIAL = multiple of SORT_AREA_SIZE + DB_BLOCK_SIZE; NEXT = INITIAL

    D. INITIAL = 2 ∴ SORT_AREA_SIZE; NEXT = SORT_AREA_SIZE

17. Which parameter specified in the DEFAULT STORAGE clause of CREATE TABLESPACE cannot be altered after you create the tablespace?

A. `INITIAL`

B. `NEXT`

C. `MAXEXTENTS`

D. None

18. How would you determine how much sort space is used by a user session?

A. Query the `DBA_SORT_SEGMENT` view.

B. Query the `V$SORT_SEGMENT` view.

C. Query the `V$SORT_USAGE` view.

D. You can obtain only the total sort segment size; you cannot find information on individual session sort space usage.

19. If you issue `ALTER TABLESPACE USERS OFFLINE IMMEDIATE`, which of the following statements is true? (Choose two.)

A. All data files belonging to the tablespace must be online.

B. Does not ensure that the data files are available.

C. Need not do media recovery when bringing the tablespace online.

D. Need to do media recovery when bringing the tablespace online.

20. Which format strings does Oracle use to generate OMF file names? (Choose three.)

A. %s

B. %t

C. %g

D. %a

E. %u

F. %%

Answers to Review Questions

1. C, A. To make a tablespace read-only, all the data files belonging to the tablespace must be online and available. So, bring the tablespace online, and then make it read-only.

2. B. The sort segment or temporary segment created in a temporary tablespace is released only when the instance is shut down. Each instance can have one sort segment in the tablespace; the sort segment is created when the first sort for the instance is started.

3. B, C, D. When the tablespace has automatic segment space management, Oracle manages free space automatically using bitmaps. For manual segment space management, Oracle uses free lists.

4. D. When the segment is created, it will have three extents; the first extent is 2MB, the second is 2MB, and the third is 3MB. So the total size of the segment is 7MB.

5. A, B. You can add more space to a tablespace either by adding a data file or by increasing the size of an existing data file. Option A does not specify a file name and uses the OMF feature to generate file name.

6. A. The third extent size will be `NEXT + 0.5 * NEXT`, which is 12KB, but the block size is 8KB, so the third extent size will be 16KB. The initial extent allocated will be 16KB (the minimum size for `INITIAL` is two blocks), and the total segment size is 16 + 8 + 16 = 40KB.

7. B, C. Set `DB_CACHE_SIZE` for the standard block size, and set `DB_16K_CACHE_SIZE` for the non-standard block size. You must not set the `DB_8K_CACHE_SIZE` parameter because the standard block size is 8KB.

8. C. You create locally managed temporary tablespaces using the `CREATE TEMPORARY TABLESPACE` command. The data files (temporary files) belonging to these tablespaces are in the `DBA_TEMP_FILES` view. The `EXTENT_MANAGEMENT` column of the `DBA_TABLESPACES` view shows the type of the tablespace. You can query the data files belonging to locally managed permanent tablespaces and dictionary-managed (permanent and temporary) tablespaces from `DBA_DATA_FILES`. Locally managed temporary tablespaces reduce contention on the data dictionary tables.

9. C. The SMON process automatically coalesces free extents in the tablespace when the tablespace's PCTINCREASE is set to a nonzero value. You can manually coalesce a tablespace by using ALTER TABLESPACE *<TABLESPACE NAME> COALESCE*.

10. B. A table can be dropped from a read-only tablespace. When a table is dropped, Oracle does not have to update the data file; it updates the dictionary tables. Any change to data or creation of new objects is not allowed in a read-only tablespace.

11. D. You use the INCLUDING CONTENTS clause to drop a tablespace that is not empty. Oracle does not remove the data files that belong to the tablespace, if the files are not Oracle managed; you need to do it manually using an operating system command. Oracle updates only the control file. To remove the files, you include the INCLUDING CONTENTS AND DATAFILES clause.

12. A. You can use the ALTER TABLESPACE command to rename a file that belongs to the tablespace, but you handle all other file management operations through the ALTER DATABASE command. To enable auto-extension, use ALTER DATABASE DATAFILE *<FILENAME> AUTOEXTEND ON NEXT <INTEGER> MAXSIZE <INTEGER>*.

13. D. When you create a tablespace with no default storage parameters, Oracle assigns (5 × DB_BLOCK_SIZE) to INITIAL and NEXT; PCTINCREASE is 50. So the third extent would be 50 percent more than the second. The first extent is 20KB, the second is 20KB, and the third is 32KB (because the block size is 4KB).

14. B. You can change the size of a temporary file using ALTER DATABASE TEMPFILE *<FILENAME> RESIZE <INTEGER>*. You cannot rename a temporary file.

15. C. You can rename the data files that belong to the SYSTEM tablespace when the database is in the MOUNT state by using the ALTER DATABASE RENAME FILE statement.

16. C. The recommended storage for a TEMPORARY tablespace is a multiple of SORT_AREA_SIZE + DB_BLOCK_SIZE. For example, if the sort area size is 100KB and the block size is 4KB, the sort extents should be sized 104KB, 204KB, 304KB, and so on. The disk is sorted only when there is not enough space available in memory. Memory sort size is specified by the SORT_AREA_SIZE parameter. Therefore, when the sorting is done on disk, the minimum area required is as big as the SORT_AREA_SIZE, and one block is added for the overhead. The INITIAL and NEXT storage parameters should be the same for the TEMPORARY tablespace, and PCTINCREASE should be zero. You can achieve these storage settings by creating a locally managed temporary tablespace with uniform extent sizes.

17. D. You can change all the default storage parameters defined for the tablespace using the ALTER TABLESPACE command. Once objects are created, you cannot change their INITIAL and MINEXTENTS values.

18. C. The V$SORT_USAGE view provides the number of EXTENTS and number of BLOCKS used by each sort session. This view provides the username also. It can be joined with V$SESSION or V$SQL to obtain more information on the session or the SQL statement causing the sort.

19. B, D. When you take a tablespace offline with the IMMEDIATE clause, Oracle does not perform a checkpoint and does not make sure that all data files are available. You must perform a media recovery when the tablespace is brought online.

20. B, C, E. The data file names have the format ora_%t_%u.dbf, redo log files have the format ora_%g_%u.log, and control files have the format ora_%u.ctl. %t is the tablespace name and can be a maximum of 8 characters, %u is an 8-character unique string, and %g is the redo log group number.

Segments and Storage Structures

ORACLE9i DBA FUNDAMENTALS I EXAM OBJECTIVES OFFERED IN THIS CHAPTER:

- ✓ Describe the logical structure of segments within the database
- ✓ Describe the segment types and their uses
- ✓ List the keywords that control block space usage
- ✓ Obtain information about storage structures from the data dictionary
- ✓ Describe the purpose of undo data
- ✓ Implement Automatic Undo Management

Exam objectives are subject to change at any time without prior notice and at Oracle's sole discretion. Please visit Oracle's Training and Certification website (`http://www.oracle.com/education/certification/`) for the most current exam objectives listing.

Segments are logical storage units that fit between a tablespace and an extent in the logical storage hierarchy. A segment has one or more extents, and it belongs to a tablespace. This chapter covers in detail segments, extents, and blocks. This chapter also discusses the types of segments and the type of information stored in these segments.

Oracle Objective | **Describe the logical structure of segments within the database**

Data Blocks

A *data block* is the smallest logical unit of storage in Oracle. You define the block size with the `DB_BLOCK_SIZE` initialization parameter when you create the database, and the block size cannot be changed. The block size is a multiple of the operating system block size and is the unit of I/O used in the database. The format of the data block is the same, whether it is used to store a table, index, or cluster. A data block consists of the following:

Common and variable header The header portion contains information about the type of block and block address. The block type can be data, index, or undo. The common block header can take 24 bytes, and the variable (transaction) header occupies (24 × `INITRANS`) bytes. By default, the value of `INITRANS` for tables is 1 and for indexes is 2.

Table directory This portion of the block has information about tables that have rows in this block. The table directory occupies 4 bytes.

Row directory Contains information (such as the row address) about the actual rows in the block. The space allocated for the row directory is not reclaimed, even if you delete all rows in the block. The space is reused when new rows are added to the block. The row directory occupies (4 × number of rows) bytes.

Row data The actual rows are stored in this area.

Free space This space is available for new rows or for extending the existing rows through updates. Deletions and updates may cause fragmentation in the block; this free space is coalesced by the Oracle Server when deemed necessary.

The space used for the common and variable header, table directory, and row directory in a block is collectively known as the *block overhead*. The overhead varies, but mostly it is between 84 and 107 bytes. If more rows are inserted into the block (row directory increases) or a large INITRANS is specified (header increases), this overhead size might be greater.

Block Storage Parameters

Oracle Objective

List the keywords that control block space usage

When you create objects such as tables or indexes, you can specify the block storage options. Choosing proper values for these storage parameters can save you a lot of space and provide better performance. The storage parameters affecting the block are as follows:

PCTFREE and PCTUSED These two space management parameters control the free space available for inserts and updates on the rows in the block. You can specify these parameters when you create an object.

INITRANS and MAXTRANS These two transaction entry parameters control the number of concurrent transactions that can modify or create data in the block. You can specify these parameters when you create an object. Based on these parameters, space is reserved in the block for transaction entries.

FREELIST Each segment has one or more *free lists* that list the available blocks for future inserts. The FREELIST parameter specifies the number of desired free lists for a segment. By default, one free list is allocated for each segment.

PCTFREE and *PCTUSED*

Before discussing these parameters, let's consider two important aspects of storing rows in a block: row chaining and row migration. If the table row length is bigger than a block, or if the table has LONG or LOB columns, it is difficult to fit one row entirely in one block. Oracle stores such rows in more than one block. This situation is unavoidable, and storing such rows in multiple blocks is known as *row chaining*.

In some cases, the row will fit into a block with other rows, but due to an update activity, the row length increases and no free space remains available to accommodate the modified row. Oracle then moves the entire row from its original block to a new block, leaving a pointer in the original block to refer to the new block. This process is known as *row migration*.

Both row migration and row chaining affect the performance of queries, because Oracle has to read more than one block to retrieve the row. You can avoid row migration if you plan the block's free space properly using the PCTFREE and PCTUSED parameters. PCTFREE and PCTUSED are specified in percentages of the data block.

PCTFREE specifies what percentage of the block should be allocated as free space for future updates. If the table can undergo a lot of updates and the updates increase the size of the row, set a higher value for the PCTFREE parameter, so that even if the row length increases due to an update, the rows are not moved out of the block (no row migration). Whenever a new row is added to a block, Oracle determines whether the free space will fall below the PCTFREE threshold. If it does, the block is removed from the free list, and the row is stored in another block.

PCTUSED specifies when the block can be considered for adding new rows. After the block becomes full as determined by the PCTFREE parameter, Oracle considers adding new rows to the block only when the used space falls below the percent value set by PCTUSED. When the used space in a block falls below the PCTUSED threshold, the block is added to the free list.

To understand the usage of the PCTFREE and PCTUSED parameters, consider an example. The table EMP is created with a PCTFREE value of 10 and a PCTUSED value of 40. When you insert rows into the EMP table, Oracle adds rows to a block until it is 90 percent full (including row data and overhead), leaving 10 percent of the block free for future updates. During an update operation, Oracle uses the free space available if the row length increases. Once no free space is available, Oracle moves the row out of the block and provides a pointer to the new location (row migration). If you delete rows from the table (or update the rows such that the row length decreases), more free space will be available in the block. Oracle starts inserting new rows into the block only when the used space falls below PCTUSED, which is 40 percent. Therefore, when the row data and overhead is below 40 percent of the block, new rows are inserted into the block. Such inserts will continue until the block is 90 percent full. When the block has only PCTFREE (or less) percent free space available, it is removed from the free list. The block is added back to the free list only when the used space in the block falls below PCTUSED percent.

The default value of PCTFREE is 10, and the default for PCTUSED is 40. The sum of PCTFREE and PCTUSED cannot be more than 100. If the rows in a table are subject to a lot of updates, and the updates increase the row length, set a higher PCTFREE. If the table has a large number of inserts and deletes, and the updates do not cause the row length to increase, set the PCTFREE low and set the PCTUSED high. A high value for PCTUSED will help to reuse the space freed by deletes faster. If the table row length is larger, or if the table rows are never updated, set the PCTFREE very low so that a row can fit into one block and you fill each block.

You can specify PCTFREE when you create a table, an index, or a cluster, and you can specify PCTUSED while creating tables and clusters, but not indexes.

INITRANS and *MAXTRANS*

These transaction entry settings reserve space for transactions in the block. Base these parameters on the maximum number of transactions that can touch a block at any given point in time. *INITRANS* reserves space in the block header for DML transaction entries. If you do not specify INITRANS, Oracle defaults the value to 1 for table data blocks and to 2 for index blocks and cluster blocks.

When multiple transactions access the data block, space is allocated in the block header for each transaction. When no pre-allocated space is available, Oracle allocates space from the free area of the block for the transaction entry. The space allocated from the free space thus becomes part of the block overhead and is never released. The *MAXTRANS* parameter limits the number of transaction entries that can concurrently use data in a data block. Therefore, you can limit the amount of free space that can be allocated for transaction entries in a data block by using MAXTRANS. The default value is operating system specific, and the maximum value you can specify is 255.

Base the values for INITRANS and MAXTRANS on the number of transactions that can simultaneously update/insert/delete the rows in a block. If the row length is large or the number of users accessing the table is low, set INITRANS to a low value. Some tables, such as an application's control tables, are accessed frequently by the users, and chances are high that more than one user can access a block simultaneously to update, insert, or delete. If a sufficient amount of transaction entry space is not reserved, Oracle dynamically allocates transaction entry space from the free space available in the block (this is an expensive operation, and the space allocated in this way cannot be reclaimed). When you set MAXTRANS, Oracle limits the number of transaction entries in a block.

You can specify INITRANS and MAXTRANS when you create a table, an index, or a cluster. Set a higher INITRANS value for tables and indexes that are queried most often by the application, such as application control tables.

Automatic Space Management

If a segment will not contain LOBs (Large OBject types containing large blocks of unstructured data, such as Binary Large OBjects [BLOBs] or Character Large OBjects [CLOBs]), there is an alternative to using PCTUSED and FREELISTS to manage data blocks: *Automatic Space Management*. In short, bitmaps are used instead of free lists to manage free and used space.

The advantages are many. You no longer have to guess at optimal values for PCTUSED and FREELISTS. The space is managed more efficiently, and the performance is greatly enhanced for many INSERT statements occurring concurrently on the same segment.

Other than the restrictions on segments containing LOBs, the only other major restriction is on the tablespace that contains the segments that will be automatically managed—the tablespace has to be locally managed, and the automatic management is defined for the entire tablespace and can't be enabled for individual segments.

The following is an example of a statement that creates a tablespace with automatic segment space management:

```
CREATE TABLESPACE APPL_DATA2
   DATAFILE '/disk4/oradata/DB01/appl_data02.dbf'
   SIZE 200M
   EXTENT MANAGEMENT LOCAL UNIFORM SIZE 512K
   SEGMENT SPACE MANAGEMENT AUTO;
```

Real World Scenario

Limitations of OEM

You are a busy Oracle DBA, and you like to use OEM for most of your day-to-day tasks. You want to make your life even easier by creating new tablespaces whose segment space is automatically managed, so you bring up OEM and browse the tablespaces. Right-clicking Tablespaces, you select Create…, and you find out that there is no option for setting segment space management!

In a mild panic, you dig through your documentation and manually construct a `CREATE TABLESPACE` statement to create the tablespace with the desired characteristics.

OEM doesn't always cover every possible option when creating database objects, so it's important to keep your command-line SQL*Plus skills sharp. In this scenario, you could set all the basic options for the creation of the tablespace and then click the Show SQL button to at least give you the basics for running the command manually. In fact, for any database operation, it's a good idea to click the Show SQL button to make sure you know what's going on behind the scenes, as well as stay on top of your SQL DDL syntax.

Extents

An *extent* is a logical storage unit that is made up of contiguous data blocks. An extent is first allocated when a segment is created, and subsequent extents are allocated when all the blocks in the segment are full. Oracle can manage the extent's allocated and free information through the data dictionary or locally by using the bitmaps on data files. Dictionary-managed tablespaces and locally managed tablespaces are discussed in Chapter 6, "Logical and Physical Database Structures."

You have also seen the parameters that control the size of the extents. To refresh your memory, these are as follows:

INITIAL The first extent size for a segment, allocated when the segment (object) is first created.

NEXT The second extent size for a segment.

PCTINCREASE The size by which the extents should be increased based on the previously allocated extent size. This parameter affects the third extent onward in a segment.

MINEXTENTS The minimum number of extents to be allocated when creating the segment.

MAXEXTENTS The maximum number of extents that are allowed in a segment. You can set no extent limits by specifying UNLIMITED.

When the extents are managed locally, the storage parameters do not affect the size of the extents. For locally managed tablespaces, you can either have uniform extent sizes or variable extent sizes managed completely by Oracle.

Once an object (such as a table or an index) is created, its INITIAL and MINEXTENTS values cannot be changed. Changes to NEXT and PCTINCREASE take effect when the next extent is allocated for the object—already allocated extent sizes are not changed.

The header block of each segment contains a directory of the extents in that segment.

Allocating Extents

Oracle allocates an extent when an object is first created or when all the blocks in the segment are full. For example, when you create a table, contiguous blocks specified by INITIAL are allocated for the table. If the MINEXTENTS value is more than 1, that many extents are allocated at the time of creation. Even though the table has no data, space is allocated for the table. When all the blocks allocated for the table are completely filled, Oracle allocates another extent. The size of this extent depends on the values of the NEXT and PCTINCREASE parameters.

New extents in locally managed tablespaces are allocated by searching the data file's bitmap for the amount of contiguous free space required. Oracle looks at each file's bitmap to find contiguous free space; Oracle returns an error if none of the files have enough free space.

In dictionary-managed tablespaces, Oracle allocates extents based on the following rules:

1. If the extent requested is more than 5 data blocks, Oracle adds one more block to reduce internal fragmentation. For example, if the number of blocks requested is 24, Oracle adds one more block and searches the tablespace where the segment belongs for a free extent with 25 blocks.

2. If an exact match fails, Oracle searches the contiguous free blocks again for a free extent larger than the required value. When it finds one, Oracle allocates the entire extent for the segment if the number of blocks above the required size is less than or equal to 5 blocks. Using our example, if the free contiguous blocks found is 28 blocks, Oracle allocates 28 blocks to the segment to eliminate fragmentation. If the number of blocks above the required size is more than 5 blocks, Oracle breaks the free extent into two and allocates the required space for the segment. The rest of the contiguous blocks are added to the free list. In our example, Oracle allocates 25 blocks to the segment as an extent and 15 blocks are marked as a free extent if the free extent size is 40 blocks.

3. If step 2 fails, Oracle coalesces the free space in the tablespace and repeats step 2.

4. If step 3 fails, Oracle checks to see if the files are defined as auto-extensible; if so, Oracle tries to extend the file and repeats step 2. If Oracle cannot extend the file or cannot allocate an extent even after resizing the data file to its maximum size specified, Oracle issues an error and does not allocate an extent to the segment.

Extents are normally de-allocated when you drop an object. To free up the extents allocated to a table or a cluster, use the TRUNCATE <NAME> DROP STORAGE command to remove all rows. The TRUNCATE command can be used to remove all rows from a table or cluster. The DROP STORAGE clause is the default, and it removes all the extents higher than MINEXTENTS after removing all rows. The REUSE STORAGE clause does not de-allocate extents; it just removes all the rows from the table/cluster. Rows deleted using the TRUNCATE command cannot be rolled back. Deleting rows by using DELETE does not free up the extents. You can also manually de-allocate extents by using the command ALTER [TABLE/INDEX/CLUSTER] *<NAME> DEALLOCATE UNUSED* (discussed in Chapter 8, "Managing Tables, Indexes, and Constraints").

Querying Extent Information

You can query extent information from the data dictionary by using the following views.

Oracle Objective

Obtain information about storage structures from the data dictionary

DBA_EXTENTS

This view lists the extents allocated in the database for all segments. It shows the size, segment name, and tablespace name where it resides.

```
SQL>   select owner, segment_type, tablespace_name, file_id, bytes
  2*   from dba_extents where owner='HR'
  3  ;

OWNER   SEGMENT_TYPE   TABLESPACE_NAME   FILE_ID   BYTES
------- -------------- ----------------- -------- --------
HR      TABLE          EXAMPLE                 5    65536
HR      TABLE          EXAMPLE                 5    65536
HR      TABLE          EXAMPLE                 5    65536
HR      TABLE          EXAMPLE                 5    65536
HR      TABLE          EXAMPLE                 5    65536
HR      TABLE          EXAMPLE                 5    65536
HR      INDEX          EXAMPLE                 5    65536
HR      INDEX          EXAMPLE                 5    65536
HR      INDEX          EXAMPLE                 5    65536
```

DBA_FREE_SPACE

This view lists information about the free extents in a tablespace.

```
SQL>  select tablespace_name, max(bytes) largest,
  2   min(bytes) smallest, count(*) ext_count
  3  from dba_free_space
  4* group by tablespace_name
SQL> /

TABLESPACE_NAME           LARGEST    SMALLEST  EXT_COUNT
----------------- ------------ ----------- ----------
CWMLITE                14680064    14680064          1
DRSYS                  12845056    12845056          1
EXAMPLE                  196608      196608          1
INDX                   26148864    26148864          1
OEM_REPOSITORY         36634624    36634624          1
SYSTEM                 85872640    85872640          1
TOOLS                   4390912     4390912          1
UNDOTBS               207880192       65536          8
USERS                  26083328    26083328          1
```

All free space in the operating system files must be represented in either DBA_FREE_SPACE or DBA_EXTENTS.

Segments

A *segment* is a logical storage unit that is made up of one or more extents. Every object in the database that requires space to store data is allocated a segment. The size of the segment is the total of the size of all extents in that segment. When you create a table, an index, a cluster, or a materialized view (snapshot), a segment is allocated for the object (for partitioned tables and indexes, a segment is allocated for each partition). A segment can belong to only one tablespace, but may spread across multiple data files belonging to the tablespace.

Oracle Objective **Describe the segment types and their uses**

There are many types of segments:

Table This is the most common type of segment in a database. All data in a table segment must reside in the same tablespace, unlike partitioned tables. Tables that have LOB or VARRAY columns do not store these columns in the same segment.

Table Partition To support large enterprise databases that need high levels of availability and performance, a table may be split into partitions, stored in separate tablespaces. The partitions may be accessed by a distinct key range (range partitioning), by a hashing algorithm (hash partitioning), or by both. Each part of the table that resides in a different tablespace is considered a segment.

Cluster As the name implies, a cluster segment is a single segment that is composed of one or more tables. The data is stored in key order, and all tables within the cluster have the same storage characteristics. Typically, tables stored in a cluster are joined; for example, an order table and a line-item table.

Nested Table If a table has columns that are tables themselves (nested tables), each column is stored in its own segment. Each segment may have its own storage parameters.

Index All index entries for a table index are stored in the same segment.

Index Organized Table (IOT) An IOT segment is essentially a table and an index combined into a single segment, stored in index order. Access to an IOT is very fast because a query accessing a particular row need only traverse one segment to find the results.

Index Partition An index partition segment is similar to a table partition segment in that the index segments are usually stored in separate tablespaces to enhance availability, performance, and scalability.

Temporary In a nutshell, *temporary segments* hold overflow information from sort operations that don't fit in memory. User-initiated sort operations are usually the result of DML operations such as `CREATE INDEX`, `SELECT ... GROUP BY`, or `SELECT DISTINCT`. These segments are allocated in the temporary tablespace assigned to the user that runs these statements. Since the activity from these operations causes frequent allocation and de-allocation, it is recommended that a separate tablespace be allocated just for temporary segments. Having a separate tablespace prevents fragmentation on the SYSTEM or other application tablespaces. Entries made to the temporary segment blocks are not recorded in the redo log files.

LOB For LOBs in a table that are larger than about 4 KB, space is allocated in a LOB segment, separate from the segment containing the elements of the rest of the table. The only piece of information remaining in the table for a LOB is a pointer to the segment containing the LOB itself.

Undo Transactions that change rows in a table also store information in *undo segments*, specifically, the information that would be needed to restore the row to its original state in case of a rollback or an instance failure. For automatic undo management, all user undo information must reside in an undo tablespace.

Bootstrap A special system segment that is used to initialize the data dictionary upon instance startup. It cannot be queried, needs no maintenance, and is basically transparent to all users and administrators of the database.

Segment Storage Parameters

Storage parameters for segments generally take preference over storage parameters specified at the tablespace or database level. If no segment-level storage parameters are specified, the default tablespace parameters are used; if these do not exist, the database server defaults are used.

Changes to storage parameters at any of these three levels will only affect new extents and will not affect any extents in existing segments.

Querying Segment Information

You can obtain segment information from the data dictionary by using the following views.

DBA_SEGMENTS

This view shows the segments created in the database, their size, tablespace, type, storage parameters, and so on. Notice that the LOB segment types are listed as LOBINDEX for index and LOBSEGMENT for data.

```
SQL> select tablespace_name, segment_type, count(*)
  2    seg_cnt from dba_segments
  3  where owner != 'SYS'
  4  group by tablespace_name, segment_type;

TABLESPACE_NAME    SEGMENT_TYPE          SEG_CNT
------------------ ------------------ ---------
CWMLITE            INDEX                     67
CWMLITE            TABLE                     28
DRSYS              INDEX                     76
DRSYS              LOBINDEX                   2
DRSYS              LOBSEGMENT                 2
DRSYS              TABLE                     43
EXAMPLE            INDEX                    132
EXAMPLE            INDEX PARTITION           84
EXAMPLE            LOBINDEX                  23
EXAMPLE            LOBSEGMENT                23
EXAMPLE            NESTED TABLE               3
EXAMPLE            TABLE                     61
EXAMPLE            TABLE PARTITION           24
SYSTEM             INDEX                    181
SYSTEM             INDEX PARTITION           17
SYSTEM             LOBINDEX                  22
SYSTEM             LOBSEGMENT                22
SYSTEM             TABLE                    150
SYSTEM             TABLE PARTITION           19
TOOLS              INDEX                     63
TOOLS              TABLE                     29
USERS              TABLE                      1
```

V$SORT_SEGMENT

This view contains information about every sort segment in a given instance. The view is updated only when the tablespace is of the TEMPORARY type. It shows the number of active users, sort segment size, extents used, extents not used, and so on.

```
SQL> select tablespace_name, extent_size, current_users,
  2  total_blocks, used_blocks, free_blocks, max_blocks
  3  from v$sort_segment;

TABLESPACE_NAME EXTENT_SIZE CURRENT_USERS TOTAL_BLOCKS USED_BLOCKS FREE_BLOCKS MAX_BLOCKS
--------------- ----------- ------------- ------------ ----------- ----------- ----------
TEMP                      8             0         1552           0        1552       1552
```

Managing Undo Segments

Undo segments record old values of data that were changed by a transaction. Undo segments provide read consistency and the ability to undo changes, as well as assist in crash recovery. Information in an undo segment consists of several entries called undo entries. Before updating or deleting rows, Oracle stores the row as it existed before the operation (known as the before-image data) in an undo segment. An *undo entry* consists of the before-image data along with the block ID and data file number. The undo entries that belong to a transaction are all linked together, so that the transaction can be rolled back, if necessary. The data block header is also updated with the undo segment information to identify where to find the undo information. This information provides a read-consistent view of the data at a given point in time. The changes to data in a serial transaction are stored in a single undo segment. When the transaction is complete (either by a COMMIT or by a ROLLBACK), Oracle finds a new undo segment for the session.

Oracle Objective

Describe the purpose of undo data

When a user performs an update or a delete operation, the before-image data is saved in the undo segments; then the blocks corresponding to the data are modified. For inserts, the undo entries include the ROWID of the row inserted, because to undo an insert operation, the rows inserted must be deleted. If the transaction modifies an index, the old index keys also will be stored in the undo segments. The undo segments are freed when the transaction ends, but the undo information is not destroyed immediately. The undo segments are used to provide a read-consistent view of relevant data for queries in other sessions that started before the transaction is committed.

Oracle records changes to the original data block and undo segment block in the redo log. This second recording of the undo information is important for transactions that are not yet committed or rolled back at the time of a system crash. If a system crash occurs, Oracle automatically restores the undo segment information, including the undo entries for active transactions, as part of instance or media recovery. Once the recovery is complete, Oracle performs the actual rollbacks of transactions that had been neither committed nor rolled back at the time of the system crash.

Creating Undo Segments

When you create the database, Oracle creates the SYSTEM undo segment in the SYSTEM tablespace. Every database should have an *undo tablespace* for non-SYSTEM undo segments, other than the SYSTEM undo segment, if the database contains more than one tablespace. Oracle uses the SYSTEM undo segment primarily for transactions involving objects in the SYSTEM tablespace. For changes involving objects in the non-SYSTEM tablespace, use undo segments in an undo tablespace.

Oracle Objective

Implement Automatic Undo Management

Although multiple undo tablespaces can exist in a database, only one can be active at any given time. The currently active undo tablespace must be large enough to handle the workload for all concurrent transactions.

Two initialization parameters control the use of automatic undo management in the database: UNDO_MANAGEMENT and UNDO_TABLESPACE. The parameter UNDO_MANAGEMENT can be set to AUTO or MANUAL and cannot be dynamically altered after the database is started.

The parameter UNDO_TABLESPACE specifies the tablespace to be used for undo segments, and unlike the UNDO_MANAGEMENT parameter, it can be changed dynamically while the instance is running. If no undo tablespace is specified at system startup, the Oracle Server will automatically create one called SYS_UNDOTBS, with a system-assigned data file name in the directory $ORACLE_HOME/dbs.

Maintaining Undo Segments

After you create the database, you can create additional undo tablespaces, as in the following example:

```
CREATE UNDO TABLESPACE SYS_UNDOTBS_NIGHT
     DATAFILE 'undo2.dbf' SIZE 15M;
```

Figure 7.1 shows how to create an undo tablespace using OEM.

FIGURE 7.1 Using OEM to create an undo tablespace

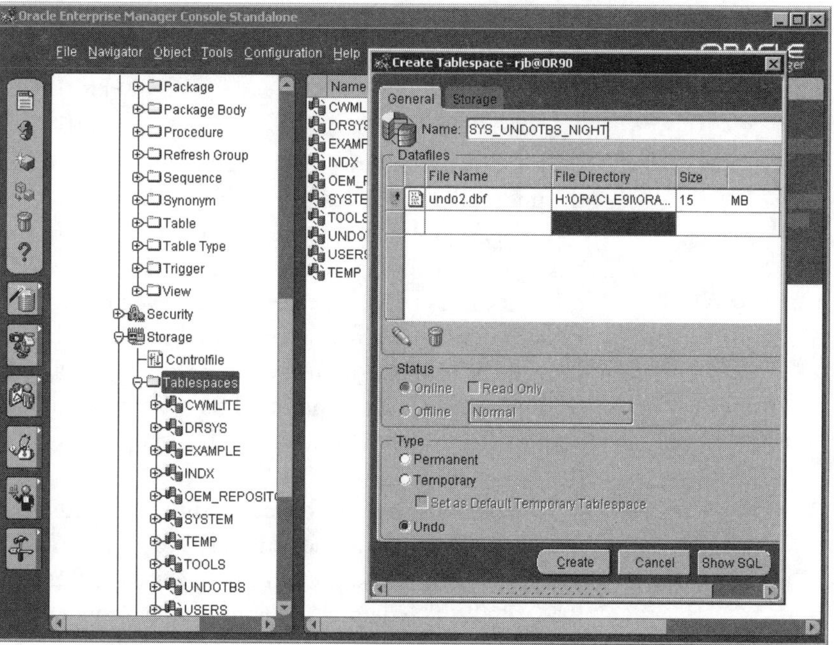

Most of the other clauses that apply to regular tablespaces also apply to undo tablespaces, such as ADD DATAFILE, ONLINE/OFFLINE, BEGIN BACKUP, END BACKUP, and RENAME.

Switching undo tablespaces is also very straightforward:

```
ALTER SYSTEM SET UNDO_TABLESPACE = SYS_UNDOTBS_NIGHT;
```

An undo tablespace can be dropped like any other tablespace, but not until all transactions within the tablespace are complete. First, specify a new undo tablespace as in the previous example. To see if the tablespace has any pending transactions, run the following query:

```
SQL> select rn.name, rs.status
       from v$rollname rn, v$rollstat rs
       where rn.name in
          (select segment_name from dba_segments
           where tablespace_name = 'UNDOTBS')
       and rn.usn = rs.usn
       ;

NAME                           STATUS
------------------------------ ---------------
_SYSSMU2$                      PENDING OFFLINE
_SYSSMU8$                      PENDING OFFLINE
```

If lines with a status of PENDING OFFLINE are returned from this query, the undo tablespace cannot be dropped.

An undo tablespace may need to be enlarged to support long-running queries against the database that need *consistent reads*. These queries need the original values of the rows of a table, even though another transaction may have changed and already committed rows in the same table; undo segments provide the mechanism to save the original values of the rows and provide this read-consistency. The amount of time that undo data is retained for consistent reads is controlled with the initialization parameter UNDO_RETENTION, specified in seconds.

To control system resources and prevent individual users or groups of users from using too much undo space, you can use Resource Manager to place limits on a resource group. Specify the Resource Manager parameter UNDO_POOL. The default value for this parameter is UNLIMITED. The following is an example of specifying UNDO_POOL:

```
EXEC DBMS_RESOURCE_MANAGER.CREATE_PLAN_DIRECTIVE
```

```
(PLAN => 'QPS',
 GROUP_OR_SUBPLAN => 'DirectMarketing',
 COMMENT => 'Restrict undo space usage',
 SWITCH_TIME => 3, SWITCH_ESTIMATE => TRUE,
 CPU_P1 => 60, UNDO_POOL => 450);
```

In this example, the resource group `DirectMarketing` under the resource plan `QPS` will be limited to a total of 450KB of undo information.

Snapshot Too Old Error

An `ORA-1555 snapshot too old` error occurs when Oracle cannot produce a read-consistent view of the data. This error usually happens when a transaction commits after a long-running query has started, and the undo information is overwritten or the undo extents are de-allocated. Here's an example. User `SCOTT` has updated the `EMP` table and has not committed the changes. The old values of the rows updated by `SCOTT` are written to the undo segment. When user `JAKE` queries the `EMP` table, Oracle uses the undo segment to produce a read-consistent view of the table. If `JAKE` initiated a long query, Oracle fetches the blocks in multiple iterations. User `SCOTT` can commit his transaction, and the undo segment is marked committed. If another transaction overwrites the same undo segment, `JAKE`'s transaction will not be able to get the view of the `EMP` table when the transaction started. This produces a *snapshot too old* error. You can reduce the chances of generating a `Snapshot too old` error by estimating the amount of undo activity during peak usage periods and adjusting the size of the undo tablespace.

Querying Undo Information

You can query the following dictionary views to obtain information about the undo segments and transactions.

DBA_ROLLBACK_SEGS

This view provides information about all undo segments (online or offline), their status, tablespace name, sizes, and so on. Note that some of the following code has been reformatted to fit on our page. The table will appear as a single, long table on your screen.

```
SQL>  select segment_name, owner, tablespace_name, initial_extent ini,
  2     next_extent next, min_extents min, status stat
  3* from dba_rollback_segs
SQL> /
```

```
SEGMENT_NAME  OWNER   TABLESPACE_NAME     INI    NEXT  MIN  STAT
------------  ------  ---------------  -------  -----  ---  -------
SYSTEM        SYS     SYSTEM             53248  53248    2  ONLINE
_SYSSMU1$     PUBLIC  UNDOTBS           131072           2  ONLINE
_SYSSMU2$     PUBLIC  UNDOTBS           131072           2  ONLINE
_SYSSMU3$     PUBLIC  UNDOTBS           131072           2  ONLINE
_SYSSMU4$     PUBLIC  UNDOTBS           131072           2  OFFLINE
```

V$ROLLNAME

This view lists all online undo segments. The USN is the undo segment number, which can be used to join with the V$ROLLSTAT view.

```
SQL> select * from v$rollname;

       USN  NAME
----------  -------------------------
         0  SYSTEM
         1  _SYSSMU1$
         2  _SYSSMU2$
         3  _SYSSMU3$
         4  _SYSSMU4$
```

V$ROLLSTAT

This view lists the undo statistics. You can join this view with the V$ROLLNAME view to get the undo segment name. The view shows the segment size, OPTIMAL value, number of shrinks since instance start-up, number of active transactions, extents, status, and so on.

```
SQL> select * from v$rollstat
  2  where usn = 1

USN  EXTENTS   RSSIZE  WRITES  XACTS  GETS  WAITS  OPTSIZE  HWMSIZE
---  -------  -------  ------  -----  ----  -----  -------  -------
  1        8  4186112  152556      0  1008      0  4194304  4186112

SHRINKS  WRAPS  EXTENDS  AVESHRINK  AVEACTIVE  STATUS  CUREXT  CURBLK
-------  -----  -------  ---------  ---------  ------  ------  ------
      0      0        0          0          0  ONLINE       3      40
```

V$UNDOSTAT

This view collects 10-minute snapshots that reflect the performance of the undo tablespace to aid in adjusting the undo tablespace size to support changing system load requirements.

```
SQL>  select begin_time, end_time, undoblks, maxquerylen
  2*  from v$undostat
SQL> /

BEGIN_TIME         END_TIME           UNDOBLKS MAXQUERYLEN
------------------ ------------------ -------- -----------
19-OCT-01  8:05:01 19-OCT-01  8:15:01        1           0
19-OCT-01  7:55:01 19-OCT-01  8:05:01        1           0
19-OCT-01  7:45:01 19-OCT-01  7:55:01        0           0
19-OCT-01  7:35:01 19-OCT-01  7:45:01        0           2
19-OCT-01  7:25:01 19-OCT-01  7:35:01        0           1
19-OCT-01  7:15:01 19-OCT-01  7:25:01       15           1
```

Summary

This chapter discussed the logical storage structures in detail. A data block is the smallest logical storage unit in Oracle. The data block overhead is the space used to store the block information and row information. The overhead consists of a common and variable header, a table directory, and a row directory. The rows are stored in the row data area, and the free space is the space available to accommodate new rows or the space available for the existing rows to expand.

The free space can be managed by two parameters: PCTFREE and PCTUSED. PCTFREE determines the amount of free space that should be maintained in a block for future row expansion due to updates. When the used space in a block reaches the PCTFREE threshold, the block is removed from the free list. The block is added back to the free list when the used space drops below PCTUSED. The INITRANS and MAXTRANS parameters specify the concurrent transactions that can access a block. INITRANS reserves transaction space for the specified number of transactions, and MAXTRANS specifies the maximum number of concurrent transactions for the block.

Extents are logical storage units consisting of contiguous blocks. Sizes of extents are specified by the INITIAL, NEXT, and PCTINCREASE parameters.

The minimum value of INITIAL should be two blocks. A segment consists of one or more extents, and there are four types of segments. *Data segments* store the table rows. *Index segments* store index keys. (The data and index segments used to store LOB or VARRAY data types are known as LOB segment and LOB index segments, respectively.) Temporary segments are used for sort operations, and undo segments are used to store undo information.

When the database is created, Oracle creates a SYSTEM undo segment. You should create an undo tablespace for the non-system undo segments. Undo tablespaces are similar to other tablespaces in that they can be modified, added, dropped, backed-up, and switched. You can control the amount of undo space used by a user or consumer group with the Resource Manager directive UNDO_POOL.

DBA_EXTENTS and DBA_SEGMENTS are views that can be queried to get information on extents and segments. Undo segment information can be queried from the DBA_ROLLBACK_SEGS, V$ROLLNAME, V$ROLLSTAT, and V$UNDOSTAT views.

Exam Essentials

Understand what a segment is and how it fits into the hierarchy of logical database objects. Enumerate the different types of segments in the database, and explain how they are used to enhance the functionality and availability of the database.

Describe how the storage clause is applied to different database objects. Know when to specify storage parameters and how storage parameters are determined if they are omitted at segment creation.

List the components of a database block and their attributes. Describe the purpose of each database block component and explain how each of the storage parameters changes the characteristics of each component.

Understand the features and benefits of automatic segment space management. Describe the benefits of automatic segment space management over manual space configuration. Be able to create a tablespace that is managed automatically. Describe how the server process allocates and frees blocks, and describe the mechanism used for block management.

Enumerate the key data dictionary views used to manage segment and extents. Be able to retrieve the amount of free and used space in the database.

Understand the purpose and structure of undo data. Define undo data and explain how it aids in rollback and instance recovery. Describe the structure of an undo segment and how data is written to and read from an undo segment.

Differentiate between SYSTEM and non-SYSTEM undo segments. Identify the locations where these two types of segments are stored, and discuss which Oracle processes use them.

Identify initialization parameters used for undo management. List the initialization parameters used for undo management and the possible values, and explain when these parameters can be changed.

Be able to create and maintain undo segments. Understand when an undo tablespace can be created and how the server can automatically create an undo tablespace. Identify the valid operations to an undo tablespace, and understand the scenarios under which switching undo tablespaces is advantageous.

Know how to monitor undo tablespace usage. Identify the views used to extract undo segment usage for the purpose of optimizing the size of the undo tablespace. Be able to restrict the amount of undo space used by a user or group.

Key Terms

Before you take the exam, make sure you're familiar with the following terms:

Automatic Space Management	PCTUSED
consistent reads	row chaining
data block	row migration
data segments	segment
free lists	snapshot too old
Index segments	temporary segments
INITRANS	undo entry
MAXTRANS	undo segments
PCTFREE	undo tablespace

Review Questions

1. Place the following logical storage structures in order—from the smallest logical storage unit to the largest.

   A. Segment

   B. Block

   C. Tablespace

   D. Extent

2. When a table is updated, where is the before-image information (which can be used for undoing the changes) stored?

   A. Temporary segment

   B. Redo log buffer

   C. Undo buffer

   D. Undo segment

3. Which parameter specifies the number of transaction slots in a data block?

   A. `MAXTRANS`

   B. `INITRANS`

   C. `PCTFREE`

   D. `PCTUSED`

4. Select the statement that is not true regarding undo tablespaces.

   A. Undo tablespaces will not be created if they are not specified in the `CREATE DATABASE` statement.

   B. Two undo tablespaces may be active if a new undo tablespace was specified and there are pending transactions on the old one.

   C. You can switch from one undo tablespace to another.

   D. `UNDO_MANAGEMENT` cannot be changed dynamically while the instance is running.

5. Which of the following database objects consists of more than one segment?

A. Nested Table

B. Partitioned table

C. Index Partition

D. Undo segment

E. None of the above

6. Which of the following segment allocation parameters is ignored when automatic segment space management is in effect for a tablespace?

A. `FREELISTS`

B. `PCTFREE`

C. `INITRANS`

D. `MAXTRANS`

7. Which data dictionary view would you query to see the free extents in a tablespace?

A. `DBA_TABLESPACES`

B. `DBA_FREE_SPACE`

C. `DBA_EXTENTS`

D. `DBA_SEGMENTS`

8. Which two data dictionary views can account for the total amount of space in a data file?

A. `DBA_FREE_SEGMENTS`

B. `DBA_FREE_SPACE`

C. `DBA_SEGMENTS`

D. `DBA_EXTENTS`

9. Which portion of the data block stores information about the table having rows in this block?

   A. Common and variable header

   B. Row directory

   C. Table directory

   D. Row data

10. When does Oracle stop adding rows to a block?

    A. When free space reaches the PCTFREE threshold

    B. When row data reaches the PCTFREE threshold

    C. When free space drops below the PCTUSED threshold

    D. When row data drops below the PCTUSED threshold

11. What main restriction is placed on tablespaces defined with automatic segment space management?

    A. The tablespace cannot contain nested tables.

    B. The tablespace cannot be transportable.

    C. The tablespace cannot contain LOBs.

    D. The bootstrap segment cannot reside in a tablespace that has automatic segment space management enabled.

12. Which dynamic performance view can help you adjust the size of an undo tablespace?

    A. V$UNDOSTAT

    B. V$ROLLSTAT

    C. V$SESSION

    D. V$ROLLNAME

13. What is the default value of PCTFREE?

A. 40

B. 0

C. 100

D. 10

14. Which data dictionary view can you query to see the OPTIMAL value for a rollback segment?

A. DBA_ROLLBACK_SEGS

B. V$ROLLSTAT

C. DBA_SEGMENTS

D. V$ROLLNAME

15. What is row migration?

A. A single row spread across multiple blocks

B. Moving a table from one tablespace to another

C. Storing a row in a different block when there is not enough room in the current block for the row to expand

D. Deleting a row and adding it back to the same table

16. What can cause the `Snapshot too old` error?

A. Smaller rollback extents

B. Higher MAXEXTENTS value

C. Larger rollback extents

D. Higher OPTIMAL value

17. The sum of the values PCTFREE and PCTUSED cannot exceed which of the following:

    A. 255

    B. DB_BLOCK_SIZE

    C. The maximum is operating system dependent.

    D. 100

18. Which of the following statements may require a temporary segment?

    A. CREATE TABLE

    B. CREATE INDEX

    C. UPDATE

    D. CREATE TABLESPACE

19. How does Oracle determine the extent sizes for a temporary segment?

    A. From the initialization parameters

    B. From the tables involved in the sort operation

    C. Using the default storage parameters for the tablespace

    D. The database block size

20. Fill in the blank: The parameter MAXTRANS specifies the maximum number of concurrent transactions per _________.

    A. Table

    B. Segment

    C. Extent

    D. Block

Answers to Review Questions

1. B, D, A, and C. A data block is the smallest logical storage unit in Oracle. An extent is a group of contiguous blocks. A segment consists of one or more extents. A segment can belong to only one tablespace. A tablespace can have many segments.

2. D. Before any DML operation, the undo information (before-image of data) is stored in the undo segments. This information is used to undo the changes and to provide a read-consistent view of the data.

3. B. INITRANS specifies the number of transaction slots in a data block. Oracle uses a transaction slot when the data block is being modified. INITRANS reserves space for the transactions in the block. MAXTRANS specifies the maximum number of concurrent transactions allowed in the block. The default for a block in a data segment is 1, and the default for the block in an index segment is 2.

4. A. If a specific undo tablespace is not defined in the CREATE DATABASE statement, Oracle automatically creates one with the name SYS_UNDOTBS.

5. B. A partitioned table consists of multiple table partition segments in different tablespaces.

6. A. Enabling automatic segment space management uses bitmaps instead of freelists to manage free space.

7. B. DBA_FREE_SPACE shows the free extents in a tablespace. DBA_EXTENTS shows all the extents that are allocated to a segment.

8. B, D. The sum of the free space in DBA_FREE_SPACE plus the space allocated for extents in DBA_EXTENTS should add up to the total space specified for that tablespace. DBA_FREE_SEGMENTS is not a valid data dictionary view, and DBA_SEGMENTS only contains the number of extents and blocks allocated to each segment.

9. C. The table directory portion of the block stores information about the table having rows in the block. The row directory stores information such as row address and size of the actual rows stored in the row data area.

10. A. The PCTFREE and PCTUSED parameters are used to manage the free space in the block. Oracle inserts rows into a block until the free space falls below the PCTFREE threshold. PCTFREE is the amount of space reserved for future updates. Oracle considers adding more rows to the block only when the free space falls below the PCTUSED threshold.

11. C. Table segments that have LOBs cannot reside in a locally managed tablespace that has automatic segment space management enabled.

12. A. The V$UNDOSTAT view, in conjunction with the value for UNDO_RETENTION and DB_BLOCK_SIZE parameters, can be used to calculate an optimal undo tablespace size when database activity is at its peak.

13. D. The default value of PCTFREE is 10, and the default for PCTUSED is 40.

14. B. You can query the OPTIMAL value from the V$ROLLSTAT view. This view does not show the offline rollback segments.

15. C. Row migration is the movement of a row from one block to a new block. Row migration occurs when a row is updated and its new size cannot fit into the free space of the block; Oracle moves the row to a new block, leaving a pointer in the old block to the new block. You can avoid this problem by either setting a higher PCTFREE value or specifying a larger block size at database creation.

16. A. Smaller rollback extents can cause the Snapshot too old error if there are long-running queries in the database.

17. D. These two numbers are percentages that are defined as the percentage of a given block, and since these areas cannot overlap, the sum cannot be greater than 100 percent.

18. B. Operations that require a sort may need a temporary segment (when the sort operation cannot be completed in the memory area specified by SORT_AREA_SIZE). Queries that use DISTINCT, GROUP BY, ORDER BY, UNION, INTERSECT, or MINUS clauses also need a sort of the result set.

19. C. The default storage parameters for the tablespace determine the extent sizes for temporary segments.

20. D. MAXTRANS specifies the maximum allowed concurrent transactions per block. Oracle needs transaction space for each concurrent transaction in the block's variable header. You can pre-allocate space by specifying INITRANS.

Managing Tables, Indexes, and Constraints

ORACLE9i DBA FUNDAMENTALS I EXAM OBJECTIVES OFFERED IN THIS CHAPTER:

- ✓ Identify the various methods of storing data
- ✓ Describe Oracle datatypes
- ✓ Distinguish between an extended versus a restricted ROWID
- ✓ Describe the structure of a row
- ✓ Create regular and temporary tables
- ✓ Manage storage structures within a table
- ✓ Reorganize, truncate, drop a table
- ✓ Drop a column within a table
- ✓ List different types of indexes and their uses
- ✓ Create various types of indexes
- ✓ Reorganize indexes
- ✓ Drop indexes
- ✓ Get index information from the data dictionary
- ✓ Monitor the usage of an index

- ✓ **Implement data integrity constraints**
- ✓ **Maintain integrity constraints**
- ✓ **Obtain constraint information from the data dictionary**

Exam objectives are subject to change at any time without prior notice and at Oracle's sole discretion. Please visit Oracle's Training and Certification website (`http://www.oracle.com/education/certification`) for the most current exam objectives listing.

The previous chapters have discussed Oracle's architecture: physical and logical structures of the database. Data is stored in Oracle as rows and columns. This chapter covers the options available when creating tables, shows how to quickly retrieve data by using indexes, and discusses how the Oracle database can enforce business rules by using integrity constraints.

Some of the material in this chapter is similar to material in Chapter 7 of Sybex's *OCA/OCP: Introduction to Oracle9i SQL Study Guide*. For more in-depth information about the objectives covered in the Introduction to Oracle9i: SQL exam, see *OCA/OCP: Introduction to Oracle9i SQL Study Guide* by Chip Dawes and Biju Thomas, Sybex 2002.

Storing Data

Oracle Objective

Identify the various methods of storing data

A table is the basic form of data storage in Oracle. You can think of a table as a spreadsheet having column headings and many rows of information. A schema, or a user, in the database owns the table. The table columns have a defined datatype—the data stored in the columns should satisfy the characteristics of the column. You can also define rules for storing data in the columns using integrity constraints. Oracle9i has various types of tables to suit your data storage needs. A table by default means a relational permanent table. The following types of tables are available in Oracle9i to store data.

Relational Simply known as a table, the relational table is the most common method for storing data. These tables are permanent and can be partitioned. When you partition a table, you break it into multiple smaller pieces, which improves performance and makes the table easier to manage. To create a relational table, you use the `CREATE TABLE ... ORGANIZATION HEAP` statement. Since `ORGANIZATION HEAP` is the default, it can be omitted.

Temporary Temporary tables store private data or data that is specific to a session. Other users in the database cannot use these data. Temporary tables are used for temporary data manipulation or for storing intermediary results. To create a temporary table, you use the `CREATE GLOBAL TEMPORARY TABLE` statement.

Index Organized Index Organized Tables (IOTs) store the data in a structured primary key sorted manner. You must define a primary key for each IOT. These tables are similar to relational tables that have a primary key, but they do not use separate storage for the table and primary key as relational tables do. To create an IOT, you use the `CREATE TABLE ... ORGANIZATION INDEX` statement.

External The external table type is new to Oracle9i. As the name indicates, data is stored outside the Oracle database in flat files. External tables are read-only, and no indexes are allowed on external tables. Column names defined in the Oracle database are mapped to the columns in the external file. The default driver used to read external table is SQL*Loader. To create an external table, you use the `CREATE TABLE ... ORGANIZATION EXTERNAL` statement.

Object Object tables are a special kind of tables that support the object-oriented features of the Oracle9i database. In an object table, each row represents an object. We have already discussed in the previous chapters the logical storage structures and parameters. Let's see how these structures can be related to a table. The following sections discuss how to create and manipulate the types of tables in Oracle9i.

Creating Tables

Oracle Objective

Create regular and temporary tables

To create a table, you use the CREATE TABLE command. You can create a table under the username used to connect to the database, or, with proper privileges, you can create a table under another username. A database user can be referred to as a schema or as an owner, when the user owns objects in the database. The simplest form of creating a table is as follows:

```
CREATE TABLE ORDERS (
ORDER_NUM     NUMBER,
ORDER_DATE    DATE,
PRODUCT_CD    VARCHAR2 (10),
QUANTITY      NUMBER (10,3),
STATUS        CHAR);
```

ORDERS is the table name; the columns in the table are specified in parentheses separated by commas. The table is created under the username used to connect to the database; to create the table under another schema, you need to qualify the table with the schema name. For example, if you want to create the ORDERS table as being owned by SCOTT, create the table by using CREATE TABLE SCOTT.ORDERS (   ).

A column name and a datatype identify each column. For certain datatypes, you can specify a maximum width. You can specify any Oracle built-in datatype or user-defined datatype for the column definition. When specifying user-defined datatypes, the user-defined type must exist before creating the table.

Oracle Objective

Describe Oracle datatypes

Oracle9i has three categories of built-in *datatypes*: scalar, collection, and relationship. Collection and relationship datatypes are used for object-relational functionality of Oracle9i. Table 8.1 lists the built-in scalar datatypes in Oracle.

TABLE 8.1 Oracle Built-in Scalar Datatypes

Datatype	Description
CHAR (<*size*> [BYTE | CHAR])	Fixed-length character data with length specified inside parentheses. Data is space padded to fit the column width. You can also include the optional keywords BYTE and CHAR inside parentheses along with size to indicate if the size specified is in bytes or in characters. BYTE is the default. Size defaults to 1 byte if not defined. Maximum is 2000 bytes.
VARCHAR (<*size*> [BYTE | CHAR])	Same as VARCHAR2.
VARCHAR2 (<*size*> [BYTE | CHAR])	Variable-length character data. Maximum allowed length is specified in parentheses. You must specify a size; there is no default value. Maximum is 4000 bytes. Unlike the CHAR datatype, VARCHAR2 columns are not blank padded with trailing spaces if the column value is shorter than its maximum specified length. You can specify the size in bytes or characters; by default the size is in bytes.
NCHAR (<*size*>)	Similar to CHAR, but used to store Unicode character set data. NCHAR datatype is fixed length, maximum size 2000 bytes, and default size 1 character.
NVARCHAR2 (<*size*>)	Same as VARCHAR2; stores Unicode variable length data. The size is specified in characters, and the maximum allowed size is 4000 bytes.
LONG	Stores variable-length character data up to 2GB. Use CLOB or NCLOB datatypes instead. Provided in Oracle9i for backward compatibility. Can have only one LONG column per table.

TABLE 8.1 Oracle Built-in Scalar Datatypes *(continued)*

Datatype	Description
NUMBER (*<precision>*, *<scale>*)	Stores fixed and floating-point numbers. You can optionally specify a precision (total length including decimals) and scale (digits after decimal point). The default is 38 digits of precision, and the valid range is between -1×10^{-130} and $9.999\ 99^{125}$.
DATE	Stores date data. Has century, year, month, date, hour, minute, and seconds internally. Can be displayed in various formats. You can store the dates from January 1, 4712 BC to December 31, 9999 AD. If you specify a date value without the time component, the default time is 12AM (midnight 00:00:00 hrs).
TIMESTAMP [(<precision>)]	TIMESTAMP datatype stores date and time information with fractional seconds precision. The only difference between DATE and TIMESTAMP datatypes is the ability to store fractional seconds up to a precision of 9 digits. The default precision is 6 and can range from 0 to 9.
TIMESTAMP [(<precision>)] WITH TIME ZONE	TIMESTAMP WITH TIME ZONE is similar to the TIMESTAMP datatype, but stores the *time zone displacement.* Displacement is the difference between the local time and the Universal Time Coordinate (UTC), also known as Greenwich Mean Time. The displacement is represented in hours and minutes.
TIMESTAMP [(<precision>)] WITH LOCAL TIME ZONE	TIMESTAMP WITH LOCAL TIME ZONE is similar to the TIMESTAMP datatype, but includes the time zone displacement. TIMESTAMP WITH LOCAL TIME ZONE does not store the displacement information in the database, but stores the time as a normalized form of database time zone. The data is always stored in the database time zone, but when the user retrieves data, it is shown in the users local session time zone.

TABLE 8.1 Oracle Built-in Scalar Datatypes *(continued)*

Datatype	Description
INTERVAL YEAR [(precision)] TO MONTH	Used to represent a period of time as years and months. The precision specifies the precision needed for the year field, and its default is 2. The precision can have values from 0 to 9. This datatype can be used to store the difference between two date time values, in which the only significant portions are the year and month.
INTERVAL DAY [(precision)] TO SECOND	Used to represent a period of time as days, hours, minutes, and seconds. The precision specifies the precision needed for the day field, and its default is 6. The precision can have values from 0 to 9. Larger precision allows the difference between the dates to be larger. This datatype can be used to store the difference between two date time values, with seconds precision.
RAW (*<size>*)	Variable-length datatype used to store unstructured data, without a character set conversion. Provided for backward compatibility. Use BLOB or BFILE instead.
LONG RAW	Same as RAW, can store up to 2GB of binary data. LONG RAW is supported in Oracle9i for backward compatibility; you must use BLOB instead.
BLOB	Stores up to 4GB of unstructured binary data.
CLOB	Stores up to 4GB of character data.
NCLOB	Stores up to 4GB of Unicode character data.
BFILE	Stores unstructured binary data in operating system files outside the database. The external file size can be up to 4GB. Oracle stores only the file pointer in the database; the actual file is in the operating system.

TABLE 8.1 Oracle Built-in Scalar Datatypes *(continued)*

Datatype	Description
ROWID	Stores binary data representing a physical row address of a table's row. Occupies 10 bytes.
UROWID	Stores binary data representing any type of row address: physical, logical, or foreign. Up to 4000 bytes.

Collection types are used to represent more than one element, such as an array. There are two collection datatypes: VARRAY and TABLE. Elements in the VARRAY datatype are ordered and have a maximum limit. Elements in a TABLE datatype (nested table) are not ordered, and there is no upper limit to the number of elements, unless restricted by available resources.

REF is the relationship datatype, which defines a relationship with other objects by using a reference. It actually stores pointers to data stored in different object tables.

Specifying Storage

Oracle Objective

Manage storage structures within a table

If you create a table without specifying the storage parameters and tablespace, the table will be created in the default tablespace of the user, and the storage parameters used will be those of the default specified for the tablespace. It is always better to estimate the size of the table and specify appropriate storage parameters when creating the table. If the table is too large, you might need to consider partitioning (discussed later) or creating the table in a separate tablespace to help manage the table.

Oracle allocates a segment to the table when the table is created. This segment will have the number of extents specified by the storage parameter MINEXTENTS. Oracle allocates new extents to the table as required. Although you can have an unlimited number of extents for a segment, a little planning can improve the performance of the table. The presence of numerous extents affects the operations on the table, such as truncating a table or scanning a full table. A larger number of extents may cause additional I/Os in the data file and therefore may affect performance.

To create the ORDERS table using explicit storage parameters in the USER_DATA tablespace, use the following:

```
CREATE TABLE JAKE.ORDERS (
ORDER_NUM     NUMBER,
ORDER_DATE    DATE,
PRODUCT_CD    VARCHAR2 (10),
QUANTITY      NUMBER (10,3),
STATUS        CHAR)
TABLESPACE USER_DATA
PCTFREE    5
PCTUSED    75
INITRANS   1
MAXTRANS   255
STORAGE   (INITIAL 512K   NEXT 512K   PCTINCREASE 0
           MINEXTENTS 1   MAXEXTENTS 100
           FREELISTS 1    FREELIST GROUPS 1
           BUFFER_POOL KEEP);
```

The table will be owned by JAKE and will be created in the USER_DATA tablespace (JAKE should have appropriate space quota privileges in the tablespace; privileges and space quotas are discussed in Chapter 9, "Managing Users and Security"). None of the storage parameters are mandatory to create a table; Oracle assigns default values if you omit them. Let's discuss the clauses used in the table creation.

The TABLESPACE clause specifies where the table is to be created. If you omit the STORAGE clause or any parameters in the STORAGE clause, the default is taken from the tablespace's default storage (if applicable). If you omit the TABLESPACE clause, the table is created in the default tablespace of the user.

The PCTFREE and PCTUSED clauses are block storage parameters. The PCTFREE clause specifies the amount of free space that should be reserved in each block of the table for future updates. In this example, you specify a low PCTFREE for the ORDERS table, because not many updates to the table increase the row length. PCTUSED specifies when the block should be considered for inserting new rows once the PCTFREE threshold is reached. Here we specified 75, so when the used space falls below 75 (as the result of updates or deletes), new rows will be added to the block.

The INITRANS and MAXTRANS clauses specify the number of concurrent transactions that can update each block of the table. Oracle reserves space in the block header for the INITRANS number of concurrent transactions. For each additional concurrent transaction, Oracle allocates space from the free space—which has an overhead of dynamically allocating transaction entry space. If the block is full, and no space is available, the transaction waits until a transaction entry space is available. MAXTRANS specifies the maximum number of concurrent transactions that can touch a block. This specification prevents unnecessarily allocating transaction space in the block header, because the transaction space allocated is never reclaimed. In most cases, the Oracle defaults of INITRANS 1 and MAXTRANS 255 are sufficient.

The STORAGE clause specifies the extent sizes, free lists, and buffer pool values. In Chapter 6, "Logical and Physical Database Structures," we discussed the INITIAL, NEXT, MINEXTENTS, MAXEXTENTS, and PCTINCREASE parameters. These five parameters control the size of the extents allocated to the table. If the table is created on a locally managed uniform extent tablespace, these storage parameters are ignored.

The FREELIST GROUPS clause specifies the number of free list groups that should be created for the table. The default and minimum value is 1. Each free list group uses one data block (that's why the minimum value for INITIAL is two database blocks) known as the segment header, which contains information about the extents, free blocks, and high-water mark of the table.

The FREELISTS clause specifies the number of lists for each free list group. The default and minimum value is 1. The free list manages the list of blocks that are available to add new rows. A block is removed from the free list if the free space in the block is below PCTFREE. The block remains out of the free list as long as the used space is above PCTUSED. Create more free lists if the volume of inserts to the table is high. An appropriate number would be the number of concurrent transactions performing inserts to the table. Oracle recommends having FREELISTS and INITRANS be the same value. The FREELIST GROUPS parameter is mostly used for parallel server configuration, in which you can specify a group for each instance.

The BUFFER_POOL parameter of the STORAGE clause specifies the area of the database buffer cache to keep the blocks of the table when read from the data file while querying or for update/delete. There are three buffer pools: KEEP, RECYCLE, and DEFAULT. The default value is DEFAULT. Specify KEEP if the table is small and is frequently accessed. The blocks in the KEEP pool are always available in the data buffer cache of SGA (System Global Area), so I/O will be faster. The blocks assigned to the RECYCLE buffer pool are removed from memory as soon as they are not needed. Specify RECYCLE for large tables or tables that are seldom accessed. If you do not specify KEEP or RECYCLE, the blocks are assigned to the DEFAULT pool, where they will be aged out using an LRU algorithm.

If you create the tablespace with the SEGMENT SPACE MANAGEMENT AUTO clause, the parameters PCTUSED, FREELISTS, and FREELIST GROUPS are ignored.

Storing LOB Structures

A table can contain columns of type CLOB, BLOB, or NCLOB. These internal large object (LOB) columns can have storage settings that are different from those of the table, and these settings can be stored in a different tablespace for easy management and performance improvement. The following example specifies storage for a LOB column when creating the table.

```
CREATE TABLE LICENSE_INFO
(DRIVER_ID   VARCHAR2 (20),
 DRIVER_NAME VARCHAR2 (30),
 DOB         DATE,
 PHOTO       BLOB)
TABLESPACE APP_DATA STORAGE (INITIAL 4M NEXT 4M PCTINCREASE 0)
LOB (PHOTO) STORE AS PHOTO_LOB
    (TABLESPACE APP_LARGE_DATA
    DISABLE STORAGE IN ROW
    STORAGE (INITIAL 128M NEXT 128M PCTINCREASE 0)
    CHUNK 4000
    PCTVERSION 20
    NOCACHE LOGGING);
```

The table LICENSE_INFO is created with a BLOB datatype column. The table is stored in the APP_DATA tablespace, and the BLOB column PHOTO is stored in the APP_LARGE_DATA tablespace. Let's look at the various clauses specified for the LOB storage.

The lob segment is given the name of PHOTO_LOB. If a name is not given, Oracle generates a name. You can specify multiple LOB columns in parentheses following the LOB keyword, if they all have the same storage characteristics. In such cases, you cannot specify a name for the LOB segment. For example, if the table has three LOB columns and all have the same characteristics, you may specify the following:

```
LOB (PHOTO, VIDEO, AUDIO) STORE AS
(TABLESPACE APP_LARGE_DATA
 CACHE READS NOLOGGING);
```

The TABLESPACE clause specifies the tablespace where the lob segment(s) should be stored. The tablespace can be managed locally or by the dictionary. If the LOB column is larger than 4000 bytes, data is stored in the LOB segment. Storing data in the LOB segment is known as out of line storage. If the LOB column data is less than 4000 bytes, it is stored inline, along with the other column data of the table. If you omit the TABLESPACE clause, the LOB segment is created in the table's tablespace.

The DISABLE/ENABLE STORAGE IN ROW clause specifies whether LOB data should be stored inline or out of line. ENABLE is the default and stores LOB data along with the other columns if the LOB data is less than 4000 bytes. DISABLE stores the LOB data in the LOB segment regardless of it size. Whether the LOB data is stored inline or out of line, the LOB locator is always stored along with the row.

The STORAGE clause specifies the extent sizes and growth parameters. These parameters are the same, as those you would use with a table.

The CHUNK clause specifies the total number of bytes of data that will be read or written during LOB manipulation. CHUNK must be a multiple of the database block size. If you specify a value other than a multiple of the block size, Oracle uses the next higher value that is a multiple of block size. For example, if you specify 4000 for CHUNK and the database block size is 2048, Oracle will take the value of 4096. The default value for CHUNK is the database block size, and the maximum value is 32KB. The INITIAL and NEXT values specified in the STORAGE clause must be higher than the value for CHUNK.

The PCTVERSION clause specifies the percentage of all used LOB data space that can be occupied by old versions of LOB data pages. Since LOB data changes are not written to the rollback segments, PCTVERSION specifies the percentage of old information that should be kept in the LOB segment for consistent reads. The default is 10, and the percentage can range from 0 through 100.

The CACHE / NOCACHE / CACHE READS clause specifies whether to cache the LOB reads. If the LOB is read and updated frequently, use the CACHE clause. NOCACHE is the default, and it is useful for a LOB that is read infrequently and never updated. CACHE READS caches only the read operation, which is useful for a LOB that is read frequently, but never updated.

The LOGGING / NOLOGGING clause specifies whether redo information should be generated for LOB data. NOLOGGING does not write redo and is useful for faster data loads. You cannot specify CACHE and NOLOGGING together.

Creating a Table from a Query

Oracle Objective — **Create regular and temporary tables**

You can create a table using existing tables or views by specifying a subquery instead of defining the columns. The subquery can refer to more than one table or view. The table is created with the rows returned from the subquery. You can specify new column names for the table, but Oracle derives the datatype and maximum width based on the query result—you cannot specify the datatype with this method. You can specify the storage parameters for the tables created by using the subquery. For example, let's create a new table from the ORDERS table for the orders that are accepted. Notice that the new column names are specified.

```
CREATE TABLE ACCEPTED_ORDERS
  (ORD_NUMBER, ORD_DATE, PRODUCT_CD, QTY)
  TABLESPACE USERS
  PCTFREE 0
  STORAGE (INITIAL 128K NEXT 128K PCTINCREASE 0)
AS
  SELECT ORDER_NUM, ORDER_DATE, PRODUCT_CD, QUANTITY
  FROM   ORDERS
  WHERE  STATUS = 'A';
```

The `CREATE TABLE...AS SELECT...` will not work if the query refers to columns of `LONG` datatype. When you create a table using the subquery, only the `NOT NULL` constraints associated with the columns are copied to the new table. Other constraints and column default definitions are not copied.

Partitioning Tables

When tables are very large, you can manage them better by using partitioning. *Partitioning* is breaking a large table into manageable pieces based on the values in a column (or multiple columns) known as the partition key. If you have a very large table spread across many data files, and one disk fails, you have to recover the entire table. However, if the table is partitioned, you need to recover only that partition. SQL statements can access the required partition(s) rather than reading the entire table. Four partitioning methods are available:

Range You can create a range partition in which the partition key values are in a range—for example, you can partitions a transaction table on the transaction date, and you can create a partition for each month or each quarter. The partition column list can be one or more columns.

Hash Hash partitions are more appropriate when you do not know how much data will be in a range or whether the sizes of the partition vary. Hash partitions use a hash algorithm on the partitioning columns. The number of partitions required should be specified preferably as a power of two (such as 2, 4, 8, 16, and so on).

List If you know all the values that are supposed to be stored in the column and want to create a partition for each value, use the list partition method. You must specify a list of values when defining the partition, and you can group one or more values together. List partitioning gives explicit control over how each row maps to a partition, whereas in range partition a range of values map to a partition. List partitioning is good for managing partitions using discrete values, which may not be possible using range partitioning.

Composite This method uses the range partition method to create partitions and the hash partition method to create subpartitions.

The *logical attributes* for all partitions remain the same (such as column name, datatype, constraints, and so on), but each partition can have its own *physical attributes* (such as tablespace, storage parameters, and so on). Each partition in the partitioned table is allocated a segment. You can place these partitions on different tablespaces, which can help you to balance the I/O by placing the data files appropriately on disk. Also, by having the partitions in different tablespaces, you can make a partition tablespace read-only. You can specify the storage parameters at the table level or for each partition.

Partitioned tables cannot have any columns with LONG or LONG RAW datatypes.

Range-Partitioned Table

To create a range-partitioned table, you specify the PARTITION BY RANGE clause in the CREATE TABLE command. As stated earlier, range partitioning is suitable for tables that have column(s) with a range of values. For example, your transaction table might have the transaction date column, with which you can create a partition for every month or for a quarter. Consider the following example:

```
CREATE TABLE ORDER_TRANSACTION (
 ORD_NUMBER  NUMBER(12),
 ORD_DATE    DATE,
 PROD_ID     VARCHAR2 (15),
 QUANTITY    NUMBER (15,3))
PARTITION BY RANGE (ORD_DATE)
(PARTITION FY2001Q4 VALUES LESS THAN
          (TO_DATE('01012002','MMDDYYYY'))
          TABLESPACE ORD_2001Q4,
 PARTITION FY2002Q1 VALUES LESS THAN
          (TO_DATE('04012002','MMDDYYYY'))
          TABLESPACE ORD_2002Q1 STORAGE (INITIAL 500M NEXT 500M)
          INITRANS 2 PCTFREE 0,
 PARTITION FY2002Q2 VALUES LESS THAN
          (TO_DATE('07012002','MMDDYYYY'))
          TABLESPACE ORD_2002Q2,
 PARTITION FY2002Q3 VALUES LESS THAN
          (TO_DATE('10012002','MMDDYYYY'))
          TABLESPACE ORD_2002Q3 STORAGE (INITIAL 10M NEXT 10M))
STORAGE (INITIAL 200M NEXT 200M PCTINCREASE 0 MAXEXTENTS 4096)
NOLOGGING;
```

This example creates a range-partitioned table named ORDER_TRANSACTION. PARTITION BY RANGE specifies that the table be range partitioned; the partition column is provided in parentheses (separate multiple columns with commas), and the partition specifications are defined. Each partition specification begins with the keyword PARTITION. You can optionally provide a name for the partition. The VALUES LESS THAN clause defines values for the partition columns that should be in the partition. In the example, each partition is created on different tablespaces; partitions FY2001Q4 and FY2002Q2 inherit the storage parameter values from the table definition, whereas FY2002Q1 and FY2002Q3 have the storage parameters explicitly defined. Records with ORD_DATE prior to 01-Jan-2002 will be stored in partition FY2001Q4; since you did not specify a partition for records with ORD_DATE after 31-Sep-2002, Oracle rejects those rows. NULL value is treated greater than all other values. If the partition key can have NULL values or records with a higher ORD_DATE than the highest upper range in the partition specification list, you must create a partition for the upper range. The MAXVALUE parameter specifies that the partition bound is infinite. In this example, an upper-bound partition can be specified as follows:

```
CREATE TABLE ORDER_TRANSACTION (    )
PARTITION BY RANGE (ORD_DATE)
(PARTITION FY1999Q4 VALUES LESS THAN
          (TO_DATE('01012002','MMDDYYYY'))
          TABLESPACE ORD_2001Q4,
 PARTITION FY2999Q4 VALUES LESS THAN (MAXVALUE)
          TABLESPACE ORD_2999Q4 )
STORAGE (INITIAL 200M NEXT 200M PCTINCREASE 0 MAXEXTENTS 4096)
NOLOGGING;
```

Hash-Partitioned Table

You create a hash-partitioned table by specifying the PARTITION BY HASH clause in the CREATE TABLE command. Hash partitioning is suitable for any large table to take advantage of Oracle9i's performance improvements even if you do not have column(s) with a range of values. Hash partitioning is suitable when you do not know how many rows will be in the table. Choose a column with unique values or more distinct values for the partition key.

The following example creates a hash-partitioned table with four partitions. The partitions are created in tablespaces DOC101, DOC102, and DOC103. Since there are four partitions and only three tablespaces listed, Oracle reuses the DOC101 tablespace for the fourth partition. Oracle creates the partition names as SYS_*XXXX*. Physical attributes are specified at the table level only.

```
CREATE TABLE DOCUMENTS1 (
 DOC_NUMBER  NUMBER(12),
 DOC_TYPE    VARCHAR2 (20),
 CONTENTS    VARCHAR2 (600))
PARTITION BY HASH (DOC_NUMBER, DOC_TYPE)
PARTITIONS 4 STORE IN (DOC101, DOC102, DOC103)
STORAGE (INITIAL 64K NEXT 64K PCTINCREASE 0 MAXEXTENTS 4096);
```

The following example creates a hash-partitioned table with named partitions in the tablespaces.

```
CREATE TABLE DOCUMENTS2 (
 DOC_NUMBER  NUMBER(12),
 DOC_TYPE    VARCHAR2 (20),
 CONTENTS    VARCHAR2 (600))
PARTITION BY HASH (DOC_NUMBER, DOC_TYPE)
( PARTITION DOC201 TABLESPACE DOC201,
  PARTITION DOC202 TABLESPACE DOC202,
  PARTITION DOC203 TABLESPACE DOC203,
  PARTITION DOC204 TABLESPACE DOC204 )
STORAGE (INITIAL 64K NEXT 64K PCTINCREASE 0 MAXEXTENTS 4096);
```

List-Partitioned Table

To create a list-partitioned table, you specify the `PARTITION BY LIST` clause in the `CREATE TABLE` command. List partitioning gives explicit control over the rows that are stored in each partition. You can specify `NULL` as a valid list value. If you insert a row that has a partition column value not defined in the list, Oracle rejects the row. You can specify only one column name as the partition key. The following example creates a list-partitioned table.

```
CREATE TABLE POPULATION_STATS
(STATE  VARCHAR2 (2),
 COUNTY VARCHAR2 (30),
 CITY   VARCHAR2 (30),
 MEN    NUMBER,
 WOMEN  NUMBER,
 BCHILD NUMBER,
 GCHILD NUMBER)
```

```
PARTITION BY LIST (STATE)
(PARTITION SC VALUES ('TX','LA','OK') TABLESPACE SC_DATA,
 PARTITION SW VALUES ('NM','AZ') TABLESPACE SW_DATA,
 PARTITION SE VALUES ('AR','MS','AL') TABLESPACE SE_DATA);
```

Composite-Partitioned Table

Composite partitions have range partitions and hash subpartitions. Only subpartitions are physically created on the disk (tablespace); partitions are logical representations only. Composite partitioning gives the flexibility of range and hash for tables with a smaller range of values.

In the following example, the table is range partitioned on the MAKE_YEAR column; each partition is subdivided based on the MODEL into 4 subpartitions on 4 tablespaces. Each tablespace will have one subpartition from each partition, that is, 3 subpartitions per tablespace, thereby having 12 subpartitions.

```
CREATE TABLE CARS (
  MAKE_YEAR  NUMBER(4),
  MODEL      VARCHAR2 (30),
  MANUFACTR  VARCHAR2 (50),
  QUANTITY   NUMBER)
  PARTITION BY RANGE (MAKE_YEAR)
  SUBPARTITION BY HASH (MODEL) SUBPARTITIONS 4
  STORE IN(TSMK1, TSMK2, TSMK3, TSMK4)
   ( PARTITION M2001 VALUES LESS THAN (2002),
     PARTITION M2002 VALUES LESS THAN (2003),
     PARTITION M9999 VALUES LESS THAN (MAXVALUE))
STORAGE (INITIAL 64K NEXT 64K PCTINCREASE 0 MAXEXTENTS 4096);
```

The following example shows how to name the subpartitions and store each subpartition in a different tablespace. Subpartitions for partition M2001 have explicit storage parameters specified.

```
CREATE TABLE CARS2 (
  MAKE_YEAR  NUMBER(4),
  MODEL      VARCHAR2 (30),
  MANUFACTR  VARCHAR2 (50),
  QUANTITY   NUMBER)
  PARTITION BY RANGE (MAKE_YEAR)
  SUBPARTITION BY HASH (MODEL) SUBPARTITIONS 4
```

```
   ( PARTITION M2001 VALUES LESS THAN (2002)
     STORAGE (INITIAL 128K NEXT 128K)
     ( SUBPARTITION M2001_SP1 TABLESPACE TS011,
       SUBPARTITION M2001_SP2 TABLESPACE TS012,
       SUBPARTITION M2001_SP3 TABLESPACE TS013,
       SUBPARTITION M2001_SP4 TABLESPACE TS014 ),
     PARTITION M2002 VALUES LESS THAN (2003)
     ( SUBPARTITION M2002_SP1 TABLESPACE TS021,
       SUBPARTITION M2002_SP2 TABLESPACE TS022,
       SUBPARTITION M2002_SP3 TABLESPACE TS023,
       SUBPARTITION M2002_SP4 TABLESPACE TS024 ),
     PARTITION M9999 VALUES LESS THAN (MAXVALUE)
     ( SUBPARTITION M2999_SP1 TABLESPACE TS991,
       SUBPARTITION M2999_SP2 TABLESPACE TS992,
       SUBPARTITION M2999_SP3 TABLESPACE TS993,
       SUBPARTITION M2999_SP4 TABLESPACE TS994 ))
STORAGE (INITIAL 64K NEXT 64K PCTINCREASE 0 MAXEXTENTS 4096);
```

Using Other Create Clauses

You can specify the following additional clauses while creating a table. These clauses help to manage various types of operations on the table.

LOGGING/NOLOGGING LOGGING is the default for the table and tablespace, but if the tablespace is defined as NOLOGGING, the table uses NOLOGGING. LOGGING specifies that table creation and direct-load inserts should be logged to the redo log files. Creating the table by using a subquery and the NOLOGGING clause can dramatically reduce the time to create large tables. If the table creation, initial data population (using a subquery), and direct-load inserts are not logged to the redo log files when using the NOLOGGING clause, you must back up the table (or better yet, the entire tablespace) after such operations are performed. Media recovery will not create or load tables created with the NOLOGGING attribute. You can also specify a separate LOGGING or NOLOGGING attribute for indexes and LOB storage of the table, independent of the table's attribute. The following example creates a table with the NOLOGGING clause.

```
CREATE TABLE MY_ORDERS (... ...)
TABLESPACE USER_DATA STORAGE (... ...)
NOLOGGING;
```

PARALLEL/NOPARALLEL NOPARALLEL is the default. PARALLEL causes the table creation (if created using a subquery) and the DML statements on the table to execute in parallel. Normally, a single-server process performs operations on tables in a transaction (serial operation). When the PARALLEL attribute is set, Oracle uses multiple processes to complete the operation for a full table scan. You can specify a degree for the parallelism; if a degree is not specified, Oracle calculates the optimum degree of parallelism. The parameter PARALLEL_THREADS_PER_CPU determines the number for parallel degree per CPU; usually the default is 2. If you do not specify the degree, Oracle calculates the degree based on this parameter and the number of CPUs available. The following example creates a table by using a subquery. The table creation will not be logged in the redo log file, and multiple processes will query the JAKE.ORDERS table and create the MY_ORDERS table.

```
CREATE TABLE MY_ORDERS (... ...)
TABLESPACE USER_DATA STORAGE (... ...)
NOLOGGING PARALLEL
AS SELECT * FROM JAKE.ORDERS;
```

CACHE/NOCACHE NOCACHE is the default. For small look-up tables that are frequently accessed, you can specify the CACHE clause to have the blocks retrieved using a full table scan placed at the MRU end of the LRU list in the buffer cache; the blocks are not aged out of the buffer cache immediately. The default behavior (NOCACHE) is to place the blocks from a full table scan at the tail end of the LRU list, where they are moved out of the list as soon as a different process or query needs these blocks for storing another table's blocks in the cache.

Creating Temporary Tables

Temporary tables hold information that is available only to the session that created the data. The definition of the temporary table is available to all sessions. To create a temporary table, you use the CREATE GLOBAL TEMPORARY TABLE statement. The data in the table can be session-specific or transaction-specific. The ON COMMIT clause specifies which. The following statement creates a temporary table that is transaction-specific.

```
CREATE GLOBAL TEMPORARY TABLE INVALID_ORDERS
(ORDER#   NUMBER (8),
 ORDER_DT DATE,
 VALUE    NUMBER (12,2))
ON COMMIT DELETE ROWS;
```

Oracle deletes rows or truncates the table after each commit. To define the table as session-specific, use the ON COMMIT PRESERVE ROWS clause.

Storage for temporary tables is allocated in the temporary tablespace of the user. Segments are created only when the first insert statement is performed on the table. The temporary segments allocated to temporary tables are deallocated at the end of the transaction for transaction-specific tables and at the end of session for session-specific tables.

You can create indexes on temporary tables. DML (Data Manipulation Language) statements on temporary tables do not generate redo information, but undo information is generated.

Altering Tables

Oracle Objective

Reorganize, truncate, and drop a table

You can alter a table by using the ALTER TABLE command to change it's the table's storage settings, add or drop columns, or modify the column characteristics such as default value, datatype, and length. You can also move the table from one tablespace to another, disable constraints and triggers, and change the clauses such as PARALLEL, CACHE, and LOGGING. In this section, we will discuss altering the storage and space used by the table.

You cannot change the STORAGE parameters INITIAL and MINEXTENTS by using the ALTER TABLE command. You can change NEXT, PCTINCREASE, MAXEXTENTS, FREELISTS, and FREELIST GROUPS. The changes will not affect the extents that are already allocated. When you change NEXT, the next extent allocated will have the new size. When you alter PCTINCREASE, the next extent allocated will be based on the current value of NEXT, but further extent sizes will be calculated with the new PCTINCREASE value. Here is an example of changing the storage parameters:

```
ALTER TABLE ORDERS
STORAGE (NEXT 512K PCTINCREASE 0 MAXEXTENTS UNLIMITED);
```

Allocating and Deallocating Extents

You can allocate new extents to a table or a partition manually by using the ALTER TABLE command. You can optionally specify a filename if you want to allocate the extent in a particular data file. You can specify the size of the extent in bytes (use K or M to specify the size in KB or MB). If you omit the size of the extent, Oracle uses the NEXT size. For example, to manually allocate the next extent, use the following:

```
ALTER TABLE ORDERS ALLOCATE EXTENT;
```

To specify the size of the extent to be allocated, use the following:

```
ALTER TABLE ORDERS ALLOCATE EXTENT (SIZE 200K);
```

To specify the data file where the extent should be allocated, use the following:

```
ALTER TABLE ORDERS ALLOCATE EXTENT (SIZE 200K
DATAFILE 'C:\ORACLE\ORADATA\USER_DATA01.DBF');
```

The data file should belong to the tablespace where the table or the partition resides.

Sometimes the storage space estimated for the table is too high. The table may be created with large extent sizes, or if you do not set the PCTINCREASE size properly, the space allocated to the table may be large. Any other table or object cannot use the space once allocated. You can free up such unused free space by manually deallocating the unused blocks above the *high-water mark (HWM)* of the table. The HWM indicates the historically highest amount of used space in a segment. The HWM moves only in the forward direction, that is, when new blocks are used to store data in a table, the HWM is increased. When rows are deleted, and even if a block is completely empty, the HWM is not decreased. The HWM is reset only when you TRUNCATE the table.

You can use the UNUSED_SPACE procedure of the DBMS_SPACE package to find the HWM of the segment. The following listing shows the parameters for the procedure.

```
PROCEDURE UNUSED_SPACE
 Argument Name                  Type       In/Out Default?
 ------------------------------ ---------- ------ --------
 SEGMENT_OWNER                  VARCHAR2   IN
 SEGMENT_NAME                   VARCHAR2   IN
 SEGMENT_TYPE                   VARCHAR2   IN
 TOTAL_BLOCKS                   NUMBER     OUT
 TOTAL_BYTES                    NUMBER     OUT
 UNUSED_BLOCKS                  NUMBER     OUT
 UNUSED_BYTES                   NUMBER     OUT
 LAST_USED_EXTENT_FILE_ID       NUMBER     OUT
 LAST_USED_EXTENT_BLOCK_ID      NUMBER     OUT
 LAST_USED_BLOCK                NUMBER     OUT
 PARTITION_NAME                 VARCHAR2   IN     DEFAULT
```

You can execute the procedure by specifying the owner, type (table, index, table partition, table subpartition, and so on), and name. The HWM is TOTAL_BYTES – UNUSED_BYTES. Here is an example:

```
SQL> variable vtotalblocks number
SQL> variable vtotalbytes number
SQL> variable vunusedblocks number
SQL> variable vunusedbytes number
SQL> variable vlastusedefid number
SQL> variable vlastusedebid number
SQL> variable vlastusedblock number
SQL> EXECUTE DBMS_SPACE.UNUSED_SPACE ('JOHN', -
> 'ORDERS', 'TABLE', :vtotalblocks, :vtotalbytes, -
> :vunusedblocks, :vunusedbytes, -
> :vlastusedefid, :vlastusedebid, :vlastusedblock);

PL/SQL procedure successfully completed.

SQL> select :vtotalbytes, :vunusedbytes from dual;

:VTOTALBYTES :VUNUSEDBYTES
------------ -------------
     1224288       8507904

SQL>
```

You can use the DEALLOCATE UNUSED clause of the ALTER TABLE command to free up the unused space allocated to the table. For example, to free up all blocks above the HWM, use this statement:

```
ALTER TABLE ORDERS DEALLOCATE UNUSED;
```

You can use the KEEP parameter in the UNUSED clause to specify the number of blocks you want to keep above the HWM after deallocation. For example, to have 100KB of free space available for the table above the HWM, specify the following:

```
ALTER TABLE ORDERS DEALLOCATE UNUSED KEEP 100K;
```

If you do not specify KEEP, and the HWM is below MINEXTENTS, Oracle keeps MINEXTENTS extents. If you specify KEEP, and the HWM is below MINEXTENTS, Oracle adjusts the MINEXTENTS to match the number of extents. If the HWM is less than the size of INITIAL, and KEEP is specified, Oracle adjusts the size of INITIAL.

Table 8.2 shows some examples of freeing up space. Let's assume that the table is created with (INITIAL 1024K NEXT 1024K PCTINCREASE 0 MINEXTENTS 4) and now the table has 10 extents (total size 10,240KB).

TABLE 8.2 DEALLOCATE Clause Examples

HWM	DEALLOCATE Clause	Resulting Size	Extent Count
7000KB	UNUSED;	7000KB	Seven; the seventh extent will be split at the HWM.
200KB	UNUSED;	4096KB	Four, because the KEEP clause is not specified.
200KB	UNUSED KEEP 100K;	300KB	One; the initial extent is split at the HWM.
2000KB	UNUSED KEEP 0K;	2000KB	Two; the second extent is split at the HWM.

When a full table scan is performed, Oracle reads each block up to the table's high-water mark.

You use the TRUNCATE command to delete all rows of the table and to reset the HWM of the table. You can keep the space allocated to the table or deallocate the extents when using TRUNCATE. By default, Oracle deallocates all the extents allocated above MINEXTENTS of the table and the associated indexes. To preserve the space allocated, you must specify the REUSE clause (DROP is the default), as in this example:

```
TRUNCATE TABLE ORDERS REUSE STORAGE;
```

To truncate a table, you must disable all referential integrity constraints.

Reorganizing Tables

You can use the MOVE clause of the ALTER TABLE command on a nonpartitioned table to reorganize or to move from one tablespace to another. You can reorganize the table to reduce the number of extents by specifying larger extent sizes or to prevent row migration. When you move a table, Oracle creates a new segment for the table, copies the data, and drops the old segment. The new segment can be in the same tablespace or in a different tablespace. Since the old segment is dropped only after you create the new segment, you need to make sure you have sufficient space in the tablespace, if you're not changing to a different tablespace. The MOVE clause can specify a new tablespace, new storage parameters for the table, new free space management parameters, and new transaction entry parameters. You can use the NOLOGGING clause to speed up the reorganization by not writing the changes to the redo log file.

The following example moves the ORDERS table to another tablespace named NEW_DATA. New storage parameters are specified, and the operation is not logged in the redo log files (NOLOGGING).

```
ALTER TABLE ORDERS MOVE
TABLESPACE NEW_DATA
STORAGE (INITIAL 50M NEXT 5M PCTINCREASE 0)
PCTFREE 0 PCTUSED 50
INITRANS 2 NOLOGGING;
```

Prior to Oracle8i, you reorganized a table using the export-drop-import method. Queries are allowed on the table while the move operation is in progress, but no insert, update, or delete operations are allowed. The granted permissions on the table are retained.

Dropping a Table

If a table is no longer used, you can drop it to free up space. Once you drop a table, the action cannot be undone. The syntax follows:

```
DROP TABLE [schema.]table_name [CASCADE CONSTRAINTS]
```

When you drop a table, the data and definition of the table are removed. The indexes, constraints, triggers, and privileges on the table are also dropped. Oracle does not drop the views, materialized views, or other stored programs that reference the table, but it marks them as invalid. You must specify the CASCADE CONSTRAINTS clause if there are referential integrity constraints referring to the primary key or unique key of this table. Here's how to drop the table TEST owned by user SCOTT:

```
DROP TABLE SCOTT.TEST;
```

Truncating a Table

The TRUNCATE statement is similar to the DROP statement, but it does not remove the structure of the table, so none of the indexes, constraints, triggers, and privileges on the table are dropped. By default, the space allocated to the table and indexes is freed. If you do not want to free up the space, include the REUSE STORAGE clause. You cannot roll back a truncate operation. Also, you cannot selectively delete rows using the TRUNCATE statement. The syntax of TRUNCATE statement is:

```
TRUNCATE {TABLE|CLUSTER} [<schema>.]<name>
[{DROP|REUSE} STORAGE]
```

You cannot truncate the parent table of an enabled referential integrity constraint. You must first disable the constraint and then truncate the table, even if the child table has no rows. The following example demonstrates this process:

```
SQL> CREATE TABLE t1 (
 2   t1f1 NUMBER CONSTRAINT pk_t1 PRIMARY KEY);
Table created.

SQL> CREATE TABLE t2 (t2f1 NUMBER CONSTRAINT fk_t2
                             REFERENCES t1 (t1f1));
Table created.

SQL> TRUNCATE TABLE t1;
truncate table t1
               *
ERROR at line 1:
```

```
ORA-02266: unique/primary keys in table referenced by enabled foreign keys

SQL> ALTER TABLE t2 DISABLE CONSTRAINT fk_t2;
Table altered.

SQL> TRUNCATE TABLE t1;
Table truncated.

SQL>
```

TRUNCATE versus DELETE

The TRUNCATE statement is similar to a DELETE statement without a WHERE clause, except for the following:

- TRUNCATE is very fast on both large and small tables. DELETE will generate undo information, in case a rollback is issued, but TRUNCATE will not generate undo.
- TRUNCATE is DDL and, like all DDL, performs an implicit commit—you cannot roll back a TRUNCATE. Any uncommitted DML changes will also be committed with the TRUNCATE.
- TRUNCATE resets the high-water mark in the table and all indexes. Since full table scans and index fast-full scans read all data blocks up to the high-water mark, full-scan performance after a DELETE will not improve; after a TRUNCATE, performance will be very fast.
- TRUNCATE does not fire any DELETE triggers.
- There is no object privilege that can be granted to allow a user to truncate another user's table. The DROP ANY TABLE system privilege is required to truncate a table in another schema.
- When a table is truncated, the storage for the table and all indexes can be reset back to the initial size. A DELETE will never shrink the size of a table or its indexes.

TRUNCATE versus DROP TABLE

Using TRUNCATE is also different from dropping and re-creating a table. Compared with dropping and recreating a table, TRUNCATE does not do the following:

- Invalidate dependent objects
- Drop indexes, triggers, or referential integrity constraints
- Require privileges to be re-granted

Use the TRUNCATE statement to delete all rows from a large table; it does not write the rollback entries and is much faster than the DELETE statement when deleting a large number of rows.

Dropping Columns

Oracle Objective

Drop a column within a table

You can drop a column that is not used immediately, or you can mark the column as not used and drop it later.

Here is the syntax for dropping a column:

```
ALTER TABLE [<schema>.]<table_name>
DROP {COLUMN <column_name> | (<column_names>)}
[CASCADE CONSTRAINTS]
```

DROP COLUMN drops the column name specified from the table. You can provide more than one column name separated by commas inside parentheses. The indexes and constraints on the column are also dropped. You must specify CASCADE CONSTRAINTS if the dropped column is part of a multicolumn constraint; the constraint will be dropped.

Here is the syntax for marking a column as unused:

```
ALTER TABLE [<schema>.]<table_name>
SET UNUSED {COLUMN <column_name> | (<column_names>)}
[CASCADE CONSTRAINTS]
```

You usually mark a column as unused instead of dropping it immediately if the table is very large and consumes a lot of resources at peak hours. In such cases, you would mark the column as unused and drop it at off-peak hours. Once the column is marked as unused, you will not see it as part of the table definition. Let's mark the UPDATE_DT column in the ORDERS table as unused:

```
ALTER TABLE orders SET UNUSED COLUMN update_dt;
```

The syntax for dropping a column already marked as unused is:

```
ALTER TABLE [<schema>.]<table_name>
DROP {UNUSED COLUMNS | COLUMNS CONTINUE}
```

Use the COLUMNS CONTINUE clause to continue a DROP operation that was previously interrupted. You cannot specify selected column names to drop after marking the column as unused. The DROP UNUSED COLUMNS clause will drop all the columns that are marked as unused. To clear data from the UPDATE_DT column from the ORDERS table, use the following statement:

```
ALTER TABLE orders DROP UNUSED COLUMNS;
```

Analyzing Tables

You can analyze a table to verify the blocks in it, to find the chained and migrated rows, and to collect statistics on the table. You can specify the PARTITION or SUBPARTITION clause to analyze a specific partition or subpartition of the table.

Validating Structure

As the result of hardware problems, disk errors, or software bugs, some blocks can become corrupted (logical corruption). Oracle returns a corruption error only when the rows are accessed. (The Export utility identifies logical corruption in tables, because it does a full table scan.) You can use the ANALYZE command to validate the structure or check the integrity of the blocks allocated to the table. If Oracle finds blocks or rows that are not readable, it returns an error. The ROWIDs of the bad rows are inserted into a table. You can specify the name of the table in which you want the ROWIDs to be saved; by default, Oracle looks for the table named INVALID_ROWS. You can create the table using the script utlvalid.sql supplied from Oracle, located in the rdbms/admin directory of the software installation. The structure of the table is as follows:

```
SQL>  @c:\oracle\ora90\rdbms\admin\utlvalid.sql


Table created.

SQL> desc invalid_rows
```

```
Name                          Null?    Type
----------------------- -------- ------------
OWNER_NAME                             VARCHAR2(30)
TABLE_NAME                             VARCHAR2(30)
PARTITION_NAME                         VARCHAR2(30)
SUBPARTITION_NAME                      VARCHAR2(30)
HEAD_ROWID                             ROWID
ANALYZE_TIMESTAMP                      DATE
```

This example validates the structure of the ORDERS table:

```
ANALYZE TABLE ORDERS VALIDATE STRUCTURE;
```

If Oracle encounters bad rows, it inserts them into the INVALID_ROWS table. To specify a different table name, use the following syntax.

```
ANALYZE TABLE ORDERS VALIDATE STRUCTURE
INTO SCOTT.CORRUPTED_ROWS;
```

You can also validate the blocks of the indexes associated with the table by specifying the CASCADE clause.

```
ANALYZE TABLE ORDERS VALIDATE STRUCTURE CASCADE;
```

To analyze a partition by name MAY2002 in table GLEDGER, specify

```
ANALYZE TABLE GLEDGER PARTITION (MAY2002) VALIDATE STRUCTURE;
```

Finding Migrated Rows

A row is *migrated* if the row is moved from its original block to another block because there was not enough free space available in its original block to accommodate the row, which was expanded due to an update. Oracle keeps a pointer in the original block to indicate the new block ID of the row. When there are many migrated rows in a table, performance of the table is affected, because Oracle has to read two blocks instead of one for a given row retrieval or update. You can prevent this problem by specifying an efficient PCTFREE value.

A row is *chained* if the row is bigger than the block size of the database. Normally, the rows of a table with LOB datatypes are more likely to become chained.

You can use the LIST CHAINED ROWS clause of the ANALYZE command to find the chained and migrated rows of a table. Oracle writes the ROWID of such rows to a specified table. If no table is specified, Oracle looks for the CHAINED_ROWS table. You can create this table using the script utlchain.sql supplied from Oracle, located in the rdbms/admin directory of the software installation. The structure of the table is as follows:

```
SQL> @c:\oracle\ora90\rdbms\admin\utlchain.sql

Table created.

SQL> DESC CHAINED_ROWS
 Name                          Null?    Type
 ----------------------------- -------- ------------
 OWNER_NAME                             VARCHAR2(30)
 TABLE_NAME                             VARCHAR2(30)
 CLUSTER_NAME                           VARCHAR2(30)
 PARTITION_NAME                         VARCHAR2(30)
 SUBPARTITION_NAME                      VARCHAR2(30)
 HEAD_ROWID                             ROWID
 ANALYZE_TIMESTAMP                      DATE
```

Only the ROWIDs are listed in the CHAINED_ROWS table. You can use this information to save these chained rows to a different table, delete them from the source table, and insert them back from the second table. Here is one way to fix migrated rows in a table:

1. Analyze the table to find migrated rows.

   ```
   ANALYZE TABLE ORDERS LIST CHAINED ROWS;
   ```

2. Find the number of migrated rows.

   ```
   SELECT COUNT(*)
   FROM CHAINED_ROWS
   WHERE OWNER_NAME = 'SCOTT'
   AND  TABLE_NAME = 'ORDERS';
   ```

3. If there are migrated rows, create a temporary table to hold the migrated rows.

   ```
   CREATE TABLE TEMP_ORDERS AS
   SELECT * FROM ORDERS
   WHERE ROWID IN (SELECT HEAD_ROWID
           FROM CHAINED_ROWS
           WHERE OWNER_NAME = 'SCOTT'
           AND   TABLE_NAME = 'ORDERS');
   ```

4. Delete the rows from the ORDERS table.

```
DELETE FROM ORDERS
WHERE ROWID IN (SELECT HEAD_ROWID
      FROM   CHAINED_ROWS
      WHERE OWNER_NAME = 'SCOTT'
      AND   TABLE_NAME = 'ORDERS');
```

5. Insert the rows back into the ORDERS table.

```
INSERT INTO ORDERS
SELECT * FROM TEMP_ORDERS;
```

Before deleting the rows, make sure you disable any foreign key constraints referring to the ORDERS table. You will not be able to delete the rows if there are child rows, and most important, defining the constraints with the CASCADE option deletes the child rows! See the "Managing Constraints" section later in this chapter to learn about the foreign key constraints and how to enable/disable them.

Collecting Statistics

You can collect statistics about a table and save them in the dictionary tables by using the ANALYZE command. The cost-based optimizer also uses the statistics to generate the execution plan of SQL statements. You can calculate the exact statistics (COMPUTE) of the table or sample a few rows and estimate the statistics (ESTIMATE). By default, Oracle collects statistics for all the columns and indexes in the table. For large tables, you may want to estimate, because when you compute the statistics, Oracle reads each block of the table. The following information is collected and saved in the dictionary when you use the ANALYZE command to collect statistics:

- The total number of rows in the table and the number of chained rows
- The total number of blocks allocated, the total number of unused blocks, and the average free space in each block
- The average row length

Here is an example of analyzing a table using the COMPUTE clause:

```
ANALYZE TABLE ORDERS COMPUTE STATISTICS;
```

When using the ESTIMATE option, you can either specify a certain number of rows or specify a certain percentage of rows in the table. If the rows specified are more than 50 percent of the table, Oracle does a COMPUTE. If you do not specify the SAMPLE clause, Oracle samples 1064 rows. To specify the number of rows, use the following:

```
ANALYZE TABLE ORDERS ESTIMATE STATISTICS
SAMPLE 200 ROWS;
```

To specify a percentage of the table to sample, use the following:

```
ANALYZE TABLE ORDERS ESTIMATE STATISTICS
SAMPLE 20 PERCENT;
```

To remove statistics collected on a table, use the DELETE STATISTICS option, as follows:

```
ANALYZE TABLE ORDERS DELETE STATISTICS;
```

You can also collect the statistics using the DBMS_STATS package. You have the option of collecting the statistics into a non-dictionary table.

Querying Table Information

Several data dictionary views are available to provide information about the tables. We will discuss certain views and their columns that you should be familiar with before taking the test.

DBA_TABLES

You primarily use the DBA_TABLES, USER_TABLES, and ALL_TABLES views to query for information about tables (TABS is a synonym for USER_TABLES). The views contain the following information (the columns that can be used in the query are provided in parentheses):

- Identity (OWNER, TABLE_NAME)
- Storage (TABLESPACE_NAME, PCT_FREE, PCT_USED, INI_TRANS, MAX_TRANS, INITIAL_EXTENT, NEXT_EXTENT, MAX_EXTENTS, MIN_EXTENTS, PCT_INCREASE, FREELISTS, FREELIST_GROUPS, BUFFER_POOL)
- Statistics (NUM_ROWS, BLOCKS, EMPTY_BLOCKS, AVG_SPACE, CHAIN_CNT, AVG_ROW_LEN, AVG_SPACE_FREELIST_BLOCKS, NUM_FREELIST_BLOCKS, SAMPLE_SIZE, LAST_ANALYZED)

- Miscellaneous create options (LOGGING, DEGREE, CACHE, PARTITIONED, NESTED)

DBA_TAB_COLUMNS

Use the DBA_TAB_COLUMNS, USER_TAB_COLUMNS, and ALL_TAB_COLUMNS views to display information about the columns in a table. You can query the following information:

- Identity (OWNER, TABLE_NAME, COLUMN_NAME, COLUMN_ID)
- Column characteristics (DATA_TYPE, DATA_LENGTH, DATA_PRECISION, DATA_SCALE, NULLABLE, DEFAULT_LENGTH, DATA_DEFAULT)
- Statistics (AVG_COL_LEN, NUM_DISTINCT, HIGH_VALUE, LOW_VALUE, NUM_NULLS, LAST_ANALYZED, SAMPLE_SIZE)

Table 8.3 lists other dictionary views that show information about the tables in the database.

TABLE 8.3 Dictionary Views with Table Information

View Name	Contents
ALL_ALL_TABLES DBA_ALL_TABLES USER_ALL_TABLES	Similar information as in DBA_TABLES; shows information about relational tables and object tables.
ALL_TAB_PARTITIONS DBA_TAB_PARTITIONS USER_TAB_PARTITIONS	Partitioning information, storage parameters, and partition-level statistics gathered.
ALL_TAB_SUBPARTITIONS DBA_TAB_SUBPARTITIONS USER_TAB_SUBPARTITIONS	Subpartition information for composite partitions in the database.
ALL_OBJECTS DBA_OBJECTS USER_OBJECTS	Information about the objects. For table information such as creation timestamp and modification date, query this view. The OBJECT_TYPE column shows the type of the object, such as table, index, trigger, etc.

TABLE 8.3 Dictionary Views with Table Information *(continued)*

View Name	Contents
ALL_EXTENTS DBA_EXTENTS USER_EXTENTS	Information about the extents allocated to the table. Shows the tablespace, data file, number of blocks, extent size, etc.

The Structure of a Row

Oracle Objective

Describe the structure of a row

Oracle stores data in the form of rows. Rows are stored in blocks. You define the size of the block when you create the database, but you can override the size when you create tablespaces. If the entire row can be inserted into a block, the row is stored as a row piece. If the row to be stored is bigger than the block size, the row is stored using multiple row pieces. The same is true for rows that grow beyond the free space available in a block during updates.

A row piece contains a maximum of only 255 columns. If there is data beyond the 255th column in a row, the row is stored as multiple row pieces, a practice known as *intra-block chaining*. Intra-block chaining does not affect IO performance.

A row piece has two parts—a row header and column data. A row header is about 3 bytes for a row piece that is fully contained in a block. The row header includes information about the row piece such as the columns, whether any rows are chained, and whether any cluster keys are present. After the row header is the column data. Column data has two pieces—length and data. The column length occupies 1 byte for data less than 251 bytes and 3 bytes for data over 250 bytes. To conserve space, Oracle does not store null values; only the column length is marked as zero. If the NULL columns are toward the end of the row, Oracle does not even store the column length.

Using *ROWID*

Oracle Objective | **Distinguish between an extended versus a restricted ROWID**

ROWID uniquely identifies each row of the table. ROWID is a pseudo-column in all tables that is not implicitly selected—you must specify ROWID in the query. The ROWID is an 18-byte structure that stores the physical location of the row. Since ROWIDs contain the exact block ID where the row is located, using ROWID is the fastest way to access a row. There are two categories of ROWIDs:

Physical Identifies each row of a table, partition, subpartition, or cluster

Logical Identifies the rows of an Index Organized Table (IOT—discussed later in this chapter)

Unless explicitly specified, ROWID in this chapter means a physical ROWID. There are two formats for the ROWID:

Extended This format uses a base-64 encoding scheme to display the ROWID consisting of the characters A–Z, a–z, 0–9, +, and –. The ROWID is an 18-character representation that is stored in 10 bytes. The format is *OOOOOOFFFBBBBBBRRR*:

- *OOOOOO* is the object number.
- *FFF* is the relative data file number where the block is located; the file number is relative to the tablespace.
- *BBBBBB* is the block ID where the row is located.
- *RRR* is the row in the block.

```
SQL> SELECT ROWID, ORDER_NUM
  2  FROM   ORDERS;

ROWID               ORDER_NUM
------------------  ---------
AAAFqsAADAAAAfTAAA    5934343
AAAFqsAADAAAAfTAAB     343433
```

Restricted This format is the pre-Oracle8 format, carried forward for compatibility. The restricted format is *BBBBBBB.RRRR.FFFF* (in base-16 or hexadecimal format):

- *BBBBBBB* is the data block.
- *RRRR* is the row number.
- *FFFF* is the data file.

```
SQL> SELECT DBMS_ROWID.ROWID_TO_RESTRICTED(ROWID,0),
  2         ORDER_NUM
  3  FROM   ORDERS;

DBMS_ROWID.ROWID_T  ORDER_NUM
------------------ ---------
000007D3.0000.0003   5934343
000007D3.0001.0003    343433
```

DBMS_ROWID

You can use the DBMS_ROWID package to read and convert the ROWID information. This package has several useful functions that you can use to convert the ROWID between extended and restricted formats. You use the function ROWID_TO_RESTRICTED to convert the extended ROWID format to restricted format. The two parameters to this function are the extended ROWID and the conversion type. Conversion type is an integer: 0 to return the ROWID in an internal format, and 1 to return it in a character string.

Oracle7 used restricted ROWID format, and Oracle8 and later versions use the extend ROWID format. If the database is upgraded from Oracle7 to Oracle8i, and there are some tables with a ROWID defined as the type of an explicit column in the table, you can convert the restricted ROWID to extended format by using the function ROWID_TO_EXTENDED. There are four parameters to this function: the old ROWID, the object owner, the object name, and the conversion type. The object owner and object name parameters are optional.

```
SQL> SELECT ROWID,
  2  DBMS_ROWID.ROWID_TO_EXTENDED(ROWID,
  2  NULL, NULL, 0) EXT_ROWID,
  3  DBMS_ROWID.ROWID_TO_RESTRICTED(ROWID,1) RES_ROWID
  4  FROM   ORDERS
SQL> /
```

```
ROWID              EXT_ROWID          RES_ROWID
------------------ ------------------ ------------------
AAAFqsAADAAAAfTAAA AAAFqsAADAAAAfTAAA 000007D3.0000.0003
AAAFqsAADAAAAfTAAB AAAFqsAADAAAAfTAAB 000007D3.0001.0003
```

The ROWID_TO_VERIFY function takes the same parameters as the ROWID_TO_EXTENDED function. This function verifies whether a restricted format ROWID can be converted to extended format by using the ROWID_TO_EXTENDED function. If the ROWID can be converted, it returns 0; otherwise, it returns 1.

Managing Indexes

Oracle Objective | **Describe the different types of indexes and their uses**

Indexes are used to access data more quickly than reading the whole table, and they reduce disk I/O considerably when the queries use the available indexes. As with tables, you can specify storage parameters for indexes, create partitioned indexes, and analyze the index to verify structure and collect statistics. You can create any number of indexes on a table. A column can be part of multiple indexes, and you can specify as many as 30 columns in an index. When you specify more than one column, the index is known as a *composite index*. You can have more than one index with the same index columns, but in a different order.

You can create and drop indexes without affecting the base data of the table—indexes and table data are independent. Oracle maintains the indexes automatically: when new rows are added to the table, updated, or deleted, Oracle updates the corresponding indexes. You can create the following types of indexes:

Bitmap A *bitmap index* does not repeatedly store the index column values. Each value is treated as a key, and a bit is set for the corresponding ROWIDs. Bitmap indexes are suitable for columns with low cardinality, such as the SEX column in an EMPLOYEE table, in which the possible values are M or F. The *cardinality* is the number of distinct column values in a column. In the EMPLOYEE table example, the cardinality of the SEX column is 2. You cannot create unique or reverse key bitmap indexes.

b-tree This type of index is the default. You create the index by using the b-tree algorithm. The *b-tree* includes nodes with the index column values and the ROWID of the row. The ROWIDs identify the rows in the table. You can create the following types of b-tree indexes:

Non-unique This is the default b-tree index; the index column values are not unique.

Unique You create this type of b-tree index by specifying the UNIQUE keyword: each column value entry of the index is unique. Oracle guarantees that the combination of all index column values in the composite index is unique. Oracle returns an error if you try to insert two rows with the same index column values.

Reverse key To specify the *reverse key index* you use the REVERSE keyword. The bytes of each column indexed are reversed, but the column order is retained. For example, if column ORDER_NUM has value 54321, Oracle reverses the bytes to 12345 and then adds the column to the index. You can use this type of indexing for unique indexes when inserts to the table are always in the ascending order of the indexed columns. This type of indexing helps to distribute the adjacent valued columns to different leaf blocks of the index and, as a result, improve performance by retrieving fewer index blocks. *Leaf blocks* are the blocks at the lowest level of the b-tree.

Function-based You can create the *function-based index* on columns with expressions. For example, creating an index on the SUBSTR(EMPID, 1,2) can speed up the queries using SUBSTR(EMPID, 1, 2) in the WHERE clause.

Oracle does not include the rows with NULL values in the index columns when storing the b-tree index. Bitmap indexes store NULL values.

Creating Indexes

Oracle Objective

Create various types of indexes

The CREATE INDEX statement creates a non-unique b-tree index on the columns specified. You must specify a name for the index and the table name on which the index should be built. For example, to create an index on the ORDER_DATE column of the ORDERS table, specify the following:

```
CREATE INDEX IND1_ORDERS
ON ORDERS (ORDER_DATE);
```

To create a unique index, you must specify the keyword UNIQUE immediately after CREATE. For example:

```
CREATE UNIQUE INDEX IND2_ORDERS
ON ORDERS (ORDER_NUM);
```

To create a bitmap index, you must specify the keyword BITMAP immediately after CREATE. Bitmap indexes cannot be unique. For example:

```
CREATE BITMAP INDEX IND3_ORDERS
ON ORDERS (STATUS);
```

Specifying Storage

If you do not specify the TABLESPACE clause in the CREATE INDEX statement, Oracle creates the index in the default tablespace of the user. If you don't specify the STORAGE clause, Oracle inherits the default storage parameters defined for the tablespace. All the storage parameters discussed in the "Managing Tables" section are applicable to indexes and have the same meaning except for PCTUSED. You cannot specify PCTUSED for indexes. Keep the INITRANS for the index more than that specified for the corresponding table, because the index blocks can hold a larger number of rows than a table.

Here is an example of creating an index and specifying the storage:

```
CREATE UNIQUE INDEX IND2_ORDERS
ON ORDERS (ORDER_NUM)
TABLESPACE USER_INDEX
PCTFREE    25
INITRANS   2
MAXTRANS   255
STORAGE   (INITIAL 128K   NEXT 128K    PCTINCREASE 0
           MINEXTENTS 1   MAXEXTENTS 100
           FREELISTS 1    FREELIST GROUPS 1
           BUFFER_POOL KEEP);
```

When creating indexes for a table with rows, Oracle writes the data blocks with index values up to PCTFREE. The free space reserved by specifying PCTFREE is used when inserting into the table a new row (or updating a row that changes the corresponding index key column value) that needs to be placed between two index key values of the leaf node. If no free space is available in the block, Oracle uses a new block. If many new rows are inserted into the table, keep the PCTFREE of the index high.

Using Other Create Clauses

You can use the NOLOGGING clause to specify that information is not written to the redo log files, which speeds index creation. The default is LOGGING.

You can also collect statistics about the index while creating the index by specifying the COMPUTE STATISITCS clause. Using this clause avoids another ANALYZE on the index later.

The ONLINE clause specifies that the table will be available for DML operations when the index is built.

If data is loaded to the table in the order of an index, you can specify the NOSORT clause. Oracle does not sort the rows, but if the data is not sorted, Oracle returns an error. Specifying this clause saves time and temporary space.

For multicolumn indexes, eliminating the repeating key columns can save storage space. Specify the COMPRESS clause when creating the index. NOCOMPRESS is the default. This clause can be used only with non-partitioned indexes. Index performance may be affected when using this clause.

Specify PARALLEL to create the index using multiple server processes. NOPARALLEL is the default.

The following is an example of creating an index by specifying some of the miscellaneous clauses:

```
SQL> CREATE INDEX IND5_ORDERS ON ORDERS
     (ORDER_NUM, ORDER_DATE)
     TABLESPACE INDX
     NOLOGGING
     NOSORT
     COMPRESS
     SORT
     COMPUTE STATISTICS;

Index created.

SQL>
```

Partitioning

As with tables, you can partition indexes for better manageability and performance. Partitioned tables can have partitioned and/or non-partitioned indexes, and partitioned indexes can be created on partitioned or nonpartitioned tables. When all the index partitions correspond to the table partitions (equipartitioning), the index is called a local partitioned index. Specifying the `LOCAL` keyword creates local indexes. For local indexes, Oracle maintains the index partition keys automatically, in synch with the table partition. A global partitioned index specifies different partition range values; the partition column values need not belong to a single table partition. Specifying the `GLOBAL` keyword creates global indexes.

You can create four types of partitioned indexes:

Local prefixed Local index with leading columns (leftmost column in index) in the order of the partition key.

Local non-prefixed Partition key columns are not leading columns, but the index is local.

Global prefixed Global index, with leading columns in the order of the partition key.

Global non-prefixed Global index, with leading columns not in the partition key order.

Bitmap indexes created on partitioned tables must be local. You cannot create a partitioned bitmap index on a non-partitioned table.

Reverse Key Indexes

Specifying the REVERSE keyword creates a reverse key index. Reverse key indexes improve performance of certain OLTP (Online Transaction Processing) applications using the parallel server. The following example creates a reverse key index on the ORDER_NUM and ORDER_DATE column of the ORDERS table.

```
CREATE UNIQUE INDEX IND2_ORDERS
ON ORDERS (ORDER_DATE, ORDER_NUM)
TABLESPACE USER_INDEX
REVERSE;
```

Function-Based Indexes

Function-based indexes are created as regular b-tree or bitmap indexes. Specify the expression or function when creating the index. Oracle precalculates the value of the expression and creates the index. For example, to create a function based on SUBSTR(PRODUCT_ID,1,2), use the following:

```
CREATE INDEX IND4_ORDERS
ON ORDERS (SUBSTR(PRODUCT_ID,1,2))
TABLESPACE USER_INDEX;
```

To use the function-based index, you must set the instance initialization parameter QUERY_REWRITE_ENABLED to TRUE and the parameter QUERY_REWRITE_INTEGRITY to TRUSTED. Also, set the COMPATIBLE parameter to 8.1.0 or higher. A query can use this index if its WHERE clause specifies a condition by using SUBSTR(PRODUCT_ID,1,2), as in the following example:

```
SELECT * FROM ORDERS
WHERE SUBSTR(PRODUCT_ID,1,2) = 'BT';
```

You must gather statistics for function-based indexes for the cost-based optimizer to use the index. The rule-based optimizer does not use function-based indexes.

Index Organized Tables

You can store index and table data together in a structure known as an *Index Organized Table (IOT)*. IOTs are suitable for tables in which the data access is mostly through its primary key, such as look-up tables, which have a code and a description. An IOT is a b-tree index, and instead of storing the ROWID of the table where the row belongs, the entire row is stored as part of the index. You can build additional indexes on the columns of an IOT. You access the data in an IOT in the same way you access the data in a table.

Since the row is stored along with the b-tree index, there is no physical ROWID for each row. The primary key identifies the rows in an IOT. Oracle "guesses" the location of the row and assigns a logical ROWID for each row, which permits the creation of secondary indexes. You can partition an IOT, but the partition columns should be a subset of the primary key columns.

To build additional indexes on the IOT, Oracle uses a logical ROWID, which is derived from the primary key values of the IOT. The logical ROWID can include a guessed physical location of the row in the data files. This guessed location is not valid when a row is moved from one block to another. If the logical ROWID does not include the guessed location of the ROWID, Oracle has to perform two index scans when using the secondary index. The logical ROWIDs can be stored in columns with the datatype UROWID.

To create an IOT, you use the CREATE TABLE command with the ORGANIZATION INDEX keyword. You must specify the primary key for the table when creating the table.

```
SQL> CREATE TABLE IOT_EXAMPLE (
     PK_COL1    NUMBER (4),
     PK_COL2    VARCHAR2 (10),
     NON_PK_COL1 VARCHAR2 (40),
     NON_PK_COL2 DATE,
     CONSTRAINT PK_IOT PRIMARY KEY
             (PK_COL1, PK_COL2))
     ORGANIZATION INDEX
     TABLESPACE INDX
     STORAGE (INITIAL 32K NEXT 32K PCTINCREASE 0);

Table created.

SQL>
```

Altering Indexes

Using the ALTER INDEX command, you can make the following alterations in an index:

- Change its STORAGE clause, except for the parameters INITIAL and MINEXTENTS
- Deallocate unused blocks
- Rebuild the index
- Coalesce leaf nodes
- Manually allocate extents
- Change the PARALLEL/NOPARALLEL, LOGGING/NOLOGGING clauses
- Modify partition storage parameters, rename partitions, drop partitions, and so on
- Specify the ENABLE/DISABLE clause to enable or disable function-based indexes
- Mark the index or index partition as UNUSABLE, thereby disabling the index or index partition
- Rename the index

Since the rules for changing the storage parameters, allocating extents, and deallocating extents are similar to those for altering a table, we will provide only some short examples here.

To change storage parameters, use the following:

```
ALTER INDEX SCOTT.IND1_ORDERS
STORAGE (NEXT 512K MAXEXTENTS UNLIMITED);
```

To allocate an extent, use the following:

```
ALTER INDEX SCOTT.IND1_ORDERS
ALLOCATE EXTENT SIZE 200K;
```

To deallocate unused blocks, use the following:

```
ALTER INDEX SCOTT.IND1_ORDERS
DEALLOCATE UNUSED KEEP 100K;
```

If you disable an index by specifying the UNUSABLE clause, you must rebuild the index to make it valid.

Rebuilding/Coalescing Indexes

Oracle Objective

Reorganize indexes

Over time, blocks in an index can become fragmented and leave behind free space in leaf blocks. You can compress these indexes and gain space that can be used for new leaf blocks. You can use the COALESCE clause to free up index leaf blocks within the same branch of the tree. The index storage parameters and tablespace values remain the same. Here is an example:

```
ALTER INDEX IND1_ORDERS COALESCE;
```

If you want to re-create the index on a different tablespace or specify different storage parameters and free up leaf blocks, you can use the REBUILD clause. When you rebuild an index, Oracle drops the original index when the rebuild is complete. (A new index is created even if you do not change the tablespace or storage.) Users can access the index if you specify the ONLINE parameter. Optionally, you can collect statistics while rebuilding the index by using the COMPUTE STATISTICS parameter, and you can specify NOLOGGING so that redo log entries are not generated. You can also specify REVERSE or NOREVERSE to convert a normal index to a reverse key index or vice versa.

The following example moves the index to a new tablespace, collecting the statistics while rebuilding, and makes the table available for insert/update/delete operations by specifying the ONLINE clause.

```
ALTER INDEX IND1_ORDERS REBUILD
TABLESPACE NEW_INDEX_TS
STORAGE (INITIAL 25M NEXT 5M PCTINCREASE 0)
PCTFREE 20 INITRANS 4
COMPUTE STATISTICS
ONLINE NOLOGGING;
```

Dropping Indexes

Oracle Objective

Drop indexes

You can drop indexes using the DROP INDEX command. Oracle frees up all the space used by the index when the index is dropped. When a table is dropped, the indexes built on the table are automatically dropped. For example:

```
DROP INDEX SCOTT.IND5_ORDERS;
```

You cannot drop the indexes used to enforce the uniqueness or primary key of a table. Such indexes can be dropped only after disabling the primary and unique keys.

Analyzing Indexes

As you can with tables, you can analyze indexes to validate their structure (to find block corruption) and to collect statistics. You cannot use the ANALYZE command on an index with the LIST CHAINED ROWS clause. You can use the COMPUTE or ESTIMATE clause when collecting statistics. Here are some examples.

To validate the structure of an index, use the following:

```
ANALYZE INDEX IND5_ORDERS VALIDATE STRUCTURE;
```

To collect statistics by sampling 40 percent of the entries in the index, use the following:

```
ANALYZE INDEX IND5_ORDERS ESTIMATE STATISTICS
SAMPLE 40 PERCENT;
```

To delete statistics, use the following:

```
ANALYZE INDEX IND5_ORDERS DELETE STATISTICS;
```

Monitoring Index Usage

Oracle Objective — **Monitor the usage of an index**

Oracle9i provides a method for detecting whether an index is used. You can drop unused indexes from the database to free up space and resources. Each index causes an overhead when DML statements are performed on the table. To enable index monitoring, you use the MONITORING USAGE clause of the ALTER INDEX statement.

```
ALTER INDEX <index name> MONITORING USAGE;
```

The V$OBJECT_USAGE view contains information about index usage. If the index is used after the monitoring begins, the USED column will have a value of YES. The following example illustrates index monitoring. It enables monitoring of index PK_DEPT.

```
SQL> alter index pk_dept monitoring usage;

Index altered.

SQL> select * from v$object_usage;

INDEX_NAME   TABLE_NAME    MON   USE    START_MONITORING     END_MONITORING
----------   -----------   ----- ----   -------------------  --------------
PK_DEPT      DEPT          YES   NO     11/23/2001 23:54:05

SQL>
```

The START_MONITORING column has the timestamp of when the monitoring began. Each time you start monitoring, this timestamp is reset. Using the NOMONITORING clause can stop the monitoring of the index.

```
ALTER INDEX <index name> NOMONITORING USAGE;
```

Let's now query the DEPT table and see how the USED column value changes.

```
SQL> select /*+ index (dept pk_dept) */ * from dept
  2  where deptno = 10;

    DEPTNO  DNAME           LOC
----------  ------------    -------------
        10  ACCOUNTING      NEW YORK

SQL> alter index pk_dept nomonitoring usage;

Index altered.

SQL> select * from v$object_usage;

INDEX_NAME  TABLE_NAME  MON  USE      START_MONITORING       END_MONITORING
----------- ----------- ---- ---- -------------------- -------------------
PK_DEPT     DEPT        NO   YES  11/23/2001 23:54:05  11/24/2001 23:54:05

SQL>
```

Querying Index Information

Oracle Objective

Get index information from the data dictionary

Several data dictionary views are available to query information about indexes. This section covers certain views and their columns that you should be familiar with before taking the exam.

DBA_INDEXES

The DBA_INDEXES, USER_INDEXES, and ALL_INDEXES views are the primary views you can use to query for information about indexes (IND is a synonym for USER_INDEXES). The views have the following information (the columns that can be used in the query are provided in parentheses):

- Identity (OWNER, INDEX_NAME, INDEX_TYPE, TABLE_OWNER, TABLE_NAME, TABLE_TYPE)

- Storage (TABLESPACE_NAME, PCT_FREE, PCT_USED, INI_TRANS, MAX_TRANS, INITIAL_EXTENT, NEXT_EXTENT, MAX_EXTENTS, MIN_EXTENTS, PCT_INCREASE, FREELISTS, FREELIST_GROUPS, BUFFER_POOL)
- Statistics (BLEVEL, LEAF_BLOCKS, DISTINCT_KEYS, AVG_LEAF_BLOCKS_PER_KEY, AVG_DATA_BLOCKS_PER_KEY, NUM_ROWS, SAMPLE_SIZE, LAST_ANALYZED)
- Miscellaneous create options (UNIQUENESS, LOGGING, DEGREE, CACHE, PARTITIONED)

DBA_IND_COLUMNS

Use the DBA_IND_COLUMNS, USER_IND_COLUMNS, and ALL_IND_COLUMNS views to display information about the columns in an index. The following information can be queried:

- Identity (INDEX_OWNER, INDEX_NAME, TABLE_OWNER, TABLE_NAME, COLUMN_NAME)
- Column characteristics (COLUMN_LENGTH, COLUMN_POSITION, DESCEND)

Table 8.4 lists other dictionary views that show information about the indexes in the database.

TABLE 8.4 Dictionary Views with Index Information

View Name	Contents
ALL_IND_PARTITIONS DBA_IND_PARTITIONS USER_IND_PARTITIONS	Index partitioning information, storage parameters, and partition-level statistics gathered
ALL_IND_SUBPARTITIONS DBA_IND_SUBPARTITIONS USER_IND_SUBPARTITIONS	Sub-partition information for composite index partitions in the database
ALL_IND_EXPRESSIONS DBA_IND_EXPRESSIONS USER_IND_EXPRESSIONS	Columns or expressions used to create the function-based index
INDEX_STATS	Statistical information from the ANALYZE INDEX VALIDATE STRUCTURE command

Managing Constraints

Constraints are created in the database to enforce a business rule and to specify relationships between various tables. You can also enforce business rules by using database triggers and application code. *Integrity constraints* prevent bad data from being entered into the database.

Oracle allows you to create five types of integrity constraints:

NOT NULL Prevents NULL values from being entered into the column. These types of constraints are defined on a single column.

CHECK Checks whether the condition specified in the constraint is satisfied.

UNIQUE Ensures that there are no duplicate values for the column(s) specified. Every value or set of values is unique within the table.

PRIMARY KEY Uniquely identifies each row of the table. Prevents NULL values. A table can have only one primary key constraint.

FOREIGN KEY Establishes a parent-child relationship between tables by using common columns.

Creating Constraints

Oracle Objective

Implement data integrity constraints

To create constraints, you use the CREATE TABLE or ALTER TABLE statements. You can specify the constraint definition at the column level if the constraint is defined on a single column. You define multiple column constraints at the table level; specify the columns in parentheses separated by a comma. If you do not provide a name for the constraints, Oracle assigns a system-generated name. To provide a name for the constraint, specify the keyword CONSTRAINT followed by the constraint name. In this section, we will discuss the rules for each constraint type and give you some examples of creating constraints.

NOT NULL

NOT NULL constraints have the following characteristics:

- You define the constraint at the column level.
- Use CREATE TABLE to define constraints when creating the table. The following example shows a named constraint on the ORDER_NUM column; for ORDER_DATE, Oracle generates a name.

```
CREATE TABLE ORDERS (
 ORDER_NUM   NUMBER (4) CONSTRAINT NN_ORDER_NUM NOT NULL,
 ORDER_DATE  DATE NOT NULL,
 PRODUCT_ID)
```

- Use ALTER TABLE MODIFY to add or remove a NOT NULL constraint on the columns of an existing table. The following code shows examples of removing a constraint and adding a constraint.

```
ALTER TABLE ORDERS MODIFY ORDER_DATE NULL;
ALTER TABLE ORDERS MODIFY PRODUCT_ID NOT NULL;
```

CHECK

CHECK constraints have the following characteristics:

- They can be defined at the column level or table level.
- The condition specified in the CHECK clause should evaluate to a Boolean result and can refer to values in other columns of the same row; the condition cannot use queries.
- Environment functions such as SYSDATE, USER, USERENV, UID, and pseudo-columns such as ROWNUM, CURRVAL, NEXTVAL, or LEVEL cannot be used to evaluate the check condition.
- One column can have more than one CHECK constraint defined. The column can have a NULL value.
- They can be created using CREATE TABLE or ALTER TABLE.

```
CREATE TABLE BONUS (
 EMP_ID     VARCHAR2 (40) NOT NULL,
 SALARY     NUMBER (9,2),
 BONUS      NUMBER (9,2),
CONSTRAINT CK_BONUS CHECK (BONUS > 0));
```

```
ALTER TABLE BONUS
ADD CONSTRAINT CK_BONUS2 CHECK (BONUS < SALARY);
```

UNIQUE

UNIQUE constraints have the following characteristics:

- They can be defined at the column level for single-column unique keys. For a multiple-column unique key (composite key—the maximum number of columns specified can be 32), the constraint should be defined at the table level.
- Oracle creates a unique index on the unique key columns to enforce uniqueness. If a unique index or a non-unique index already exists on the table with the same columns in the index, Oracle uses the existing index. To use the existing non-unique index, the table must not contain any duplicate keys.
- Unique constraints allow NULL values in the constraint columns.
- Storage can be specified for the implicit index created when creating the key. If no storage is specified, the index is created on the default tablespace with the default storage parameters of the tablespace. You can specify the LOGGING and NOSORT clauses, as you would when creating an index. The index created can be a local or a global partitioned index. The index will have the same name as the unique constraint. Following are two examples. The first one defines a unique constraint with two columns and specifies the storage parameters for the index. The second example adds a new column to the EMP table and creates a unique key at the column level.

  ```
  ALTER TABLE BONUS
  ADD CONSTRAINT UQ_EMP_ID UNIQUE (DEPT, EMP_ID)
  USING INDEX TABLESPACE INDX
  STORAGE (INITIAL 32K NEXT 32K PCTINCREASE 0);

  ALTER TABLE EMP ADD
  SSN VARCHAR2 (11) CONSTRAINT UQ_SSN UNIQUE;
  ```

PRIMARY KEY

PRIMARY KEY constraints have the following characteristics:

- All characteristics of the UNIQUE key are applicable except that NULL values are not allowed in the primary key columns.
- A table can have only one primary key.
- Oracle creates a unique index and NOT NULL constraints for each column in the key. Oracle can use an existing index if all the columns of the primary key are in the index. The following example defines a primary key when creating the table. Storage parameters are specified for both the table and the primary key index.

```
CREATE TABLE EMPLOYEE (
 DEPT_NO VARCHAR2 (2),
 EMP_ID  NUMBER (4),
 NAME    VARCHAR2 (20) NOT NULL,
 SSN     VARCHAR2 (11),
 SALARY  NUMBER (9,2) CHECK (SALARY > 0),
CONSTRAINT PK_EMPLOYEE PRIMARY KEY (DEPT_NO, EMP_ID)
 USING INDEX TABLESPACE INDX
 STORAGE (INITIAL 64K NEXT 64K)
 NOLOGGING,
CONSTRAINT UQ_SSN UNIQUE (SSN)
 USING INDEX TABLESPACE INDX)
TABLESPACE USERS
STORAGE (INITIAL 128K NEXT 64K);
```

- Indexes created to enforce unique keys and primary keys can be managed as any other index. However, these indexes cannot be dropped explicitly.

You cannot drop indexes created to enforce the primary key or unique constraints.

FOREIGN KEY

The foreign key is the column or columns in the table (child table) in which the constraint is created; the referenced key is the primary key, the unique key column, or columns in the table (parent table) that is referenced by the constraint. The following rules are applicable to foreign key constraints:

- You can define a foreign key constraint at the column level or table level. Define multiple-column foreign keys at the table level.
- The foreign key column(s) and referenced key column(s) can be in the same table (self-referential integrity constraint).
- `NULL` values are allowed in the foreign key columns. The following is an example of creating a foreign key constraint on the `COUNTRY_CODE` and `STATE_CODE` columns of the `CITY` table, which refers to the `COUNTRY_CODE` and `STATE_CODE` columns of the `STATE` table (the composite primary key of the `STATE` table).

  ```
  ALTER TABLE CITY ADD CONSTRAINT FK_STATE
   FOREIGN KEY (COUNTRY_CODE, STATE_CODE)
   REFERENCES STATE (COUNTRY_CODE, STATE_CODE);
  ```

- The `ON DELETE` clause specifies the action to be taken when a row in the parent table is deleted and child rows exist with the deleted parent primary key. You can delete the child rows (`CASCADE`) or set the foreign key column values to `NULL` (`SET NULL`). If you omit this clause, Oracle will not allow you to delete from the parent table if child records exist. You must delete the child rows first and then the parent row. Following are two examples of specifying the delete action in a foreign key.

  ```
  ALTER TABLE CITY ADD CONSTRAINT FK_STATE
   FOREIGN KEY (COUNTRY_CODE, STATE_CODE)
   REFERENCES STATE (COUNTRY_CODE, STATE_CODE)
   ON DELETE CASCADE;

  ALTER TABLE CITY ADD CONSTRAINT FK_STATE
   FOREIGN KEY (COUNTRY_CODE, STATE_CODE)
   REFERENCES STATE (COUNTRY_CODE, STATE_CODE)
   ON DELETE SET NULL;
  ```

Creating Disabled Constraints

When you create a constraint, it is enabled automatically. You can create a *disabled* constraint by specifying the DISABLE keyword after the constraint definition. For example:

```
ALTER TABLE CITY ADD CONSTRAINT FK_STATE
 FOREIGN KEY (COUNTRY_CODE, STATE_CODE)
 REFERENCES STATE (COUNTRY_CODE, STATE_CODE) DISABLE;

ALTER TABLE BONUS
ADD CONSTRAINT CK_BONUS CHECK (BONUS > 0) DISABLE;
```

Dropping Constraints

To drop constraints, you use ALTER TABLE. You can drop any constraint by specifying the constraint name.

```
ALTER TABLE BONUS DROP CONSTRAINT CK_BONUS2;
```

To drop unique key constraints with referenced foreign keys, specify the CASCADE clause to drop the foreign key constraints and the unique constraint. Specify the unique key columns(s). For example:

```
ALTER TABLE EMPLOYEE DROP UNIQUE (EMP_ID) CASCADE;
```

To drop primary key constraints with referenced foreign key constraints, use the CASCADE clause to drop all foreign key constraints and then the primary key.

```
ALTER TABLE BONUS DROP PRIMARY KEY CASCADE;
```

Enabling and Disabling Constraints

Oracle Objective

Maintain integrity constraints

When you create a constraint, the constraint is automatically enabled (unless you specify the DISABLE clause). You can disable a constraint by using the DISABLE clause of the ALTER TABLE statement. When you disable the UNIQUE or PRIMARY KEY constraints, Oracle drops the associated unique index. When you re-enable these constraints, Oracle builds the index.

You can disable any constraint by specifying the clause DISABLE CONSTRAINT followed by the constraint name. Specifying UNIQUE and the column name(s) can disable unique keys, and specifying PRIMARY KEY can disable the table's primary key. You cannot disable a primary key or a unique key if foreign keys that are enabled reference it. To disable all the referenced foreign keys and the primary or unique key, specify CASCADE. Following are three examples that illustrate disabling.

```
ALTER TABLE BONUS DISABLE CONSTRAINT CK_BONUS;

ALTER TABLE EMPLOYEE DISABLE CONSTRAINT UQ_EMPLOYEE;

ALTER TABLE STATE DISABLE PRIMARY KEY CASCADE;
```

Using the ENABLE clause of the ALTER TABLE statement enables a constraint. When you enable a disabled unique or primary key, Oracle creates an index if an index with the unique or primary key columns (prefixed) does not already exist. You can specify storage for the unique or primary key when enabling these constraints. For example:

```
ALTER TABLE STATE ENABLE PRIMARY KEY USING INDEX
TABLESPACE USER_INDEX STORAGE (INITIAL 2M NEXT 2M);
```

You can use the EXCEPTIONS INTO clause to find the rows that violate a referential integrity or uniqueness condition. The ROWIDs of the invalid rows are inserted into a table. You can specify the name of the table in which you want the ROWIDs to be saved; by default, Oracle looks for the table named EXCEPTIONS. You can create the table using the script utlexcpt.sql supplied from Oracle, located in the rdbms/admin directory of the software installation. The structure of the table is as follows:

```
SQL>  @c:\oracle\ora90\rdbms\admin\utlexcpt.sql

Table created.

SQL> desc exceptions
 Name                      Null?    Type
 ------------------------- -------- --------------
 ROWID                              ROWID
 OWNER                              VARCHAR2(30)
 TABLE_NAME                         VARCHAR2(30)
 CONSTRAINT                         VARCHAR2(30)
```

The following example enables the primary key constraint and inserts the ROWIDs of the bad rows into the EXCEPTIONS table:

```
ALTER TABLE STATE ENABLE PRIMARY KEY
EXCEPTIONS INTO EXCEPTIONS;
```

You can also use the MODIFY CONSTRAINT clause of the ALTER TABLE statement to enable/disable constraints. Specify the constraint name followed by the MODIFY CONSTRAINT keywords. Following are examples.

```
ALTER TABLE BONUS MODIFY CONSTRAINT CK_BONUS DISABLE;

ALTER TABLE STATE MODIFY CONSTRAINT PK_STATE
DISABLE CASCADE;

ALTER TABLE BONUS MODIFY CONSTRAINT CK_BONUS ENABLE;

ALTER TABLE STATE MODIFY CONSTRAINT PK_STATE USING INDEX
TABLESPACE USER_INDEX STORAGE (INITIAL 2M NEXT 2M) ENABLE;
```

Validated Constraints

You have seen how to enable and disable a constraint. ENABLE and DISABLE affect only future data that will be added/modified in the table. In contrast, the VALIDATE and NOVALIDATE keywords in the ALTER TABLE command act on the existing data. Therefore, a constraint can have four states:

ENABLE VALIDATE This is the default for the ENABLE clause. The existing data in the table is validated to verify that it conforms to the constraint.

ENABLE NOVALIDATE This constraint does not validate the existing data, but enables the constraint for future constraint checking.

DISABLE VALIDATE The constraint is disabled (any index used to enforce the constraint is dropped), but the constraint remains valid. No DML operation is allowed on the table because future changes cannot be verified.

DISABLE NOVALIDATE This is the default for the DISABLE clause. The constraint is disabled, and no checks are done on future or existing data.

Let's look at an example of how these clauses can be used. Say that you have a large data warehouse table, on which bulk data loads are performed every night. This table has a primary key enforced using a non-unique index—because Oracle does not drop the non-unique index when disabling the constraint. When you do batch loads, you can disable the primary key constraint as follows:

```
ALTER TABLE WH01 MODIFY CONSTRAINT PK_WH01
DISABLE NOVALIDATE;
```

After the batch load completes, you can enable the primary key as follows:

```
ALTER TABLE WH01 MODIFY CONSTRAINT PK_WH01
ENABLE NOVALIDATE;
```

Oracle does not allow any inserts/updates/deletes on a table with a DISABLE VALIDATE constraint. Changing the constraint status to DISABLE VALIDATE is a quick way to make a table read-only.

Real World Scenario

Creating a Table, Indexes, and Constraints for a Customer Maintenance Application

You, the DBA, must create the tables that are needed to manage a customer database. You are given the physical structure of the tables, the relationship between the tables, and the following information:

- Columns of the CUSTOMER_MASTER table and the type of data stored. CUST_ID is the unique identifier of the table—the primary key. This table contains customer name, e-mail address, date of birth, primary contact address type, and status flag.
- The CUSTOMER_ADDRESS table keeps the addresses of the customers. Each customer can have a maximum of four addresses—business1, business2, home1, and home2.
- CUSTOMER_REFERENCES table keeps information about the new customers introduced by a customer. This table simply keeps the customer ID of the referring customer and the new customer.

- Each table has record creation date, created user name, update date, and update username.

You decide to keep the tables and indexes in separate tablespaces and to use the uniform extent feature of the tablespace. This arrangement helps to manage the space on the tablespace more effectively. Data is kept in CUST_DATA tablespace, and indexes are maintained in the CUST_INDX tablespace. You create the tablespaces as follows:

```
CREATE TABLESPACE CUST_DATA DATAFILE
'C:\ORACLE\ORADATA\CUST_DATA01.DBF' SIZE 512K
AUTOEXTEND ON NEXT 128K MAXSIZE 2000K
EXTENT MANAGEMENT LOCAL UNIFORM SIZE 64K
SEGMENT SPACE MANAGEMENT AUTO;
CREATE TABLESPACE CUST_INDX DATAFILE
'C:\ORACLE\ORADATA\CUST_INDX.DBF' SIZE 256K
AUTOEXTEND ON NEXT 128K MAXSIZE 2000K
EXTENT MANAGEMENT LOCAL UNIFORM SIZE 32K
SEGMENT SPACE MANAGEMENT AUTO;
```

Now you need to create the `CUSTOMER_MASTER` table. The table needs to have a primary key `CUST_ID` and a unique key `EMAIL`. You create a non-unique index on the `EMAIL` column, which is used to enforce the `UNIQUE` key. You also want to create an index on the DOB column because each week the firm sends greetings to all customers who are celebrating a birthday that week. The check constraint on the ADD_TYPE ensures that no other values are inserted into the column.

```
CREATE TABLE CUSTOMER_MASTER (
CUST_ID        VARCHAR2 (10),
CUST_NAME      VARCHAR2 (30),
EMAIL          VARCHAR2 (30),
DOB            DATE,
```

```
ADD_TYPE      CHAR (2) CONSTRAINT CK_ADD_TYPE
              CHECK (ADD_TYPE IN ('B1','B2','H1','H2')),
CRE_USER      VARCHAR2 (5) DEFAULT USER,
CRE_TIME      TIMESTAMP (3) DEFAULT SYSTIMESTAMP,
MOD_USER      VARCHAR2 (5),
MOD_TIME      TIMESTAMP (3),
CONSTRAINT PK_CUSTOMER_MASTER PRIMARY KEY (CUST_ID)
  USING INDEX TABLESPACE CUST_INDX)
TABLESPACE CUST_DATA;
CREATE INDEX CUST_EMAIL ON CUSTOMER_MASTER (EMAIL)
TABLESPACE CUST_INDX;
ALTER TABLE CUSTOMER_MASTER ADD CONSTRAINT UQ_CUST_EMAIL
UNIQUE (EMAIL) USING INDEX CUST_EMAIL;
```

Now you are ready to create the CUSTOMER_ADDRESSES table. You create the table first and then add the primary key and the foreign key. You create the foreign key with an option to defer its checking until commit time.

```
CREATE TABLE CUSTOMER_ADDRESSES (
CUST_ID     VARCHAR2 (10),
ADD_TYPE    CHAR (2),
ADD_LINE1   VARCHAR2 (40) NOT NULL,
ADD_LINE2   VARCHAR2 (40),
CITY        VARCHAR2 (40) NOT NULL,
STATE       VARCHAR2 (2) NOT NULL,
ZIP         NUMBER (5) NOT NULL)
TABLESPACE CUST_DATA;
ALTER TABLE CUSTOMER_ADDRESSES ADD CONSTRAINT
PK_CUST_ADDRESSES PRIMARY KEY (CUST_ID, ADD_TYPE)
USING INDEX TABLESPACE CUST_INDX;
ALTER TABLE CUSTOMER_ADDRESSES ADD CONSTRAINT
FK_CUST_ADDRESSES FOREIGN KEY (CUST_ID)
```

```
REFERENCES CUSTOMER_MASTER;
ALTER TABLE CUSTOMER_ADDRESSES ADD CONSTRAINT
CK_ADD_TYPE2 CHECK (ADD_TYPE IN ('B1','B2','H1','H2'));
```

You forgot, however, to enable the constraint deferrable clause and to delete records from CUSTOMER_ADDRESSES table when the row is deleted from CUSTOMER_MASTER table, so you do that now as follows:

```
ALTER TABLE CUSTOMER_ADDRESSES
DROP CONSTRAINT FK_CUST_ADDRESSES;
ALTER TABLE CUSTOMER_ADDRESSES ADD CONSTRAINT
FK_CUST_ADDRESSES FOREIGN KEY (CUST_ID)
REFERENCES CUSTOMER_MASTER
ON DELETE CASCADE DEFERRABLE INITIALLY IMMEDIATE;
```

Now you create the CUSTOMER_REFERENCES table. Since this table row never grows with updates, you set the PCTFREE of the table to 0.

```
CREATE TABLE CUSTOMER_REFERENCES (
CUST_ID      VARCHAR2 (10) REFERENCES CUSTOMER_MASTER,
CUST_REF_ID  VARCHAR2 (10) REFERENCES CUSTOMER_MASTER,
CRE_USER     VARCHAR2 (5),
CRE_TIME     TIMESTAMP (3) DEFAULT SYSTIMESTAMP,
MOD_USER     VARCHAR2 (5) DEFAULT USER,
MOD_TIME     TIMESTAMP (3),
CONSTRAINT PK_CUST_REFS PRIMARY KEY (CUST_ID, CUST_REF_ID))
TABLESPACE CUST_DATA
PCTFREE 0;
```

By reviewing the creating, you find that the CUSTOMER_ADDRESSES table does not have the created and modified user information and that the CUSTOMER_REFERENCES table has a DEFAULT value assigned to the wrong column. You fix these problems as follows:

```
ALTER TABLE CUSTOMER_ADDRESSES ADD (
CRE_USER     VARCHAR2 (5) DEFAULT USER,
CRE_TIME     TIMESTAMP (3) DEFAULT SYSTIMESTAMP,
```

```
MOD_USER      VARCHAR2 (5),
MOD_TIME      TIMESTAMP (3));
ALTER TABLE CUSTOMER_REFERENCES MODIFY
MOD_USER DEFAULT NULL;
ALTER TABLE CUSTOMER_REFERENCES MODIFY
CRE_USER DEFAULT USER;
```

Also, the primary key for the CUSTOMER_REFERENCES table did not specify a tablespace for the primary key index, so it was created in the default tablespace of the table. You correct this as follows:

```
SQL> SELECT TABLESPACE_NAME FROM DBA_INDEXES WHERE
  2  INDEX_NAME = 'PK_CUST_REFS';
TABLESPACE_NAME
------------------------------
CUST_DATA
SQL> ALTER INDEX PK_CUST_REFS REBUILD TABLESPACE CUST_INDX;
Index altered.
SQL> SELECT TABLESPACE_NAME FROM DBA_INDEXES WHERE
  2  INDEX_NAME = 'PK_CUST_REFS';
TABLESPACE_NAME
------------------------------
CUST_INDX
SQL>
```

Now you query the dictionary views to see the table information.

```
SQL> SELECT TABLE_NAME, TABLESPACE_NAME
  2  FROM   USER_TABLES
  3  WHERE  TABLE_NAME LIKE 'CUST%';
TABLE_NAME                     TABLESPACE_NAME
------------------------------ ------------------------
CUSTOMER_ADDRESSES             CUST_DATA
CUSTOMER_MASTER                CUST_DATA
CUSTOMER_REFERENCES            CUST_DATA
```

```
SQL> SELECT SEGMENT_NAME, SEGMENT_TYPE, TABLESPACE_NAME, BYTES
  2  FROM   DBA_SEGMENTS
  3  WHERE  OWNER = 'CM'
  4  AND    SEGMENT_NAME LIKE '%CUST%';
SEGMENT_NAME         SEGMENT_TYPE       TABLESPACE      BYTES
-------------------- ------------------ ---------- ----------
CUSTOMER_MASTER      TABLE              CUST_DATA       65536
CUSTOMER_ADDRESSES   TABLE              CUST_DATA       65536
CUSTOMER_REFERENCES  TABLE              CUST_DATA       65536
PK_CUSTOMER_MASTER   INDEX              CUST_INDX       32768
CUST_EMAIL           INDEX              CUST_INDX       32768
PK_CUST_ADDRESSES    INDEX              CUST_INDX       32768
PK_CUST_REFS         INDEX              CUST_INDX       65536
7 rows selected.
SQL>
SQL> SELECT INDEX_NAME, COLUMN_NAME, COLUMN_POSITION
  2  FROM   USER_IND_COLUMNS
  3  WHERE  INDEX_NAME LIKE '%CUST%'
  4  ORDER BY 1,3;
INDEX_NAME           COLUMN_NAME          COLUMN_POSITION
-------------------- -------------------- ---------------
CUST_EMAIL           EMAIL                              1
PK_CUSTOMER_MASTER   CUST_ID                            1
PK_CUST_ADDRESSES    CUST_ID                            1
PK_CUST_ADDRESSES    ADD_TYPE                           2
PK_CUST_REFS         CUST_ID                            1
PK_CUST_REFS         CUST_REF_ID                        2
6 rows selected.
SQL>
```

Next you query the dictionary views to see the constraint information. Notice that the two foreign key constraints on CUSTOMER_REFERENCES table and the NOT NULL constraints in the CUSTOMER_ADDRESSES table have system generated names.

```
SQL> SELECT CONSTRAINT_NAME, CONSTRAINT_TYPE, TABLE_NAME,
  2         R_CONSTRAINT_NAME
  3  FROM   USER_CONSTRAINTS
  4  WHERE  TABLE_NAME LIKE 'CUST%';

CONSTRAINT_NAME      C TABLE_NAME           R_CONSTRAINT_NAME
-------------------- - -------------------- -------------------
SYS_C002792          C CUSTOMER_ADDRESSES
SYS_C002793          C CUSTOMER_ADDRESSES
SYS_C002794          C CUSTOMER_ADDRESSES
SYS_C002795          C CUSTOMER_ADDRESSES
PK_CUST_ADDRESSES    P CUSTOMER_ADDRESSES
FK_CUST_ADDRESSES    R CUSTOMER_ADDRESSES   PK_CUSTOMER_MASTER
CK_ADD_TYPE2         C CUSTOMER_ADDRESSES
CK_ADD_TYPE          C CUSTOMER_MASTER
PK_CUSTOMER_MASTER   P CUSTOMER_MASTER
UQ_CUST_EMAIL        U CUSTOMER_MASTER
PK_CUST_REFS         P CUSTOMER_REFERENCES
SYS_C002804          R CUSTOMER_REFERENCES  PK_CUSTOMER_MASTER
SYS_C002805          R CUSTOMER_REFERENCES  PK_CUSTOMER_MASTER
13 rows selected.
SQL>
SQL> SELECT CONSTRAINT_NAME, GENERATED, INDEX_NAME
  2  FROM   USER_CONSTRAINTS
  3  WHERE  TABLE_NAME LIKE 'CUST%';
CONSTRAINT_NAME      GENERATED      INDEX_NAME
-------------------- -------------- --------------------
SYS_C002792          GENERATED NAME
SYS_C002793          GENERATED NAME
SYS_C002794          GENERATED NAME
SYS_C002795          GENERATED NAME
```

```
PK_CUST_ADDRESSES    USER NAME       PK_CUST_ADDRESSES
FK_CUST_ADDRESSES    USER NAME
CK_ADD_TYPE2         USER NAME
CK_ADD_TYPE          USER NAME
PK_CUSTOMER_MASTER   USER NAME       PK_CUSTOMER_MASTER
UQ_CUST_EMAIL        USER NAME       CUST_EMAIL
PK_CUST_REFS         USER NAME       PK_CUST_REFS
SYS_C002804          GENERATED NAME
SYS_C002805          GENERATED NAME
13 rows selected.
SQL>
```

Deferring Constraint Checks

By default, Oracle checks whether the data conforms to the constraint when the statement is executed. Oracle allows you to change this behavior if the constraint is created using the `DEFERRABLE` clause (`NOT DEFERRABLE` is the default). Oracle specifies that the transaction can set the constraint-checking behavior. `INITIALLY IMMEDIATE` specifies that the constraint be checked for conformance at the end of each SQL statement (this is the default). `INITIALLY DEFERRED` specifies that the constraint be checked for conformance at the end of the transaction. You cannot change the `DEFERRABLE` status of a constraint using `ALTER TABLE MODIFY CONSTRAINT`; you must drop and re-create the constraint, and you can change the `INITIALLY [DEFERRED/IMMEDIATE]` clause using `ALTER TABLE`.

If the constraint is `DEFERRABLE`, you can change the behavior by using the `SET CONSTRAINTS` command or by using the `ALTER SESSION SET CONSTRAINT` command. You can enable or disable deferred constraint checking by listing all the constraints or by specifying the `ALL` keyword. You use the `SET CONSTRAINTS` command to set the constraint-checking behavior for the current transaction, and you use the `ALTER SESSION` command to set the constraint-checking behavior for the current session.

Let's look at an example. Create a primary key constraint on the `CUSTOMER` table and a foreign key constraint on the `ORDERS` table as `DEFERRABLE`.

Although the constraints are created DEFERRABLE, they are not deferred because of the INITIALLY IMMEDIATE clause.

```
ALTER TABLE CUSTOMER ADD CONSTRAINT PK_CUST_ID
PRIMARY KEY (CUST_ID) DEFERRABLE
INITIALLY IMMEDIATE;

ALTER TABLE ORDERS ADD CONSTRAINT FK_CUST_ID
FOREIGN KEY (CUST_ID)
REFERENCES CUSTOMER (CUST_ID)
ON DELETE CASCADE DEFERRABLE;
```

If you try to add a row to the ORDERS table with a CUST_ID that is not available in the CUSTOMER table, Oracle returns an error immediately, even though you plan to add the CUSTOMER row soon. Since the constraints are verified for conformance at each SQL statement, you must insert the CUSTOMER row first and then insert the row to the ORDERS table. Because the constraints are defined as DEFERRABLE, you can change this behavior by using the following command:

```
SET CONSTRAINTS ALL DEFERRED;
```

Now, you can insert rows in these tables in any order. Oracle checks the constraint conformance only at commit time.

If you want deferred constraint checking as the default, create/modify the constraint by using INITIALLY DEFERRED. For example:

```
ALTER TABLE CUSTOMER MODIFY CONSTRAINT PK_CUST_ID
INITIALLY DEFERRED;
```

Querying Constraint Information

Oracle Objective

Obtain constraint information from the data dictionary

You can query constraints, their columns, type, status, and so on from the dictionary, using the following views.

DBA_CONSTRAINTS

You can query the ALL_CONSTRAINTS, DBA_CONSTRAINTS, and USER_CONSTRAINTS views to get information about the constraints. The CONSTRAINT_TYPE column shows the type of constraint—C for check, P for primary key, U for unique key, and R for referential (foreign key); V and O are associated with views. For check constraints, the SEARCH_CONDITION column shows the check condition. NOT NULL constraints are listed in this view as CHECK constraints. NOT NULL constraint information can also be found in the NULLABLE column of the DBA_TAB_COLUMNS view. Here is a sample query to get the constraint information:

```
SQL> SELECT CONSTRAINT_NAME, CONSTRAINT_TYPE, DEFERRED,
  2         DEFERRABLE, STATUS
  3  FROM   DBA_CONSTRAINTS
  4  WHERE  TABLE_NAME = 'ORDERS';

CONSTRAINT_NAME    C DEFERRED  DEFERRABLE     STATUS
------------------ - --------- -------------- --------
CK_QUANTITY        C IMMEDIATE NOT DEFERRABLE DISABLED
PK_ORDERS          P DEFERRED  DEFERRABLE     ENABLED

SQL>
```

DBA_CONS_COLUMNS

The ALL_CONS_COLUMNS, DBA_CONS_COLUMNS, and USER_CONS_COLUMNS views show the columns associated with the constraints.

```
SQL> SELECT CONSTRAINT_NAME, COLUMN_NAME, POSITION
  2  FROM   DBA_CONS_COLUMNS
  3  WHERE  TABLE_NAME = 'ORDERS';

CONSTRAINT_NAME                COLUMN_NAME      POSITION
------------------------------ --------------- ----------
CK_QUANTITY                    QUANTITY
PK_ORDERS                      ORDER_NUM               2
PK_ORDERS                      ORDER_DATE              1

SQL>
```

Summary

This chapter discussed the various options available for creating tables, indexes, and constraints. You create tables using the CREATE TABLE command. By default, the table is created in the current schema. To create the table in another schema, you qualify the table with the schema name. You can create storage parameters when creating the table. The storage parameters that specify the extent sizes are INITIAL, NEXT, and PCTINCREASE. Once the table is created, you cannot change the INITIAL and MINEXTENTS parameters. PCTFREE controls the free space in the data block.

Partitioning the tables lets you manage large tables more easily and results in better query performance. Partitioning is breaking a large table into smaller, more manageable pieces. Four partitioning methods are available: range, hash, list and composite. You can also create indexes on partitioned tables. The indexes can be equipartitioned, which results in what is also known as a local index, meaning index partitions will have the same partition keys and number of partitions as the partitioned table. You can create partitioned indexes on partitioned tables or non-partitioned tables. Similarly, partitioned tables can have partitioned local, partitioned global, or nonpartitioned indexes.

You can alter tables and indexes to deallocate extents or unused blocks. You use the DEALLOCATE clause of the ALTER TABLE statement to release the free blocks that are above the high-water mark (HWM). You can also manually allocate space to a table or an index by using the ALLOCATE EXTENT clause. You move or reorganize tables can be using the MOVE clause. You can specify new tablespace and storage parameters.

You can use the ANALYZE command on tables and indexes to validate the structure and to identify corrupt blocks. You can also use the ANALYZE command to collect statistics and to find and fix the chained rows in a table. The ROWID of the table is an 18-character representation of the physical location of the row. You can use the DBMS_ROWID package to convert ROWIDs between restricted and extended formats. You can query information on tables from DBA_TABLES, DBA_TAB_COLUMNS, DBA_TAB_PARTITIONS, and so on.

You can create indexes as b-tree or bitmap. Bitmap indexes save storage space for low cardinality columns. You can create reverse key or function-based indexes. An Index Organized Table (IOT) stores the index and row data in the b-tree structure. Specify tablespace and storage when creating indexes. When you create indexes ONLINE, the table is available for insert/update/delete operations during indexing. You can use the REBUILD clause of the ALTER INDEX command to move the index to a different tablespace or to reorganize the index. You can also change a reverse key index to a normal index and vice versa. You can monitor index usage and then drop unused indexes from the database to save resources.

You create constraints on tables to enforce business rules. There are five types of constraints: not null, check, unique, primary key, and foreign key.

You can create the constraints to check conformance at each SQL statement or when committing the changes—checking for conformance at each statement is the default. You can enable and disable constraints. Enable constraints with the NOVALIDATE clause to save time after large data loads.

Exam Essentials

Understand the Oracle datatypes. Know the datatypes that you can use when creating/altering tables. Learn the new datatypes introduced in Oracle9i—TIMESTAMP and INTERVAL. Know the default width and precision of each datatype.

Know the row. Learn the structure of the row and its components. The row header normally occupies 3 bytes; columns with length less than 251 bytes occupy 1 byte for column length storage, and columns with length of more than 250 bytes occupy 2 bytes for storing the column length in the row piece.

Know the ROWID. ROWID is the physical location of the row. Understand the components that constitute the ROWID and the datatypes available to store the ROWID information.

Know the syntax for creating tables. The CREATE TABLE statement is a complex statement. Understand all the clauses available to specify its storage, segment space management, and logging characteristics.

Know how to create the different types of tables. Understand the keywords that appear in the ORGANIZATION clause of the CREATE TABLE statement. HEAP is the default and is used to create regular tables. INDEX creates an IOT, and EXTERNAL creates an external table.

Know how to rebuild a table. You can reorganize a table by using the MOVE clause of the ALTER TABLE statement. The table can be rebuilt on the same tablespace or on a different tablespace with new storage parameters.

Drop a column from table. Dropping a column from table was introduced in Oracle8i. For large tables, you can mark a column as unused and later drop the column. Dropping the column saves disk space.

Understand how to use the data dictionary to find table information. Know the dictionary views that contain information about the tables, its storage segments and extents, partitions, creation /modification timestamps, and so on. The most commonly used views to query table information are DBA_TABLES, DBA_TAB_COLUMNS, DBA_SEGMENTS, and DBA_OBJECTS.

Understand the different types of indexes available. Know the different types of indexes and when to use them. The most commonly used index is the b-tree index. Bitmap, reverse-key, and function-based are the other types of indexes.

Understand how to manage indexes. Indexes over time grow large and contain a lot of free space. Such indexes can be coalesced. You can also reorganize indexes using the ALTER INDEX REBUILD statement. You can move the index to a different tablespace, and you can use new storage parameters.

Monitor index usage. The ability to monitor index usage is new in Oracle9i. It is good to know which indexes are not used over a period of time, so that you can drop them and save resources. Use the MONITORING USAGE clause of the ALTER INDEX statement to monitor indexes.

Know the different types of constraints that can be created on a table. Understand their purpose and syntax of creation. NOT NULL is a column level constraint, and the other constraints can be defined at the column level or table level.

Know the dictionary views to get constraint information. You use the data dictionary views DBA_CONSTRAINTS and DBA_CONS_COLUMNS to get constraint information. The INDEX_OWNER and INDEX_NAME columns of DBA_CONSTRAINTS provide the index used to enforce uniqueness or primary key constraint.

Key Terms

Before you take the exam, make sure you're familiar with the following terms:

- bitmap index
- b-tree
- datatypes
- function-based index
- high-water mark (HWM)
- Index Organized Table
- integrity constraints
- intra-block chaining
- logical attributes
- partitioning
- physical attributes
- reverse key index
- `ROWID`

Review Questions

1. A table is created as follows:

```
CREATE TABLE MY_TABLE (COL1 NUMBER)
STORAGE (INITIAL 2M NEXT 2M MINEXTENTS 6 PCTINCREASE 0);
```

When you issue the following statement, what will be the size of the table, if the high-water mark of the table is 200KB?

```
ALTER TABLE MY_TABLE DEALLOCATE UNUSED KEEP 1000K;
```

A. 1000KB

B. 200KB

C. 1200KB

D. 2MB

E. 13MB

2. Which command is used to drop a constraint?

A. `ALTER TABLE    MODIFY CONSTRAINT`

B. `DROP CONSTRAINT`

C. `ALTER TABLE    DROP CONSTRAINT`

D. `ALTER CONSTRAINT    DROP`

3. When you define a column with datatype `TIMESTAMP WITH LOCAL TIME ZONE`, what is the precision of seconds stored?

A. 2

B. 6

C. 9

D. 0

4. Which data dictionary view has the timestamp of the table creation?

   A. DBA_OBJECTS

   B. DBA_SEGMENTS

   C. DBA_TABLES

   D. All the above

5. What happens when you issue the following statement and the CHAINED_ROWS table does not exist in the current schema?

   ```
   ANALYZE TABLE EMPLOYEE LIST CHAINED ROWS;
   ```

   A. Oracle creates the CHAINED_ROWS table.

   B. Oracle updates the dictionary with the number of chained rows in the table.

   C. Oracle creates the CHAINED_ROWS table under the SYS schema; if one already exists under SYS, Oracle uses it.

   D. The statement fails.

6. The following statement is issued against the primary key constraint (PK_BONUS) of the BONUS table. (Choose two statements that are true.)

   ```
   ALTER TABLE BONUS MODIFY CONSTRAINT PK_BONUS DISABLE VALIDATE;
   ```

   A. No new rows can be added to the BONUS table.

   B. Existing rows of the BONUS table are validated before disabling the constraint.

   C. Rows can be modified, but the primary key columns cannot change.

   D. The unique index created when defining the constraint is dropped.

7. Which clause in the `ANALYZE` command checks for the integrity of the rows in the table?

A. `COMPUTE STATISTICS`

B. `VALIDATE STRUCTURE`

C. `LIST INVALID ROWS`

D. None of the above

8. Which statement is not true?

A. A partition can be range-partitioned.

B. A subpartition can be range-partitioned.

C. A partition can be hash-partitioned.

D. A subpartition can be hash-partitioned.

9. A table is created with an `INITRANS` value of 2. Which value would you choose for `INITRANS` of an index created on this table?

A. 4

B. 2

C. 1

10. When validating a constraint, why would you specify the `EXCEPTIONS` clause?

A. To display the `ROWID`s of the rows that do not satisfy the constraint

B. To move the bad rows to the table specified in the `EXCEPTIONS` clause

C. To save the `ROWID`s of the bad rows in the table specified in the `EXCEPTIONS` clause

D. To save the bad rows in the table specified in the `EXCEPTIONS` clause

11. Which keyword is not valid for the BUFFER_POOL parameter of the STORAGE clause?

A. DEFAULT

B. LARGE

C. KEEP

D. RECYCLE

12. Which clause in the ALTER TABLE command do you use to reorganize a table?

A. REORGANIZE

B. REBUILD

C. RELOCATE

D. MOVE

13. Which line in the following code has an error?

```
1  ALTER TABLE MY_TABLE
2  STORAGE (
3  MINEXTENTS 4
4  NEXT 512K)
5  NOLOGGING;
```

A. 2

B. 3

C. 4

D. 5

14. Which component is not part of the ROWID?

A. Tablespace

B. Data file number

C. Object ID

D. Block ID

15. Which keyword do you use in the `CREATE INDEX` command to create a function-based index?

A. `CREATE FUNCTION INDEX`

B. `CREATE INDEX   ORGANIZATION INDEX`

C. `CREATE INDEX   FUNCTION BASED`

D. None of the above

16. Which data dictionary view shows statistical information from the `ANALYZE INDEX VALIDATE STRUCTURE` command?

A. `INDEX_STATS`

B. `DBA_INDEXES`

C. `IND`

D. None; `VALIDATE STRUCTURE` does not generate statistics.

17. A constraint is created with the `DEFERRABLE INITIALLY IMMEDIATE` clause. What does this mean?

A. Constraint checking is done only at commit time.

B. Constraint checking is done after each SQL statement, but you can change this behavior by specifying `SET CONSTRAINTS ALL DEFERRED`.

C. Existing rows in the table are immediately checked for constraint violation.

D. The constraint is immediately checked in a DML operation, but subsequent constraint verification is done at commit time.

18. Which script creates the `CHAINED_ROWS` table?

A. `catproc.sql`

B. `catchain.sql`

C. `utlchain.sql`

D. No script is necessary; `ANALYZE TABLE LIST CHAINED ROWS` creates the table.

19. What is the difference between a unique constraint and a primary key constraint?

A. A unique key constraint requires a unique index to enforce the constraint, whereas a primary key constraint can enforce uniqueness using a unique or non-unique index.

B. A primary key column can be `NULL`, but a unique key column cannot be `NULL`.

C. A primary key constraint can use an existing index, but a unique constraint always creates an index.

D. A unique constraint column can be `NULL`, but primary key column(s) cannot be `NULL`.

20. You can monitor an index for its usage by using the `MONITORING USAGE` clause of the `ALTER INDEX` statement. Which data dictionary view do you use to query the index usage?

A. `USER_INDEX_USAGE`

B. `V$OBJECT_USAGE`

C. `V$INDEX_USAGE`

D. `DBA_INDEX_USAGE`

Answers to Review Questions

1. C. You use the KEEP parameter in the DEALLOCATE clause to specify the amount of space you want to keep in the table above the HWM. If you do not specify the KEEP parameter, Oracle deallocates all the space above the HWM if the HWM is above MINEXTENTS; otherwise, free space is de-allocated above MINEXTENTS.

2. C. Constraints are defined on the table and are dropped using the ALTER TABLE command DROP clause. For dropping the primary key, you can also specify PRIMARY KEY instead of the constraint name. Similarly, to drop a unique constraint, you can also specify UNIQUE (*<COLUMN_NAMES>*).

3. B. The TIMESTAMP datatypes have a default precision of 6 digits. The range of values can be from 0 to 9.

4. A. The DBA_OBJECTS view has information about all the objects created in the database and has the timestamp and status of the object in the column CREATED. DBA_TABLES does not show the timestamp.

5. D. If you do not specify a table name to insert the ROWID of chained/migrated rows, Oracle looks for a table named CHAINED_ROWS in the user's schema. If the table does not exist, Oracle returns an error. The dictionary (the DBA_TABLES view) is updated with the number of chained rows when you do a COMPUTE STATISTICS on the table.

6. A and D. DISABLE VALIDATE disables the constraint and drops the index, but keeps the constraint valid. No DML operation is allowed on the table.

7. B. The VALIDATE STRUCTURE clause of the ANALYZE TABLE command checks the structure of the table and makes sure all rows are readable.

8. B. Subpartitions can only be hash-partitioned. A partition can be range-partitioned or hash-partitioned.

9. A. Since index blocks hold more entries per block than table data blocks hold, you should provide a higher value of INITRANS to the index than to the table.

10. C. If you specify the EXCEPTIONS INTO clause when validating or enabling a constraint, the ROWIDs of the rows that do not satisfy the constraint are saved in the table specified in the EXCEPTIONS clause. You can remove the bad rows or fix the column values and enable the constraint.

11. B. The BUFFER_POOL parameter specifies a buffer pool cache for the table or index. The KEEP pool retains the blocks in the SGA. RECYCLE removes blocks from the SGA as soon as the operation is completed, and the DEFAULT pool is for objects for which KEEP or RECYCLE is not specified.

12. D. You use the MOVE clause to reorganize a table. You can specify new tablespace and storage parameters. Queries are allowed on the table, but no DML operations are allowed during the move.

13. B. When you change the storage parameters for an existing index or table, you cannot change the MINEXTENTS and INITIAL values.

14. A. The format of a ROWID is *OOOOOOFFFBBBBBBRRR*; *OOOOOO* is the object number, *FFF* is the relative data file number where the block is located, *BBBBBB* is the block ID where the row is located, and *RRR* is the row in the block.

15. D. You don't need to specify a keyword to create a function-based index; you need only to specify the function itself. To enable a function-based index, you set the parameter QUERY_REWRITE_ENABLED to TRUE, and you set QUERY_REWRITE_INTEGRITY to TRUSTED.

16. A. The INDEX_STATS and INDEX_HISTOGRAMS views show statistical information from the ANALYZE INDEX VALIDATE STRUCTURE statement.

17. B. DEFERRABLE specifies that the constraint can be deferred using the SET CONSTRAINTS command. INITIALLY IMMEDIATE specifies that the constraint's default behavior is to validate the constraint for each SQL statement.

18. C. The utlchain.sql script, located in the rdbms/admin directory for the Oracle software installation, creates the table. When chained or migrated rows are found in the table after you issue the ANALYZE TABLE LIST CHAINED ROWS command, the ROWIDs of such chained/migrated rows are inserted into the CHAINED_ROWS table.

19. D. Columns that are part of the primary key cannot accept `NULL` values.

20. B. The `V$OBJECT_USAGE` view has information about the indexes that are monitored. The START_MONITORING and END_MONITORING columns give the start and end timestamp of monitoring. If an index is used, the USED column will have a value YES.

Managing Users, Security, and Globalization Support

ORACLE9i DBA FUNDAMENTALS I EXAM OBJECTIVES OFFERED IN THIS CHAPTER:

- ✓ Manage passwords using profiles
- ✓ Administer profiles
- ✓ Control use of resources using profiles
- ✓ Obtain information about profiles, password management, and resources
- ✓ Create new database users
- ✓ Alter and drop existing database users
- ✓ Monitor information about existing users
- ✓ Identify system and object privileges
- ✓ Grant and revoke privileges
- ✓ Identify auditing capabilities
- ✓ Create and modify roles
- ✓ Control availability of roles
- ✓ Remove roles
- ✓ Use predefined roles
- ✓ Display role information from the data dictionary
- ✓ Choose database character set and national character set for a database

- ✓ **Specify the language-dependent behavior using initialization parameters, environment variables, and the ALTER SESSION command**
- ✓ **Use the different types of National Language Support (NLS) parameters**
- ✓ **Explain the influence on language-dependent application behavior**
- ✓ **Obtain information about Globalization Support usage**

Exam objectives are subject to change at any time without prior notice and at Oracle's sole discretion. Please visit Oracle's Training and Certification Web site (`http://www.oracle.com/education/certification/`) for the most current exam objectives listing.

Controlling database access and resource limits is an important aspect of the DBA's function. You use profiles to manage the database and system resources and to manage database passwords and password verification. You control database and data access using privileges, and you create roles to manage the privileges. This chapter covers creating users and assigning proper resources and privileges. It also discusses the auditing capabilities of the database and using Globalization Support.

Profiles

You use *profiles* to control the database and system resource usage. Oracle provides a set of predefined resource parameters that you can use to monitor and control database resource usage. You can define limits for each resource by using a database profile. You also use profiles for password management. You can create profiles for different user communities and then assign a profile to each user. When you create the database, Oracle creates a profile named DEFAULT, and if you do not specify a profile for the user, Oracle assigns the user the DEFAULT profile.

Managing Resources

Oracle Objective	Control use of resources using profiles

Oracle lets you control the following types of resource usage through profiles:

- Concurrent sessions per user
- Elapsed and idle time connected to the database
- CPU time used
- Private SQL and PL/SQL area used in the SGA (System Global Area)
- Logical reads performed
- Amount of private SGA space used in Shared Server configurations

Resource limits are enforced only if you have set the parameter RESOURCE_LIMIT to TRUE. Even if you have defined profiles and assigned profiles to users, Oracle enforces them only when this parameter is set to TRUE. You can set this parameter in the initialization parameter file so that every time the database starts, the resource usage is controlled for each user using the assigned profile. You enable or disable resource limits using the ALTER SYSTEM command. The default value of RESOURCE_LIMIT is FALSE.

The limits for each resource are specified as an integer; you can set no limit for a given resource by specifying UNLIMITED, or you can use the value specified in the DEFAULT profile by specifying DEFAULT. The DEFAULT profile initially has the value UNLIMITED for all resources. After you create the database, you can modify the DEFAULT profile.

Most resource limits are set at the session level; a session is created when a user connects to the database. You can control certain limits at the statement level (but not at the transaction level). If a user exceeds a resource limit, Oracle aborts the current operation, rolls back the changes made by the statement, and returns an error. The user has the option of committing or rolling back the transaction, because the statements issued earlier in the transaction are not aborted. No other operation is permitted when a session-level limit is reached. The user *can* disconnect, in which case the transaction is committed. You use the following parameters to control resources:

SESSIONS_PER_USER Limits the number of concurrent user sessions. No more sessions from the current user are allowed when this threshold is reached.

CPU_PER_SESSION Limits the amount of CPU time a session can use. The CPU time is specified in hundredths of a second.

CPU_PER_CALL Limits the amount of CPU time a single SQL statement can use. The CPU time is specified in hundredths of a second. This parameter is useful for controlling runaway queries, but you should be careful to specify this limit for batch programs.

LOGICAL_READS_PER_SESSION Limits the number of data blocks read in a session, including the blocks read from memory and from physical reads.

LOGICAL_READS_PER_CALL Limits the number of data blocks read by a single SQL statement, including the blocks read from memory and from physical reads.

PRIVATE_SGA Limits the amount of space allocated in the SGA for private areas, per session. Private areas for SQL and PL/SQL statements are created in the SGA in the multithreaded architecture. You can specify K to indicate the size in KB or M to indicate the size in MB. If you specify neither K or M, the size is in bytes. This limit does not apply to dedicated server architecture connections.

CONNECT_TIME Specifies the maximum number of minutes a session can stay connected to the database (total elapsed time, not CPU time). When the threshold is reached, the user is automatically disconnected from the database; any pending transaction is rolled back.

IDLE_TIME Specifies the maximum number of minutes a session can be continuously idle, that is, without any activity for a continuous period of time. When the threshold is reached, the user is disconnected from the database; any pending transaction is rolled back.

COMPOSITE_LIMIT A weighted sum of four resource limits: CPU_PER_SESSION, LOGICAL_READS_PER_SESSION, CONNECT_TIME, and PRIVATE_SGA. You can define a *cost* for the system resources (the resource cost on one database may be different from another, based on the number of transactions, CPU, memory, and so on) known as the *composite limit*. The upcoming section "Managing Profiles" discusses setting the resource cost.

Managing Passwords

Oracle Objective

Manage passwords using profiles

You also use profiles to manage passwords. You can set the following by using profiles:

Account locking Number of failed login attempts, and the number of days the password will be locked.

Password expiration How often passwords should be changed, whether passwords can be reused, and the grace period after which the user is warned that the password change is due.

Password complexity Use of a customized function to verify the password complexity—for example, the password should not be the same as the user ID, cannot include commonly used words, and so on.

You can use the following parameters in profiles to manage passwords:

FAILED_LOGIN_ATTEMPTS Specifies the maximum number of consecutive invalid login attempts (providing an incorrect password) allowed before the user account is locked.

PASSWORD_LOCK_TIME Specifies the number of days the user account will remain locked after the user has made FAILED_LOGIN_ATTEMPTS number of consecutive failed login attempts.

PASSWORD_LIFE_TIME Specifies the number of days a user can use one password. If the user does not change the password within the number of days specified, all connection requests return an error. The DBA then has to reset the password.

PASSWORD_GRACE_TIME Specifies the number of days the user will get a warning before the password expires. This is a reminder for the user to change the password.

PASSWORD_REUSE_TIME Specifies the number of days a password cannot be used again after changing it.

PASSWORD_REUSE_MAX Specifies the number of password changes required before a password can be reused. You cannot specify a value for both PASSWORD_REUSE_TIME and PASSWORD_REUSE_MAX; one should always be set to UNLIMITED, because you can enable only one type of password history method.

PASSWORD_VERIFY_FUNCTION Specifies the function you want to use to verify the complexity of the new password. Oracle provides a default script, which you can modify.

You can specify minutes or hours as a fraction or expression in parameters that require days as a value. One hour can be represented as 0.042 days or 1/24, and one minute can be specified as 0.000694 days, 1/24/60, or 1/1440.

Managing Profiles

Oracle Objective

Administer profiles

You can create many profiles in the database that specify both resource management parameters and password management parameters. However, you can assign a user only one profile at any given time. To create a profile, you use the CREATE PROFILE command. You need to provide a name for the profile and then specify the parameter names and their values separated by space(s).

As an example, let's create a profile to manage passwords and resources for the accounting department users. The users are required to change their password every 60 days, and they cannot reuse a password for 90 days. They are allowed to make a typo in the password only six consecutive times while connecting to the database; if the login fails a seventh time, their account is locked forever (until the DBA or security department unlocks the account). The accounting department users are allowed a maximum of six database connections; they can stay connected to the database for 24 hours, but an inactivity of 2 hours will terminate their session. To prevent users from performing runaway queries, in this example we will set the maximum number of blocks they can read per SQL statement to 1 million.

```
SQL> CREATE PROFILE ACCOUNTING_USER LIMIT
      SESSIONS_PER_USER        6
      CONNECT_TIME             1440
      IDLE_TIME                120
      LOGICAL_READS_PER_CALL   1000000
      PASSWORD_LIFE_TIME       60
      PASSWORD_REUSE_TIME      90
      PASSWORD_REUSE_MAX       UNLIMITED
      FAILED_LOGIN_ATTEMPTS    6
      PASSWORD_LOCK_TIME       UNLIMITED

Profile created.
```

In the example, parameters such as PASSWORD_GRACE_TIME, CPU_PER_SESSION, and PRIVATE_SGA are not used. They will have a value of DEFAULT, which means the value will be taken from the DEFAULT profile.

The DBA or security officer can unlock a locked user account by using the ALTER USER command. The following example shows the unlocking of SCOTT's account.

```
SQL> ALTER USER SCOTT ACCOUNT UNLOCK;

User altered.
```

Composite Limit

The composite limit specifies the total resource cost for a session. You can define a weight for each resource based on the available resources. The following resources are considered for calculating the composite limit:

- CPU_PER_SESSION
- LOGICAL_READS_PER_SESSION
- CONNECT_TIME
- PRIVATE_SGA

The costs associated with each of these resources are set at the database level by using the ALTER RESOURCE COST command. By default, the resources have a cost of 0, which means they should not be considered for a composite limit (they are inexpensive). A higher cost means that the resource is expensive. If you do not specify any of these resources in ALTER RESOURCE COST, Oracle will keep the previous value. For example:

```
SQL> ALTER RESOURCE COST
  2  LOGICAL_READS_PER_SESSION 10
  3  CONNECT_TIME 2;

Resource cost altered.
```

Here CPU_PER_SESSION and PRIVATE_SGA will have a cost of 0 (if they have not been modified before).

You can define limits for each of the four parameters in the profile as well as set the composite limit. The limit that is reached first is the one that takes effect. The following statement adds a composite limit to the profile you created earlier.

```
SQL> ALTER PROFILE ACCOUNTING_USER LIMIT
  2  COMPOSITE_LIMIT 1500000;

Profile altered.
```

The cost for the composite limit is calculated as follows:

Cost = (10 × LOGICAL_READS_PER_SESSION) + (2 × CONNECT_TIME)

If the user has performed 100,000 block reads and was connected for two hours, the cost thus far would be (10 × 100,000) + (2 × 120) = 1,000,240. The user will be restricted when this cost exceeds 1,500,000 or when the values for LOGICAL_READS_PER_SESSION or CONNECT_TIME set in the profile are reached.

Password Verification Function

You can create a function to verify the complexity of the passwords and assign the function name to the PASSWORD_VERIFY_FUNCTION parameter in the profile. When a password is changed, Oracle checks to see whether the supplied password satisfies the conditions specified in this function. Oracle provides a default verification function, known as VERIFY_FUNCTION, which is in the rdbms/admin directory of your Oracle software installation; the script is named utlpwdmg.sql. The password verification function should be owned by SYS and should have the following characteristics.

```
FUNCTION SYS.<function_name>
( <userid_variable> IN VARCHAR2 (30),
  <password_variable> IN VARCHAR2 (30),
  <old_password_variable> IN VARCHAR2 (30) )
RETURN BOOLEAN
```

Oracle's default password verification function checks that the password conforms to the following:

- Is not the same as the username
- Has a minimum length
- Is not too simple; a list of words is checked
- Contains at least one letter, one digit, and one punctuation mark
- Differs from the previous password by at least three letters

If the new password satisfies all the conditions, the function returns a Boolean result of TRUE, and the user's password is changed.

Altering Profiles

Using the ALTER PROFILE command changes profile values. You can change any parameter in the profile using this command. The changes take effect the next time the user connects to the database. For example, to add a password verification function and set a composite limit to the profile you created in the previous example, use the following:

```
SQL> ALTER PROFILE ACCOUNTING_USER LIMIT
  2  PASSWORD_VERIFY_FUNCTION VERIFY_FUNCTION
  3  COMPOSITE_LIMIT 1500

Profile altered.
```

Dropping Profiles

To drop a profile, you use the DROP PROFILE command. If any user is assigned the profile you want to drop, Oracle returns an error. You can drop such profiles by specifying CASCADE, in which case the users who have that profile will be assigned the DEFAULT profile.

```
SQL> DROP PROFILE ACCOUNTING_USER CASCADE;

Profile dropped.
```

Assigning Profiles

To assign profiles to users, you use the CREATE USER or ALTER USER command. These commands are discussed later in the chapter. This example assigns the ACCOUNTING_USER profile to an existing user named SCOTT:

```
SQL> ALTER USER SCOTT
  2  PROFILE ACCOUNTING_USER;

User altered.
```

Querying Profile Information

Oracle Objective

Obtain information about profiles, password management, and resources

You can query profile information from the DBA_PROFILES view. The following example shows information about the profile created previously. The RESOURCE_TYPE column indicates whether the parameter is KERNEL (resource) or PASSWORD.

```
SQL> SELECT RESOURCE_NAME, LIMIT
  2  FROM   DBA_PROFILES
  3  WHERE  PROFILE = 'ACCOUNTING_USER'
  4  AND    RESOURCE_TYPE = 'KERNEL';

RESOURCE_NAME             LIMIT
------------------------- ----------
COMPOSITE_LIMIT           1500
SESSIONS_PER_USER         6
CPU_PER_SESSION           DEFAULT
CPU_PER_CALL              DEFAULT
LOGICAL_READS_PER_SESSION DEFAULT
LOGICAL_READS_PER_CALL    10000000
IDLE_TIME                 120
```

```
CONNECT_TIME                   UNLIMITED
PRIVATE_SGA                    DEFAULT

9 rows selected.
```

The view USER_RESOURCE_LIMITS shows the limit defined for the current user for resource, and the view USER_PASSWORD_LIMITS shows the limit defined for the password.

```
SQL> SELECT * FROM USER_PASSWORD_LIMITS;

RESOURCE_NAME              LIMIT
-------------------------- ---------------
FAILED_LOGIN_ATTEMPTS      6
PASSWORD_LIFE_TIME         60
PASSWORD_REUSE_TIME        90
PASSWORD_REUSE_MAX         UNLIMITED
PASSWORD_VERIFY_FUNCTION   VERIFY_FUNCTION
PASSWORD_LOCK_TIME         UNLIMITED
PASSWORD_GRACE_TIME        UNLIMITED

7 rows selected.
```

You can query the system resource cost from the RESOURCE_COST view.

```
SQL> SELECT * FROM RESOURCE_COST;

RESOURCE_NAME               UNIT_COST
-------------------------- ----------
CPU_PER_SESSION                    10
LOGICAL_READS_PER_SESSION           0
CONNECT_TIME                        2
PRIVATE_SGA                         0
```

Users

Access to the Oracle database is provided using database accounts known as usernames (users). If the user owns database objects, the account is known as a *schema*, which is a logical grouping of all the objects owned by the user. Persons requiring access to the database should have a valid username created in the database. The following properties are associated with a database user account:

Authentication method Each user must be authenticated to connect to the database by using a password, through the operating system, or via the Enterprise Directory Service. Operating system authentication is discussed in the "Privileges and Roles" section.

Default and temporary tablespaces The default tablespace specifies a tablespace for the user to create objects if another tablespace is not explicitly specified. The user needs a quota assigned in the tablespace to create objects, even if the tablespace is the user's default. You use the temporary tablespace to create the temporary segments; the user need not have any quota assigned in this tablespace.

Space quota The user needs a *space quota* assigned in each tablespace in which they want to create the objects. By default, a newly created user does not have any space quota allocated on any tablespace to create schema objects. For the user to create schema objects such as tables or materialized views, you must allocate a space quota in tablespaces.

Profile The user can have a profile to specify the resource limits and password settings. If you don't specify a profile when you create the user, the `DEFAULT` profile is assigned.

When you create the database, the `SYS` and `SYSTEM` users are created. `SYS` is the schema that owns the data dictionary.

Managing Users

Oracle Objective

Create new database users

To create users in the database, you use the CREATE USER command. Specify the authentication method when you create the user. A common authentication method is using the database; the username is assigned a password, which is stored encrypted in the database. Oracle verifies the password when establishing a connection to the database. As an example, let's create a user JOHN with the various clauses available in the CREATE USER command.

```
SQL> CREATE USER JOHN
     IDENTIFIED BY "B1S2!"
     DEFAULT TABLESPACE USERS
     TEMPORARY TABLESPACE TEMP
     QUOTA UNLIMITED ON USERS
     QUOTA 1M ON INDX
     PROFILE ACCOUNTING_USER
     PASSWORD EXPIRE
     ACCOUNT UNLOCK

User created.
```

The IDENTIFIED BY clause specifies that the user will be authenticated using the database. To authenticate the user using the operating system, specify IDENTIFIED EXTERNALLY. The password specified is not case sensitive.

If you do not specify the DEFAULT TABLESPACE clause, the SYSTEM tablespace is assigned as the default tablespace. When you create the database, you can specify a default temporary tablespace (DEFAULT TEMPORARY TABLESPACE clause of the CREATE DATABASE statement, discussed in Chapter 4). You can also define it later using the ALTER DATABASE statement. If such default temporary tablespace is specified and you do not specify the TEMPORARY TABLESPACE clause in the CREATE USER command, the database's default temporary tablespace is assigned to the user. If the database does not have a default temporary tablespace defined, SYSTEM tablespace is assigned as the temporary tablespace by default. You cannot specify the undo tablespace as the default or temporary tablespace. The following query shows whether a default temporary tablespace is defined for the database.

```
SQL> SELECT * FROM DATABASE_PROPERTIES
     WHERE  PROPERTY_NAME = 'DEFAULT_TEMP_TABLESPACE';
```

```
PROPERTY_NAME             PROPERTY_VALUE
------------------------- -------------------------
DESCRIPTION
---------------------------------------------------
DEFAULT_TEMP_TABLESPACE    TEMP
Name of default temporary tablespace
SQL>
```

Although the default and temporary tablespaces are specified, JOHN does not initially have any space quota on the USERS tablespace (or any tablespace). You allocate quotas on the USERS and INDX tablespaces through the QUOTA clause. You can specify the QUOTA clause any number of times with the appropriate tablespace name and space limit. The space limit is specified in bytes, but can be followed by K or M to indicate KB or MB. To create extents, the user should have a sufficient space quota in the tablespace. UNLIMITED specifies that the quota on the tablespace is not limited.

The PROFILE clause specifies the profile to be assigned. PASSWORD EXPIRE specifies that the user will be prompted (if using SQL*Plus, otherwise the DBA should change the password) for a new password at the first login. ACCOUNT UNLOCK is the default; you can specify ACCOUNT LOCK to initially lock the account.

The user JOHN can connect to the database only if he has the CREATE SESSION privilege. Granting privileges and roles is discussed later, in the section "Privileges and Roles." The CREATE SESSION privilege is granted to user JOHN by specifying the following:

```
SQL> GRANT CREATE SESSION TO JOHN;

Grant succeeded.
```

To create extents, a user with the UNLIMITED TABLESPACE system privilege does not need any space quota in any tablespace.

Modifying User Accounts

Oracle Objective

Alter and drop existing database users

You can modify all the characteristics you specified when creating a user by using the ALTER USER command. You can also assign or modify the default roles assigned to the user (discussed later in this chapter). Changing the default tablespace of a user affects only the objects created in the future. The following example changes the default tablespace of JOHN and assigns a new password.

```
ALTER USER JOHN
IDENTIFIED BY SHADOW2#
DEFAULT TABLESPACE APPLICATION_DATA;
```

You can lock or unlock a user's account as follows:

```
ALTER USER <username> ACCOUNT [LOCK/UNLOCK]
```

You can also expire the user's password:

```
ALTER USER <username> PASSWORD EXPIRE
```

Users must change the password the next time they log in, or you must change the password. If the password is expired, SQL*Plus prompts for a new password at login time.

In the following example, setting the quota to 0 revokes the tablespace quota assigned. The objects created by the user in the tablespace remain there, but no new extents can be allocated in that tablespace.

```
ALTER USER JOHN QUOTA 0 ON USERS;
```

Users can change their password by using the ALTER USER command; they do not need the ALTER USER privilege to do so. They can also change their password using the PASSWORD command in SQL*Plus.

Dropping Users

You can drop a user from the database by using the DROP USER command. If the user (schema) owns objects, Oracle returns an error. If you specify the CASCADE keyword, Oracle drops all the objects owned by the user and then drops the user. If other schema objects, such as procedures, packages, or views, refer to the objects in the user's schema, they become invalid. When you drop objects, space is freed up immediately in the relevant tablespaces. The following example shows how to drop the user JOHN, with all the owned objects.

```
DROP USER JOHN CASCADE;
```

You cannot drop a user who is currently connected to the database.

Authenticating Users

In this section, we will discuss two widely used user-authenticating methods:

- Authentication by the database
- Authorization by the operating system

When you use database authentication, you define a password for the user (the user can change the password), and Oracle stores the password in the database (encrypted). When users connect to the database, Oracle compares the password supplied by the user with the password in the database.

By default, the password supplied by the user is not encrypted when sent over the network. To encrypt the user's password, you must set the ORA_ENCRYPT_LOGIN environment variable to TRUE on the client machine. Similarly, when using database links, the password sent across the network is not encrypted. To encrypt such connections, you must set the DBLINK_ENCRYPT_LOGIN initialization parameter to TRUE. Passwords are encrypted using the data encryption standard (DES) algorithm.

When you use authorization by the operating system, Oracle verifies the operating system login account and connects to the database—users need not specify a username and password. Oracle does not store the passwords of such operating-system authenticated users, but they must have a username in the database. The initialization parameter OS_AUTHENT_PREFIX determines the prefix used for operating system authorization. By default, the value is OPS$. For example, if your operating system login name is ALEX, the database username should be OPS$ALEX. When Alex specifies CONNECT / or does not specify a username to connect to the database, Oracle tries to connect Alex to the OPS$ALEX account. You can set the OS_AUTHENT_PREFIX parameter to a null string " "; this will not add any prefix. To create an operating-system authenticated user, use the following:

```
SQL> CREATE USER OPS$ALEX IDENTIFIED EXTERNALLY;
```

To connect to a remote database using operating system authorization, set the REMOTE_OS_AUTHENT parameter to TRUE. You must be careful in using this parameter, because connections can be made from any computer.

For example, if you have an operating system account named ORACLE and a database account OPS$ORACLE, you can connect to the database from the machine where the database resides. If you set REMOTE_OS_AUTHENT to TRUE, you can log in to any server with the ORACLE operating system account and connect to the database over the network. If a user creates an operating system ID named ORACLE and is on the network, the user can connect to the database using operating system authorization.

Complying with Oracle Licensing Terms

The DBA is responsible for ensuring that the organization complies with the Oracle licensing agreement. Chapter 4, "Creating a Database and Data Dictionary," discussed the parameters that can be set in the initialization file to enforce license agreements. They are as follows:

LICENSE_MAX_SESSIONS Maximum number of concurrent user sessions. When this limit is reached, only users with the RESTRICTED SESSION privilege are allowed to connect. The default is 0—unlimited. Set this parameter if your license is based on concurrent database usage.

LICENSE_SESSIONS_WARNING A warning limit on the number of concurrent user sessions. The default value is 0—unlimited. A warning message is written in the alert file when the limit is reached.

LICENSE_MAX_USERS Maximum number of users that can be created in the database. The default is 0—unlimited. Set this parameter if your license is based on the total number of database users.

You can change the value of these parameters dynamically by using the ALTER SYSTEM command. For example:

```
ALTER SYSTEM
   SET LICENSE_MAX_SESSIONS = 256
   LICENSE_SESSIONS_WARNING = 200;
```

The high-water mark (HWM) column of the V$LICENSE view shows the maximum number of concurrent sessions created since instance start-up and the limits set. A value of 0 indicates that no limit is set.

```
SQL> SELECT * FROM V$LICENSE;

SESSIONS_MAX SESSIONS_WARNING SESSIONS_CURRENT SESSIONS_HIGHWATER USERS_MAX
------------ ---------------- ---------------- ------------------ ---------
         256              200              105                115         0
```

You can obtain the total number of database users from the DBA_USERS view:

```
SELECT COUNT(*) FROM DBA_USERS;
```

Querying User Information

Oracle Objective

Monitor information about existing users

You can query user information from the data dictionary views DBA_USERS and USER_USERS. USER_USERS shows only one row: information about the current user. You can obtain the user account status, password expiration date, account locked date (if locked), encrypted password, default and temporary tablespaces, profile name, and creation date from this view. Oracle creates a numeric ID and assigns it to the user when the user is created. SYS has an ID of 0.

```
SQL> SELECT USERNAME, DEFAULT_TABLESPACE,
  2         TEMPORARY_TABLESPACE, PROFILE,
  3         ACCOUNT_STATUS, EXPIRY_DATE
  4  FROM   DBA_USERS
  5  WHERE  USERNAME = 'JOHN';

USERNAME DEFAULT_TABLESPACE TEMPORARY_TABLESPACE PROFILE         ACCOUNT_ST EXPIRY_DA
-------- ------------------ -------------------- --------------- ---------- ---------
JOHN     USERS              TEMP                 ACCOUNTING_USER OPEN       22-OCT-00
```

The view ALL_USERS shows the username and creation date.

```
SQL> SELECT * FROM ALL_USERS
  2  WHERE USERNAME LIKE 'SYS%';
```

```
USERNAME     USER_ID CREATED
-------- ---------- ---------
SYS                0 13-JUL-00
SYSTEM             5 13-JUL-00
```

The views DBA_TS_QUOTAS and USER_TS_QUOTAS list the tablespace quota assigned to the user. A value of –1 indicates an unlimited quota.

```
SQL> SELECT TABLESPACE_NAME, BYTES, MAX_BYTES, BLOCKS,
  2         MAX_BLOCKS
  3  FROM   DBA_TS_QUOTAS
  4  WHERE  USERNAME = 'JOHN';

TABLESPACE      BYTES  MAX_BYTES     BLOCKS MAX_BLOCKS
---------- ---------- ---------- ---------- ----------
INDX                0    1048576          0        128
USERS               0         -1          0         -1
```

The V$SESSION view shows the users currently connected to the database, and V$SESSTAT shows the session statistics. You can find the description for the statistic codes from V$SESSTAT in V$STATNAME.

```
SQL> SELECT USERNAME, OSUSER, MACHINE, PROGRAM
  2  FROM   V$SESSION
  3  WHERE  USERNAME = 'JOHN';

USERNAME OSUSER  MACHINE       PROGRAM
-------- ------- ------------- -----------------
JOHN     KJOHN   USA.CO.AU     SQLPLUSW.EXE

SQL> SELECT A.NAME, B.VALUE
  2  FROM   V$STATNAME A, V$SESSTAT B, V$SESSION C
  3  WHERE  A.STATISTIC# = B.STATISTIC#
  4  AND    B.SID        = C.SID
  5  AND    C.USERNAME   = 'JOHN'
  6  AND    A.NAME LIKE '%session%';
```

```
NAME                                     VALUE
---------------------------------------- ----------
session logical reads                           729
session stored procedure space                    0
CPU used by this session                         12
session connect time                              0
session uga memory                            98368
session uga memory max                       159804
session pga memory                           296416
session pga memory max                       296416
session cursor cache hits                         0
session cursor cache count                        0
```

The current username connected to the database is available in the system variable USER. Using SQL*Plus, you can run SHOW USER to get the username.

```
SQL> SHOW USER
USER is "JOHN"
SQL>
```

Real World Scenario

Copying User Accounts from One Database to Another

The password provided with the IDENTIFIED BY clause is encrypted and stored in the database. You can also provide the encrypted password using the IDENTIFIED BY VALUES clause as the user's password. Enclose such entries in single quotes. This method is useful for copying user accounts from one database to another, without compromising their password. The PASSWORD column in the DBA_USERS view provides the encrypted password.

As an example, let's create a user called BENJAMIN with the password NOICE.

```
CREATE USER benjamin IDENTIFIED BY noice
DEFAULT TABLESPACE users;
```

You can query the encrypted password from the data dictionary.

```
SELECT username, password
FROM   dba_users
WHERE  username = 'BENJAMIN';

USERNAME                       PASSWORD
------------------------------ ----------------------
BENJAMIN                       C2851F759114DCAC
```

You can drop the user from the database and create the user again by supplying the encrypted password. If you execute the same SQL statement in any Oracle database, the password assigned to user `BENJAMIN` will be `NOICE`.

```
DROP USER benjamin;

CREATE USER benjamin IDENTIFIED BY
VALUES 'C2851F759114DCAC'
DEFAULT TABLESPACE users;
```

Let's now grant the `CREATE SESSION` privilege to Benjamin and verify that his password is really NOICE.

```
SQL> GRANT CREATE SESSION TO benjamin;
Grant succeeded.
SQL>
SQL> CONNECT benjamin/noice
Connected.
SQL>
```

Now let's generate a script from the data dictionary to create all user accounts with their existing passwords. You can change the CREATE USER to ALTER USER for synchronizing passwords between databases (for example, your test and production databases).

```
SET ECHO OFF FEEDBACK OFF PAGES 0 LINES 200 TRIMS ON
SPOOL createusers.sql
SELECT 'CREATE USER '|| username || ' IDENTIFIED BY VALUES ''' ||
       password || ''';'
```

```
FROM    dba_users;
SPOOL OFF
SET FEEDBACK ON PAGES 24 LINES 80
```

The script generated will be saved in file *createusers.sql*, whose content will be similar to the following.

```
CREATE USER OE IDENTIFIED BY VALUES 'D1A2DFC623FDA40A';
CREATE USER SH IDENTIFIED BY VALUES '54B253CBBAAA8C48';
CREATE USER BENJAMIN IDENTIFIED BY VALUES 'C2851F759114DCAC';
```

Managing Privileges

Oracle Objective

Identify system and object privileges

In the Oracle database, *privileges* control access to the data and restrict the actions users can perform. Through proper privileges, users can create, drop, or modify objects in their own schema or in another user's schema. Privileges also determine the data to which a user should have access. You can grant privileges to a user by means of two methods:

- You can assign privileges directly to the user.
- You can assign privileges to a role, and then assign the role to the user.

A *role* is a named set of privileges, which eases the management of privileges. For example, if you have 10 users needing access to the data in the accounting tables, you can grant the privileges required to a role and grant the role to the 10 users. There are two types of privileges:

Object privileges *Object privileges* are granted on schema objects that belong to a different schema. The privilege can be on data (to read, modify, delete, add, or reference), on a program (to execute), or on an object (to change the structure).

System privileges *System privileges* provide the right to perform a specific action on any schema in the database. System privileges do not specify an object, but are granted at the database level. Certain system privileges are very powerful and should be granted only to trusted users. System privileges and object privileges can be granted to a role.

PUBLIC is a user group defined in the database; it is not a database user or a role. Every user in the database belongs to this group. Therefore, if you grant privileges to PUBLIC, they are available to all users of the database.

A user and a role cannot have the same name.

Object Privileges

Object privileges are granted on a specific object. The owner of the object has all privileges on the object. The owner can grant privileges on that object to any other users of the database. The owner can also authorize another user in the database to grant privileges on the object to other users. For example, user JOHN owns a table named CUSTOMER and grants read and update privileges to JAMES. (To specify multiple privileges, separate them with a comma.)

```
SQL> GRANT SELECT, UPDATE ON CUSTOMER TO JAMES;
```

JAMES cannot insert into or delete from CUSTOMER; JAMES can only query and update rows in the CUSTOMER table. JAMES cannot grant the privilege to another user in the database, because JAMES is not authorized by JOHN to do so. If the privilege is granted with the WITH GRANT OPTION, JAMES can grant the privilege to others.

```
SQL> GRANT SELECT, UPDATE ON CUSTOMER
  2  TO JAMES WITH GRANT OPTION;
```

The INSERT, UPDATE, or REFERENCES privileges can be granted on columns also. For example:

```
SQL> GRANT INSERT (CUSTOMER_ID) ON CUSTOMER TO JAMES;
```

The following are the object privileges that can be granted to users of the database:

`SELECT` Grants read (query) access to the data in a table, view, sequence, or materialized view.

`UPDATE` Grants update (modify) access to the data in a table, column, view, or materialized view.

`DELETE` Grants delete (remove) access to the data in a table, view, or materialized view.

`INSERT` Grants insert (add) access to a table, column, view, or materialized view.

`EXECUTE` Grants execute (run) privilege on a PL/SQL stored object, such as a procedure, package, or function.

`READ` Grants read access on a directory.

`INDEX` Grants index creation privilege on a table.

`REFERENCES` Grants reference access to a table or columns to create foreign keys that can reference the table.

`ALTER` Grants access to modify the structure of a table or sequence.

`ON COMMIT REFRESH` Grants the privilege to create a refresh-on-commit materialized view on the specified table.

`QUERY REWRITE` Grants the privilege to create a materialized view for query rewrite using the specified table.

`WRITE` Allows the external table agent to write a log file or a bad file to the directory. This privilege is associated only with the external tables.

`UNDER` Grants the privilege to create a sub-view under a view.

The following are some points related to object privileges that you need to remember:

- Object privileges can be granted to a user, a role, or `PUBLIC`.
- If a view refers to tables or views from another user, you must have the privilege `WITH GRANT OPTION` on the underlying tables of the view to

grant any privilege on the view to another user. For example, JOHN owns a view, which references a table from JAMES. To grant the SELECT privilege on the view to another user, JOHN should have received the SELECT privilege on the table WITH GRANT OPTION.

- Any object privilege received on a table provides the grantee the privilege to lock the table.
- The SELECT privilege cannot be specified on columns; to grant column-level SELECT privileges, create a view with the required columns and grant SELECT on the view.
- You can specify ALL or ALL PRIVILEGES to grant all available privileges on an object (for example, GRANT ALL ON CUSTOMER TO JAMES).
- Unless you have the DBA role or the system privilege GRANT ANY OBJECT PRIVILEGE, to grant privileges on objects owned by another user you must have been granted the appropriate privilege on the object WITH GRANT OPTION.
- Multiple privileges can be granted to multiple users and/or roles in one statement. For example, GRANT INSERT, UPDATE, SELECT ON CUSTOMER TO ADMIN_ROLE, JULIE, SCOTT;

System Privileges

System privileges are the privileges that enable the user to perform an action; they are not specified on any particular object. Like object privileges, system privileges also can be granted to a user, a role, or PUBLIC. There are many system privileges in Oracle; Table 9.1 summarizes the privileges used to manage objects in the database. The CREATE, ALTER, and DROP privileges provide the ability to create, modify, and drop the object specified in the user's schema. When a privilege is specified with ANY, the user is authorized to perform the action on any schema in the database. Table 9.2 shows the types of privileges that are associated with certain types of objects. For example, the SELECT ANY TABLE privilege gives the user the ability to query all tables or views in the database, regardless of who owns them; the SELECT ANY SEQUENCE privilege gives the user the ability to select from all sequences in the database.

TABLE 9.1 System Privileges for Managing Objects

OBJECT TYPE	CREATE	CREATE ANY	ALTER	ALTER ANY	DROP	DROP ANY	EXECUTE ANY	QUERY REWRITE	GLOBAL QUERY REWRITE
Cluster	✓	✓		✓		✓			
Context		✓				✓			
Database link	✓								
Public database link	✓				✓				
Dimension	✓	✓		✓		✓			
Directory		✓				✓			
Indextype	✓	✓		✓		✓			
Index		✓		✓		✓		✓	✓
Library	✓	✓			✓	✓			
Materialized view	✓	✓		✓		✓			
Operator	✓	✓				✓	✓		
Outline		✓		✓		✓			
Procedure	✓	✓		✓		✓	✓		
Profile	✓		✓		✓				

TABLE 9.1 System Privileges for Managing Objects *(continued)*

OBJECT TYPE	CREATE	CREATE ANY	ALTER	ALTER ANY	DROP	DROP ANY	EXECUTE ANY	QUERY REWRITE	GLOBAL QUERY REWRITE
Role	√			√		√			
Rollback segment	√		√		√				
Sequence	√	√		√		√			
Snapshot	√	√		√		√			
Synonym	√	√				√			
Public synonym	√				√				
Table	√	√		√		√			
Tablespace	√		√		√				
Trigger	√	√		√		√			
Type	√	√		√		√	√		
User	√		√		√				
View	√		√			√			

Table 9.2 lists other system privileges that do not fall into the categories outlined in Table 9.1.

TABLE 9.2 Additional System Privileges

If you have	You'll be able to
SELECT ANY TABLE/ SEQUENCE/ OUTLINE	Select from table, sequence or create a clone private outline from a public outline.
SELECT ANY DICTIONARY	Query data dictionary schema objects owned by the SYS schema.
ALTER DATABASE	Change the database configuration by using the ALTER DATABASE command.
ALTER SYSTEM	Use the ALTER SYSTEM command.
AUDIT SYSTEM	Audit SQL statements.
CREATE SESSION	Connect to the database.
ALTER RESOURCE COST	Use the ALTER RESOURCE COST command to set up resource costs.
ALTER SESSION	Change session properties by using ALTER SESSION.
RESTRICTED SESSION	Connect to the database when the database is in restricted mode.
BACKUP ANY TABLE	Export tables that belong to other users.
DELETE ANY TABLE	Delete rows from tables or views owned by any user in the database.
INSERT ANY TABLE	Insert rows into tables or views owned by any user into the database.
LOCK ANY TABLE	Lock tables or views owned by any user in the database.
UPDATE ANY TABLE	Update rows in tables or views owned by any user in the database.

TABLE 9.2 Additional System Privileges *(continued)*

If you have	You'll be able to
MANAGE TABLESPACE	Perform tablespace management operations such as taking them offline or online and beginning or ending backup.
UNLIMITED TABLESPACE	Create objects in any tablespace; space in the database is not restricted.
ADMINISTER DATABASE TRIGGER	Create a trigger in the database (you still need the CREATE TRIGGER or CREATE ANY TRIGGER privilege).
BECOME USER	Become another user while doing a full import.
ANALYZE ANY	Use the ANALYZE command on any table, index, or cluster in any schema in the database.
AUDIT ANY	Audit any object or schema in the database.
COMMENT ANY TABLE	Create comments on any tables in the database.
GRANT ANY PRIVILEGE	Grant any system privilege.
GRANT ANY ROLE	Grant any role.
ON COMMIT REFRESH	Create a refresh-on-commit materialized view on any table in the database.
UNDER ANY VIEW	Create sub-views under object views
SYSOPER	Start up and shut down the database; mount, open, or back up the database; use ARCHIVELOG and RECOVER commands; use the RESTRICTED SESSION privilege.
SYSDBA	Perform all SYSOPER actions plus create or alter a database.

Privileges with the ANY parameter are powerful and should be granted to responsible users. Privileges with the ANY parameter provide access to all such objects in the database, including SYS-owned dictionary objects. For example, if you give a user the ALTER ANY TABLE privilege, that user can use the privilege on a data dictionary table. To protect the dictionary, Oracle provides an initialization parameter, O7_DICTIONARY_ACCESSIBILITY, that controls access to the data dictionary. If this parameter is set to TRUE (the Oracle7 behavior, default is FALSE), a user with the ANY privilege can exercise that privilege on the SYS dictionary objects. It is not possible to access the dictionary with the ANY privilege if this parameter is set to FALSE. For example, a user with SELECT ANY TABLE can query the DBA_ views, but when O7_DICTIONARY_ACCESSIBILITY is set to FALSE, the user cannot query the dictionary views. You can, however, grant the user specific access to the dictionary views (via object privileges). When we discuss roles later in this chapter, you'll learn how to provide query access to the dictionary.

Here are some points to remember about system privileges:

- To connect to the database, you need the CREATE SESSION privilege.
- To truncate a table that belongs to another schema, you need the DROP ANY TABLE privilege.
- The CREATE ANY PROCEDURE (or EXECUTE ANY PROCEDURE) privilege allows the user to create, replace, or drop (or execute) procedures, packages, and functions; this includes Java classes.
- The CREATE TABLE privilege gives you the ability to create, alter, drop, and query tables in a schema.
- SELECT, INSERT, UPDATE, and DELETE are object privileges, but SELECT ANY, INSERT ANY, UPDATE ANY, and DELETE ANY are system privileges (in other words, they do not apply to a particular object).

Granting System Privileges

Oracle Objective

Grant and revoke privileges

System privileges are also granted to a user, a role, or PUBLIC by using the GRANT command. The WITH ADMIN OPTION clause gives the grantee the privilege to grant the privilege to another user, role, or PUBLIC. For example, if JOHN needs to create a table under JAMES's schema, he needs the CREATE ANY TABLE privilege. This privilege not only allows JOHN to create a table under JAMES's schema, but also allows the creation of a table under any schema in the database.

```
SQL> GRANT CREATE ANY TABLE TO JOHN;
```

If John must be able to grant this privilege to others, he should be granted the privilege with the WITH ADMIN OPTION clause (or should have the GRANT ANY PRIVILEGE privilege).

```
SQL> GRANT CREATE ANY TABLE TO JOHN WITH ADMIN OPTION;
```

Revoking Privileges

You can revoke a user's object privileges and system privileges by using the REVOKE statement. You can revoke a privilege if you have granted it to the user or if you have been granted that privilege with the WITH ADMIN OPTION (for system privileges) or the WITH GRANT OPTION (for object privileges) clauses. Here are some examples of revoking privileges.

To revoke the UPDATE privilege granted to JAMES from JOHN on JOHN's CUSTOMER table, use the following:

```
SQL> REVOKE UPDATE ON CUSTOMER FROM JAMES;
```

To revoke the SELECT ANY TABLE and CREATE TRIGGER privileges granted to JULIE, use the following:

```
SQL> REVOKE SELECT ANY TABLE, CREATE TRIGGER
  2   FROM JULIE;
```

To revoke the REFERENCES privilege, specify the CASCADE CONSTRAINTS clause, which will drop the referential integrity constraint created using the privilege. You must use this clause if any constraints exist.

```
SQL> REVOKE REFERENCES ON CUSTOMER
  2   FROM JAMES CASCADE CONSTRAINTS;
```

The following statement revokes all the privileges granted by JAMES on the STATE table to JULIE. JAMES executes this statement.

```
SQL> REVOKE ALL ON STATE FROM JULIE;
```

Keep the following in mind when revoking privileges:

- If multiple users (or administrators) have granted an object privilege to a user, revoking the privilege by one administrator will not prevent the user from performing the action, because the privileges granted by the other administrators are still valid.
- To revoke the WITH ADMIN OPTION or WITH GRANT OPTION, you must revoke the privilege and re-grant the privilege without the clause.
- You cannot selectively revoke column privileges; you must revoke the privileges from the table and grant them again with the appropriate columns.

- If a user has used their system privileges to create or modify an object, and subsequently the user's privilege is revoked, no change is made to the objects that the user has already created or modified. The user just can no longer create or modify the object.
- If a PL/SQL program or view is created based on an object privilege (or a DML system privilege such as SELECT ANY, UPDATE ANY, and so on), revoking the privilege will invalidate the object.
- If user A is granted a system privilege WITH ADMIN OPTION, and grants the privilege to user B, user B's privilege still remains when user A's privilege is revoked.
- If user A is granted an object privilege WITH GRANT OPTION, and grants the privilege to user B, user B's privilege is also automatically revoked when user A's privilege is revoked, and the objects that use the privileges under user A and user B are invalidated.

Querying Privilege Information

You can query privilege information from the data dictionary by using various views. Table 9.3 lists and describes the views that provide information related to privileges.

TABLE 9.3 Privilege Information

View Name	Description
ALL_TAB_PRIVS DBA_TAB_PRIVS USER_TAB_PRIVS	Lists the object privileges. ALL_TAB_PRIVS shows only the privileges granted to the user and to PUBLIC.
ALL_TAB_PRIVS_MADE USER_TAB_PRIVS_MADE	Lists the object grants made by the current user or grants made on the objects owned by the current user.
ALL_TAB_PRIVS_RECD USER_TAB_PRIVS_RECD	Lists the object grants received by the current user or PUBLIC.
ALL_COL_PRIVS DBA_COL_PRIVS USER_COL_PRIVS	Lists column privileges.

TABLE 9.3 Privilege Information *(continued)*

View Name	Description
ALL_COL_PRIVS_MADE USER_COL_PRIVS_MADE	Lists column privileges made by the current user.
ALL_COL_PRIVS_RECD USER_COL_PRIVS_RECD	Lists column privileges received by the current user.
DBA_SYS_PRIVS USER_SYS_PRIVS	Lists system privilege information.
SESSION_PRIVS	Lists the system privileges available for the current session.

Here are some sample queries using the dictionary views to query privileges information.

To list information about privileges granted on the table CUSTOMER, use the following:

```
SQL> SELECT * FROM DBA_TAB_PRIVS
  2  WHERE TABLE_NAME = 'CUSTOMER';

GRANTEE         OWNER  TABLE_NAME  GRANTOR PRIVILEGE GRA
--------------- ------ ----------- ------- --------- ---
SCOTT           JOHN   CUSTOMER    JAMES   SELECT    NO
JAMES           JOHN   CUSTOMER    JOHN    SELECT    YES
JAMES           JOHN   CUSTOMER    JOHN    UPDATE    YES
ACCOUNTS_MANAGE JOHN   CUSTOMER    JOHN    SELECT    NO
```

To list system privileges granted to JOHN:

```
SQL> SELECT * FROM DBA_SYS_PRIVS
  2  WHERE  GRANTEE = 'JOHN';

GRANTEE         PRIVILEGE            ADM
--------------- -------------------- ---
JOHN            CREATE SESSION       NO
JOHN            UNLIMITED TABLESPACE NO
```

 **Real World Scenario**

Fixing an Insufficient Privilege Error after Querying the Dictionary

User Benjamin is getting an error message when he tries to do the following update. As a DBA, you need to understand the roles and privileges and grant Benjamin the appropriate privilege.

```
SQL> UPDATE COUNTRIES
  2  SET    COUNTRY_NAME = 'USA'
  3  WHERE  COUNTRY_ID = 'US';
UPDATE COUNTRIES
       *
ERROR at line 1:
ORA-01031: insufficient privileges
SQL>
```

Since Benjamin is not qualifying the table name with a username, a synonym must exist. Let's find the synonym definition and the owner of the COUNTRIES table.

```
SQL> SELECT * FROM DBA_SYNONYMS
  2  WHERE  SYNONYM_NAME = 'COUNTRIES';

OWNER     SYNONYM_NAME    TABLE_OWNER   TABLE_NAME
--------- --------------- ------------- -------------
DB_LINK
---------------------------------------------
PUBLIC    COUNTRIES       HR             COUNTRIES


OE        COUNTRIES       HR             COUNTRIES


SQL>
```

Two synonyms are created; one is a private synonym owned by OE and the other is a public synonym. Benjamin must be using the public synonym. Both synonyms refer to the COUNTRIES table owned by the HR schema. Let's query and find out which privilege on the HR.COUNTRIES table is assigned to Benjamin.

```
SQL> SELECT PRIVILEGE
  2  FROM    DBA_TAB_PRIVS
  3  WHERE   GRANTEE = 'BENJAMIN'
  4  AND     TABLE_NAME = 'COUNTRIES'
  5  AND     OWNER = 'HR';

no rows selected
SQL>
```

No privileges are assigned on table HR.COUNTRIES to Benjamin. Let's query and find out whether the privileges on this table are granted to any role.

```
SQL> SELECT GRANTEE, PRIVILEGE
  2  FROM    DBA_TAB_PRIVS
  3  WHERE   TABLE_NAME = 'COUNTRIES'
  4  AND     OWNER = 'HR'
  5  AND     GRANTEE IN (SELECT ROLE FROM DBA_ROLES);
GRANTEE                        PRIVILEGE
------------------------------ ---------------------
HR_SELECT                      SELECT
HR_UPDATE                      DELETE
HR_UPDATE                      INSERT
HR_UPDATE                      SELECT
HR_UPDATE                      UPDATE
SQL>
```

The HR_SELECT role has query privileges, and the HR_UPDATE role has all privileges on this table. Query to find out which roles are assigned to Benjamin.

```
SQL> SELECT * FROM DBA_ROLE_PRIVS
  2  WHERE  GRANTEE = 'BENJAMIN';
GRANTEE       GRANTED_ROLE       ADM DEF
------------- ------------------ --- ---
BENJAMIN      CONNECT            NO  YES
BENJAMIN      HR_SELECT          NO  YES
SQL>
```

Benjamin has two roles assigned, CONNECT and HR_SELECT. To fix Benjamin's problem, you can either grant him the HR_UDPATE role or grant update privileges on the HR.COUNTRIES table.

```
GRANT HR_UPDATE TO BENJAMIN;
```

Or

```
CONNECT HR/HR
GRANT UPDATE ON COUNTRIES TO BENJAMIN;
```

Managing Roles

Oracle Objective — **Create and modify roles**

A *role* is a named group of privileges that you can use to ease the administration of privileges. For example, if your accounting department has 30 users and all need similar access to the tables in the accounts receivable application, you can create a role and grant the appropriate system and object privileges to the role. You can grant the role to each user of the accounting department, instead of granting each object and system privilege to individual users.

Using the CREATE ROLE command creates the role. No user owns the role; it is owned by the database. When a role is created, no privileges are associated with it. You must grant the appropriate privileges to the role. For example, to create a role named ACCTS_RECV and grant certain privileges to the role, use the following:

```
CREATE ROLE ACCTS_RECV;
```

```
GRANT SELECT ON GENERAL_LEDGER TO ACCTS_RECV;
GRANT INSERT, UPDATE ON JOURNAL_ENTRY TO ACCTS_RECV;
```

Similar to users, roles can also be authenticated. The default is NOT IDENTIFIED, which means no authorization is required to enable or disable the role. The following authorization methods are available:

Database Using a password associated with the role, the database authorizes the role. Whenever such roles are enabled, the user is prompted for a password if the role is not one of the default roles for the user. In the following example, a role ACCOUNTS_MANAGER is created with a password.

```
SQL> CREATE ROLE ACCOUNTS_MANAGER IDENTIFIED BY ACCMGR;
```

Operating system The role is authorized by the operating system. This is useful when the operating system can associate its privileges with the application privileges, and information about each user is configured in operating system files. To enable operating system role authorization, set the parameter OS_ROLES to TRUE. The following example creates a role, authorized by the operating system.

```
SQL> CREATE ROLE APPLICATION_USER IDENTIFIED EXTERNALLY;
```

You can change the role's password or authentication method by using the ALTER ROLE command. You cannot rename a role. For example:

```
SQL> ALTER ROLE ACCOUNTS_MANAGER IDENTIFIED BY MANAGER;
```

To drop a role, use the DROP ROLE command. Oracle will let you drop a role even if it is granted to users or other roles. When you drop a role, it is immediately removed from the users' role lists.

```
SQL> DROP ROLE ACCOUNTS_MANAGER;
```

Using Predefined Roles

Oracle Objective

Use predefined roles

When you create the database, Oracle creates six predefined roles. These roles are defined in the sql.bsq script, which is executed when you run the

CREATE DATABASE command. The following roles are predefined:

CONNECT Privilege to connect to the database, to create a cluster, a database link, a sequence, a synonym, a table, and a view, and to alter a session.

RESOURCE Privilege to create a cluster, a table, and a sequence, and to create programmatic objects such as procedures, functions, packages, indextypes, types, triggers, and operators.

DBA All system privileges with the ADMIN option, so the system privileges can be granted to other users of the database or to roles.

SELECT_CATALOG_ROLE Ability to query the dictionary views and tables.

EXECUTE_CATALOG_ROLE Privilege to execute the dictionary packages (SYS-owned packages).

DELETE_CATALOG_ROLE Ability to drop or re-create the dictionary packages.

Also, when you run the catproc.sql script as part of the database creation, the script executes catexp.sql, which creates two more roles:

EXP_FULL_DATABASE Ability to make full and incremental exports of the database using the Export utility.

IMP_FULL_DATABASE Ability to perform full database imports using the Import utility. This is a very powerful role.

Removing Roles

Oracle Objective

Remove roles

You can remove roles from the database using the DROP ROLE statement. When you drop a role, all privileges that users had through the role are lost. If they used the role to create objects in the database or to manipulate data, those objects and changes remain in the database. To drop a role named HR_UPDATE, use the following statement:

```
DROP ROLE HR_UPDATE;
```

To drop a role, you must have been granted the role with the ADMIN OPTION, or you must have the DROP ANY ROLE system privilege.

Enabling and Disabling Roles

Oracle Objective | **Control availability of roles**

If a role is not the default role for a user, it is not enabled when the user connects to the database. You use the ALTER USER command to set the default roles for a user. You can use the DEFAULT ROLE clause with the ALTER USER command in four ways, as illustrated in the following examples.

To specify the named roles CONNECT and ACCOUNTS_MANAGER as default roles, use the following:

```
ALTER USER JOHN DEFAULT ROLE
CONNECT, ACCOUNTS_MANAGER;
```

To specify all roles granted to the user as the default, use the following:

```
ALTER USER JOHN DEFAULT ROLE ALL;
```

To specify all roles except certain roles as the default, use the following:

```
ALTER USER JOHN DEFAULT ROLE ALL
EXCEPT RESOURCE, ACCOUNTS_ADMIN;
```

To specify no roles as the default, use the following:

```
ALTER USER JOHN DEFAULT ROLE NONE;
```

You can specify only roles granted to the user as default roles. The DEFAULT ROLE clause is not available in the CREATE USER command. Default roles are enabled when the user connects to the database and do not require a password.

You enable or disable roles using the SET ROLE command. You specify the maximum number of roles that can be enabled in the initialization parameter MAX_ENABLED_ROLES (the default is 20). You can enable or disable only roles granted to the user. If a role is defined with a password, you must supply the password when you enable the role. For example:

```
SET ROLE ACCOUNTS_ADMIN IDENTIFIED BY MANAGER;
```

To enable all roles, specify the following:

```
SET ROLE ALL;
```

To enable all roles, except the roles specified, use the following:

```
SET ROLE ALL EXCEPT RESOURCE, ACCOUNTS_USER;
```

To disable all roles, including the default roles, use the following:

```
SET ROLE NONE;
```

Real World Scenario

How Can You Establish a Security Policy Using Default Roles?

You have an application that was developed in house, and you want to control the application's security through roles. Your users are smart and use tools such as Microsoft Access and SQL*Plus to access the database. You do not want any updates to the database outside the application, but at the same time you do not want to limit the users' ability to use these other tools. The application tracks data changes, so you want all users to use their own ID to connect to the application and make changes. The application uses the database privileges of the user to make changes.

Solution:

You need at least two roles defined in the database—one to query the application tables and another to update data. The role that updates data needs to be password protected. Let's create two roles.

```
CREATE ROLE APP_QUERY;
CREATE ROLE APP_UPDATE IDENTIFIED BY FNDMYPSWD;
```

Now, grant `SELECT` privileges on tables to the `APP_QUERY` role, and grant `INSERT`, `UPDATE`, and `DELETE` privileges on tables to the `APP_UPDATE` role. Grant the necessary roles to users.

```
GRANT APP_QUERY, APP_UPDATE TO CHRIS;
```

Next, change the users default role to only `APP_QUERY`.

```
ALTER USER CHRIS DEFAULT ROLE APP_QUERY;
```

If you have other roles that you want to establish as the default for the user, you can use the following:

```
ALTER USER CHRIS DEFAULT ROLE ALL EXCEPT APP_UPDATE;
```

You can query the DBA_ROLE_PRIVS view to see default and non-default roles for the user. The DEFAULT_ROLE column will display NO for non-default roles. In the application, you must set the appropriate role that gives the privilege to manipulate the data.

```
SET ROLE APP_UPDATE IDENTIFIED BY FNDMYPSWD;
```

If you need to set more than one role, you can specify all the required roles in the SET command.

```
SET ROLE APP_UPDATE IDENTIFIED BY FNDMYPSWD, APP_ADMIN;
```

You can develop methods to encrypt and decrypt passwords, instead of hard coding them in the application.

Querying Role Information

Oracle Objective

Display role information from the data dictionary

The data dictionary view DBA_ROLES lists the roles defined in the database. The column PASSWORD specifies the authorization method.

```
SQL> SELECT * FROM DBA_ROLES;

ROLE                           PASSWORD
------------------------------ --------
CONNECT                        NO
RESOURCE                       NO
DBA                            NO
SELECT_CATALOG_ROLE            NO
EXECUTE_CATALOG_ROLE           NO
DELETE_CATALOG_ROLE            NO
```

```
EXP_FULL_DATABASE              NO
IMP_FULL_DATABASE              NO
APPLICATION_USER               EXTERNAL
ACCOUNTS_MANAGER               YES
```

The view SESSION_ROLES lists the roles that are enabled in the current session.

```
SQL> SELECT * FROM SESSION_ROLES;

ROLE
------------------------------
CONNECT
DBA
SELECT_CATALOG_ROLE
HS_ADMIN_ROLE
EXECUTE_CATALOG_ROLE
DELETE_CATALOG_ROLE
EXP_FULL_DATABASE
IMP_FULL_DATABASE
JAVA_ADMIN
```

The view DBA_ROLE_PRIVS (or USER_ROLE_PRIVS) lists all the roles granted to users and roles.

```
SQL> SELECT * FROM DBA_ROLE_PRIVS
  2  WHERE GRANTEE = 'JOHN';

GRANTEE     GRANTED_ROLE        ADM DEF
----------- ------------------- --- ---
JOHN        ACCOUNTS_MANAGER    YES NO
JOHN        RESOURCE            NO  YES
```

The view ROLE_ROLE_PRIVS lists the roles granted to the roles, ROLE_SYS_PRIVS lists the system privileges granted to roles, and ROLE_TAB_PRIVS shows information on the object privileges granted to roles.

```
SQL> SELECT * FROM ROLE_ROLE_PRIVS
  2  WHERE  ROLE = 'DBA';

ROLE    GRANTED_ROLE                   ADM
------- ------------------------------ ---
DBA     DELETE_CATALOG_ROLE            YES
DBA     EXECUTE_CATALOG_ROLE           YES
```

```
DBA     EXP_FULL_DATABASE           NO
DBA     IMP_FULL_DATABASE           NO
DBA     JAVA_ADMIN                  NO
DBA     SELECT_CATALOG_ROLE         YES

SQL> SELECT * FROM ROLE_SYS_PRIVS
  2  WHERE  ROLE = 'CONNECT';

ROLE          PRIVILEGE              ADM
------------- ---------------------- ---
CONNECT       ALTER SESSION          NO
CONNECT       CREATE CLUSTER         NO
CONNECT       CREATE DATABASE LINK   NO
CONNECT       CREATE SEQUENCE        NO
CONNECT       CREATE SESSION         NO
CONNECT       CREATE SYNONYM         NO
CONNECT       CREATE TABLE           NO
CONNECT       CREATE VIEW            NO

SQL> SELECT * FROM ROLE_TAB_PRIVS
  2  WHERE  TABLE_NAME = 'CUSTOMER';


ROLE        OWNER  TABLE_NAME COLUMN_NAME PRIVILEGE GRA
----------- ------ --------------------- --------- ---
ACC_MANAGER JOHN   CUSTOMER               SELECT    NO
```

Auditing the Database

Oracle Objective

Identify auditing capabilities

Auditing is storing information about database activity. You can use auditing to monitor suspicious database activity and to collect statistics on database usage. When you create the database, Oracle creates the SYS.AUD$ table, known as the *audit trail*, which stores the audited records. To enable auditing, set the initialization parameter AUDIT_TRAIL to TRUE or DB. When this parameter is set to OS, Oracle writes the audited records to an operating system file instead of inserting them into the SYS.AUD$ table. You use the AUDIT command to specify the audit actions. Oracle has three types of auditing capabilities:

Statement auditing Audits SQL statements. (Example: AUDIT SELECT BY SCOTT audits all SELECT statements performed by SCOTT.)

Privilege auditing Audits privileges. (Example: AUDIT CREATE TRIGGER audits all users who exercise their CREATE TRIGGER privilege.)

Object auditing Audits the use of a specific object. (Example: AUDIT SELECT ON JOHN.CUSTOMER monitors the SELECT statements performed on the CUSTOMER table.)

You can restrict the auditing scope by specifying the user list in the BY clause. You can use the WHENEVER SUCCESSFUL clause to specify that only successful statements are to be audited. The WHENEVER NOT SUCCESSFUL clause limits auditing to failed statements. You can also specify BY SESSION or BY ACCESS; BY SESSION as the default. BY SESSION specifies that one audit record is inserted for one session, regardless of the number of times the statement is executed. BY ACCESS specifies that one audit record is inserted each time the statement is executed. Following are some examples of auditing.

To audit the connection and disconnection to the database, use the following:

```
AUDIT SESSION;
```

To audit only successful logins, use the following:

```
AUDIT SESSION WHENEVER SUCCESSFUL;
```

To audit only failed logins, use the following:

```
AUDIT SESSION WHENEVER NOT SUCCESSFUL;
```

To audit successful logins of specific users, use the following:

```
AUDIT SESSION BY JOHN, ALEX WHENEVER SUCCESSFUL;
```

To audit the successful updates and deletes on the CUSTOMER table, use the following:

```
AUDIT UPDATE, DELETE ON JOHN.CUSTOMER
```

```
BY ACCESS WHENEVER SUCCESSFUL;
```

To turn off auditing, use the NOAUDIT command. You can specify all options available in the AUDIT statement to turn off auditing except BY SESSION and BY ACCESS. When you turn off auditing, Oracle turns off the action, regardless of its BY SESSION or BY ACCESS specification. To turn off the object auditing enabled on the CUSTOMER table, use the following:

```
NOAUDIT UPDATE, DELETE ON JOHN.CUSTOMER;
```

Oracle always monitors certain database activities and writes them to operating system files, even if auditing is disabled. Oracle writes audit records when the instance starts up and shuts down and when a user connects to the database with administrator privileges.

Using Globalization Support

Oracle Objective | **Choose database character set and national character set for a database**

You use *Globalization Support*, known as *National Language Support (NLS)* in the previous release of Oracle, to store and retrieve data in a native language and format. Oracle supports a wide variety of languages and character sets. Globalization support lets you communicate with end users in their native language using their familiar date formats, number formats, and sorting sequence. Oracle uses Unicode (a worldwide encoding standard for computer usage) to support the languages.

You define the database character set when you create the database using the CHARACTER SET clause of the CREATE DATABASE command. The character set stores data in the CHAR, VARCHAR2, CLOB, and LONG columns, and stores table names, column names, and so on in the dictionary, stores

PL/SQL variables in memory, and so on. If you do not specify a character set when you create the database, Oracle uses the US7ASCII character set. US7ASCII is a seven-bit ASCII character set that uses a single byte to store a character, and it can represent 128 characters (2^7).

Other widely used single-byte character sets are WE8ISO8859P1 (the Western European eight-bit ISO [International Organization for Standardization] standard 8859 Part I) and UTF8. These character sets use eight bits to represent a character and can represent 256 characters (2^8). Oracle also supports multibyte character encoding. Multibyte encoding is used to represent languages such as Japanese, Chinese, Hindi, and so on. Multibyte encoding schemes can be fixed-width encoding schemes or variable-width encoding schemes. In a variable-width encoding scheme, certain characters are represented using one byte, and two or more bytes represent other characters.

The options to change the database character set after you create the database are limited. You can change the database character set only if the new character set is a superset of the current character set; that is, all the characters represented in the current character set must be available in the new character set. WE8ISO8859P1 and UTF8 are a superset of US7ASCII. To change the database character set, use the following:

```
ALTER DATABASE CHARACTER SET WE8ISO8859P1;
```

You must be careful when changing the database character set; be sure to back up of the database before the change. You cannot roll back this action, which may result in loss of data or data corruption.

Oracle lets you choose an additional character set for the database that enhances the character-processing capabilities. You specify the second character set when you create the database using the `NATIONAL CHARACTER SET` clause. If you do not specify `NATIONAL CHARACTER SET`, Oracle uses the Unicode character set AF16UTF16. The national character set stores data in `NCHAR`, `NVARCHAR2`, and `NCLOB` data type columns.

The national character set can be either AF16UTF16 or UTF8. AF16UTF16 is the default. AF16UTF16 and UTF8 are Unicode character sets. You cannot specify AF16UTF16 as the database character set. When choosing a multibyte character set for your database, remember that, by default, the VARCHAR2, CHAR, NVARCHAR2, and NCHAR data types specify the maximum length in bytes, not in characters. You can change this default behavior by setting the NLS_LENGTH_SEMANTICS=CHAR or by providing the semantic information along with the column definition (as in VARCHAR2 (20 CHAR)). If the character set used is two bytes, `VARCHAR2 (10)` can hold a maximum of five characters.

The client machine can specify a character set different from the database character set by using local environment variables. The database character set should be a superset to the client character set. Oracle converts the character set automatically, but there is some overhead associated with this conversion.

Certain character sets can support multiple languages. For example, the character set WE8ISO8859P1 can support all western European languages such as English, Finnish, Italian, Swedish, Danish, French, German, Spanish, and so on.

The Unicode Character Set

Unicode is a universal character encoding scheme that allows you to store information from any major language using a single character set. Unicode provides a unique code value for every character, regardless of the platform, program, or language. Unicode has both 16-bit and 8-bit encoding.

UTF-16 is the 16-bit encoding of Unicode. It is a fixed-width multibyte encoding in which the character codes 0x00 through 0x7F have the same meaning as they do in ASCII. One Unicode character is 2 bytes in this encoding. Characters from both European and Asian scripts are represented in 2 bytes. AF16UTF16 is UTF-16 encoded character set.

UTF-8 is the 8-bit encoding of Unicode. It is a variable-width multibyte encoding in which the character codes 0x00 through 0x7F have the same meaning as they do in ASCII. One Unicode character can be 1 byte, 2 bytes, or 3 bytes in this encoding. Characters from the European scripts are represented in either 1 or 2 bytes, and characters from most Asian scripts are represented in 3 bytes. AL32UTF8, UTF8, and UTFE are UTF-8 encoded character sets. You can specify a UTF-8 encoded character set as a database character set; such a database is known as a *Unicode database*.

Using NLS Parameters

Oracle Objective

Specify the language-dependent behavior using initialization parameters, environment variables, and the ALTER SESSION command

Oracle provides several NLS parameters to customize the database and client workstations to suit the native format. These parameters have a default value based on the database and national character set chosen to create the database. Specifying the NLS parameters can change the default values. You can customize the NLS parameters in the following ways:

- By specifying the initialization file, which will be used at the instance startup (Example: `NLS_DATE_FORMAT = "YYYY-MM-DD"`)
- By setting the parameter as an environment variable (Example on Unix: `csh: setenv NLS_DATE_FORMAT YYYY-MM-DD` or using the MS-Windows registry)
- By setting the parameter in the Oracle session using the `ALTER SESSION` command (Example: `ALTER SESSION SET NLS_DATE_FORMAT = "YYYY-MM-DD"`)
- By using certain SQL functions (Example: `TO_CHAR (SYSDATE, 'YYYY-MM-DD', 'NLS_DATE_LANGUAGE = AMERICAN')`)

The parameter specified in SQL functions has the highest priority; the next highest is the parameter specified using `ALTER SESSION`, then the environment variable, then the initialization parameters, and finally the database default parameters have the lowest priority. You cannot change certain parameters using `ALTER SESSION`, and you cannot specify certain parameters as environment variables. Parameter specification areas are discussed in the following sections.

Oracle Objective

Use the different types of National Language Support (NLS) parameters

NLS_LENGTH_SEMANTICS Specified at the session level (using ALTER SESSION) or as an initialization parameter. Defines the character length semantics as byte or character. The default is BYTE. NLS_LENGTH_SEMANTICS does not apply to tables in SYS and SYSTEM; they are always in BYTE semantic.

NLS_LANG Specified only as an environment variable. NLS_LANG has three parts: the language, the territory, and the character set. None of the parts are mandatory. The format to specify NLS_LANG is *<LANGUAGE>_<TERRITORY>.<CHARACTER SET>*. The language specifies the language to be used for displaying Oracle error messages, day names, month names, and so on. The territory specifies the default date format, numeric formats, and monetary formats. The character set specifies the character set to be used by the client machine—for example, AMERICAN_AMERICA.WE8ISO8859P1, in which AMERICAN is the language, AMERICA is the territory, and WE8ISO8859P1 is the character set.

NLS_LANGUAGE Specified at the session level or as an initialization parameter. Sets the language to be used. The session value overrides the NLS_LANG setting. The default values for the NLS_DATE_LANGUAGE and NLS_SORT parameters are derived from NLS_LANGUAGE.

NLS_TERRITORY Specified at the session level or as an initialization parameter. Sets the territory. The session value overrides the NLS_LANG setting. The default values for parameters such as NLS_CURRENCY, NLS_ISO_CURRENCY, NLS_DATE_FORMAT, and NLS_NUMERIC_CHARACTERS are derived from NLS_TERRITORY.

NLS_DATE_FORMAT Specified at the session level, as an environment variable, or as an initialization parameter. Sets a default format for date displays.

NLS_DATE_LANGUAGE Specified at the session level, as an environment variable, or as an initialization parameter. Sets a language explicitly for day and month names in date values.

NLS_TIMESTAMP_FORMAT Specified at the session level, as an environment variable, or as an initialization parameter. This parameter defines the default timestamp format to use with the TO_CHAR and TO_TIMESTAMP functions.

NLS_TIMESTAMP_TZ_FORMAT Specified at the session level, as an environment variable, or as an initialization parameter. This parameter defines the default timestamp with time zone format to use with the TO_CHAR and TO_TIMESTAMP_TZ functions

NLS_CALENDAR Specified at the session level, as an environment variable, or as an initialization parameter. Sets the calendar Oracle uses.

NLS_NUMERIC_CHARACTERS Specified at the session level, as an environment variable, or as an initialization parameter. Specifies the decimal character and group separator (for example, in `234,224.99`, the comma is the group separator and the period is the decimal character).

NLS_CURRENCY Specified at the session level, as an environment variable, or as an initialization parameter. Specifies a currency symbol.

NLS_ISO_CURRENCY Specified at the session level, as an environment variable, or as an initialization parameter. Specifies the ISO currency symbol. For example, when the `NLS_ISO_CURRENCY` value is `AMERICA`, the currency symbol for U.S. dollars is $, and the ISO currency symbol is `USD`.

NLS_DUAL_CURRENCY Specified at the session level, as an environment variable, or as an initialization parameter. Specifies an alternate currency symbol. Introduced to support the Euro.

NLS_SORT Specified at the session level, as an environment variable, or as an initialization parameter. Specifies the language to use for sorting. You can specify any valid language. The `ORDER BY` clause in a SQL statement uses this value for the sort mechanism. For example:

```
   ALTER SESSION SET NLS_SORT = GERMAN;
   SELECT * FROM CUSTOMERS
ORDER BY NAME;
```

In this example, the `NAME` column will be sorted using the German linguistic sort mechanism. You can also explicitly set the sort language by using the `NLSSORT` function, rather than altering the session parameter. The following example demonstrates this method:

```
SELECT * FROM CUSTOMERS
ORDER BY NLSSORT(NAME, "NLS_SORT= GERMAN");
```

NCHAR Considerations When Migrating to Oracle9i

The Oracle8i Server introduced a national character (NCHAR, NVARCHAR2, NCLOB) datatype that allows for an alternate character set in addition to the original database character set. NCHAR datatypes support a number of special, fixed-width Asian character sets that were introduced to provide for higher performance when processing of Asian character data.

In Oracle9i, the NCHAR datatypes are limited to the Unicode character set encoding (UTF8 and AL16UTF16) only. Any other Oracle8i Server character sets that were available under the NCHAR datatype, including Asian character sets (for example, JA16SJISFIXED), are not supported.

So, if your Oracle8i database has NCHAR, NVARCHAR2, and NCLOB columns, when migrating to Oracle9i, you have to use the export/import utility when converting these to the Unicode character set. The process is as follows:

1. Export all tables containing NCHAR columns from Oracle8i.
2. Drop the tables (or the NCHAR Columns).
3. Upgrade the database to Oracle9i.
4. Import the tables (or columns) into Oracle9i.

Using NLS To Change Application Behavior

Oracle Objective

Explain the influence on language-dependent application behavior

Globalization Support enables applications to use local symbols and semantics regardless of where the database resides. The various NLS parameters define locale specific to the country and language. Oracle9i supports many languages. The user of the application need not know any other culture or language or conventions to use the application. You can set the following NLS parameters so that everything is in local format for the user.

Language You can store, retrieve, and manipulate data in local native languages. Oracle9i supports all major languages and subsets of languages using the Unicode character set. Use the NLS_LANG and the NLS_LANGUAGE parameters.

Geographical location You can set the geographic-specific information, such as currency symbol, date formats, and numeric conventions, local to the user. Use NLS_TERRITORY.

Date and time formats You can set date and time formats specific to the location or convenience. Use NLS_DATE_FORMAT, NLS_DATE_LANGUAGE, NLS_TIMESTAMP_FORMAT, and NLS_TIMESTAMP_TZ_FORMAT.

Currency and numeric formats You can display the currency symbol local to the application. Some countries use the comma (,) as a decimal separator, and some countries use the period (.) as a decimal separator. You can specify such settings using NLS_CURRENCY, NLS_DUAL_CURRENCY, NLS_ISO_CURRENCY, and NLS_NUMERIC_CHARACTERS.

Calendar and Sorting You can set local calendars and specify linguistic sorting using the NLS parameters NLS_CALENDAR and NLS_SORT.

Obtaining NLS Data Dictionary Information

Oracle Objective

Obtain information about Globalization Support usage

You can obtain NLS data dictionary information from the data dictionary using the following views:

NLS_DATABASE_PARAMETERS Shows the parameters defined for the database (the database default values)

NLS_INSTANCE_PARAMETERS Shows the parameters specified in the initialization parameter file

NLS_SESSION_PARAMETERS Shows the parameters that are in effect in the current session

V$NLS_VALID_VALUES Shows the allowed values for the language, territory, and character set definitions

The following examples show NLS information from the data dictionary views and examples of changing session NLS values.

```
SQL> SELECT * FROM NLS_DATABASE_PARAMETERS;

PARAMETER                 VALUE
------------------------- ------------------------------
NLS_LANGUAGE              AMERICAN
NLS_TERRITORY             AMERICA
NLS_CURRENCY              $
NLS_ISO_CURRENCY          AMERICA
NLS_NUMERIC_CHARACTERS    .,
NLS_CHARACTERSET          UTF8
NLS_CALENDAR              GREGORIAN
NLS_DATE_FORMAT           DD-MON-YY
NLS_DATE_LANGUAGE         AMERICAN
NLS_SORT                  BINARY
NLS_TIME_FORMAT           HH.MI.SSXFF AM
NLS_TIMESTAMP_FORMAT      DD-MON-YY HH.MI.SSXFF AM
NLS_TIME_TZ_FORMAT        HH.MI.SSXFF AM TZH:TZM
NLS_TIMESTAMP_TZ_FORMAT   DD-MON-YY HH.MI.SSXFF AM TZH:T
NLS_DUAL_CURRENCY         $
NLS_COMP                  BINARY
NLS_NCHAR_CHARACTERSET    US7ASCII
NLS_RDBMS_VERSION         9.0.1.1.1
NLS_LENGTH_SEMANTICS      BYTE
NLS_NCHAR_CONV_EXCP       FALSE

20 rows selected.

SQL> ALTER SESSION SET NLS_DATE_FORMAT =
                         'DD-MM-YYYY HH24:MI:SS';
Session altered.

SQL> ALTER SESSION SET NLS_DATE_LANGUAGE = 'GERMAN';

Session altered.
```

```
SQL> SELECT TO_CHAR(SYSDATE, 'Day, Month'),
                                        SYSDATE FROM DUAL;
TO_CHAR(SYSDATE,'DAY, SYSDATE
--------------------- -------------------
Dienstag  , August    29-08-2000 16:24:14

SQL> ALTER SESSION SET NLS_CALENDAR =  "Persian";

Session altered.

SQL> SELECT SYSDATE FROM DUAL;

SYSDATE
------------------
09 Shahruoar  1379

SQL> SELECT * FROM NLS_SESSION_PARAMETERS;

PARAMETER                 VALUE
------------------------- ------------------------------
NLS_LANGUAGE              AMERICAN
NLS_TERRITORY             AMERICA
NLS_CURRENCY              $
NLS_ISO_CURRENCY          AMERICA
NLS_NUMERIC_CHARACTERS    .,
NLS_CHARACTERSET          UTF8
NLS_CALENDAR              GREGORIAN
NLS_DATE_FORMAT           DD-MON-RR
NLS_DATE_LANGUAGE         AMERICAN
NLS_SORT                  BINARY
NLS_TIME_FORMAT           HH.MI.SSXFF AM
NLS_TIMESTAMP_FORMAT      DD-MON-RR HH.MI.SSXFF AM
NLS_TIME_TZ_FORMAT        HH.MI.SSXFF AM TZR
NLS_TIMESTAMP_TZ_FORMAT   DD-MON-RR HH.MI.SSXFF AM TZR
NLS_DUAL_CURRENCY         $
NLS_COMP                  BINARY
NLS_LENGTH_SEMANTICS      BYTE
NLS_NCHAR_CONV_EXCP       FALSE
```

```
NLS_NCHAR_CHARACTERSET      AL16UTF16
NLS_RDBMS_VERSION           9.0.1.1.1

20 rows selected
SQL>
```

Summary

This chapter discussed the security aspects of the Oracle database: profiles, privileges, and roles. You use profiles to control the database and system resource usage. You also use profiles to manage passwords. You can create various profiles for different user communities and assign a profile to each user. When you create the database, Oracle creates a profile named DEFAULT, which is assigned to the users when you do not specify a profile for the user. Profiles can monitor the resource use by session or on a per-call basis. Resource limits are enforced only when the parameter RESOURCE_LIMIT is set to TRUE.

Using profiles, you can lock an account, manage password expiration and reuse, and verify password complexity. When an account is locked, the DBA must unlock it in order for the user to connect to the database. You cannot drop profiles when they are assigned to users; you can drop such profiles only when you use the CASCADE keyword.

You create users in the database to use the database. Every user needs the CREATE SESSION privilege to be able to connect to the database. Users are assigned a default and a temporary tablespace. When the user does not specify a tablespace when creating a table, the table is created in the default tablespace. The temporary tablespace is used for creating sort segments. If you do not specify default or temporary tablespaces, Oracle assigns SYSTEM as the user's default and temporary tablespace. Users are granted a space quota on the tablespace. When they exceed this quota, no more extents can be allocated to the objects. If a user has the UNLIMITED TABLESPACE system privilege, there are no space quota restrictions.

Before connecting a user to the database, Oracle authenticates the username. The authentication method can be via the database, whereby the user specifies a password, or it can be via the operating system. The operating system authentication method uses the operating system login information to connect to the database; such users are created with the IDENTIFIED

EXTERNALLY clause. You cannot drop a user who is connected to the database. You must terminate the user session before dropping the user.

To control the actions performed by users on the database, you use privileges. A role is a named set of privileges, which makes managing privileges easy. There are two types of privileges: object and system. Object privileges specify allowed actions on a specific object (the owner of the object has to grant the privilege to other users or authorize other users to grant the privileges on the object); system privileges specify the allowed actions on the database. To manage privileges, you use the GRANT and REVOKE commands. Any privilege granted to PUBLIC is available to all users in the database.

You can monitor database actions or statements using the AUDIT command. You can audit statements, privilege usage, or object usage, and you can restrict auditing to specific users, successful statements, or failed statements. You can also limit the number of audit records generated by specifying auditing by session (one record per session) or by access (one record per DDL, DML, and so on).

Oracle can store and retrieve data in a native language and format using the Globalization Support feature. The character set used determines the default language and the conventions used. You specify the character set when you create the database. You can specify only the Unicode character set as the national character set for the database. Oracle provides several parameters that can determine the characteristics and conventions of data displayed to the user. You can specify these parameters for a session, for the instance, or in certain SQL functions. If none are specified, the database defaults are used.

Exam Essentials

Know how to differentiate between object privileges and system privileges. System privileges give the privileges to perform certain actions on the database; object privileges give privileges to perform operations on specific objects.

Learn the various privileges that can be granted on objects. Insert, update, delete, select, query rewrite, and execute are certain privileges that you can grant on schema objects. Know which privilege is applicable to which object.

Learn the various system privileges. System privileges can be granted on objects owned by a user (such as CREATE TABLE) or on any schema in the database (such as CREATE ANY TABLE). Other system privileges provide administration capabilities.

Know how to grant and revoke privileges. Understand the implications of granting and revoking privileges, especially object privileges. You use the GRANT statement to grant privileges, and you use the REVOKE statement to remove privileges. Understand the WITH ADMIN OPTION and WITH GRANT OPTION clauses.

Learn to monitor suspicious database activity. Know the database auditing capabilities of the database. You can audit sessions, DDL operations, and DML operations.

Create and manage profiles. Know the components you can control when managing resources and passwords.

Understand account locking and password verification. Accounts can be locked after unsuccessful login attempts. Passwords can be set to expire after a certain period, and new passwords can be verified against certain rules.

Understand data dictionary views. Know the dictionary views used to provide information about users, privileges, roles, and sessions.

Know how to manage users. Create new users and change the tablespace assignments and space quota of existing users.

Know how to enable and disable roles. Roles granted to users can be set as default or non-default. Roles can also be password protected. Understand the SET ROLE command.

Understand Globalization Support. Know the difference between the database character set and the national character set. Understand the datatypes that store information in the national character set. Also learn the characteristics of the Unicode character set.

Know the dictionary views with NLS information. Understand the information available in the dictionary views NLS_DATABASE_PARAMETERS, NLS_INSTANCE_PARAMETERS and NLS_SESSION_PARAMETERS.

Key Terms

Before you take the exam, make sure you're familiar with the following terms:

- audit trail
- auditing
- Globalization Support
- National Language Support (NLS)
- object privileges
- privileges
- profiles
- PUBLIC
- role
- schema
- space quota
- system privileges
- Unicode database

Review Questions

1. Profiles cannot be used to restrict which of the following?

   A. CPU time used

   B. Total time connected to the database

   C. Maximum time a session can be inactive

   D. Time spent reading blocks

2. Which command is used to assign a profile to an existing user?

   A. `ALTER PROFILE`.

   B. `ALTER USER`.

   C. `SET PROFILE`.

   D. The profile should be specified when creating the user; it cannot be changed.

3. Which resource is not used to calculate the `COMPOSITE_LIMIT`?

   A. `PRIVATE_SGA`

   B. `CPU_PER_SESSION`

   C. `CONNECT_TIME`

   D. `LOGICAL_READS_PER_CALL`

4. Choose the option that is not true.

   A. Oracle creates a profile named `DEFAULT` when the database is created.

   B. Profiles cannot be renamed.

   C. `DEFAULT` is a valid name for a profile resource.

   D. The `SESSIONS_PER_USER` resource in the `DEFAULT` profile initially has a value of 5.

5. What is the maximum number of profiles that can be assigned to a user?

   A. 1

   B. 2

   C. 32

   D. Unlimited

6. What happens when you create a new user and do not specify a profile?

   A. Oracle prompts you for a profile name.

   B. No profile is assigned to the user.

   C. The DEFAULT profile is assigned.

   D. The SYSTEM profile is assigned.

7. Which resource specifies the value in minutes?

   A. CPU_PER_SESSION

   B. CONNECT_TIME

   C. PASSWORD_LOCK_TIME

   D. All the above

8. Which password parameter in the profile definitions can restrict the user from using the old password for 90 days?

   A. PASSWORD_REUSE_TIME

   B. PASSWORD_REUSE_MAX

   C. PASSWORD_LIFE_TIME

   D. PASSWORD_REUSE_DAYS

9. Which dictionary view shows the password expiration date for a user?

   A. DBA_PROFILES

   B. DBA_USERS

   C. DBA_PASSWORDS

   D. V$SESSION

10. Which clause in the CREATE USER command can be used to specify no limits on the space allowed in tablespace APP_DATA?

    A. DEFAULT TABLESPACE

    B. UNLIMITED TABLESPACE

    C. QUOTA

    D. PROFILE

11. User JAMES has a table named JOBS created on the tablespace USERS. When you issue the following statement, what effect it will have on the JOBS table?

    ALTER USER JAMES QUOTA 0 ON USERS;

    A. No more rows can be added to the JOBS table.

    B. No blocks can be allocated to the JOBS table.

    C. No new extents can be allocated to the JOBS table.

    D. The table JOBS cannot be accessed.

12. Which view would you query to see whether John has the CREATE TABLE privilege?

    A. DBA_SYS_PRIVS

    B. DBA_USER_PRIVS

    C. DBA_ROLE_PRIVS

    D. DBA_TAB_PRIVS

13. Which clause should you specify to enable the grantee to grant the system privilege to other users?

    A. WITH GRANT OPTION

    B. WITH ADMIN OPTION

    C. CASCADE

    D. WITH MANAGE OPTION

14. Which of the following is not a system privilege?

    A. SELECT

    B. UPDATE ANY

    C. EXECUTE ANY

    D. CREATE TABLE

15. Which data dictionary view can you query to see whether a user has the EXECUTE privilege on a procedure?

    A. DBA_SYS_PRIVS

    B. DBA_TAB_PRIVS

    C. DBA_PROC_PRIVS

    D. SESSION_PRIVS

16. To grant the SELECT privilege on the table CUSTOMER to all users in the database, which statement would you use?

    A. GRANT SELECT ON CUSTOMER TO ALL USERS;

    B. GRANT ALL ON CUSTOMER TO ALL;

    C. GRANT SELECT ON CUSTOMER TO ALL;

    D. GRANT SELECT ON CUSTOMER TO PUBLIC;

17. Which role in the following list is not a predefined role from Oracle?

    A. SYSDBA

    B. CONNECT

    C. IMP_FULL_DATABASE

    D. RESOURCE

18. How do you enable a role?

    A. ALTER ROLE

    B. ALTER USER

    C. SET ROLE

    D. ALTER SESSION

19. What is accomplished when you issue the following statement?

```
ALTER USER JOHN DEFAULT ROLE ALL;
```

A. John is assigned all the roles created in the database.

B. Future roles granted to John will not be default roles.

C. All of John's roles are enabled, except the roles with passwords.

D. All of John's roles are enabled when he connects to the database.

20. Which command defines `CONNECT` and `RESOURCE` as the default roles for user `JAMES`?

A. `ALTER USER`

B. `ALTER ROLE`

C. `SET ROLE`

D. `SET PRIVILEGE`

21. Which data dictionary view shows the database character set?

A. `V$DATABASE`

B. `NLS_DATABASE_PARAMETERS`

C. `NLS_INSTANCE_PARAMETERS`

D. `NLS_SESSION_PARAMETERS`

22. Choose two NLS parameters that cannot be modified using the `ALTER SESSION` statement.

A. `NLS_CHARACTERSET`

B. `NLS_SORT`

C. `NLS_NCHAR_CHARACTERSET`

D. `NLS_TERRITORY`

Answers to Review Questions

1. D. There is no resource parameter in the profile definition to monitor the time spent reading blocks, but you can restrict the number of blocks read per SQL statement or per session.

2. B. You use the PROFILE clause in the ALTER USER command to set the profile for an existing user. You must have the ALTER USER privilege to do this.

3. D. Call-level resources are not used to calculate the COMPOSITE_LIMIT. You can set the resource cost of the four resources (the fourth is LOGICAL_READS_PER_SESSION) using the ALTER RESOURCE COST command.

4. D. All resources in the default profile have a value of UNLIMITED when the database is created. You can change these values.

5. A. A user can have only one profile assigned. You can query the profile assigned to a user from the DBA_USERS view.

6. C. The DEFAULT profile is created when the database is created and is assigned to users if you do not specify a profile for the new user. Before you can assign a profile, you must create the user in the database.

7. B. CONNECT_TIME is specified in minutes, CPU_PER_SESSION is specified in hundredths of a second, and PASSWORD_LOCK_TIME is specified in days.

8. A. PASSWORD_REUSE_TIME specifies the number of days required before the old password can be reused; PASSWORD_REUSE_MAX specifies the number of password changes required before a password can be reused. At least one of these parameters must be set to UNLIMITED.

9. B. The DBA_USERS view shows the password expiration date, account status, and locking date along with the user's tablespace assignments, profile, creation date, and so on.

10. C. You use the QUOTA clause to specify the amount of space allowed on a tablespace; you can specify a size or UNLIMITED. The user will have unlimited space if the system privilege UNLIMITED TABLESPACE is granted.

11. C. When the space quota is exceeded or quota is removed from a user on a tablespace, the tables remain in the tablespace, but no new extents can be allocated.

12. A. `CREATE TABLE` is a system privilege. You can query system privileges from `DBA_SYS_PRIVS` or `USER_SYS_PRIVS`.

13. B. The `WITH ADMIN OPTION` specified with system privileges enables the grantee to grant the privileges to others, and the `WITH GRANT OPTION` specified with object privileges enables the grantee to grant the privilege to others.

14. A. `SELECT`, `INSERT`, `UPDATE`, `DELETE`, `EXECUTE`, and `REFERENCES` are object privileges. `SELECT ANY`, `UPDATE ANY`, and so on are system privileges.

15. B. The `DBA_TAB_PRIVS`, `USER_TAB_PRIVS`, and `ALL_TAB_PRIVS` views show information about the object privileges.

16. D. `PUBLIC` is the group or class of database users to which all users of the database belong.

17. A. `SYSDBA` and `SYSOPER` are not roles; they are system privileges.

18. C. You use the `SET ROLE` command to enable or disable granted roles for the user. The view `SESSION_ROLES` shows the roles that are enabled in the session. All default roles are enabled when the user connects to the database.

19. D. Default roles are enabled when a user connects to the database even if the roles are password authorized.

20. A. The `ALTER USER` command defines the default role(s) for a user.

21. B. The `NLS_DATABASE_PARAMETERS` view shows the database character set and all the NLS parameter settings. The character set cannot be changed at the instance or session level, so the character set information does not show up in the `NLS_INSTANCE_PARAMETERS` and `NLS_SESSION_PARAMETERS` views.

22. A and C. You cannot change the character set after creating the database. The `CHARACTER SET` and `NATIONAL CHARACTER SET` clauses are used in the `CREATE DATABASE` command.

Glossary

A

alert log A log that is written to the BACKGROUND_DUMP_DEST directory that is specified in the initialization parameter file and that shows start-ups, shutdowns, ALTER DATABASE and ALTER SYSTEM commands, and a variety of error statements.

alert log file A text file that logs significant database events and messages. The alert log file stores information about block corruption errors, internal errors, and the non-default initialization parameters used at instance start-up.

archive logs Logs that are copies of the online redo logs and that are saved to another location before the online copies are reused.

ARCHIVELOG A mode of database operation. When the Oracle database is run in ARCHIVELOG mode, the online redo log files are copied to another location before they are overwritten. These archived log files can be used for point-in-time recovery of the database. They can also be used for analysis.

archiver process (ARC*n*) Copies the online redo log files to archive log files.

asynchronous I/O Multiple I/O activities performed at the same time without any dependencies.

audit trail Records generated by auditing, which are stored in the database in the table SYS.AUD$. Auditing enables the DBA to monitor suspicious database activity.

automatic archiving The automatic creation of archive logs after the appropriate redo logs have been switched. The LOG_ARCHIVE_START parameter must be set to TRUE in the init.ora file for automatic archiving to take place.

automatic space management For data block maintenance in a tablespace, using bitmaps instead of free lists to manage free and used space. An alternative to using PCTUSED, FREELISTS, and FREELIST GROUPS to manage data blocks.

B

BACKGROUND_DUMP_DEST An `init.ora` parameter that determines the location of the alert log and Oracle background process trace files.

base tables The lowest-level tables in the data dictionary. They are highly normalized and contain cryptic, version-specific information. The data dictionary views are based on these tables.

before image Image of the transaction data before the transaction occurred. This image is stored in the rollback (undo) segments when DML operations are performed.

bitmap index An indexing method used by Oracle to create the index by using bitmaps. Used for low-cardinality columns.

block The smallest unit of storage in an Oracle database. Data is stored in the database in blocks. The block size is defined when the database is created and is a multiple of the operating system block size.

b-tree An algorithm used for creating indexes.

C

cache recovery The part of instance recovery in which all the data that is not in the data files is reapplied to the data files from the online redo logs.

change vectors A description of a change made to a single block in the database.

checkpoint process (CKPT) A checkpoint is an event that flushes the modified data from the buffer cache to the disk and updates the control file and data files. The checkpoint process updates the headers of data files and control files; the actual blocks are written to the file by the DBW*n* process.

checkpointing The process of updating the SCN in all the data files and control files in the database in conjunction with all necessary data blocks in the data buffers being written to disk. This is done for the purposes of ensuring database consistency and synchronization.

CKPT See *checkpoint process*.

coalesce Combine neighboring free extents to form a single extent on a tablespace.

commit To save or permanently store the results of a transaction to the database.

control file Maintains information about the physical structure of the database. The control file contains the database name and timestamp of database creation, backup information, and the name and location of every data file and redo log file.

current online redo logs Logs that are actively being written to by the LGWR process.

D

data block The smallest unit of data storage in Oracle. The block size is specified when the database is created.

data block buffers Memory buffers containing data blocks that get flushed to disk if modified and committed.

data dictionary A collection of database tables and views containing metadata about the database, its structures, its privileges, and its users. Oracle accesses the data dictionary frequently during the parsing of SQL statements.

data dictionary cache An area in the shared pool that holds the most recently used database dictionary information. The data dictionary cache is also known as the *row cache* because it holds data as rows instead of buffers (which hold entire blocks of data).

data file The data files in a database contain all the database data. One data file can belong to only one database and to one tablespace. Tablespaces can consist of more than one data file.

data segment A segment that stores table or cluster data.

data types Used to specify certain characteristics for table columns, such as numeric, alphanumeric, date, and so on.

database The physical structure that stores the actual data. The Oracle server consists of the database and the instance.

database buffer cache The area of memory that caches the database data. It holds the recent blocks that are read from the database data files, and it holds new or modified blocks that are to be written to the database data files.

database buffers See *data block buffers.*

database writer process (DBW*n*) The DBW*n* process writes the changed database blocks from the SGA to the data file. There can be a maximum of 10 database writer processes (DBW0 through DBW9).

DBA tools GUI tools integrated with the OEM. Administrators can use these tools for complete database administration rather than using SQL*Plus.

DBW*n* See *database writer process.*

degree of parallelism The number of parallel processes you choose to enable for a particular parallel activity such as recovery.

DICTIONARY A data dictionary view that contains the name and description of all the data dictionary views in the database.

dictionary-managed tablespace A tablespace in which the extent allocation and de-allocation information is managed through the data dictionary.

dirty buffers The blocks in the database buffer cache that are changed, but not yet written to the disk.

distributed transactions Transactions that occur in remote databases.

DUAL A dummy table owned by SYS; it has one column and one row and is useful for computing a constant expression with a SELECT statement.

dump file The file where the logical backup is stored. This file is created by the Export utility and read by the Import utility.

dynamic performance views Data dictionary views that are continuously updated while a database is open and in use. Their contents relate primarily to performance. These views have the prefix V$.

E

environment variables Operating system variables, usually on Unix, that define file locations and other parameters for the database.

execute The stage in SQL processing that runs the parsed SQL code from the library cache.

extent A contiguous allocation of blocks for data or index storage. An extent has multiple blocks, and a segment can have multiple extents.

extent management Extents allocated to tablespaces can be managed locally in the data files or through the data dictionary. You can specify the extent management clause when creating a tablespace. The default is dictionary-managed.

F

fetch The stage in SQL query processing that returns the data to the user process.

free buffers The blocks in the database buffer cache that can be overwritten.

free lists A logical storage structure within each segment that maintains the list of available blocks for future inserts into that segment.

function-based index Indexes created on functions or expressions, to speed up queries containing `WHERE` clauses with a particular function or expression.

G

Globalization Support See *National Language Support*.

H

header block The first block in a data file; it contains information about the data file, such as freelist and checkpoint information.

high-water mark (HWM) The maximum number of blocks used by the table. The high-water mark is not reset when you delete rows.

I

Index Organized Table (IOT) Table rows stored in a b-tree index, using a primary key. Avoids duplication of storage for table data and index information.

index segment A segment that stores index information.

INITRANS A segment data block parameter that controls the number of concurrent transactions that can modify or create data in the block.

instance The memory structures and background processes of the Oracle server.

integrity constraints Structures built into the database to enforce business rules.

J

Java pool An optional area in the SGA used for processing server-side Java language procedures.

L

large pool An optional area in the SGA used for specific database operations, such as backup, recovery, or the User Global Area (UGA) space when using a Shared Server configuration.

LGWR See *log writer process.*

library cache An area in the shared pool of the SGA that stores the parsed SQL statements. When a SQL statement is submitted, the server process searches the library cache for a matching SQL statement; if it finds one, re-parsing of the SQL statement is not necessary.

locally managed tablespace A tablespace that has the extent allocation and de-allocation information managed through bitmaps in the associated data files of the tablespace.

log buffers Memory buffers containing the entries that are written to the log files.

log file group Two or more log files, usually stored on different physical disks, that are written to in parallel and are considered multiplexed for the purposes of database recovery. For the purposes of log file creation and recovery, a single, non-multiplexed log file is still considered part of a log group.

log sequence number A sequence number assigned to each redo log file.

log writer process (LGWR) The LGWR process writes the redo log buffer entries (change vectors) to the online redo log files. A redo log entry is any change, or transaction, that has been applied to the database, committed or not.

LOG_ARCHIVE_DEST An `init.ora` parameter that determines the destination of the archive logs.

LOG_ARCHIVE_DEST_*n* An `init.ora` parameter that determines the other destinations of the archive logs, remote or local. This parameter supports a maximum of five locations, *n* being a number from 1 through 5. Only one of these destinations can be remote.

LOG_ARCHIVE_DUPLEX_DEST An `init.ora` parameter that determines the duplexed, or second, destination of archive logs in a two-location archive log configuration.

LOG_ARCHIVE_START An `init.ora` parameter that enables automatic archiving.

logging The recording of DML statements, creation of new objects, and other changes in the redo logs.

logical attributes For tables and indexes, logical attributes are the columns, data types, constraints, and so on.

logical structures The database structures as seen by the user. Tablespaces, segments, extents, blocks, tables, and indexes are all examples of logical structures.

LogMiner A utility that can be used to analyze the redo log files. It can provide a fix for logical corruption by building redo and undo SQL statements from the contents of the redo logs. LogMiner is a set of PL/SQL packages and dynamic performance views.

M

Management Server The middle tier between the console GUI and managed nodes in the Enterprise Manager setup. It processes and coordinates all system management tasks and distributes these tasks to Intelligent Agents on the nodes.

MAXTRANS A segment data block parameter that specifies the maximum number of concurrent transactions that can modify or create data in the block.

metadata Information about the objects that are available in the database. The data dictionary information is the metadata for the Oracle database.

mount A stage in starting up the database. When the instance started mounts a database, the control file is opened to read the data file and redo log file information before the database can be opened.

multiplexing Oracle's mechanism for writing to more than one copy of the redo log file or control file. It involves mirroring, or making duplicate copies. Multiplexing ensures that even if you lose one member of the redo log group or one control file, you can recover using the other one. It intersperses blocks from Oracle data files within a backup set.

multithreaded configuration A database configuration whereby one shared server process takes requests from multiple user processes. In a dedicated server configuration, there will be one server process for one user process. In Oracle 9i, this is known as a Shared Server configuration, formerly known as MTS.

N

National Language Support (NLS) Enables Oracle to store and retrieve information in a format and language that can be understood by users anywhere in the world. The database character set and various other parameters are used to enhance this capability.

NOARCHIVELOG Mode of database operation, whereby the redo log files are not preserved for recovery or analysis purposes.

Nologging Not recording DML statements, the creation of new objects, and other changes in the redo logs—therefore making the changes unrecoverable until the next physical backup.

non-current online redo logs Online redo logs that are not in the current or active group being written to.

O

object privileges Privileges granted on an object for users other than the object owner. They allow these users to manipulate data in the object or to modify the object.

online redo logs Redo logs that are being written to by the LGWR process at some point in time. See *archive logs*.

Optimal Flexible Architecture (OFA) A standard that defines the optimal way to set up an Oracle database. It includes guidelines for specifying database file locations for better performance and management.

ORA_NLS33 An environment variable to set if using a character set other than US7ASCII.

Oracle Enterprise Manager (OEM) A DBA system management tool that performs a variety of DBA tasks, including running the RMAN utility in GUI mode, managing different components of Oracle, and administering the databases at one location.

Oracle Managed Files (OMF) A method to ease the maintenance of database file locations for data files, control files, and online redo log files. Two new initialization parameters define the location of files in the operating system: `DB_CREATE_FILE_DEST` and `DB_CREATE_ONLINE_LOG_DEST_`*n*.

Oracle Real Application Cluster (RAC) An Oracle database that consists of at least two servers, or nodes, each with an instance but sharing one database. Formerly known as Oracle Parallel Server.

Oracle Recovery Manager (RMAN) The Recovery Manager utility, which is responsible for the backup and recovery of Oracle databases.

Oracle Universal Installer (OUI) A Java-based GUI tool used to install all Oracle products.

`ORACLE_HOME` The environment variable that defines the location where the Oracle software is installed.

`ORACLE_SID` The environment variable that defines the database instance name. If you are not using OracleNet, connections are made to this database instance by default.

operating system authentication An authentication method used to connect administrators and operators to the database to perform administrative tasks. Connection is made to the database by verifying the operating system privileges.

P

package A stored PL/SQL program that holds a set of other programs such as procedures, functions, cursors, variables, and so on.

parallel query processes Oracle background processes that process a portion of a query. Each parallel query process runs on a separate CPU.

PARALLEL_MAX_SERVERS An `init.ora` parameter that determines the maximum number of parallel query processes at any given time.

parameter file A binary or text file with parameters to configure memory, database file locations, and limits for the database. This file is read when the database is started. When you are using utilities such as SQL*Loader or Export or Import, you can specify the command-line parameters in a parameter file, which can be reused for other exports or imports.

parsing A stage in SQL processing wherein the syntax of the SQL statement, object names, and user access are verified. Oracle also prepares an execution plan for the statement.

partitioning Breaking the table or index into multiple smaller, more manageable chunks.

password file authentication An authentication method used to connect administrators and operators to the database to perform administrative tasks. Oracle creates a file on the server with the SYS password; users are added to this file when they are granted SYSOPER or SYSDBA privilege.

PCTFREE A segment block parameter that specifies what percentage of the block should be allocated as free space for future updates.

PCTUSED A segment block parameter that specifies when a block can be considered for adding new rows. New rows can be added to the block only when the used space falls below this percentage.

PFILE A text-based file containing the initial values for memory, file locations, and other parameters in the instance.

PGA See *Program Global Area.*

physical attributes For tables and indexes, physical attributes are the physical storage characteristics, such as the extent size, tablespace name, and so on.

physical structures The database structures that store the actual data and operation of the database. Data files, control files, and redo log files constitute the physical structure of the database.

pinned buffers The blocks in the database buffer cache that are being accessed.

PMON See *process monitor process.*

Private Global Area See *Program Global Area.*

privileges Authorization granted on an object in the database or an authorization to perform an activity.

procedure or function A PL/SQL program that is stored in the database in a compiled form. A function always returns one value; a procedure does not. You can pass a parameter to and from the procedure or function.

process A daemon, or background program, that performs certain tasks.

process monitor process (PMON) Performs recovery of failed user processes. This process is mandatory and is started by default when the database is started. It frees up all the resources held by the failed processes.

profiles A set of named parameters used to control the use of resources and to manage passwords.

Program Global Area (PGA) A non-shared memory area allocated to the server process. Also known as the Process Global Area or Private Global Area.

PUBLIC A users group available in all databases of which all users are members. When a privilege is granted to PUBLIC, it is available to all users in the database.

R

read-consistent image Image of the transaction data before the transaction occurred. This image is available to all users not executing the transaction.

read-only tablespace A tablespace that allows only read activity, such as SELECT statements. It is available only for querying. The data is static and doesn't change. No write activity (for example, INSERT, UPDATE, and DELETE statements) is allowed. Read-only tablespaces need to be backed up only once.

read-write tablespace A tablespace that allows both read and write activity, including SELECT, INSERT, UPDATE, and DELETE statements. By default, a tablespace is opened in read-write mode.

record sections Logical areas within the control file. The two types of record sections are *reusable* and *not reusable*.

recoverer process (RECO) An optional background process used with distributed transactions to resolve failures.

recovery catalog Information stored in a database used by the RMAN utility to back up and restore databases.

Recovery Manager (RMAN) An automated tool from Oracle that can perform and manage the backup and recovery process.

redo buffers See *log buffers*.

redo entry See *redo record*.

redo log buffer The area in the SGA that records all changes to the database. The changes are known as redo entries, or change vectors, and are used to reapply the changes to the database in case of a failure.

redo log file The redo log buffers from the SGA are periodically copied to the redo log files. Redo log files are critical to database recovery.

redo logs Record all changes to the database, whether the transactions are committed or rolled back. Redo logs are classified as online redo logs or offline redo logs (also called archive logs), which are simply copies of online redo logs.

redo record A group of change vectors. Redo entries record data that you can use to reconstruct all changes to the database, including the rollback segments.

Redundant Array of Inexpensive Disks (RAID) The storage of data on multiple disks for fault tolerance, to protect against individual disk crashes. If one disk fails, that disk can be rebuilt from the other disks. RAID is available in variations, termed RAID 0 through 5 in most cases.

report A query of the catalog that is more detailed than a list and that describes what may need to be done.

reverse key index An index in which column values are reversed before being added to the index entry.

role A named group of system and object privileges used to ease the administration of privileges to users.

roll back To undo a transaction from the database.

roll-forward-and-roll-back process Applying all the transactions, committed or not committed, to the database and then undoing all uncommitted transactions.

row cache See *data dictionary cache*.

row chaining Storing a row in multiple blocks because the entire row cannot fit in one block. Usually row chaining occurs when the table has large `VARCHAR2` or `LOB columns`.

row migration Moving a row from one block to another due to an update operation, because not enough free space is available to accommodate the updated row.

`ROWID` Exact physical location of the row on disk. `ROWID` is a pseudo-column in all tables.

S

schema A logical structure used to group a set of database objects owned by a user.

segment A logical structure that holds data. Every object created to store data is allocated a segment. A segment has one or more extents.

server process A background process that takes requests from the user process and applies them to the Oracle database.

session A job or a task that Oracle manages. When you log in to the database by using SQL*Plus or any tool, you start a session.

SGA See *System Global Area*.

Shared Global Area See *System Global Area*.

shared pool An area in the SGA that holds information such as parsed SQL, PL/SQL procedures and packages, the data dictionary, locks, character set information, security attributes, and so on.

SMON See *system monitor process*.

sort area An area in the PGA that is used for sorting data during query processing.

space quota Maximum space allowed for a user in a tablespace for creating objects.

SPFILE A binary file containing instance parameter values, such as memory, file locations, and other database modes of operation. It is not meant to be edited by a standard text editor; it is created from a standard PFILE and then modified by the `ALTER SYSTEM` command thereafter. See also *PFILE*.

sql.bsq The SQL commands automatically run when the `CREATE DATABASE` command is executed. These commands create the minimal set of tables, indexes, user accounts, and roles for proper database operation.

standard block size Block size specified when creating the database. The system tablespace and temporary tablespaces use this block size. Other tablespaces can use a non-standard block size.

structure Either a physical or a logical object that is part of the database, such as files or database objects themselves.

system change number (SCN) A unique number generated at the time of a `COMMIT`, acting as an internal counter to the Oracle database and used for recovery and read consistency.

System Global Area (SGA) A memory area in the Oracle instance that is shared by all users.

system monitor process (SMON) Performs instance recovery at database start-up by using the online redo log files. It is also responsible for cleaning up temporary segments in the tablespaces that are no longer used and for coalescing the contiguous free space in the tablespaces.

system privileges Privileges granted to perform an action, as opposed to a privilege on an object.

T

tablespace A logical storage structure at the highest level. A tablespace can have many segments that may be used for data, index, sorting (temporary), or rollback information. The data files are directly related to tablespaces. A segment can belong to only one tablespace.

tempfile Physical file associated with the locally managed temporary tablespace.

templates A logical structure created with the Oracle Database Creation Assistant (DBCA) to make it easier to create a similar database on the same or a different server. It can be created from scratch, or it can be generated from an existing database.

temporary segment A segment created for sorting data. Temporary segments are also created when an index is built or a table is built using `CREATE TABLE AS`.

temporary tablespace A tablespace that stores temporary segments for sorting and creating tables and indexes.

U

undo entries The block and row information used to undo the changes made to a row.

undo segment A database segment containing undo entries.

undo tablespace A database tablespace used only for holding undo segments. Only one undo tablespace can be active at a time.

Unicode Character set that allows you to store information from any language using a single character set.

user process A process that is started by the application tool that communicates with the Oracle server process.

USER_DUMP_DEST An `init.ora` parameter that determines the location of the user process trace files.

V

V$CONTROLFILE The dictionary view that gives the names of the control files. It provides information about the control files that can be useful in the backup and recovery process.

V$DATAFILE The view that provides information about the data files.

V$LOG_HISTORY A V$ view that displays history regarding the redo log files.

V$LOGFILE The dictionary view that gives the redo log file names and status of each redo log file. It provides information about the online redo log files.

V$TABLESPACE The view providing information about the tablespaces in the database.

Index

Note to Reader: Bolded page numbers refer to definitions and main discussions of a topic. *Italicized* page numbers refer to illustrations and tables.

A

B

C

D

E

F

G

J

K

L

M

N

O

P

Q

R

S

T

U

V

W